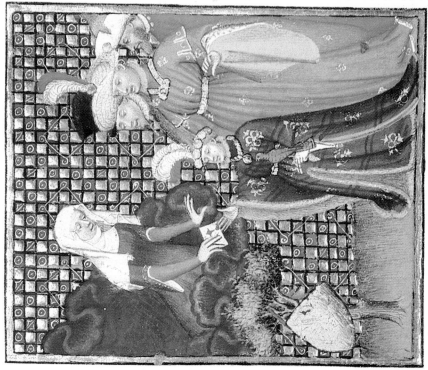

A. Christine presenting her book to Louis of Orleans.

B. Othea presenting her letter to Hector.

L'Epistre Othéa, London, BL, Harley MS 4431, fol. 95r & v.

C. Christine presenting her book to Louis of Orleans.   D. Othea presenting her letter to Hector.

L'Epistre Othéa, Paris, BN MS fr. 606, fol. 1r & v.

Sandra L. Hindman

CHRISTINE DE PIZAN'S "EPISTRE OTHÉA"
PAINTING AND POLITICS AT THE COURT OF CHARLES VI

This study examines the political views of Christine de Pizan as reflected in illuminated manuscripts of her writings. It is well established that Christine, who wrote between the years 1390 and 1429 mostly for those prominent in the royal court of the mad king, Charles VI, commented on the sensitive political issues of her day. The newness of this approach lies in its claim that her political commentaries may be understood better by analyzing the miniatures that accompany manuscripts of her texts. Among her writings, the *Epistre Othéa*, an epistolary allegory written from the goddess of wisdom, Othea, to the Trojan hero, Hector, is most extensively illuminated; its one hundred and one miniatures far exceed the numbers in her other illuminated works.

Three manuscripts of the *Epistre* dating within ten years of one another are the focus of this investigation. The first, executed around 1400, was decorated with only six miniatures. The second (probably begun around 1406 and completed around 1408) and third (around the same time or perhaps a little later), which present a slightly changed version of the text, were each decorated with one hundred and one miniatures. Each of the three manuscripts has autograph features: the first and second were penned by Christine and the third was supervised by her. It can now be demonstrated that she also determined the contents of the pictures in all three manuscripts. Thus the pictures reflect her views rather than those of her painters.

Christine's political allegory in these illuminated manuscripts of the *Epistre* was at first centered on the person to whom she dedicated the work, Louis of Orleans, likening him to Hector. She urged Hector (Louis) to practice political moderation based on wisdom, of which Othea (Christine) is the goddess. The political allegory is expressed in part through the very choice of the epistolary form, a mode of allegorical writing developed at the court of Charles VI to advise the king and the princes. The allegory is also conveyed through the miniatures, through details of heraldry, color, and costume, and through the selection and treatment of certain idiosyncratic subjects for illustration. Originally fulfilled in the figure of Louis, the allegory was adaptable to different figures from within the royal circle because of the special links between the kingdoms of France and Troy from which the genealogy of Hector issued through the French royal line. Anxious about the future welfare of France, Christine urged her influential readers to practice wise politics.

Together with two other authors, Philip of Mézières and Honoré Bouvet, Christine created an image of monarchy that was a timely response to the tragic circumstances of a particular reign, during which the king suffered forty-two fits of insanity and the question of his succession was pressing. However, the image they formulated was to serve later Valois kings as well, who, having emerged triumphant from the period of the Hundred Years' War, sought to regenerate national self-esteem. The legacy of the *Epistre Othéa* lies in these later inflated expressions of monarchy, especially in the royal entries which mixed verbal and visual imagery to communicate political thought. The *Epistre* belongs to an early stage in the process of forging and celebrating ideas about statehood that were to last through the Old Regime.

STUDIES AND TEXTS 77

CHRISTINE DE PIZAN'S "EPISTRE OTHÉA"

Painting and Politics at the Court of Charles VI

BY

SANDRA L. HINDMAN

PONTIFICAL INSTITUTE OF MEDIAEVAL STUDIES

PQ
1575
.E53
H5
1986

Acknowledgment

The publication of this book has been
made possible by a donation from the
Samuel H. Kress Foundation of New York.

CANADIAN CATALOGUING IN PUBLICATIONS DATA

Hindman, Sandra, 1944-
  Christine de Pizan's "Epistre Othea"

(Studies and texts, ISSN 0082-5328 ; 77)
Bibliography: p.
Includes index.
ISBN 0-88844-077-4

1. Christine, de Pisan, ca. 1364-ca. 1431.   Epistre Othea.   2. Christine, de Pisan, ca.
1364-ca. 1431 – Political and social views.   3. Christine, de Pisan, ca. 1364-ca. 1431 –
Manuscripts.   4. Christine, de Pisan, ca. 1364-ca. 1431 – Illustrations.   I. Pontifical
Institute of Mediaeval Studies.   II. Title.   III. Series: Studies and texts (Pontifical Institute
of Mediaeval Studies) ; 77.

PQ1575.E5H56   841'.1   C86-093473-X

Permission to reproduce the photographs in this volume has been received from the following
institutions: the Archives Nationales, Paris; the Bibliothèque de l'Arsenal, Paris; the Bibliothè-
que Nationale, Paris; the Bibliothèque Publique et Universitaire, Geneva; the Bibliothèque
Royale, Brussels; the Bodleian Library, Oxford; the British Library, London; the Johns
Hopkins University Special Collections, Baltimore; the Newnham College Library, Cam-
bridge; the Österreichisches Nationalbibliothek, Vienna; the Pierpont Morgan Library, New
York; the Rothschild Collection, Waddesdon Manor; the Staatsarchiv, Vienna; and the
Universitätsbibliothek, Erlangen.

© 1986

Pontifical Institute of Mediaeval Studies
59 Queen's Park Crescent East
Toronto, Ontario, Canada M5S 2C4

PRINTED BY UNIVERSA, WETTEREN, BELGIUM

Distributed outside North America by
E. J. Brill, Postbus 9000,
2300 PA Leiden, The Netherlands
Brill ISBN 90 04 07916 5

To Howard

Contents

Color Plates

(See Frontispiece)

List of Figures

Preface

This book examines the political views of Christine de Pizan as they are reflected in illuminated manuscripts of her writings. It is widely held that Christine, who wrote between the years 1390 and 1429 mostly for individuals prominent in the royal court of King Charles VI, commented in her writings on the sensitive political issues of her day.[1] But what of the miniatures illustrating her writings? It is generally assumed that these splendid miniatures, which were executed by some of the best and most original illuminators working in Paris, accommodated the taste for luxury commodities among Christine's aristocratic patrons and thus contributed substantially to the popularity of her work. This view considers the illuminations as little more than mere ornament added to delight prospective clients. In a more serious vein, it is sometimes suggested that certain subjects and their treatment in these miniatures demonstrate an awareness of Italian "humanism." Yet this interpretation only applies to a few miniatures and hardly takes into account the texts; it seems to be motivated by certain biases about French pre-Renaissance art (or non-Italian art) and by the fact of Christine's Italian heritage. Surprisingly, it has never been suggested that the miniatures might also provide political commentaries. Since it is now believed that illuminated manuscripts of Christine's writings were produced under her direction, it seems reasonable to suppose that the pictures were designed – at least in part – in order to amplify the political views presented in the texts.

In examining Christine's political thought, I shall focus on manuscripts of one of her writings, the *Epistre Othéa*, an epistolary allegory written around 1400 from the goddess of wisdom, Othea, to the Trojan hero, Hector, when he was fifteen years old. Certain manuscripts of the *Epistre*

---

[1] C. Gauvard, "Christine de Pisan a-t-elle eu une pensée politique? À propos d'ouvrages récents," *Revue historique* 250 (1973) 417-430; G. Mombello, "Quelques aspects de la pensée politique de Christine de Pisan d'après ses œuvres publiées," in *Culture et politique en France à l'époque de l'humanisme et de la Renaissance. Atti del convegno internazionale promosso dall'Accademia delle scienze di Torino, 1971,* ed. F. Simone (Turin, 1974), pp. 43-153; and J. Wisman, "L'Éveil du sentiment national au Moyen Âge: la pensée politique de Christine de Pisan," *Revue historique* 257 (1977) 289-297.

include one hundred and one miniatures, a number far in excess of that
in any of Christine's other illuminated works, none of which is adorned
with more than seven miniatures. Because of the large number of
miniatures in the *Epistre*, a study of these manuscripts provides a virtually
unique opportunity to investigate whether and how the extended programs of illustration in Christine's manuscripts function as political
commentaries.

Those who are familiar with scholarship on the *Epistre* may immediately object, pointing out that the *Epistre* is not usually thought of as a
political work. Instead, it has typically been judged to be a moral allegory,
a system of instruction that Christine wrote while thinking of her son,
Jean de Castel, who was at the time fifteen years old, like Hector.[2] As a
woman addressing her son, Christine would thus follow other medieval
women writers who include Dhuoda, writing in the ninth century to her
son at the Carolingian court of Charles the Bald.[3] As a book of chivalry,
the *Epistre* would thus be classed with numerous courtesy books, which
include Dhuoda's manual which teaches Christian behavior in a secular
world. In challenging this understanding of the *Epistre*, I shall analyze the
contemporary manuscripts, their textual and pictorial contents, to show
that they can be read as conveying an intricate political allegory, one that
is appropriate for specific individuals at the French court and one that is
ultimately unsuitable for Christine's son.

In the light of my proposed revision of the meaning of the *Epistre
Othéa*, the established view of the *Epistre* as a work addressed to Jean de
Castel demands further attention. The persistence of this understanding
of the *Epistre* may result from a lingering reluctance to appreciate fully
Christine's role as a commentator on politics, a still-uncommon role for
a woman, and a simultaneous readiness to perceive her as a mother
concerned about the welfare of her child. In other words, Christine's
concerns as an author have been interpreted essentially through a patriarchal critical vision, one that understands Christine as fulfilling societal

---

[2] E.g., R. Tuve, *Allegorical Imagery, Some Mediaeval Books and Their Posterity*
(Princeton, 1966), p. 286; and C. C. Willard, *Christine de Pizan, Her Life and Works*
(New York, 1984), p. 94. This view is most widely held, notwithstanding the fact that
different identities of the fifteen-year-old recipient have been proposed, as summarized
by G. Mombello, "Per un'edizione critica dell'*Epistre Othéa* di Christine de Pizan," *Studi
francesi* 8 (1964) 414-416.

[3] On Dhuoda's life and her *Manualis* (which have certain striking characteristics in
common with Christine's life and her *Epistre*, which have passed unobserved), see
P. Dronke, *Women Writers of the Middle Ages, A Critical Study of Texts from Perpetua
(†203) to Marguerite Porete (†1310)* (Cambridge, Eng., 1984), pp. 36-54.

stereotypes. What may seem initially paradoxical is that the women writers who have largely dominated scholarship both on Christine and on the *Epistre*, notably the late Rosemond Tuve and more recently Charity Cannon Willard, are among those individuals who have characterized the *Epistre* in this conventional way. Being women writers themselves, they might be expected to entertain more pluralistic views of women's situations. But this does not always happen, as feminist theorists have been quick to point out.[4] "Reading as a woman" is not conditioned by gender, for women, learning within a patriarchal society, often look toward male models and may read as men. Rather, "reading as a woman" is generated by a raised literary consciousness about the act of reading that, as Jonathan Culler has recently put it, entails learning "to question the literary and political assumptions on which ... reading has been based."[5] The main assumption I am questioning here is one that clings to the image of Christine the author primarily as a mother, especially when there is no substantive evidence for this position (the fact that Hector and Jean are both fifteen seems, as we shall see, inconsequential).

The male-oriented bias that informs readings of the *Epistre* seems all the more evident when we realize that concrete historical evidence should have long ago called into question the idea that the *Epistre Othéa* was written for Jean de Castel. This evidence is another work by Christine, the *Enseignements moraulx*, or the Moral Teachings, which is expressly addressed to Jean for the purpose of teaching him useful moral precepts. As a moral guide, like a schoolbook, the *Enseignements moraulx* is similar to what scholars would have us believe the *Epistre* to be. A comparison of these two texts reveals that the *Epistre* reflects other concerns. In the course of uncovering those other concerns and exposing the political ideology of the *Epistre*, my primary intention is not to offer a feminist reading, but rather to call attention to those obstacles that have in the past stood in the way of a political reading of the work.

Another objection to a political reading might also be raised. It might be correctly pointed out that, even if the *Epistre* was not written with Jean de Castel in mind, it is nevertheless a moral allegory, a "double courtesy book," as Rosemond Tuve described it. In her analysis of the *Epistre*, Tuve proposed that the popularity of the work was due partly to Christine's successful mingling of two allegories, a poetic one and a

---

[4] See especially J. Fetterley, *The Resisting Reader, A Feminist Approach to American Fiction* (Bloomington, Ind., 1978).

[5] J. Culler, *On Deconstruction. Theory and Criticism after Structuralism* (Ithaca, NY, 1982), pp. 43-64 ("Reading as a Woman").

theological one, for her readers. According to Tuve's reading, one allegory teaches those virtues appropriate for good conduct in a secular world to a figure whom Christine calls the "good knight," and a second, imposed allegory teaches related spiritual values to the "good spirit." My interpretation does not displace Tuve's. Indeed I am prepared to accept Tuve's interrelated claims that the *Epistre* reflects Christine's knowledge of religious exegesis and that late medieval readers of the work may well have been delighted by its novel mixture of religious didacticism and classical imagery. But I believe that a political allegory coexists with those which Tuve identified and, moreover, that in the original manuscripts of the *Epistre* (but not in later copies) this political reading is the privileged one. Basing her argument primarily on the text, Tuve made little distinction between those manuscripts that were executed during Christine's lifetime and under her direction and those that were executed later. Had she focused her analysis on the original manuscripts, her conclusions might have been different, for a study of the texts and pictures in these manuscripts yields a rich reading of contemporary French politics as seen from a woman's point of view.

The willingness to accept the *Epistre* as a "double courtesy book" and to look no further for other meanings (like the willingness to see Jean de Castel as the intended reader) may result from an implicit bias that accepts courtesy literature as a more fitting genre than political allegory for a woman writer. Such a bias undoubtedly has existed and may still exist. But the view of the *Epistre* as a courtesy book has also gained support from a study of the manuscript tradition of the *Epistre*. Later manuscripts and early printed books of the *Epistre*, ones that were executed within a century of the original composition of Christine's work, are virtually unanimous in presenting the *Epistre* as a courtesy book. Thus, what has happened is this: readings of later versions of the *Epistre* have helped to shape the contemporary ideology about the work. In rereading the *Epistre*, today's reader is faced with a forceful alliance between those who contend on the basis of historical "evidence," that the *Epistre* has been regarded for centuries as a courtesy book and those who maintain, on the basis of male-oriented assumptions that operate while reading, that we should continue to regard it as a courtesy book.

The issue of Christine de Pizan's feminism comes up inevitably in the course of the reconsideration of her politics that results from my rereading of the *Epistre* as a political work. This issue is a complex one. The litany most frequently rehearsed in the literature is that, while not a feminist in a modern-day sense of the word largely because of the conservative nature of many of her values, Christine is an antecedent of feminism, its earliest

forerunner.[6] It is pointed out that the circumstances of her life and certain
themes in her writings are anomalous for women of her day and share
more with those of women as a social group today. In this respect, a good
deal has been written on Christine as a promoter of women's accom-
plishments and worth, and somewhat less has been written on her as a
feminist writer who manipulated language in novel ways to re-present
women.[7] But very little has been written on her feminism from a political
perspective. To my mind, the crucial questions are: What role(s) does she
envision for women in political life, and where does she stand on the issue
of the political power of women? I will argue that a rereading of the
Epistre provides in part a fascinating perspective on Christine's feminist
thought, by redefining her political stance vis-à-vis the ruling class for
whom she wrote.

A few final remarks about where this book fits in the scholarship on
the *Epistre* are in order here. There is still no modern edition of the
Epistre,[8] with the result that those interested in the *Epistre* must study it
in manuscript form. Although this circumstance might have produced an
awareness of the *Epistre* as a book composed of both text and miniatures,
this has not been the case, and those who have studied the *Epistre* have
concentrated either on its text or on its miniatures. Those interested in
its text have studied its sources and, like Tuve, have concluded that it is

---

[6] For example, see L. Richardson, *The Forerunners of Feminism in French Literature
of the Renaissance: From Christine de Pisan to Marie de Gournay* (Baltimore, 1929);
Christine de Pizan, *The Book of the City of Ladies*, tr. E. J. Richards (New York, 1982);
and Willard, *Christine de Pizan*, esp. pp. 222-223. A somewhat different view is held by
Joan Kelly-Gadol, "Early Feminist Theory and the *Querelle des femmes*, 1400-1789,"
Signs 8 (1982) 4-28, reprinted in Joan Kelly, *Women, History and Theory: The Essays
of Joan Kelly* (Chicago, 1984), pp. 65-109.
[7] Especially interesting in this regard are the following: Sylvia Huot, "Seduction and
Sublimation: Christine de Pizan, Jean de Meun, and Dante," *Romance Notes* 25 (1985)
361-373; and E. J. Richards, "Christine de Pizan and the Question of Feminist Rheto-
ric," *Modern Language Association Conference* 22 (1983) 15-24.
[8] G. Mombello, *La tradizione manoscritta dell'"Epistre Othéa" di Christine de Pizan.
Prolegomeni all'edizione del testo*, Memorie dell'Accademia delle scienze di Torino,
Classe di Scienze morali, storiche e filologiche, Series 4, 15 (Turin, 1967) has promised
an edition. A transcription of the version in London appeared as part of a thesis by
H. Loukopoulos, "Classical Mythology in the Works of Christine de Pisan with an
Edition of *L'Epistre Othéa* from the Manuscript Harley 4431," Unpublished doctoral
dissertation, Wayne State University, 1977. There is an edition of Stephen Scrope's
fifteenth-century English translation, *The Epistle of Othea*, ed. C. Bühler, Early English
Text Society, 264 (London, 1970). My references are to the manuscript in London,
although for the convenience of readers I have also included citations to Bühler's edition
of the published English translation, cited hereafter as *Epistle of Othea*, tr. Scrope.

a courtesy book.[9] Those interested in its miniatures have concerned themselves mostly with questions of style,[10] with the exception of Tuve, who brought to a reading of selected pictures the understanding she had of the text as religious exegesis. Thus, there has been no systematic attempt to explain the meaning of the miniatures in manuscripts of the *Epistre* and, further, apart from Tuve's book, no attempt has been made to explain the meaning of the miniatures in relationship to the meaning of the text and to the medieval readers of the manuscripts. In this present book I have tried to fill this gap by attempting to interpret the *Epistre* as Christine and her readers thought of it, when they read it as an illuminated manuscript.

An important assumption – namely, that medieval writings can be understood best when they are studied in their manuscript forms—underlies this investigation.[11] It should come as no surprise to find that medieval authors referred to texts as manuscripts, as we might refer today to a biography or a mystery as, say, a hardcover or a paperback edition, thereby conveying some sense of the physical form in which we read the text. For example, Gontier Col, writing to Christine on the subject of Jehan de Meun's *Roman de la Rose*, sent her a manuscript copy of another of Jehan's works, *Le Trésor de maistre Jehan de Meung ou les Septs Articles de la Foi*, so that she would better understand the master's writings, but Col cautioned her about the scribal errors in the manuscript, which he supposed she would be able to recognize and amend.[12] Also writing on the subject of the *Roman de la Rose*, Jean Gerson criticized Jehan de Meun's slanders in the *Roman*, pointing out that his defamations were all the more serious because he had them "portrayed skilfully and lavishly in words and pictures, the more quickly to allure people into hearing, seeing, and holding fast to these things."[13] In each of these

---

[9] P. G. C. Campbell, *L'Épître d'Othéa. Étude sur les sources de Christine de Pisan* (Paris, 1924).

[10] See M. Meiss, *French Painting in the Time of Jean de Berry. The Limbourgs and their Contemporaries*, 2 vols. (London, 1974), 1: 23-41, 292-296, 377-382, 388-389, where the author's views on the "humanism" of the miniatures are also found; and L. Schaefer, "Die Illustrationen zu den Handschriften der Christine de Pizan," *Marburger Jahrbuch für Kunstwissenschaft* 10 (1937) 119-208; and P. de Winter, "Christine de Pizan, ses enlumineurs et ses rapports avec le milieu bourguignon," *Actes du 104ᵉ congrès national des sociétés savantes (1979)*, (Paris, 1982), pp. 335-375.

[11] A similar view of medieval reading is argued by John Fleming, *The 'Roman de la Rose': A Study in Allegory and Iconography* (Princeton, 1969).

[12] Christine de Pizan, *"La Querelle de la Rose": Letters and Documents*, ed. J. L. Baird and J. R. Kane, North Carolina Studies in the Romance Languages and Literatures, 199 (Chapel Hill, N.C., 1978), p. 58.

[13] *Ibid.*, p. 73.

instances the meaning of the work was thought of as being bound up in the form of the manuscript, which in the first case was a poorly corrected copy by an ill-informed scribe and in the second was a lavishly illuminated copy produced under the direction of the author.

There is evidence that Christine was involved more extensively than was usual in the activity of bookmaking and so would have been especially alert to the manuscript as a form for expressing her ideas. Since she wrote out and edited her own works, including the most deluxe manuscripts of her writings, she may have supervised all stages of the production of her manuscripts.[14] Thus she may have determined the contents of the pictures, a possibility I have had to explore before asserting that the pictures reflect her views rather than those of her painters. Her active role in the production of her manuscripts certainly makes it likely that she took into account her medieval readers, her patrons, for whom the illustrated copies were made, as she went about producing copies of her manuscripts. Because so much is already known or can be uncovered about the circumstances surrounding the execution and ownership of manuscripts of the *Epistre*, I have been able to speculate from a firmer historical ground than is often possible about the interchange between the author and her readers. The vehicles in which this interchange is reflected are her illuminated manuscripts, and for this reason they, not only their words or only their pictures, are the "texts" on which I base my reading.

Three manuscript copies of the *Epistre* dating within ten years of one another are the focus of my study.[15] The first was executed around 1400, perhaps for Duke Louis of Orleans, to whom the work was dedicated (Paris, BN MS fr. 848). This one was decorated with only six miniatures. The second and third copies, which present a slightly changed version of the text, were each decorated with one hundred and one miniatures. The second copy was probably begun around 1406 and completed around 1408 as part of a deluxe corpus of Christine's "Collected Works" for Duke John of Berry (Paris, BN MS fr. 606). The third copy was executed around the same time or perhaps a little later and was incorporated into another deluxe volume of her "Collected Works," one that she presented to Queen Isabeau of Bavaria between 1410 and 1415 (London, BL Harley MS 4431). All three manuscripts have autograph features; the first and

---

[14] G. Ouy and C. Reno, "Identification des autographes de Christine de Pizan," *Scriptorium* 34 (1980) 221-238.

[15] These manuscripts are studied, in relation to the manuscript tradition, by G. Mombello, *La tradizione manoscritta*, pp. 13-31, 199-210.

third were written entirely by Christine, while the writing of the second was supervised by her.[16]

I will argue that Christine fashioned a political allegory in these illuminated manuscripts of the *Epistre*, one that was centered on the person to whom she dedicated the work, Louis of Orleans, likening him to Hector even in the earliest, sparsely illustrated, copy. She urged Louis (Hector) to practice political moderation based on wisdom, of which Othea (Christine) is the goddess. But Louis was not the only reader Christine addressed in the *Epistre*. Both manuscript copies with one hundred and one pictures were completed after Louis's death in 1407. I believe that these later copies upheld the dead duke as an example, while they impelled other readers, those still in power — the duke of Berry, the queen, and the dauphin — to the practice of wise politics on which the future welfare of France depended. The allegory, originally fulfilled in the figure of Louis, was adaptable to different figures within the royal circle because of the special links between the kingdoms of France and Troy, from which the genealogy of Hector issued through the French royal line.

* * *

Initially struck by the apparent discrepancy between the content of the pictures and the usual interpretation of the text of the London copy of the *Epistre Othéa* and intrigued, at the same time, by the potential of studying a luxury manuscript produced by an author-scribe, I began work on this project in 1974. Preliminary findings were delivered, with Susan Noakes, in a joint lecture in May 1974. Entitled "Text and Illustration: Christine de Pizan's *Epistre Othéa*," this lecture was presented at a conference on "The Genealogy of the Epic" at The Johns Hopkins University and then, in a shorter version, at the meetings of the First Courtly Literature Society. Some of our findings have been incorporated into chapter 3, "The Ideological Programs of the Manuscripts." As I continued to work on the project, I became interested in exploring the nature of Christine's political views as reflected in the *Epistre*, the subject of my book as it now stands.

Many institutions and individuals have contributed in various ways to this project. In particular, the staffs of the Bibliothèque Nationale in Paris and the British Library in London were unceasingly helpful in answering questions, providing technical facilities for the study of the manuscripts,

---

[16] Ouy and Reno, "Identification des autographes," pp. 227, 230.

and meeting demands for photographs and slides. I owe special debts of gratitude to François Avril, Conservateur, Salle des Manuscrits, Bibliothèque Nationale, Paris, and Janet Backhouse, Assistant Keeper of Manuscripts, the British Library, London. Among the staffs of other institutions where I was freely provided access to manuscripts, I thank those of Newnham College Library, Cambridge; the Bibliothèque Municipale, Beauvais; the Bibliothèque Royale, Brussels; the Universitätsbibliothek, Erlangen; the Biblioteca Bodmeriana, Cologny-Geneva; the Koninklijke Bibliotheek, The Hague; the Rothschild Collection, Waddesdon Manor; the Musée Condé, Chantilly; the Bodleian Library, Oxford; and the Bibliothèque de l'Arsenal, Paris.

Individuals who read drafts of the manuscript and whose comments I have tried to incorporate include Gilbert Ouy, Gabrielle Spiegel, Anne D. Hedeman, Anne van Buren, and Riccardo Famiglietti. It would be difficult to thank sufficiently Gilbert Ouy, whose enthusiasm for this project never waned and whose work on French humanism at the court of Charles VI, on Christine de Pisan, and on manuscript production has provided a constant inspiration for this study. I am grateful also to David Hult for assistance with the medieval French translations and to Christine Reno for sharing with me her unpublished transcription of Phillipps MS 128.

A number of grants and fellowships supported my research at various stages, funding trips to Europe to study the manuscripts, subsidizing the purchase of photographs, and facilitating the leave that was used to write a first draft of the book. Research grants from the American Philosophical Society made possible two trips to Europe (Summers 1977, 1981) as well as the purchase of photographs. A grant-in-aid from the American Council for Learned Societies funded another trip to Europe (Summer 1978) and the purchase of photographs. Fellowships from the National Endowment for the Humanities and the Center for Advanced Study in the Visual Arts of the National Gallery of Art in Washington made possible a leave of absence from Johns Hopkins in 1980-1981. That year, which I spent as a Senior Fellow at the Center for Advanced Study in the Visual Arts, was invaluable; it enabled me to write a draft of the book while working in a stimulating environment that fostered a lively discourse on ideas about research and writing in art history. I am very grateful to Henry Millon, Marianna Shreve Simpson, Rosalind Krauss, and Keith Moxey, each of whom contributed insights during my stay at the center.

I would also like to acknowledge the generosity of the Samuel H. Kress Foundation, which through a gift to the Pontifical Institute of Mediaeval Studies made possible the liberal color and black-and-white illustrations that accompany this book.

My greatest debt is to Howard Lehman, who in numerous capacities assisted with the completion of this book. As editor he read and commented on the manuscript, and as friend he listened daily to the practical and intellectual problems that came up in the course of research and writing. More important, his presence made the fabric of my life as a professional woman very different from Christine's; writing as a widow in a more conventional society, Christine faced solitude and sexism. Howard shared with me a lively companionship that broke up the solitary activity of writing and a deep conviction in the equality of women that sustained me throughout this project. I am grateful to him for having given so much.

Chicago, Illinois
April 1985

Abbreviations

BEC:	Bibliothèque de l'École des Chartes
BL:	British Library
BN:	Bibliothèque Nationale
BR:	Bibliothèque Royale
JWCI:	*Journal of the Warburg and Courtauld Institutes*
ÖNB:	Österreichische Nationalbibliothek
SATF:	Société des anciens textes français
SHF:	Société de l'histoire de France

Introduction
The Historical Setting

Praised for her shrewd reasoning by the noted Jean Gerson who called her a masculine woman, accused of forgery by others who claimed that her writing was more characteristic of a man, Christine de Pizan is now regarded by many as France's first woman of letters.[1] Because she was so exceptional — an Italian living in France, a woman writing like a man, a feminist in an age of male domination, when it was unusual for women to be educated at all, much less for them to be self-supporting professional writers — scholars have focused on her individuality and isolated her from her time period.[2] Many things about Christine are, to be sure, difficult to explain. But the dominant view in this book is that she can be better understood if she is placed in a historical context.

Those who seek to learn about Christine's work will, therefore, need to gain some insight into the circumstances of her life and into the nature of the government in France from 1368, when at the age of four she moved to Paris, to around 1415, when she probably left Paris. Both were exceptional. Christine's close connection with the royal court, where first her father and then her husband worked, gave her an unusual access to material for her writings. The successive reigns of the monarchs, the "wise" Charles V, who died in 1380, and the "mad" Charles VI, who died in 1422, fostered an age of stable reconstruction followed by one of turbulent unrest. The characteristics of these two reigns contributed to shape the political thought of the period, including Christine's. The conjunction between the circumstances of Christine's life and the nature of the government in France helps to explain how, and in what ways, she came to comment on political issues.

---

[1] For Gerson's remark, see Christine "*La Querelle de la Rose*," ed. J. L. Baird and J. R. Kane, p. 148; the accusation of forgery is found in idem, *Lavision-Christine, Introduction and Text*, ed. M. L. Towner (Washington, D.C., 1932), p. 143.

[2] Modern biographies include M.-J. Pinet, *Christine de Pisan 1364-1430. Étude biographique et littéraire*, Bibliothèque du xvᵉ siècle, 35 (Paris, 1927); the somewhat more popular studies, E. McLeod, *The Order of the Rose. The Life and Ideas of Christine de Pizan* (Totowa, N.J., 1976); R. Pernoud, *Christine de Pisan* (Paris, 1982); and C. C. Willard, *Christine de Pizan, Her Life and Works*.

Born in 1364 in Venice, Christine came to Paris in 1368 to join her father, Thomas, who had three years earlier accepted the position of physician and astrologer to King Charles v.[3] The king gave Thomas money to send for his wife, who was the daughter of a Bolognese doctor, and his three children, the eldest, Christine, and her two younger brothers, Aghinolfo and Paolo. Although it is not known exactly where the family lived in Paris, their house was probably a dependency of the king's principal residence, the sprawling Hôtel Saint-Pol located in the quarter of the Marais. Little is known about Christine's early education or friendships, but presumably she participated in life at court as was customary for families of royal servants. She later wrote eye-witness accounts of the royal receptions for the sultan of Babylon and the Holy Roman emperor.[4] She admired immensely her father, the astrologer, who "took great pleasure from seeing" her "inclination to learning," whereas she described her mother as "keeping her busy with spinning and silly girlishness, following the common custom of women."[5] Growing up in the palace of the king, "nourished on his bread," she said,[6] Christine passed a happy childhood.

At the age of fifteen, in 1379, she married a nobleman, Etienne Castel, a match that, although it was arranged by her father, seems to have resulted in genuine love. King Charles v offered Christine's husband a salary and a post as "notary and secretary to the king"[7] and in 1380 he made the family a present of the Tour Barbeau, a house on the Seine.[8]

For Christine, the reign of Charles v (1364-80) was a time during which the "good wise king restored France from the state of ruin into which it had fallen before."[9] The foremost problem of Charles's reign was the Hundred Years' War between France and England.[10] The cause of the war was the English king's claim to the French throne, a claim that dated

---

[3] Christine, *Lavision*, pp. 149-150. Christine Reno is preparing a new edition, based in part on a manuscript with autograph glosses in a private collection, formerly Phillipps MS 128.

[4] Christine de Pizan, *Livre des fais et bonnes meurs du sage Roy Charles V*, ed. S. Solente, 2 vols., SHF (Paris, 1936-1940), 2: 85, 95-129.

[5] Christine, *The City of Ladies*, pp. 154-155.

[6] Christine, *Livre des fais et bonnes meurs*, 2: 193.

[7] Christine, *Lavision*, pp. 151-152.

[8] Pinet, *Christine de Pisan*, p. 11, n. 1.

[9] Christine, *Lavision*, Phillipps MS 128, fol. 6r.

[10] On the reign of Charles VI, see R. Cazelles, *Société politique, noblesse et couronne sous Jean le Bon et Charles V*, Mémoires et documents publiés par la Société de l'École des Chartes, 28 (Geneva, 1982); and the biography, R. Delachenal, *Histoire de Charles V*, 5 vols. (Paris, 1909-1931).

from 1328, when the first king of the Valois line, Philip VI, the grandson of the Capetian King Philip III, acceded to the throne.[11] When the last son of King Philip IV died in 1328, only a daughter, Isabelle, survived him. Since women and their offspring had long been excluded from the throne, according to custom that invoked the Salic law of the Frankish tribes, the throne passed to the nearest male, a Valois. But Isabelle's son, Edward III, king of England, pressed his claim to France, arguing that his blood line, through his mother, was closest to that of the deceased king, Philip IV. When a series of councils affirmed Philip VI's right to accession and upheld the Salic law, England decided to take by force what it could not acquire by law. At the accession of Charles V, England already controlled most of southwestern France, although by the terms of the Peace of Calais in 1360 the English king, Edward III, had tacitly surrendered his claim to the French throne.

Charles V was a statesman, not a warrior. He appointed a constable, the Breton Bertrand du Guesclin, to conduct the war, and under Bertrand's direction the reconquest of France was accomplished. By 1375, only Calais and a portion of Bordeaux were still in the hands of the English. Free from the duties of battle, Charles surrounded himself with able counselors who helped him conduct the day-to-day business of governing. He filled the royal administration with educated secretaries and notaries, many from among the bourgeoisie, like Pierre d'Orgemont,[12] with whom Christine's husband must have worked. And he employed theoreticians, who worked to consolidate royal power by exalting the prestige of the monarch in works of propaganda.[13] It was in this peaceful, intellectual milieu that the Pizzano family lived and worked.

Something should be said here about the illuminated manuscripts made for King Charles V in order to set the stage for Christine's illuminated manuscripts produced at the court of King Charles VI. Charles V was a sophisticated patron who commissioned translations of existing works and compositions of new works that closely reflect the political concerns of the reign.[14] For example, Jean Golein composed a treatise on the

[11] On this period, see R. Cazelles, *La Société politique et la crise de la royauté sous Philippe de Valois* (Paris, 1958).

[12] Cazelles, *Société politique, noblesse et couronne*, pp. 470ff.

[13] *Ibid.*, pp. 505-516.

[14] See especially L. Delisle, *Recherches sur la librairie de Charles V*, 2 vols. (Paris, 1907); C. R. Sherman, *The Portraits of Charles V of France (1338-1380)*, Monographs on Archaeology and Fine Arts, 20 (New York, 1969); Paris, Bibliothèque Nationale, *La Librairie de Charles V* (Paris, 1968); and J. Monfrin, "Les Traducteurs et leur publique en France au Moyen Âge," *Journal des Savants* (1964) 5-20.

ceremony of the coronation, the *Traité du Sacre*, along with a translation of the Latin *Ordo* of the coronation. Incorporating ideas that appear in Golein's treatise, the illuminated Coronation Book of Charles V and Jeanne de Bourbon is apparently the first such book to contain an extended sequence of carefully detailed miniatures, which can best be understood when we recognize the special meaning of the coronation for Charles and his queen.[15] Nicole Oresme translated into French Aristotle's *Politics* and *Ethics*, and wrote a commentary to accompany the translation, as well as a guide to the reader [the king?] to explain the prefatory miniatures.[16] Charles must have had a special interest in these works, for he possessed two illuminated copies of each, one a large "library" edition and the other a smaller "pocket" edition. Like the Coronation Book, the *Politics* and *Ethics* include pictorial and textual references to contemporary events and ideas that held particular interest for their patron. Another example of a manuscript that reflects ideas at court is Charles V's personal copy of the *Grandes Chroniques de France*, the official chronicle of the French kings. This copy was revised four times, three times during the reign of Charles V, in order to update it to refer to recent events and to respond to new political issues.[17] The royal copy of the *Grandes Chroniques*, along with copies of Aristotle and the Coronation Book, displays a sophisticated picture cycle that makes manifest the ideology of the text.

Thus, the illuminated manuscripts produced throughout the reign of Charles V reveal the collaboration of theoreticians, scribes, and illuminators, who together present a synthesis of the ideology of the Valois monarchy, a synthesis formulated at the king's express command by a small circle of advisers who worked closely with him. Along with many other, similar, royal commissions, these books were housed in the newly

---

[15] See the detailed study of this manuscript (London, BL MS Cotton Tib. B VII) by C. R. Sherman, "The Queen in the Charles V's *Coronation Book*: Jeanne de Bourbon and the *Ordo ad Reginam Benedicendam*," *Viator* 8 (1977) 255-297.

[16] See the studies by C. R. Sherman, "Some Visual Definitions in the Illustrations of Aristotle's *Nicomachean Ethics* and *Politics* in the French Translation of Nicole Oresme," *Art Bulletin* 59 (1977) 320-330; and idem, "A Second Instruction to the Reader from Nicole Oresme, Translator of Aristotle's *Politics* and *Economics*," *Art Bulletin* 61 (1979) 468-469. The relevant manuscripts are: Brussels, BR MS 9505-9506; The Hague, Museum Meermanno Westreenianum, MS 10 D 1.

[17] See the studies on this manuscript (Paris, BN MS fr. 2813) by Anne D. Hedeman, "The Illustrations of the *Grandes Chroniques de France* from 1274 to 1422," Unpublished doctoral dissertation, The Johns Hopkins University, 1984, esp. pp. 53-128, 398-411; idem, "Valois Legitimacy: Editorial Changes in Charles V's *Grandes Chroniques de France*," *Art Bulletin* 66 (1984) 97-117; and idem, "Restructuring the Narrative; The Function of Ceremonial in Charles V's *Grandes Chroniques de France*," *Studies in the History of Art* 16 (1985) 171-181.

constructed royal library in the Louvre, and they formed the basis of the library of Charles VI. As we shall see, the circumstances of patronage changed considerably at the court of the new king, for whom Christine was to work, although the patterns of production – entailing the close cooperation of theoreticians, scribes, and illuminators – remained similar.

After the death of Charles V in 1380, the fortunes of Christine's family declined. Thomas and Etienne were retained in the employ of the new king, but Thomas was poorly paid.[18] Christine's marriage flourished, however, and she gave birth to three children, two sons and a daughter, between 1381 and 1385.[19] At the end of the decade, two events radically altered her life. First, her father, Thomas, died sometime between 1384 and 1389, following a long illness. He left behind his wife and children, but only a meager legacy. Then, in 1389, Etienne died, probably a victim of an epidemic, while on a royal mission in Beauvais.[20] In less than a decade, Christine, though "still young," had entered through "the door of misfortune," as she described her plight.[21] She was only twenty-five years old at the time.

Emotionally heartbroken, Christine was also financially destitute. Later, in one of her writings, the *Livre de la Mutacion de fortune* (c. 1400-1403), she was to compare the moment of her husband's death to a voyage at sea, during which Fortune took her husband's life and transformed Christine into a man, who must take the helm on the open seas.[22] The metaphor was apt, for, like a man, she needed to support herself and her family, but, being a woman, she had no money of her own. She had difficulty securing Etienne's property, since it was in the king's name; interest was due on its mortgage; his past wages were owed to her; and she had to borrow frequently. On four separate occasions, Christine even pleaded her case before the law courts, but she was not to receive financial restitution until 1411, and then only after the powerful Guillaume de Tignonville, president of the Chamber of Accounts, interceded on her behalf.[23] Creditors came and removed her "little belongings," as

---

[18] Christine, *Lavision*, p. 152.

[19] *Ibid.*, p. 154.

[20] *Ibid.*, pp. 153-154; on the death of her husband, see also Christine de Pizan, *Le Livre du chemin de long estude*, ed. R. Püschel (Berlin, 1881), pp. 5-6; and idem, *Le Livre de la mutacion de Fortune*, ed. S. Solente, 3 vols., SATF (Paris, 1955), 1: 8-9.

[21] Christine, *Lavision*, p. 152.

[22] Christine, *La Mutacion*, 1: 52-53.

[23] *Ibid.*, pp. 154-155; see also, the documents referred to by Solente, in Christine, *Livre des fais et bonnes meurs*, 1: xvi-xvii.

she called them, including some prized oriental manuscripts that the former king had given to her father.[24] Her garments became more and more threadbare, and she, being "feeble of body and naturally afraid," fell ill.[25]

Her financial troubles gradually subsided in the 1390s and she regained her health, with the result that she was free from some of the practical worries that had plagued her in the years immediately following Etienne's death. Although it is not known precisely how she supported herself during this period, the sale of her father's properties in 1392 no doubt eased her financial burden.[26] By 1394 her brothers had returned to Italy, and in 1397 she placed her son, Jean Castel, in the service of the earl of Salisbury in England and her daughter took vows as a nun at the Abbey of Poissy outside Paris.[27] It is not known what happened to her third child; perhaps he had already died.

Most women in Christine's position would have taken religious vows, or perhaps remarried; Christine became a writer ("now I am a man," she wrote in the *Livre de la Mutacion*).[28] She began to compose love poetry in the 1390s, at first to console herself about the loss of her husband. It is sometimes said that she entered a poetry contest and was pleased with the positive reception her work received.[29] In any event, she spent most of this decade studying, a pastime she describes with pleasure, mentioning the "beautiful books" that she "snatched up" and reflecting that she had always felt the inclination to study but that she had never had the time required to pursue it, because of her duties as a wife and a mother.[30] By the end of the decade, around 1399, she had written one hundred poems, which she gathered together into a volume called the *Cent balades*.[31] She was ready to embark on her new career with a seriousness of purpose.

As Christine prepared for her career as a writer, she continued to live in Paris under the reign of the new king, Charles VI (1380-1422), whom she was to praise for his many "noble qualities" while lamenting the "pity

---

[24] Christine, *Lavision*, p. 157.

[25] *Ibid.*, pp. 156, 158.

[26] Christine, *Livre des fais et bonnes meurs*, 1: xviii; and N. Iorga, *Philippe de Mézières, 1327-1405, et la croisade au XIVᵉ siècle*, Bibliothèque de l'École des hautes études, sciences philologiques et historiques, 110 (Paris, 1896), p. 505, n. 5.

[27] Christine, *Lavision*, pp. 165, 174.

[28] Christine, *La Mutacion*, 1: 53.

[29] *Œuvres poétiques de Christine de Pisan*, ed. M. Roy, 3 vols., SATF (Paris, 1886-1896), 1: 100.

[30] Christine, *Lavision*, p. 163.

[31] Christine, *Œuvres poétiques*, 1: 1-100.

of his illness."[32] When the boy king came into power at the age of twelve,[33] three important ordinances passed at the end of the reign of Charles v were in effect.[34] The first ordinance set the age of majority at fourteen years and appointed Louis I, duke of Anjou, regent during the interregnum. The second ordinance established the queen, together with the dukes Louis I of Bourbon and Philip the Bold of Burgundy, as responsible for the king's education. The third ordinance, which has been called the "first constitutional law" in France, explicitly set down the conditions of succession: the eldest son of the deceased king would succeed him; if there was no son, the nearest male heir, descended from a male, became king; women were excluded from succession to the throne and could not transmit the right to the throne; the election to the throne could not be set aside; the nearest male heir acceded to the throne when the king died, and his accession through the coronation could not be contested. This last ordinance, coupled at first with Charles VI's youth and inexperience and later with his poor health, was to affect the course of the entire reign.

The reign was never a strong one, even in the beginning. At first there were antagonisms between the regent dukes, who also dismissed many of the counselors of Charles v. It was probably in this initial shuffle within the government that Thomas of Pizan effectively lost his power. Later in the decade, interest in the regency subsided, in part because Louis of Anjou had departed for Italy and Philip of Burgundy was occupied with his affairs in Flanders. For a time, at the end of the decade, it seemed as though the government of Charles VI might perpetuate that of his father. He married by 1385, a German princess, Isabeau of Bavaria, and then, in November 1388, at Reims, proclaimed his majority. He subsequently dismissed the former government and reappointed many of the counselors of his father. A peace treaty with England, negotiated in 1388, was renewed for three years in 1390, and King Richard II, who likewise had just announced his majority, sent several diplomatic missions to France.[35] During these years, the king's younger brother, Louis, the count of

---

[32] Christine, *Lavision*, formerly Phillipps MS 128, fol. 6r.

[33] On the reign of Charles VI, see M. Nordberg, *Les Ducs et la royauté. Études sur la rivalité des ducs d'Orléans et de Bourgogne 1392-1407*, Studia historica upsaliensia, 12 (Stockholm, 1964), the specialized studies that follow in the notes, and especially R. C. Famiglietti, *Royal Intrigue: Crisis at the Court of Charles VI, 1392-1420* (New York: AMS Press, 1986).

[34] On these ordinances, see Cazelles, *Société politique, noblesse et couronne*, pp. 577-581; and Nordberg, *Les Ducs*, pp. 61-65.

[35] On relations between France and England during these years, see J. J. N. Palmer, *England, France and Christendom, 1377-1399* (London, 1972).

Touraine, was a constant companion to the king, who awarded him in 1392 the dukedom that accompanied the appanage of Orleans.[36]

Disaster struck the monarchy in 1392, when the king experienced the first of forty-two fits of insanity that left him progressively weaker over the next thirty years.[37] Repeated attempts to cure him were unsatisfactory. According to the ordinances that had been passed under Charles V, Louis of Orleans was heir to the throne should the king die without a son. Although Queen Isabeau bore many children (totalling twelve over the years), so far her only son, Charles, had died at birth.[38] The uncles of Charles VI and Louis of Orleans, the dukes of Burgundy and Berry, began again to take an interest in the government, presumably envious of Louis's growing powers. The end result was a civil war that continued through most of the reign, producing extended uncertainty about the succession. The problem of the succession was aggravated by the resumption of the Hundred Years' War, along with renewed English claims to the throne, when Richard II was deposed in 1399. Thus, when Christine began to write seriously, which by her own account was in 1399,[39] the monarch had experienced one serious fit and two prolonged relapses, the dukes were quarreling over Louis of Orleans's power, and war with England had resumed.

Before describing Christine's writings and charting her career, it is useful to pause and outline the altered circumstances of patronage as they affected the production of illuminated manuscripts at the court of Charles VI. Unlike his father, Charles VI was not especially interested in illuminated manuscripts; a popular, perhaps apocryphal, account describes the dismay of the elder king, Charles V, when he found that his young son was delighted by a helmet and a sword but indifferent to precious objects and to contemplative study.[40] Be that as it may, the claim that Charles VI was not an attentive, powerful patron after the beginning of his long illness in 1392 would come as no great surprise. But even in the early years of his

[36] On Louis, see E. Jarry, *La Vie de Louis de France, duc d'Orléans, 1372-1407*, 2 vols. (Paris, 1889).

[37] On the madness of Charles VI, see A. Brachet, *Pathologie mentale des rois de France. Louis XI et ses ascendants. Une Vie humaine étudiée à travers six siècles d'héridité. 852-1483* (Paris, 1903), pp. 621-650; and G. Dodu, "La Folie de Charles VI," *La Revue historique* 150 (1925) 161-189.

[38] On the royal children, see Y. Grandeau, "Les enfants de Charles VI, essai sur la vie privée des princes et des princesses de la maison de France à la fin du Moyen Âge," *Bulletin philologique et historique (jusqu'en 1610) du comité des travaux historiques et scientifiques* 2 (1967) 809-849.

[39] Christine, *Lavision*, p. 164.

[40] This vignette is given by Anne Denieul-Cormier, *Wise and Foolish Kings. The First House of Valois. 1328-1498* (Garden City, N.Y., 1980), pp. 154-155.

reign before he became ill, there is no evidence that he followed in his father's footsteps and gathered around him a group of learned men from whom he commissioned illuminated theoretical treatises and vernacular translations for the purpose of enhancing through words and pictures the prestige of the monarchy. In the beginning of the reign, particularly in the 1380s and even in the 1390s, some authors did produce or had produced a few illuminated works about the monarchy that were dedicated to, and perhaps commissioned by, the still-youthful king.[41] But compared to the voluminous, lavishly illuminated, commissions that present a cohesive image of the monarchy and that were done for Charles V, such works are few and far between, and they are sparsely illustrated. After Charles VI's first attack of madness (and thus before Christine began to write seriously), there is simply no significant group of illuminated manuscripts that can be linked with his patronage.

This is not to say that no other significant patronage can be identified or that the production of illuminated manuscripts on political topics ceased. Quite the opposite is true. If anything, many individual groups of patrons can be identified and, judging from the extant manuscripts, the production of illuminated manuscripts accelerated rather than declined during the reign of Charles VI. In light of what has just been said, these phenomena call for some comment. It has been noted previously that instead of serving the common good of the monarchy, literary patronage under Charles VI served the private interests of individual benefactors.[42] The private interest groups that are most conspicuous at court include the various dukes, of Berry, Burgundy, Orleans, and Bourbon; the queen, Isabeau of Bavaria; and the dauphin, Louis of Guyenne. The political topics addressed in manuscripts for these individuals include partisan issues of particular concern to specific individuals at different moments of time. In the presence of such a diffuse political literature, we might suspect that the writing of a unified ideology of monarchy came to an end or lay dormant during the reign of Charles VI. This view is inaccurate, however. Such writing continued, but the theorists, who are to be found within the royal chancellery or the university, produced mostly unillustrated manuscripts, perhaps because in the absence of a royal patronage their writings

---

[41] Particularly Philippe de Mézières and Honoré Bouvet, who are discussed below, pp. 143-169.

[42] This view is presented by J. Monfrin, "Humanisme et traductions au Moyen Âge," *Journal des Savants* (1963) 161-190, esp. 178; and elaborated by J. Krynen, *Idéal du prince et pouvoir royal en France à la fin du Moyen Âge (1380-1440): Étude de la littérature politique du temps* (Paris, 1982), esp. 42-44, 48, and *passim*.

were no longer profitable commodities.[43] Yet in these unillustrated writings by Jean de Montreuil and Jean Gerson, among others, ideas about monarchy that had been initiated by the advisers of Charles V were perpetuated and refined.

With regard to the luxury, illuminated manuscripts produced during the reign of Charles VI, however, it is more difficult to summarize conveniently the political message or messages conveyed by their authors. In coming to terms with the ideologies of these manuscripts, we will notice that the strategies these authors used to express their ideas became more oblique. It therefore becomes especially important, in the process of disentangling the ideas from the literary forms in which they are imbedded, to identify correctly the particular interest group addressed in a given manuscript.

It was under these circumstances of patronage that Christine began to write. Her earliest works suggest that she was at first somewhat oblivious to the partisan politics of the reign, although she was alert to the need to establish a broad-based patronage that was not dependent on the king.[44] These early works are mostly in verse, like the *Cent balades*, and they include the short *Débat de deux amans* (c. 1400) for Louis of Orleans, the *Dit de Poissy* (c. 1400) for an unknown patron, and the *Livre des trois jugements* (c. 1402) for Jean de Werchin, the seneschal of Hainault. Each is a poetic debate on problems concerning love. But Christine had other ambitions as a writer. She compared her development as a writer to that of a worker learning a trade: the more he practices, the more adept he becomes.[45] So, she read voraciously, including "ancient histories," "histories of the French," and "books of the poets," gradually changing her style so that it became more subtle and adapted to "higher subject matter."[46] She made her début as a writer of prose around 1400, in the *Epistre Othéa*, in which she mixed verse with prose. Although she did not discontinue writing in verse, the subject matter of her verse compositions changed. Between 1400 and 1403, she undertook to write a long

---

[43] See Krynen, *Idéal du prince*, and Nicole Grévy-Pons, "Propagande et sentiment national pendant le règne de Charles VI: L'exemple de Jean de Montreuil," *Francia* 8 (1980) 127-145.

[44] Information on Christine's works, the manuscripts, editions, and dates, can be found in S. Solente, "Christine de Pisan," *Histoire littéraire de France* (Paris, 1969) 40: 335-415; and E. Yenal, *Christine de Pisan, A Bibliography of Writings of Her and About Her*, The Scarecrow Author Bibliographies, 63 (Metuchen, N.J., 1982).

[45] Christine, *Lavision*, p. 164.

[46] *Ibid.*, p. 163.

allegorical poem, the *Mutacion de fortune*, on the subject of fortune, which she mingled with a universal history. In 1402, she composed another verse allegory, the *Chemin de long estude*, on the subject of a universal empire.

By about 1401, she had turned her attention away from the writing of love poetry to the composition of works primarily on two subjects, the defense of women and the politics of France. These writings, mostly in the "prose style,"[47] constitute the majority of her literary output between 1401 and 1412. She took up the defense of women in the correspondence (c. 1401/1402) on Jehan de Meun's views of women in the *Roman de la Rose*, a copy of which she presented to the queen. Then, in the *Cité des dames* (1404-1405) she praised women of antiquity along with those of the present day. In the *Livre des trois vertus* (1405), an allegorical treatise on the virtues, she addressed common women, as well as high-born ladies, such as the wife of the dauphin, Margaret of Burgundy, to whom the work is dedicated. During these years she also wrote works concerned with politics, such as a biography of King Charles v, the *Livre des fais et bonnes meurs* (1404), commissioned by Duke Philip of Burgundy. By 1405, when she was forty-one years old, she had composed fifteen major works that filled "seventy quires of large format," or nearly 1,120 folio pages, as she wrote that year in her allegorical autobiography, *L'Avision Christine*.[48] She had yet to write the *Corps de policie* (1406-1407), a Mirror of Princes handbook for the dauphin; the *Livre des fais d'armes et de chevalerie* (c. 1410), a treatise on medieval warfare; or the *Livre de la Paix* (c. 1412), a treatise on the virtues, also for the dauphin.

It is not particularly surprising to see that Christine turned more and more toward political subjects during the first decade of the fifteenth century, when the government was increasingly unstable. The king, Charles vi, was suffering more frequently from spells of insanity. Driven by ambition, the quarrelling dukes of Orleans and Burgundy became increasingly more antagonistic toward each other. After Philip of Burgundy's death in 1404, the quarrel accelerated under his successor, John the Fearless; the hostility resulted in John's murder of Louis in 1407. The Burgundian-Armagnac struggle, as it came to be called, was carried on after Louis's death by John, who still aspired to control the government, and Bernard vii, count of Armagnac, who was anxious to avenge Louis's

---

[47] This is the phrase Christine uses to describe her biography of Charles v; see Christine, *Livre des fais et bonnes meurs*, 1: 5.

[48] Christine, *Lavision*, p. 164.

death. During these years, many lacked confidence in the authority of the
queen, Isabeau of Bavaria, who is thought by many modern historians to
have been Louis's lover. Most considered the dauphin, Louis of Guyenne,
who was born in 1397, to be still too young to rule (his elder brother
Charles, born 1392, died in January 1401).

Forged during this period of political turmoil, Christine's new career
was a big success, for the princes generously rewarded her efforts. She
attributed some of her success to the novelty of being a woman writer,
which, she said, caused a certain amount of curiosity among the princes,
who therefore wished to see what she wrote.[49] One of her earliest patrons
was the king's brother Louis of Orleans, to whom she dedicated the
Epistre Othéa and for whom she later wrote the *Livre de la Prod'hommie
de l'homme* (1405-1406). In the first years of the fifteenth century, she
gave a number of works to Philip of Burgundy, including copies of the
Mutacion and the *Chemin de long estude*.[50] When Philip commissioned
the biography of Charles V, he was undoubtedly expressing his approval
of these earlier works. Philip died before she finished the *Livre des fais
et bonnes meurs*, and so she offered it to his successor, John the Fearless,
who paid her for other books as well.[51] She does not seem to have
composed works with him in mind, however. She dedicated works also
to the king and queen, Charles VI and Isabeau of Bavaria, the dauphin,
Louis of Guyenne, and John, the duke of Berry,[52] who each rewarded
her — sometimes with gifts instead of money [53] — for her efforts. Writing
for a public which consisted almost entirely of individuals within the
monarchy, Christine began to concentrate on the political matters that
concerned them.

This steady patronage by persons in the royal circle indicates that she
was taken seriously as a writer. Her books were sent abroad, as well, with

---

[49] *Ibid.*, pp. 164-165.

[50] For works in the Burgundian inventories, see G. Doutrepont, *Inventaire de la
'librairie' de Philippe le Bon (1420)* (Brussels, 1906), nos. 8, 98, 109, 117, 124, 130-131.

[51] See G. Doutrepont, *La littérature française à la cour des Ducs de Bourgogne,
Philippe le Hardi — Jean sans Peur — Philippe le Bon — Charles le Téméraire*, Bibliothèque
du xvᵉ siècle, 8 (Paris, 1909), p. 277, for the documents of John the Fearless's payments
to Christine, in 1407, 1408, 1409, and 1412. The titles of the works are not specified.

[52] See, for example, in John of Berry's inventory, the items published by J. Guiffrey,
Inventaires de Jean duc de Berry (1401-1416), 2 vols. (Paris, 1894-1896), nos. 932, 949,
952, 959, 1004, 1239.

[53] Paris, Archives Nationales, Registers KK 42, fol. 34, and KK 43, fols. 81v and
109v. These accounts of Queen Isabeau's expenses show that she gave Christine on each
occasion a gilded silver goblet.

the result that offers came to her to serve the court of the duke of Milan, Gian Galeazzo Visconti, and that of the king of England, Henry IV.[54] It seems that she preferred to remain in France, however. Thus, although some accused her of having "students and monks forge her works," an accusation made out of envy, she said,[55] this cannot have been what those in the royal circle thought.

When Christine's clients admired her writings, they admired them as manuscripts produced by her or under her supervision, a factor that probably added to the novelty of Christine as a woman writer. The language used in inventories of collections and records of payment indicates that her technical role in the composition of her writings was recognized along with her intellectual role. References to books by Christine consistently specify that the book was "made by Christine" (*fait de Christine*), instead of simply "by Christine," the phrasing that was commonly employed to refer to the author of a work.[56] The technical language used by Christine to describe her writings also suggests someone who was involved with the making of manuscripts, for she counted her pages in units of quires and noted their dimensions.[57]

An examination of manuscripts of her writings undertaken by Gilbert Ouy and Christine Reno has shed considerable light on Christine's role as a scribe, even though we still may be unaware of the full extent to which she was involved in a supervisory capacity with production.[58] Ouy and Reno have identified fifty-five manuscripts that are partial or complete autographs. They found that Christine regularly worked with two scribes, whose work she oversaw, adding catchwords, signatures, rubrics, headings, or sometimes a special dedication. Her frequent intervention in the production of manuscripts written by these two scribes indicates, in fact, that the three individuals worked in one location, passing quires back and forth. What Christine's role was, insofar as the illuminators were concerned, is a subject that I shall take up later. In the meantime, based on her contributions as a scribe and editor, it is possible to view Christine as France's first woman "publisher" as well as its first woman of letters.

Three different phases of Christine's activity in book-making are represented by the three deluxe manuscripts of the *Epistre Othéa*. The first, an autograph in Paris, was produced probably a few years after 1400,

---

[54] Christine, *Lavision*, pp. 165-166.
[55] *Ibid.*, p. 143.
[56] See the references in Doutrepont and Guiffrey, cited above, notes 50, 51, 52.
[57] Christine, *Lavision*, p. 164.
[58] Ouy and Reno, "Identification des autographes."

perhaps for Louis of Orleans.[59] Of the three, it is the least lavish. Christine
alone transcribed the text, writing it on rather thick parchment in three
columns, which vary somewhat throughout the book as though she was
still grappling with a solution of disposing the text on the pages. The
result is a manuscript whose organization has been called capricious,[60]
although it has also been pointed out that the three-column format was
probably deliberately selected because it encouraged a kind of contemplative, instead of a sequential, reading of the chapters.[61] This copy is
sparsely illustrated, including only six miniatures, which were executed in
grisaille, a style of painting using grey tints of color which Christine
seemed to favor early in her career,[62] perhaps because it was less costly
than full-color illuminations (Figs. 1, 2, 3). For our purposes, what is
important is that this volume seems to be a somewhat less luxurious
version of the *Epistre*, a version in which miniatures play only a minor
role.

The second manuscript of the *Epistre*, also in Paris, belongs with the
earliest extant, deluxe collection of Christine's "Collected Works" that in
all probability is identical with an item recorded in 1413 in the duke of
Berry's inventory.[63] The *Epistre* is one work among twenty-five separate
verse and prose writings by Christine that date between about 1399 and
1406 and that are now divided between four volumes. Meiss and Off have
shown that the placement of the item in the inventory, which seems
actually to be a continuous record that was kept of books as they entered
the ducal library, can be used to date it more precisely, specifically
between 1406 and 1408.[64] Its proximity to other items listed as "recovered from the late duke of Orleans" suggested to them that it was begun for
Louis of Orleans, perhaps around 1406, but that when he was assassinated in 1407, Christine offered it to John of Berry. The manuscript was

[59] Mombello, *La tradizione manoscritta*, pp. 23-31. Mombello speculated that this
was the presentation copy given to Louis, but C. C. Willard, "Christine de Pisan's 'Clock
of Temperance'," *L'Esprit Créateur* 2 (1962) 152, cautioned against this hypothesis,
pointing out that the book later belonged to Agnes of Burgundy, daughter of John the
Fearless and wife of Charles I, duke of Bourbon, that is, to a member of a rival family.

[60] Mombello, *La tradizione manoscritta*, pp. 24 n. 1, 28.

[61] M. A. Ignatius, "Christine de Pizan's 'Epistre Othéa': An Experiment in Literary
Form," *Medievalia et Humanistica*, n.s., 9 (1979) 127-142.

[62] See Schaefer, "Illustrationen," pp. 163ff.; and de Winter, "Christine de Pizan, ses
enluminures," pp. 345-349.

[63] Mombello, *La tradizione manoscritta*, pp. 13-23; Guiffrey, *Inventaires*, 1: 252-253,
no. 959.

[64] M. Meiss and S. Off, "The Bookkeeping of Robinet d'Estampes and the Chronology of Jean de Berry's Manuscripts," *Art Bulletin* 53 (1971) 228.

already in the duke of Berry's library in 1409, since it precedes items that are described in the inventory as "recovered from John of Montaigu," who was executed in 1409. The hypothesis that the book was begun for Louis is sustained, in part, by the lavish frontispiece miniature depicting Louis of Orleans that prefaces the *Epistre* (Fig. 7; Pl. C).

Considerable care was taken with this version of Christine's "Collected Works," which must have been expensive. It was written by two scribes who worked under Christine's direction and whose work she corrected.[65] Christine wrote the running titles, which number the texts sequentially. She also intervened to write over the patched holes in the parchment, using this time a higher grade of skin than she had used in the earlier copy, where the holes were left unmended. The manuscript was lavishly illuminated with one hundred and twenty-five miniatures, of which one hundred and one decorate the *Epistre*. To paint the illuminations she employed three artists, only one of whose work can be seen in other Parisian manuscripts.[66] Perhaps by hiring workers who were not in demand in Paris, she was able to pay somewhat less for their services. In any event, the appearance of the Paris *Epistre*, decorated with full-color miniatures, is dazzling, especially when it is compared with the earlier, less luxurious volume of the same work. The Paris "Collected Works" was thus a major undertaking by an established author-publisher; it was not the work of a struggling entrepreneur.

The third and latest manuscript of the *Epistre* also forms part of a "Collected Works," the exquisite copy in London.[67] A splendid, half-page frontispiece depicts the first owner, Queen Isabeau of Bavaria, as she receives the book from Christine (Fig. 4). Then, a special dedication to the queen precedes twenty-nine separate works by Christine, which together constitute the fullest version of her revised writings.[68] The one hundred and thirty miniatures — one hundred and one illustrate the

---

[65] Ouy and Reno, "Identification des autographes," pp. 225, 228, 230.

[66] The Saffron and *Épître* Masters worked only for Christine, while the Master of Egerton 1070 worked for others as well; see Meiss, *Limbourgs,* 1: 37-38, 292-295, 384-388.

[67] Mombello, *La tradizione manoscritta,* pp. 199-210; and S. Hindman, "The Composition of the Manuscript of Christine de Pizan's Collected Works in the British Library: A Reassessment," *British Library Journal* 9 (1983) 93-123.

[68] On Christine's practice of revising her works, with special reference to the London manuscript, see F. Lecoy, "Notes sur quelques ballades de Christine de Pisan," in *Fin du Moyen Âge et Renaissance, Mélanges de Philologie française offerts à Robert Guiette* (Antwerp, 1961), pp. 107-114; and J. Laidlaw, "Christine de Pizan — An Author's Progress," *The Modern Language Review* 78 (1983) 532-550.

Epistre, as in the Paris copy — which richly embellish the London manuscript make it the most densely illustrated copy of Christine's writings. Similar to the one in the Paris copy, a frontispiece miniature depicting Louis of Orleans prefaces the *Epistre* (Fig. 5, Pl. A). The pictures reveal the fruitful collaboration between two of the best illuminators who worked in Paris often for royal patrons, the *Cité des dames* Master and the so-called Bedford Trend Master.[69] The manuscript acquires still greater importance because it was entirely written by Christine, who also supervised its production.[70] Because the London manuscript includes three roundels which are addressed to the young duke of Bourbon, it has been securely dated between 1410, when John succeeded his father, Louis, as duke, and 1415, when he died in the battle of Agincourt.[71]

It would seem, then, that the London manuscript offers an unparalleled opportunity to study Christine as an author-publisher at the height of her career, when she worked on a commission for one of her highest-ranking patrons, the queen of France. Yet Mombello, among others, has expressed doubt about the original integrity of the volume, suggesting that it was composed from preexisting segments that "perhaps originally were not destined to be gathered together in a single presentation volume for the queen of France."[72] A closer examination of the London codex confirms Mombello's doubt about the volume's unity, while providing evidence of the extraordinary skills as bookmakers that Christine and her workers had by this time acquired.

One radical alteration to the London manuscript has gone unnoticed: a parchment band was added to the margins of every folio of the *Epistre.*[73] First the top edges of the folios were trimmed, and then each outer and lower edge was scraped to dovetail with a similarly scraped piece of parchment, which was next attached with a thin layer of paste. The bevelled and pasted joints are not now perceptible to the touch, although they are visible to the naked eye through transmitted light. To disguise

---

[69] Meiss, *Limbourgs*, 1: 39, 292-296; and de Winter, "Christine de Pizan, ses enluminures," pp. 362-365.

[70] Ouy and Reno, "Identification des autographes," p. 227.

[71] Its date was first established by P. Meyer, in Christine, *Œuvres poétiques*, 1: 278; and confirmed by Schaefer, "Illustrationen," pp. 162-163.

[72] Mombello, *La tradizione manoscritta*, p. 203, n. 1; see also Schaefer, "Illustrationen," p. 122, who believed that a later owner had tampered with the volume.

[73] See Hindman, "The Composition," pp. 99-107, for a full discussion of the alteration, including references to other instances of parchment repair.

further the alteration, the final seams were colored with white lead pigment, tinted to match the fawn tone of the parchment, thereby camouflaging any discoloration produced from the glue or any irregularities in the dovetailed edges. Ironically, this application of camouflaging paint is what eventually called attention to the alteration, since the lead pigment, on exposure to the atmosphere, darkened.[74] The elaborate procedure, which was rarely employed, was painstakingly time-consuming and required considerable expertise.

Unusual circumstances must have brought about this alteration, which was made before the London "Collected Works" was assembled. Previous damage to the *Epistre* could have necessitated its repair. No evidence of earlier damage remains, however; there is no soot or shrinkage from fire, no teeth marks from animals, and no mold from humdity. The proportionate enlargement of *every* folio suggests instead that a smaller copy of the *Epistre* was enlarged for inclusion in a volume with different physical dimensions. Since the queen could certainly have afforded to commission an entirely new copy of any text, even one so richly illuminated, this particular copy must have been especially suited to her. It is thus now certain that the *Epistre* existed apart from the compendium to which it was deliberately joined through a difficult and unusual procedure. It also seems likely that this copy had always belonged to the queen.[75]

This new evidence necessitates a redating of the London *Epistre*. It must have been done before 1410 to 1415, when the volume was assembled.[76] It cannot have been done before around 1405, however, because it presents a version of the text which Mombello has been able

---

[74] *Ibid.*, p. 100. The lead pigment, composed of basic lead carbonate, on exposure to sulfur fumes, yielded lead sulfide, which is brownish-black to red in color. When lead sulfide was treated with etherol peroxide, it converted to lead sulfate, allowing the original whitish tone of the parchment to show through.

[75] *Ibid.*, pp. 108-112, where this hypothesis is confirmed, first, by the alteration of other portions of the London volume, which also once existed independently; second, by the fact that none of these portions can be found in inventories of Christine's works owned by other individuals; and third, by the language of the dedication to the queen.

[76] Although de Winter, "Christine de Pizan, ses enluminures," p. 365, n. 44, claims to have uncovered a document, dated 3 May 1411, that records the transaction between Christine and Isabeau for this work (Paris, BN, Coll. Dupuy, vol. 755, fol. 97v), nothing in the wording of the document sustains his claim. De Winter's reference is to a seventeenth-century transcription of the royal accounts made by Dupuy, citing Christine de Pizan and giving a date of payment. Dupuy's record does not indicate what Christine was paid for, how much, or by whom. Nor does Dupuy's transcription identify his source more fully, with the result that I have not been able to verify it.

to assign to that year. On the basis of a comparison of the layout in the Paris and London copies, the London copy probably dates somewhat after the Paris one, completed about 1408, since the layout of the London copy is more refined. Thus, the revised date of the London *Epistre* is between 1408 and 1410 to 1415.

The extant manuscripts of the *Epistre Othéa*, produced between about 1401 and 1415, differ most with respect to their illustration. While the first autograph, around 1401, included only six miniatures, the last autograph, made for the queen before 1415, included one hundred and one miniatures. In this respect, the queen's copy followed an intermediate version for the duke of Berry. The text changed little from copy to copy; the revised 1405 edition, which the two later manuscripts follow, incorporated changes to the style but not to the contents.[77] This suggests that Christine considered the text as it had been composed suitable at different moments for different patrons. Instead, the books were personalized by changing their miniatures. An initial set, devised around 1401, was changed and expanded between 1407 and 1408 and then changed again before 1415. In light of these transformations, it seems reasonable to declare that, if we are to understand the *Epistre Othéa*, we must understand the different picture cycles that appear in the manuscripts of it.

It should be kept in mind that these three manuscripts of the *Epistre Othéa*, made for different royal patrons, extend over Christine's entire career and over a significant portion of Charles VI's reign. When the first manuscript was produced, Christine had only just begun writing about serious matters, having recently recovered from the loss of her husband. At this time, around 1401, the reign of Charles VI still held some promise for the French, who had not yet admitted that their king's illness was incurable. When the second and third manuscripts were completed, Christine had already styled herself as a commentator on political events, about which she wrote frequently and with considerable fervor. By this time, from about 1407, Charles VI was undeniably ill, the queen seemed

---

[77] Mombello, *La tradizione manoscritta*, pp. 286-306; see also *idem*, "Per un'edizione critica dell'Epistre Othéa di Christine de Pizan," *Studi francesi* 8 (1964) 401-417 and 9 (1965) 1-12, where he published the four separate dedications to the *Epistre*, those to Louis of Orleans, John of Berry, Philip the Bold, and Charles VI. See also J. Laidlaw, "Christine de Pizan, the Earl of Salisbury and Henry IV," *French Studies* 36 (1982) 129-143, for the suggestion that the dedication to Charles VI, which does not specify the king by name, was actually written for King Henry IV of England. This seems highly unlikely, however, given that Christine thought of the English king as a usurper and given that the contents of the dedication and of the text of the *Epistre* relate so closely to ideas about the French monarchy.

incapable of carrying on in his place, the dauphin was too young to rule, and the prospective regent, the king's brother Louis of Orleans, had just been murdered. To account for the differences between the three manuscript versions of the *Epistre Othéa*, while situating them in their historical context, the hypothesis I am offering is that Christine saw, after completing her initial autograph for Louis of Orleans, a greater potential in the *Epistre* than in her other manuscripts to present her political views in miniatures. According to my hypothesis, she responded to the political upheavals of her day not only in her writings but in the different sets of miniatures designed for individual manuscripts of the *Epistre*.

To explore this hypothesis, I shall examine, in chapter 1, the meaning of the text of the *Epistre*, in order to determine how it lent itself to a political interpretation. Next, in chapter 2, I shall explore evidence for Christine's role in the creation of the miniatures, in order to determine whether the iconography was the responsibility of Christine or of her miniaturists. Then, in chapter 3, I shall analyze the ideological programs of the miniatures in the Paris and London copies of the *Epistre*, those with one hundred and one miniatures, in order to show how they express ideas about politics that were suited at different times to different patrons. Lastly, in chapter 4, I shall show that other illuminated manuscripts at the court of Charles VI, ones written by Philippe de Mézières, Honoré Bouvet, and Christine, also conveyed timely ideas about government through miniatures. Finally, in an Epilogue, I shall follow the intermingled fortunes of Christine and France after the completion of the London "Collected Works" to around 1430, the probable year of Christine's death.

1

The Meaning of the Text

The *Epistre Othéa* has come to be regarded primarily as a courtesy book,[1] one that was compiled from diverse, though readily identifiable sources. In support of this view, there is little doubt that what defines courtesy literature, namely a focus on moral teaching to influence good conduct, characterizes the *Epistre* as well. Nor is it disputable that the *Epistre* shows Christine's indebtedness to her sources, specifically the *Ovide moralisé* and the *Histoire ancienne*, as well as to various compendia of exegetical and philosophical quotations, which, taken together, account for nearly every sentence in this particular work.[2] But the *Epistre* is nevertheless a peculiar, highly idiosyncratic example of a courtesy book. It stands out among others in a genre that by the end of the Middle Ages was increasingly conventionalized.

Neither the characterization of the *Epistre Othéa* as a courtesy book nor the identification of its sources has been sufficient to explain a number of its unique features. There are four such features which can be considered important to an understanding of the meaning of the text. First, the *Epistre Othéa* deviates most strikingly from the forms of other courtesy books, not one of which was epistolary. A tri-partite system of texts and glosses comprises the one hundred chapters of the work. At the beginning of the *Epistre*, following the prologue, is found its title or incipit: "Here begins the Epistle of Othea the goddess that she sent to Hector of Troy when he was fifteen years old." As in a letter, Othea writes to Hector in a four-line verse text (*texte*) at the beginning of each chapter. Two prose passages follow the text. First in a gloss (*glose*) and next in an allegory

---

[1] Christine de Pizan, *The Epistle of Othea to Hector: a 'lytil bibill of knyghthood'*, tr. A. Babyngton, ed. J. Gordon (Philadelphia, 1942), pp. xxvi-xxvii; Tuve, *Allegorical Imagery*, pp. 44, 286; and D. Bornstein, *Mirrors of Courtesy* (Hamden, Conn., 1975), pp. 49-60.

[2] Its sources have been thoroughly studied by Campbell, *L'Épitre d'Othéa*, and Christine, *The Epistle of Othea*, tr. Scrope.

(*allégorie*), the author, Christine, intervenes to comment on Othea's letter. In the gloss she proposes a moral lesson for Hector as the "good knight." In the allegory she offers a spiritual lesson to the "good spirit" – Hector's Christian persona.

The usual characterization of the *Epistre* as a courtesy book has come about from a consideration more of the prose glosses than of the verse texts. The book's dual structure, wherein both a gloss and an allegory provide a commentary on the main text, even led Rosemond Tuve to call the *Epistre* a "double courtesy-book."[3] Through this term, Tuve meant to convey that the book's glosses address the knight's outward behavior and its allegories his Christian conscience. Tuve was correct in this, but what she and others neglected to question was why Christine invoked the epistolary format. Her use of this format entailed an esoteric, idiosyncratic method of introducing each chapter with a fragment of the serialized letter that binds the work together. It is the fragment of the letter at the beginning of each chapter that provides the springboard for the subsequent glosses and allegories.

Christine's use of the epistle seems at first unduly awkward. For instance, it entailed repeated linguistic shifts, with one use of language found in the texts and another found in the glosses and allegories. That is, the texts and their commentaries switch back and forth from verse language to prose, first person to third, and direct discourse to indirect. One way of accounting for this complicated use of language within each chapter is to say that it reveals Christine's overriding concern, along with the teaching of good conduct in the commentary, with the epistle that provides her own title for her work. We may come to understand the *Epistre* better, therefore, if we compare it with other epistolary writings rather than with courtesy books.

A second peculiarity of the *Epistre*, the use of Othea and Hector, sender and recipient of the letter, must also be explained in order to comprehend the overall meaning of Christine's text. Because the *Epistre* has been regarded primarily as a courtesy book, Hector's presence in it has been thought to have been motivated principally by the fact that for the later Middle Ages he came to stand for an ideal knight, a "worthy." As we shall see, Hector's importance as a model for knighthood was considerable, so it may well have partially inspired his inclusion in the *Epistre*. But Christine carefully situates Hector in a historical milieu, whose details are taken from the *Histoire ancienne*, rather than from other romances and allegories where he figures in more idealized terms as a "worthy."

---

[3] Tuve, *Allegorical Imagery*, p. 44.

As a historical figure, Hector was the eldest son of King Priam and Queen Hecuba of Troy, the husband of Andromache, and the renowned warrior for the Trojans in the war. For the ancient world, he had been Troy's counterpart to the Greek Achilles. His death by Achilles's hand marked the beginning of a series of events leading to the eventual downfall of Troy. A rereading of the text of the *Epistre* thus suggests that this historical Hector of Troy was as important as the figure of Hector the ideal knight. In other texts, moreover, Christine evinces an interest in Hector's historical past as a model for the present, specifically as a model for French kingship. It seems equally possible, therefore, that Hector was the recipient of Othea's epistle not only because he was a model chevalier but also because he was a model prince.

The use of Othea has not been adequately explained. Since no one with the name Othea has been found in earlier medieval literature, writers now accept that Christine invented her. Attention has thus come to be focused on the meaning of the made-up name. Othea has been thought to derive from Christine's misunderstanding of the Greek invocation to the goddess Minerva, "*O thea*" as "O goddess."[4] This interpretation would accord with Christine's own words that "Othea, according to the Greek, can be taken for wisdom of women." The preoccupation with the derivation of the name, Othea, has led writers away from her context in the *Epistre*. But, if we look again at the text, we realize that the identity of Othea the person is simple enough, whatever the actual origin of her name. Christine identifies her as Prudence. She is the first of the four cardinal virtues. Moreover, as the fictional author of the epistle, Prudence is a second voice of the author, Christine, who wrote the commentaries. In order to come to understand Othea better as the sender of the letter, it would seem important, therefore, to determine what meaning Prudence had for Christine.

The importance of the four cardinal virtues is the third feature of the *Epistre* that deserves fuller investigation. The text begins with the four cardinal virtues, among which the importance of Othea-Prudence, who dispatches the letter, has already been established. Temperance, Fortitude, and Justice follow, and their significance, with that of Prudence, is stressed partly by the fact that these chapters are longer than those of the remainder in the *Epistre*. It may be said that the cardinal virtues are such a common feature of courtesy literature that their presence here is the

---

[4] First proposed by Claude Sallier, "Notices de deux ouvrages manuscrits de Christine de Pisan, dans lesquels il se trouve quelques particularités de l'histoire de Louis d'Orléans," *Mémoires de l'Académie des Inscriptions et Belles-Lettres* 17 (1751) 515-525.

result of the relationship of the *Epistre* to that genre. But as we shall see, the unusual prominence accorded to the cardinal virtues links it with a specific type of courtesy book, the Mirror of Princes handbook.

The fourth feature of the *Epistre* to be examined here is the selection and order of the stories recounted in its chapters. Everyone who is familiar with the work has observed that the organization shows little regard for the narrative chronology of myth or history.[5] Following the four cardinal virtues come the seven planets. Then, beginning with chapter 14, mythological episodes seem randomly interspersed with historical events. Othea tells Hector stories from the *Ovide moralisé*, for example, of Jupiter and Io (chs. 29 and 30), Perseus and the Gorgon (ch. 55), and Phoebe and Daphne (ch. 87). But here the stories are not told in the order they are told in the *Ovide*. Othea recounts Theban and Trojan histories from the *Histoire ancienne*, such as the adventures of Memnon (ch. 36), Adrastus (ch. 46), and Calchas (ch. 81). But here she departs from the temporal sequence of the *Histoire*. For example, the wedding of Peleus and Thetis (ch. 60) precedes the judgment of Paris (ch. 73) that led to it. Achilles frequently reappears after his death (ch. 40): he is discovered by Ulysses (ch. 71), avenges Patroclus (ch. 85), and is again slain (ch. 93). Narrative order is followed only toward the end, where the stories follow historical chronology, from Andromache's vision of the destruction of Troy (ch. 88), through the death of Hector (ch. 91), to the burning of Ilion (ch. 97). The last two chapters again abandon the narrative to relate the stories of an ignorant queen, Ino, who planted boiled corn on infertile soil, and a wise king, Emperor Augustus, who listened to the Cumean sibyl foretell the birth of Christ.

To explain this apparent inattention to the chronology of myth or history, those who have written on the *Epistre* have noticed that chapters in the first half of the text are grouped according to another principle: the interrelationship of their allegories.[6] Six subsections emerge. The four cardinal virtues (chs. 1-4) are followed by the seven gifts of the Holy Spirit represented by the seven planets (chs. 6-12) and then by the three theological virtues as Minerva, Pallas, and Penthesilea (chs. 13-15). The seven deadly sins introduced by Narcissus (chs. 16-22) lead to a section on the lessons on the Credo that begins with Diana (chs. 23-24). Last

[5] For example, Campbell, *L'Épître d'Othéa*, pp. 36-44; and Christine, *Epistle of Othea*, ed. Gordon, pp. viii-ix.

[6] First by Gordon in his edition of Christine, *Epistle of Othea*, pp. xii-xiii, including a useful chart of the subjects of the glosses and allegories. See also Tuve, *Allegorical Imagery*, pp. 38-39, 285-287 n. 30.

come the Ten Commandments starting with Bellerophon (chs. 35-44). It has been pointed out that such a series of simple religious lessons characterizes many courtesy books, which further supports the connection of the *Epistre* with this genre.[7]

Yet this argument does not explain two features of the organization of the *Epistre*. First, it fails to account for the obvious use of narrative chronology at the end of the text, from chapter 88 on. Second, by focusing on the allegories, it ignores the texts and glosses. It does not seek to offer, therefore, possible reasons for the conjunction of certain classical figures, that are cited in the texts and glosses with specific religious lessons that are found in the allegories, for example, Penthesilea as the theological virtue of Charity or Diana, Ceres, and Isis as the first three lines of the Credo. Now, if we take notice of such oddities with regard to the organization of the text we can, without denying that the *Epistre* does exhibit some crucial features of courtesy literature, uncover other concerns on the part of its author that bear directly on an understanding of the meaning of the text.

THE EPISTOLARY FORM AS AN ADVICE-GIVING STRATEGY

The epistolary form is so striking a characteristic of the *Epistre Othéa* that it is surprising that it is the least discussed. No explanation has ever been put forward for the choice of this form. It might seem at first that it should be easy to discern Christine's reasons for selecting the letter form, since the *Epistre Othéa* joins a group of eleven letters within Christine's literary output.[8] But a closer look at these letters reveals that they are all quite different from the *Epistre Othéa* and thus reveal little about it. Nine of the eleven letters conform with the long-established classical and medieval epistolary tradition, that is, they are addressed in Christine's own name to identified recipients, such as Isabeau of Bavaria, Eustache Morel, and John of Berry. Except for attesting to a somewhat unusual penchant on Christine's part for letter-writing, often in order to give advice, these epistles share little with the *Epistre Othéa*, which is not so much a real letter as it is an allegorical fiction of one.

---

[7] Tuve, *Allegorical Imagery*, pp. 38-39.

[8] On her letters, see Pinet, *Christine de Pisan*, pp. 263-280; and C. C. Willard, "A New Look at Christine de Pizan's 'Epistre au Dieu d'Amours'," in *Seconda Miscellanea di studi e richerce sul quattrocento francese*, ed. F. Simone, J. Beck and G. Mombello (Chambéry-Turin, 1981), pp. 73-92.

Turning to the other letter written by Christine, the *Epistre au dieu d'amour*,[9] we find that it does share some features with the *Epistre Othéa*. In each, Christine turns over her work to a person of fable, Othea in the *Epistre Othéa* and Cupid in the *Epistre au dieu d'amours*. Moreover, the two dedication miniatures share general similarities: a fictional god or goddess — Othea or Cupid — hands over a letter to a courtier (Figs. 6, 85). Both works were written around 1400, and this temporal proximity alone could suggest a common inspiration. Because of the shared literary strategy of the fictional letter-writer, Christine's two allegorical letters have been linked to Ovid's *Heroïdes*, a collection of love letters exchanged between mythological persons.[10] It has been shown that Christine could have known Ovid's book in a French translation. Certainly, the *Heroïdes* may have inspired the *Epistre au dieu d'amours* since both books focus on the theme of love. In fact, one way of reading the *Epistre au dieu d'amours*, in which Cupid counters diverse complaints from women forsaken in love by deceitful men, could be as Christine's clever response to Ovid's *Heroïdes*. But even if we accept that the *Heroïdes* may lie behind the *Epistre au dieu d'amours*, it does not seem likely that it also inspired the *Epistre Othéa*. The essential differences between the two works are more striking than their superficial similarities. Instead of treating the theme of love through an epistolary fiction, the *Epistre Othéa* combines the epistle with a series of allegorical commentaries to instruct Hector as a Christian knight. Contrary to what might be expected, then, a comparison of the *Epistre Othéa* with the numerous letters among Christine's writings does little to elucidate its meaning.

Although it has not previously been suggested, the inspiration for the epistolary form in the *Epistre Othéa* can still be found close at hand, specifically among a group of letters by other authors at the court of Charles VI. For example, fictional epistles by Deschamps and Philippe de Mézières constitute a popular genre with which we know Christine to have been familiar. In Deschamps's prodigious literary output are two types of letters, each of which may have influenced the *Epistre Othéa*. The first type, called a *chançon royal*, is a political ballad that often parodied either general behavior or a specific action at court.[11] To address each

---

[9] Christine, *Œuvres poétiques*, 2: 1-27; and partially translated in Christine, *'La Querelle de la Rose'*, pp. 35-38.

[10] Willard, "A New Look," pp. 75-76.

[11] See Eustache Deschamps, *Œuvres complètes*, ed. A. de Queux de Saint-Hilaire and G. Raynaud, 11 vols. (Paris, 1878-1903), 7: 3 and 11: 21-23. Deschamps described this and other forms of verse in *L'Art de dictier...*, in *Œuvres*, 7: 266-299.

ballad to an identifiable person, the poet appended a four-line "cover letter" (*envoi*) wherein he named the recipient. Such verse "cover letters" are similar to the short poems Othea writes to Hector. Not only their four-line length, but also their complementary, quasi-independent relationship to a main text relates them to Christine's *Epistre*.

The second type of epistle, actually called a *lettre*, favored by Deschamps was a longer verse composition written to friends in octasyllabic rhymed couplets.[12] Christine twice adopted this verse structure and rhyme scheme. She used it in 1403 in her *Epistre à Eustache Morel*, a letter she wrote to Deschamps lamenting the corrupt government of France.[13] She used it also in the four-line "cover letter" that she included in the *Epistre Othéa*. Perhaps Christine even had in mind her borrowings from these epistolary compositions by Deschamps when she called herself his disciple.

Although Christine seems to have adopted certain formal features from Deschamps's verse letters, it might be objected that neither the length nor the content as a whole of the *Epistre Othéa* owes much to these compositions. With respect to these features, however, a longer prose epistle by Deschamps may serve as a better model for the *Epistre*. Entitled *Dolente et piteuse complainte de l'Eglise moult désolée au jour d'ui*, it was written originally in Latin in 1393.[14] Its primary subject was the problem of the schism within the church. Deschamps proposed a church council to end the schism and called all Christians to rally in support of a crusade against the Saracens. He blamed modern-day rulers for the failure to achieve church unity. To urge proper action on the part of present rulers he cited ancient examples of good and bad kingship. He then paraphrased the Beatitudes as a means of teaching good conduct. He concluded with a note of warning, reminding readers of the words of the prophets and the sibyls that went unheeded. The original recipient of this letter is unknown, but it was clearly addressed to an audience at court that would have been in a position to respond to Deschamps's advice, and it was translated into French at the command of Duke Philip of Burgundy.

For our purposes, it is important to note that Deschamps's letter belongs to a genre of advice literature that took the form of the epistle in order to address a contemporary political concern at the court of Charles VI. In addition to the use of the epistolary form, the strategies that we find

---

[12] *Ibid.*, 8: 3-73.
[13] Christine's letter is edited by Roy in Christine, *Œuvres poétiques*, 2: 295-301.
[14] Deschamps, *Œuvres*, 7: 293-311.

employed in this genre include the use of classical and biblical exempla, of spiritual guides, and of prophecies. The *Epistre Othéa* shares these very features with Deschamps's letter and, as we shall see, with others to which it is even closer in this genre.

Before proceeding to examine other examples of this genre of epistolary advice literature among the writings of Christine's contemporaries, it is important to point out that all of them seem to depend on a classical or pseudo-classical prototype, a letter purportedly from the Roman writer Plutarch to the Emperor Trajan. This letter is known from John of Salisbury, who in the *Policraticus* trades on the authority of Plutarch's letter, which advises Trajan on the virtues of good government, to offer his own advice on contemporary politics.[15] From John we learn that Plutarch, alarmed at the state of the kingdom, had organized and dispersed lessons on virtue in order to guide Trajan to good conduct through the use of ancestral exempla. In support of his own role as tutor to a ruler, Plutarch cites the model of Seneca who taught philosophy to Nero. Plutarch concludes that if Trajan "proceeds to ruin the empire Plutarch will not be the cause thereof." It is now thought that John may have invented the example of Plutarch's letter to sanction his own advisory literature with an authoritative classical source.[16] Further, it has been suggested that he chose Plutarch as the author because he was a typical moral philosopher and Trajan as the ideal emperor because he combined those virtues most exalted in medieval rulers. In any case, Plutarch's letter includes many of those features characteristic of later epistolary writings: the use of histories as exempla, of lessons on virtue, and of prophecies.

Whether or not such a letter by Plutarch actually existed, John of Salisbury's summary of it easily could have been known to writers at the court of Charles VI since his *Policraticus* was translated into French at the command of Charles v.[17] We find, in fact, that Plutarch's letter did carry authority for these contemporary French writers, who often cited it to sanction their own addresses to present-day rulers about government. For

---

[15] John of Salisbury, *The Statesman's Book ... Fourth, Fifth, and Sixth Books and Selections from the Seventh and Eighth Books of the Policraticus*, tr. John Dickinson (New York, 1927), p. 63.

[16] See H. Liebeschutz, "John of Salisbury and Pseudo-Plutarch," JWCI 6 (1943) 33-39, with objections to this theory raised by A. Momigliano, "Notes on Petrarch, John of Salisbury and the 'Instituto Traiani'," JWCI 12 (1949) 189-190.

[17] Paris, BN MS fr. 24287, discussed by L. Delisle, *Recherches sur la librairie de Charles v*, 2 vols. (Paris, 1907), 1: 83-88, 263-264; and Sherman, *The Portraits of Charles v*, pp. 74-77.

example, when Gerson spoke in 1405 before an audience of King Charles VI on the subject of good government, he summoned the "authority of Plutarch ... the only man who dared to write to Trajan on the manner of his government."[18] Christine de Pizan also introduced the model of Plutarch's letter in her *Le Corps de policie*, a Mirror of Princes book dedicated to Charles VI and the French princes.[19]

This Plutarchian model for advice-giving letters seems to have been important for letter writers at the royal court, but its existence alone was not enough to compel every potential writer to offer counsel to the king and princes. Two other factors were prerequisites. First, the writer needed sufficient access to, and even an intimate knowledge of, political situations. Second, he or she had to have an established audience, a patronage.

In the case of Deschamps, both prerequisites were clearly met.[20] He would have had ample opportunity to observe politics at court, having first served in the household of Philip of Orleans, predecessor of Duke Louis. He was then appointed a process-server to the king. When Louis of Orleans received his duchy in 1392, Deschamps left the king's service to enter his household. Throughout the 1390s he remained closely involved with the Orleans family. In the early fifteenth century he sought support from Duke Philip the Bold. The exact date of his death is unknown, but it must have been before Louis of Orleans's assassination in 1407. Deschamps thus spent his life in the service of the French king and princes who constituted the public for his epistolary writings.

Neither the classical model nor Deschamps's letters account for one peculiarity of the *Epistre Othéa*: its combination of the epistolary form and the use of allegory. For this characteristic, we must turn to other examples of the epistolary genre at the court of Charles VI, letters by Philippe de Mézières, who, like Deschamps, was a member of the royal household.[21] Philippe's official positions at court qualified him as an advice-giver even more than did Deschamps's, in that Philippe held positions that brought him closer to the king and covered a longer period. He began his political

---

[18] Jean Gerson, *Harangue faicte au nom de l'université de Paris devant le Roy Charles sixiesme, et tout le conseil, en 1405*, 3rd ed. (Paris, 1824), p. 10.

[19] Christine de Pizan, *Le Livre du Corps de policie*, ed. R. H. Lucas (Geneva, 1967), pp. xxi, 2. Plutarch was to remain an important model through the sixteenth and seventeenth centuries; see for example, Budé's *Institution du Prince*, written for Francis I, ed. C. Bontems, L.-P. Raybaud, and J.-P. Brancourt, *Le Prince dans la France des XVIe et XVIIe siècles*, Travaux et recherches de la Faculté de droit et des sciences économiques de Paris, Série sciences historiques, 7 (Paris, 1965), p. 81, and *passim*.

[20] On Deschamps's life, see Deschamps, *Œuvres*, 11: 9-99.

[21] On Philippe's life, see Iorga, *Philippe de Mézières*.

career working with the papacy and had served as chancellor of Cyprus, but in 1373 he joined the governmental council of King Charles V. Until this monarch's death, Philippe conferred with him daily. At the same time, he served as the tutor for the dauphin, Charles VI, for whom he even wrote in 1388 an allegorical Mirror of Princes book, the *Songe du vieil pèlerin*. Although he no longer held an official position at court during the years from 1388 to 1396, when he was living in retirement in the Abbey of the Célestines in Paris, he continued to write, counselling peace through both governmental and church unity. He died in 1405 at the advanced age of eighty-five. As tutor and counselor to the royal family, Philippe was in a position to give advice in the course of carrying out the day to day duties of his job.

An examination of Philippe's letters shows that they transform the epistolary model into an allegory comparable to the *Epistre Othéa*. The first such letter, the *Epistre au Roi Richart*, was written for Charles VI to offer to the English King Richard in 1395.[22] In fictional terms, the letter is composed by a figure called the Old Solitary, Philippe's allusion to himself because of his advanced age and solitary retirement. The Old Solitary addresses two kings, Charles VI and Richard II, each of whom he calls by the same allegorical name, King Ill-Advised. If King Ill-Advised heeds the advice of the Old Solitary, he can become King Well-Advised.

The advice of the Old Solitary centers on two subjects. First, peace between France and England, which, the Old Solitary argues, will be furthered by the impending marriage between the six-year-old French princess, Isabel, and the recently widowed English king. Second, peace throughout Christianity, which the Old Solitary envisions, will be brought about by the two Kings Ill-Advised who together will conquer the Holy Land ruled presently by King Vigilant or the Sultan of Babylon. Throughout the letter a number of parables and allegories are offered: for example, Charles and Richard are asked to choose between two orchards that stand for the monarchical realms, one representing good government and peace and the other discord and war. Composed as an epistle, Philippe's letter uses the devices of allegory to offer advice to a monarch or, in this case, two monarchs from a counselor. In spite of the fact that the letter writer and recipient are both identified in the title and the prologue, they are nevertheless presented in allegorical guises throughout the body of the work. It is this use of allegorical figures within the framework of a letter

---

[22] Philippe de Mézières, *Letter to King Richard II. A Plea Made In 1395 For Peace Between England and France*, ed. and tr. G. W. Coopland (Liverpool, 1965).

designed to give advice that forms a link between the *Epistre au Roi Richart* with the *Epistre Othéa*.

The *Epistre au Roi Richart* is not the only letter in which Philippe extended advice to the court in the form of an epistolary allegory. One other example is extant, and two additional ones have been lost.[23] The extant letter, called *L'Epistre lamentable et consolatoire*, was written in 1397 in response to news that had just reached Paris of the defeat of crusaders at Nicopolis.[24] It was written for Duke Philip of Burgundy, who had been instrumental in masterminding the failed crusade. As in the case of the earlier letter, the real author — that is, Philippe — is presented in fictional terms this time, however, as the Old Invalid, who is described as being in the last quarter of his life and as having been injured in an unsuccessful crusade. In the hopes that another crusading effort can be mounted, the Old Invalid seeks counsel on the question of the failed crusade from a figure called the Good Samaritan, who is probably also meant to be taken for Philippe.

The Good Samaritan offers a "cure" to the Old Invalid. Specifically, he proposes to found a new chivalric order, called the Order of the Passion, whose members will be better equipped to participate successfully in a forthcoming crusade. They will be more successful because they will be composed of a new generation of pious bourgeoisie who, unlike the princes and nobles, have not succumbed to the world's temptations. Then, these pious bourgeoisie are taught lessons in virtue by four intervening allegorical figures: Rule, Chivalric Discipline, Obedience, and Justice. The end of the letter finds the Old Invalid seated alone, lamenting that he has been unable to reform Christianity. At this moment, a wounded friend visits him and tells him a parable. The night before the battle, according to the wounded friend, a richly dressed woman, Lady Discipline of Chivalry, appeared in the Christian camp carrying the sword of justice and a golden measure. As she spoke to the wounded man, the torrents of a thunderstorm arose and disfigured her, symbolically announcing the Christians' annihilation the next day. We are probably meant to understand this parable as a vision of the failure at Nicopolis caused by the absence of an effective chivalric order like the Order of the Passion that Philippe proposed to found.

---

[23] Iorga, *Philippe de Mézières*, pp. 448, 452; the first, entitled *Epistola exhortatoria*, contained ecclesiastical counsel in addition to a lament on the death of Charles v; and the second, called an *épistre de doulce amonicion* or *épistre secrète*, called for a crusade.

[24] Discussed by Iorga, *Philippe De Mézières*, pp. 500-505; and edited in Jean Froissart, *Œuvres*, ed. H. Kervyn de Lettenhove, 25 vols. (Brussels, 1867-1877; repr. Osnabruck, 1967), 16: 444-523.

It is apparent that this epistle, too, effectively combines the form of the letter with the language of allegory to offer advice to a prince. The existence of these letters by Deschamps and Philippe, which Christine could easily have known, coupled with their similarities with the *Epistre Othéa*, would seem to support the interpretation of Christine's *Epistre* as yet another example of the epistolary allegory.

Because the form of the epistolary allegory seems to have originated around this time at the court of Charles VI, we can consider in a little more detail its literary sources in order to understand better the *Epistre*. Two principal sources can be identified, Plutarch's letter and the dream allegory. As we have seen, the classical authority of Plutarch's letter was evoked to justify contemporary advice-giving. The contents of Plutarch's letter, incorporating various sorts of moral teachings, also correspond with those by Deschamps, Philippe, and Christine. But the language does not. Whereas Plutarch's letter formed part of a prose didactic treatise, the French letters were written in an entirely different mode, one that was closer to the literature of fiction.

The French letters adopted the language customarily used in another type of allegory, the *songe*, or dream allegory, which also proliferated at the court of Charles VI, although it was by no means new.[25] By the end of the fourteenth century in France, the *songe* had become a common type of advice literature and was used frequently to comment on specific political situations. Because these dream allegories also addressed issues of contemporary government, their language may have been a source for the later letter allegories. In the work of both Christine and Philippe de Mézières we find statements, echoing Macrobius in his *Commentary on the Dream of Scipio*,[26] to the effect that dream literature permitted three levels of allegorical interpretation. A dream could be interpreted as it applies to each man, to the world in general, and to the kingdom of France.[27]

---

[25] On this use of the *songe* at the time, see Jeannine Quillet, "Songes et songeries dans l'art de la politique au XIVe siècle," *Les Études philosophiques* 30 (1975) 327-349; and D. M. Dougherty, "Political Literature in France during the Reigns of Charles V and Charles VI," Unpublished doctoral dissertation, Harvard University, 1932, esp. pp. 213-214. There is no interpretive study that surveys the dream allegory in late medieval French literature. On England, see A. C. Spearing, *Medieval Dream-Poetry* (Cambridge, 1976) and on earlier medieval uses of the form, see F. X. Newman, "*Somnium*, Medieval Theories of Dreaming and the Form of Vision Poetry," Unpublished doctoral dissertation, Princeton University, 1962.

[26] Macrobius, *Commentary on the Dream of Scipio*, tr. W. H. Stahl, Records of Civilization, Sources and Studies, 48 (New York, 1952).

[27] Such statements occur in the works of Philippe de Mézières, *Le Songe du vieil pèlerin*, tr. G. W. Coopland, 2 vols. (Cambridge, 1969), 1: 83-86; and Christine, *L'Avision Christine*, Phillipps MS 128, fol. 3r.

However, the letter genre is not just a variety of the dream literature, although it borrowed some linguistic devices from it. We do find in dream literature the use of histories as exempla, lessons on the virtues, and prophecies, as well as the presence of allegorical personifications. Still, regardless of how it is written, a letter functions differently as an allegory. The essential difference is that the letter is a much more direct and, therefore, more literal form of communication than the dream fiction. Although obviously it is possible to adress other types of literature to specific individuals, the very nature of the letter form underscores the fact that it is written from one specific person to another, equally specific, one.

We may well ask why these writers bothered at all to dress up their letters as allegories or, from another point of view, why they formulated their allegories as letters? In other words, why did they invent a hybrid form, instead of using either the model of Plutarch's letter or that of the dream allegory? The answer lies, I believe, in the persistent attraction of allegory and the unique potential of the letter as forms of writing. The writings of Christine and Philippe take a strong stand on the merits of allegory. At the end of the *Livre des fais et bonnes meurs*, Christine praised the language of allegory, pointing out that it was sanctioned by many meritorious classical and Christian prototypes.[28] For her, this embellished language was more understandable, more all-inclusive, and offered greater delight to readers than did the language of direct address. In the *Songe du vieil pèlerin*, Philippe explained that he wrote allegorically because old matter often finds fresh appeal under a new cloak.[29] Thus, their high regard for allegorical writing, coupled with the impact of the model of Plutarch's advice-giving letter, which held considerable authority, not surprisingly led these writers at the court of Charles VI to combine effectively the language of the *songe* with the form of the letter. It is important to underscore that the end result, the epistolary allegory, was a peculiarly literal allegory that in its directness was perhaps particularly well suited to the special demands of counsel at the court of the mad king.

OTHEA AND HECTOR: MODELS OF WISDOM AND KINGSHIP

To understand better the meaning of Christine's epistolary allegory, we can now turn to the figures of Othea and Hector. Hector's identity as a

[28] Christine, *Le livre des fais et bonnes meurs*, 2: 176-178.
[29] Philippe de Mézières, *Le Songe*, 1: 101.

worthy coupled with his historical persona permits us more easily to examine the interplay between the literal and figurative readings of the letter. We should bear in mind that all our manuscripts of the *Epistre Othéa* include dedications to Duke Louis of Orleans, who thus in a real sense should be understood to be the recipient.

We must remember that Hector was featured in the *Epistre Othéa* as an ideal knight and, further, that on the strength of Hector's association with knighthood the *Epistre* has been seen as a guide to all good chevaliers. This association can be easily confirmed. From the beginning of the fourteenth century, numerous romances and allegories singled out Hector among the nine worthies as a model for modern knighthood: Jacques de Longuyon's *Vœux de Paon*, Guillaume de Machaut's *Dit dou Lyon* and *Prise d'Alexandrie*, Froissart's *Chroniques* and *Le Temple d'Onnour*, and Thomas of Saluzzo's *Chevalier errant*, among others.[30] In these texts, Hector is the most prized of the three pagan worthies: Hector, Alexander the Great, and Julius Caesar. According to some accounts, he is even the best of all the worthies. According to legend, Hector is held in such high esteem partly because after undertaking to govern the city of Troy he killed between eight and thirty warring kings before he himself was slain. Hector, along with the pagan, Hebrew, and Christian worthies, thus came to stand not only for the virtues of modern knighthood but for heroic acts in general.

As the tradition of the worthies gained momentum at the end of the medieval era, it was elaborated in various ways that served to integrate further the worthies into the world of medieval chivalry. For example, female counterparts to the worthies were devised; Hector's counterpart, Penthesilea, had been the queen of the Amazons who attempted to avenge his death.[31] In the visual arts, each worthy was distinguished by his or her own fictional shield to denote the descent from which a knight could claim nobility.[32] Hector's shield was an enthroned gold lion who holds a

---

[30] On the relationship between these texts and the tradition of the worthies, see H. Schroeder, *Der Topos der 'Nine Worthies' in Literatur und bildender Kunst* (Göttingen, 1971); and on the iconographic tradition, see also R. Wyss, "Die neune Helden. Eine ikonographische Studie," *Zeitschrift für Schweizerische Archäologie und Kunstgeschichte* 17 (1957) 73-106.

[31] Schroeder, *Nine Worthies*, pp. 168-224.

[32] *Ibid.*, pp. 225-299. They appear standing with their shields in two miniatures in Thomas of Saluzzo's *Le Chevalier errant* (Paris, BN MS fr. 12559, fols. 125r and 125v), illustrated in Meiss, *Limbourgs*, 2: Figs. 47-48.

sword and is depicted in profile on a red ground.[33] The association of
Hector as a medieval knight had thus acquired such force that it could
account for his use in the *Epistre Othéa* as an ideal knight. With this
observation most commentators on the *Epistre Othéa* have gone no
further, believing Hector's presence in the *Epistre* to be fully explained by
it. And, indeed, we can find in the writings of Christine that she too
exalted Hector for these very virtues, calling him in the *Cité des dames*
"one of the bravest men of all the world" and "the flower and excellence
of the world's knighthood."[34]

But the conclusion that the *Epistre Othéa* belongs to a genre of
epistolary allegories that offered political advice requires that we take a
closer look at Hector's meaning for French politics. We do not need to
look far to find that Hector was not just a model knight. He bore a special
relationship to the French royal family whose historiography provided it
with a genealogy going back to Troy.[35] In the *Livre du Chemin de long
estude*, Christine explains Hector's importance for French history when
she sets him in a European context of the myths of national origin.[36]
Christine recounts that when Troy fell its princes were dispersed and
went, according to legend, to different centers. Helenus, a son of King
Priam of Troy, went to Greece, and from him was descended Alexander
the Great. Two nephews of Priam, Aeneas and Antenor, founded Rome
and Venice respectively. Brutus, a great-grandson of Aeneas, landed in
England and became the first king of Britain, while another descendant,
Corinus, founded Cornwall. Another of Priam's sons, Hector, was
survived after the fall of Troy by his own son, Francio, who founded
France. Through this historical fiction, all European nations were seen to
share a descent from Troy; that of France came through Hector.

Contrary to accounts that presented Francio as a nephew of Priam (like
Aeneas and Antenor), Christine's version identifies him as the son of
Hector who was himself the son of King Priam of Troy. In this respect,

---

[33] On the variations in Hector's heraldry, see Joseph Palermo, "Les Armoires
d'Hector dans la tradition médiévale," in *Jean Misrahi Memorial Volume. Studies in
Medieval Literature*, ed. H. R. Runte, H. Niedzielski and W. Hendrickson (Columbia,
S.C., 1977), pp. 89-99.

[34] Christine, *City of Ladies*, tr. Richards, p. 49.

[35] On the use of the Troy story by political writers at the court of Charles VI, see
J. Krynen, *Idéal du prince*, pp. 245-258. For earlier periods, see also E. Faral, *La Légende
Arthurienne. Études et documents*, Bibliothèque de l'école des hautes études, 244 (Paris,
1929), pp. 262-293.

[36] Christine, *Le Livre du chemin de long estude*, pp. 151-156.

she followed a version of the legend that first appeared in French historiography in the thirteenth century in Rigord's *Gesta Philippi Augusti Francorum regis.*[37] Rigord's version was in turn incorporated into the official organ of French history, the *Grandes chroniques de France.*[38] This slight alteration to the legendary genealogy allowed Christine to claim that the French nation could trace its origins through direct hereditary succession back to Priam of Troy. This genealogy elevated the rulers of France above those of Rome, Venice, and England. French monarchs shared their prestigious position in the world only with Alexander the Great of Greece. In the *Chemin,* the survey of the Trojan myths of origin forms part of a debate intended to resolve the question of who should serve as next emperor of the world; not surprisingly, the French kings are favored because of their royal lineage. And for Christine, Hector was the key person in this unbroken succession.

Time and time again, Christine returns to Hector's importance for the legend of the Trojan origins of the French in order to underscore the theme of dynastic continuity. Near the very beginning of her biography of King Charles v she includes another account of the founding of France, one that fills out the genealogy so that it can properly commence with France's first king, Pharamond.[39] With his Trojan companions, Francio, "son of the worthy Hector, son of King Priam of Troy," settled in Sicambria. Many years after Francio's death, descendants of his companions went from Sicambria to Gaul under the leadership of their duke, Priam, who was himself directly descended from Trojan royal stock. Priam was succeeded by Marchomires, who in turn fathered Pharamond, who was crowned the first king of France. Through this account, Christine intends to relate "the noble memory of the high genealogy of the noble kings of France, from whom this one [Charles v] is descended." Later in the text she evokes Hector as a specific dynastic model for Charles v, again stressing the unbroken line of descent.[40]

Given Hector's place in the dynastic succession, it seems reasonable to suppose that Christine had in mind the Trojan origins of the contemporary French kings when she selected Hector as the fictional recipient of

[37] Rigord, *Gesta Philippi Augusti Francorum regis, descripta a magistro Rigordo,* in *Recueil des historiens des Gaules et de France,* ed. M. Bouquet (Paris, 1878), 17: 16. Willard, *Christine de Pizan,* pp. 119-120, assumes that Christine took her account of the Trojan lineage from Bernard Gui's *Fleurs des histoires.*

[38] *Les Grandes chroniques de France,* ed. J. Viard, SHF, Publications in Octavo, 395 (Paris, 1920-1937), 1: 9-11.

[39] Christine, *Livre des fais et bonnes meurs,* 1: 12-14.

[40] *Ibid.,* 2: 220.

the *Epistre Othéa*. This is confirmed by the dedicatory prologue where she stresses a genealogical link between Hector and a specific prince, Louis of Orleans, who she says derives from "Trojan stock," like Hector.[41] In this context, it must be remembered that when Christine wrote the *Epistre*, Louis of Orleans, as brother to the king, was next in line of succession for the throne besides the king's direct heirs. Interpreted in this way, the *Epistre* celebrates, through the figure of Hector, Louis of Orleans's hereditary position in the illustrious realm of France. Through this text, along with many others by her, Christine can be seen as participating in a wave of erudite propaganda that upheld the authority of the monarchy during especially troubled times.[42]

Yet the question remains: why celebrate the French monarchy in an advice-giving letter? The answer may lie in the way in which Christine employed elsewhere the topos of France's Trojan origins. Specifically, in one of Christine's other works, *L'Avision*, she used Trojan history as a model by which she could instruct the current rulers – in other words, by which she could give advice. Her autobiographical *L'Avision*, begins with a history of France, once again introducing Francio, as the person from whom all later kings descended.[43] Then the Trojan model evolves as an allegory. In this allegory the French realm is a garden and the monarchs gardeners. Initially Francio planted a golden bough brought from Troy to signify the golden age. Subsequently, good gardeners tended the plant well and it flourished, although occasionally, bad gardeners stunted its growth. Extending her allegory to the present day, Christine invents two golden butterflies – the reigning princes Charles VI and his brother Louis of Orleans – who were capable of ruling well but who were changed by Fortune into two birds of prey who instead govern badly.[44] She laments the present lack of good government and calls for a return to the golden age of rule of the Trojan past. In this case, then, the Trojan origins serve not so much to remind the reader of dynastic continuity but to offer the glory of the Trojan past as a motif of hope for the present and future.

Extrapolating from *L'Avision* to the *Epistre Othéa*, it seems reasonable to suppose that the Trojan ruler Hector was meant to serve as a didactic

[41] London, BL Harley MS 4431, fol. 95r: "D'estoc troyan ancianne noblece...." Mombello, "Quelques aspects de la pensée politique de Christine de Pizan," pp. 86-87, has also commented on the importance of this phrase in the dedication.

[42] For this point of view, see Krynen, *Idéal du prince*, p. 52.

[43] Christine, *Lavision*, 78; and Phillipps MS 128, fol. 4v.

[44] Phillipps MS 128, fol. 6r [on ch. 12]: "Item au propos de France, ce peut segnefier le roy Charles VI⁰ ... le bien qui est en ses nobles condicions et la pitié de sa maladie et le temps qu'elle lui prist, et avec lui monseigneur le duc d'Orlians son frere."

model for the modern prince Louis of Orleans. This view does not deny that Hector was also an ideal knight on whom the prince could model himself. But considering the relationship of the *Epistre Othéa* to political allegories by Christine's contemporaries, on the one hand, and the importance of Hector for French politics as evidenced in Christine's own writings, on the other hand, it seems likely that in this text Hector of Troy was more important as a model for kingship than as a model for knighthood.

In light of this, one other point about Hector needs clarification: his age. Christine is quite specific about the fact that he is fifteen years old when he receives the letter, a detail that is even included in the lengthy title of the work. The question arises, then, whether, as most writers have assumed, his age is meant to point to an actual fifteen-year-old.[45] With regard to Hector's identity, the most persistent suggestion in the literature is that he is meant to suggest Christine's own son, Jean Castel.[46] Her son, it is true, was fifteen in 1400. It is also true that he might have been a suitable recipient for a courtesy book, having served in the princely household of the earl of Salisbury in England and seeking, in 1400, a similar position in France, perhaps in the household of the duke of Orleans. But, as we have seen, the *Epistre* can no longer be regarded as an ordinary courtesy book that might have been suitable for the writer's son. Whereas Hector the ideal knight might have been an appropriate model for Jean Castel, Hector the Trojan ruler, prototype for the kings of France, was not. We have seen, moreover, that advice-giving letters were directed almost exclusively to princes and kings.

So, if Hector's age is meant to associate him with an actual person, we might expect to find that person among the princes in the royal household instead of within Christine's family circle. But, if we turn to the royal household, we find that there are no suitable fifteen-year-olds. The most obvious candidate would be Louis of Orleans, because of the dedicatory prologue and because of his position next in line to the throne, should the king die without an heir. However, Louis was twenty-eight at the time of the writing of the *Epistre*, and his own son Charles was not yet ten. Another logical candidate would be the dauphin, Charles (d. 1401), who

---

[45] For example, Meiss, *Limbourgs*, 1: 23; Tuve, *Allegorical Imagery*, p. 286; Mombello, "Un'edizione critica," pp. 9, 414-416, for a summary of the possible identifications of Hector: Louis or Charles of Orleans, Anthony of Burgundy, Henry v of England, Duke Amadeo viii of Savoy, as well as Jean Castel. Ignatius, "Epistre Othéa," pp. 136-139, has dissented, viewing Hector in more general terms.

[46] Recently by Yenal, *Christine de Pisan*, p. 42; Laidlaw, "Christine de Pizan, the Earl of Salisbury and Henry iv," pp. 137-138; and Willard, *Christine de Pizan*, p. 94.

was actually next in line to the throne, but he was just eight years old in 1400, and the king himself was nearing his thirtieth year. All of this suggests that we need to look elsewhere, not for another fifteen-year-old but rather for the very meaning of the age.

Instead of pointing to a specific fifteen-year-old, the age of fifteen was probably meant to suggest a certain phase in Hector's life, as in the life of a French prince. Fifteen years was close to the age for induction into chivalric societies and the age at which the monarch began to rule. Age at admittance to chivalry ranged from early adolescence to early adulthood, from around eleven to twenty-one, but for royal princes a time shortly after the onset of adolescence became common.[47] For instance, in 1389, the two sons of the Duke of Anjou, King of Sicily and Naples, were knighted in a royal ceremony in Paris.[48] A chronicler informs us that since the eldest son was merely twelve at the time, the dubbing had taken place earlier than was customary.[49] The age of majority also varied during the medieval era. But an ordinance, discussed earlier, that was passed at the end of the reign of King Charles v and reaffirmed during the reign of Charles vi set the age at which the king could begin to rule at fourteen.[50]

It might be objected that Hector is fifteen, not fourteen, and therefore not at the age of majority. But this discrepancy probably does not matter since Hector is still at the right age to learn the arts of chivalry and government. As Christine says in the *Epistre Othéa*, he is in the "prime of his youth."[51] The occasions of becoming a knight and becoming king required the mastery of a certain body of knowledge. Such learning was acquired over a number of years, up to and including the fifteenth. For instance, Gerson composed a schoolbook for the dauphin Louis and sent it to his preceptor for use when Louis was thirteen.[52] And Christine wrote in 1412 a kind of Mirror of Princes, the *Livre de la Paix*, to the dauphin Louis when he was fifteen, referring to this age as a sort of rite of passage when one is "not a child ... but like a mature man, very wise."[53] It could

---

[47] L. Gautier, *Chivalry*, tr. D. C. Dunning (New York, 1959), p. 105.

[48] M. Barroux, *Les Fêtes royales de Saint-Denis* (Paris, 1936).

[49] *Ibid.*, pp. 10-11.

[50] Cazelles, *Société politique, noblesse et couronne*, pp. 579-581; and Nordberg, *Les Ducs*, pp. 61-65.

[51] London, BL Harley MS 4431, fol. 95v: "... en ta prime jeunece."

[52] Discussed and edited by A. Thomas, *Jean de Gerson et l'éducation des dauphins de France. Étude critique suivie du texte de deux de ses opuscules et de documents inédits sur Jean Majoris précepteur de Louis XI* (Paris, 1930).

[53] Christine, *The "Livre de la paix" of Christine de Pisan. A Critical Edition with Introduction and Notes*, ed. C. C. Willard (The Hague, 1958), p. 60.

be argued therefore that Hector's age is fifteen because as a consecrated knight and a prospective ruler he is now, "like a mature man, very wise." The implication is that, just like the dauphin whom Christine saw fit to instruct when he reached the age of fifteen, Hector can now master the arts of chivalry and government if he pays attention to the advice conveyed to him in the letter by Othea.

But what of Othea? How does she function in relation to Hector and with respect to the epistolary allegory? Unlike Hector, she has no actual identity to help us understand her meaning. Still, Christine tells us a number of things about Othea in one simple statement: "Othea, goddess of prudence ... according to the Greek can be taken for the wisdom of women."[54] There are three significant features about Othea to be learned from this remark. First, she is a classical fictional person, specifically a Greek. Second, she is a woman. Third, she is Prudence, the first of the four cardinal virtues.

With respect to the first feature, Othea's classical origin, this has usually been understood as referring to the derivation of her name, that is, that she is intended to be Minerva, the Greek goddess of wisdom.[55] Other meanings seem equally plausible, however. It might also be understood simply as Christine's attempt to invent a figure contemporary with those featured in her stories, that is, with Hector and the other Trojan heroes and with the mythological gods and goddesses — in other words, another Greek. Yet a more compelling possibility emerges if we think back for a moment to the model of Plutarch's letter. Now that we have identified Hector as a Greek type for a ruler — like the Roman Trajan —, could not Othea be seen as a Greek variant of the epistolary author, a Greek counterpart to the Roman Plutarch? In support of this suggestion, we should remember the tremendous authority that Plutarch held for John of Salisbury, who may even have invented the model, and then for Gerson and Christine, who thoroughly accepted it. To offer advice in her own epistle, then, Christine invents a classical authoress, the fictional Othea, whose authority derives from her antiquity which helps to recall the most powerful model of the genre of letter-writing, Plutarch's letter to Trajan.

---

[54] London, BL Harley MS 4431, fol. 95v; and Christine, *Epistle of Othea*, tr. Scrope, p. 6.

[55] See above, n. 4. See also alternative suggestions by Pinet, *Christine de Pisan*, pp. 274-275, that Othea is actually Orithea, queen of the Amazons and mother of Penthesilea; and G. Mombello, "Recherches sur l'origine du nom de la Déesse Othéa," *Atti della Accademia delle Scienze di Torino, Classe di scienze morali, storiche e filologiche* 103 (1968-1969) 343-373, who proposes that the name derives from the word "Otheos," which formed part of the Good Friday services.

The second characteristic of Othea, that she is a woman, may also be understood in the light of the allegorical letters. Philippe de Mézières used allegorical persons within the framework of his letters to represent himself as the letter-writer, the advice-giver, that is, the Old Solitary, the Old Invalid, the Good Samaritan, and others. So, it should not be surprising that Christine turned to the character of a woman, a wise woman whom she names Othea to give her the cloak of classical authority. As we shall see, this strategy also allows her to develop the theme of the wisdom of women within an allegorical framework.

The most notable feature of Othea, however, is her identity with Prudence, since this persona well qualifies her to instruct Hector to be a model prince. As the first of the four cardinal virtues, Prudence joined those virtues that had come to be called the "political" virtues in order to distinguish them from the theological virtues.[56] As political virtues, the cardinal virtues were considered by Christine as necessary for the teaching of "good policy" or government, an idea that she took from Aristotle's *Nicomachean Ethics*, newly available to her in a French translation.[57] In Aristotle, she also found a more developed notion of just how Prudence could teach the art of government. According to the Greek philosopher, Prudence had three essential traits, memory, intelligence, and foresight, which Christine neatly summarizes in the *Livre des fais et bonnes meurs*.[58] In the *Livre de la Paix*[59] and the *Cité des dames*, Christine goes on to specify what lessons Prudence can thus teach. For example, in the *Cité des dames* Christine sets out to show that women, just like men, can learn from Prudence. Addressing Reason, Christine says:

> I would gladly learn from you ... whether women can reflect on what is best to do and what is better to be avoided, and whether they remember past events and become learned from the examples they have seen, and, as a result, are wise in managing current affairs, and whether they have foresight into the future. Prudence, it seems to me, teaches those lessons.[60]

[56] For a review of writings on the cardinal virtues, see O. Lottin, *Psychologie et morale aux XII⁰ et XIII⁰ siècles*, vol. 3, *Problèmes de morale* (Louvain, 1949), 2.1: 154-155. They were apparently first called "political" by Peter the Chanter in his *Summa Abel*, quoted in *Ibid.*, p. 155.

[57] The translation by Nicole Oresme has been edited by A. D. Menut, "Le Livre des politiques d'Aristote [ed. by] Nicole Oresme," *Transactions of the American Philosophical Society*, n.s., 60, pt. 6 (1970) 3-392; and the manuscripts for Charles V studied by C. R. Sherman, "Some Visual Definitions." According to Sherman, Oresme defines *pollicie* in his glossary of difficult words as "political system, form of government, or constitutional government."

[58] Christine, *Livre des fais et bonnes meurs*, 2: 21.

[59] Christine, *Livre de la Paix*, pp. 65-67.

[60] Christine, *City of Ladies*, p. 87.

Because of her knowledge of past events and vision of future ones, Prudence is well equipped to counsel on the management of current affairs. Just how essential Prudence was to good government may be understood from Gerson who, using the metaphor of the body-politic, likened a ruler without Prudence to a head without eyes, ears, or a nose.[61]

Othea as Prudence interweaves phrases similar to those quoted above from the *Cité des dames* into the beginning of her letter to Hector: Hector should remember the events of the past, those things that are necessary to his great bravery, for Othea knows the things that will come.[62] Prudence acquires her greatest authority from her ability to see into the future, a faculty Othea stresses when she says that she teaches Hector "in the spirit of prophecy."[63] She shares this characteristic with the sibyls, like the Cumean sibyl who joins with Christine in the *Chemin de long estude* to teach good government and the Cumean sibyl who concludes the *Epistre*. Here Othea's prophetic abilities help to lend credibility to the fiction of the letter and heighten the sense of urgency about following its advice.

Within the epistolary allegory, the significance of Othea, as both the virtue of Prudence and Christine, and Hector, as both the ideal knight and Louis of Orleans, is reinforced by the first two miniatures in all three manuscripts. In each manuscript copy the first picture is a standard scene of presentation that depicts Christine kneeling before Louis of Orleans to whom she offers her book (Figs. 1, 5, 7; Pls. A, C). The second picture portrays Othea giving her letter to Hector who stands before her (Figs. 2, 6, 8; Pls. B, D). On the simplest level these miniatures can be viewed as corresponding with a single type, the presentation miniature, although there are differences in each picture. This correspondence underscores their interrelationship; just as Christine gives Louis of Orleans a book, so Othea gives Hector a letter. The actuality of book-giving is here equated with the fiction of letter-giving, something which helps us to understand the two figures as interchangeable.

The interrelationship of the principal figures is handled differently in each of the three manuscripts, however. It is most loosely drawn in the first of the three manuscripts, the earliest autograph in Paris. In this manuscript the identity of each separate figure is clearly established, but apart from the use of the cliché of the presentation model, which itself

[61] Gerson, *Harangue*, p. 32.

[62] London, BL Harley MS 4431, fols. 95v-96r; Christine, *Epistle of Othea*, tr. Scrope, pp. 4-6.

[63] *Ibid.*, fol. 96v; Christine, *Epistle of Othea*, tr. Scrope, p. 6.

naturally prompts the viewer to identify Christine as Othea and Louis as Hector, little extra effort went into making the figures interchangeable. A number of features clearly identify Louis in the first miniature (Fig. 1). First, the arms of Orleans decorate the tapestry behind him; second, the ducal baton or mace, symbolic of his position next in line to the king, is held by a prince behind him; and third, the square hat that he wears is a style often included in portrayals of him because he favored it.[64] His attendants wear garments consistent with their positions in the household of a prince. Christine wears a simpler garment suited to her bourgeois status.

In the second miniature Hector's identity is established not only by his name, which is neatly written over his head, but also by his heraldic charge, the lion, which carpets the background (Fig. 2). The heraldry makes it clear that we are confronted with Hector as a worthy, as a medieval knight. At the same time, Hector's court attire is appropriate for the royal king Priam's son. Hector's dual persona as a knight and ruler is thus secured by the visual details as well as by the text. The men who accompany him, sporting beards, wearing pointed hats, and carrying a crossbow, locate the scene in the pagan East. Othea as Prudence wears a head-covering also worn by sibyls.[65] What is important here is that whereas Louis and Christine are meant to represent actual persons, Hector and Othea clearly represent types. Hector is a model for the king and the knight, Othea the model of a wise woman.

Significant changes occur in this set of miniatures in the later two manuscripts. These changes suggest that the figures — Louis and Christine, Hector and Othea — were conceived in such a way as to make more explicit their identities as contemporary individuals. In addition, the changes more fully exploit the richness of the textual allegory. As we have seen, the principal characters of the allegory stand for the ideal models of a knight and a prince, the historical-fictional characters of Hector and Othea, and the real persons Louis and Christine. It is in the miniatures in the London copy that the multiple identities are most fully realized, although it is probable that the scheme of including details of this kind in the two miniatures was first devised for the Paris book.

---

[64] For example, he wears this hat in Salmon's *Demandes* (Paris, BN MS fr. 23279), fol. 70r; in Chantilly, Musée Condé, MS 492, fols. 108v and 184r; and Paris, BN MS fr. 12779, fol. 106v.

[65] This head-covering is worn by the Cumean sibyl who accompanies Christine in miniatures in copies of the *Chemin de long estude* illustrated by Meiss, *Limbourgs*, 2: 144; and Schaefer, "Illustrationen," Figs. 103-105, 107-109.

The London miniatures are most exceptional in the way that they emphasize the interchangeability of the figures through the use of similar details of color and costume (Figs. 5, 6; Pls. A, B). Louis and Hector both wear royal blue robes embroidered with gold designs. The robes are *houppelandes*, full, floor-length dresses fashionable for men and women alike at the French court.[66] Louis's robe is embroidered all over in gold with the motif of a wolf, for which the French word *loup* is a pun on his name.[67] Hector's is decorated with gold crowns, equally if less specifically appropriate for royalty. Each also wears gold jewelry. Louis's is again quite specific, being the collar of the Order of the Porcupine, alternately called the Order of the Mail, that he founded in 1394.[68] Through costume, the specificity of these images of Louis and Hector is thus greater than in the first Paris autograph. Changes also occur in the depiction of the attendants. Gone are the eastern-styled onlookers who accompany Hector in the first autograph. In their place appear European courtiers who wear red and white plumed hats that correspond exactly with those worn by Louis's attendants in the opening miniature. Christine and Othea are also more closely linked in the London manuscript; both wear similar, darkly coloured dresses and similar head coverings. Again, the point here is that the fictional figures of Hector and Othea no longer merely stand for types

[66] On the *houppelande*, see Joan Evans, *Dress in Mediaeval France* (Oxford, 1952), p. 41 and *passim*; V. Gay, *Glossaire archéologique du Moyen Âge et de la Renaissance*, 2 vols. (Paris, 1887), 2: 36; and Margaret Scott, *Late Gothic Europe, 1400-1500* (London, 1980), pp. 64, 73, 250, and *passim*.

[67] The wolf was added to the Orleans livery at least by 1390; see L. E. Laborde, *Les Ducs de Bourgogne: étude sur les lettres, les arts et les industries pendant le XVᵉ siècle*, Pt. II, *Preuves*, 3 vols. (Paris, 1849-1852), 2.3: 52, 61, 65-66, 70-71, and *passim*. As his personal emblem it appears with the duke's arms in a number of manuscripts including Paris, BN MSS fr. 312-314 (fr. 312, fol. 1r); Chantilly, Musée Condé, MS 277 (fol. 3r).

[68] On this order, see the summaries by A. Favyn, *The Theatre of Honour and Knighthood. Or a Compendious Chronicle and Historie of the Whole Christian World* (London, 1623), pp. 448-468; P. Helyot, *Histoire des ordres monastiques, religieux et militaires, et des congrégations séculières de l'un et de l'autre sexe, qui ont été establiés jusqu'à présent*, 8 vols. (Paris, 1718), 8: 276-279, 336-339; and F. F. Steenackers, *Histoire des ordres de chevalerie et des distinctions honorifiques en France* (Paris, 1867), pp. 75-90.

Studies in depth have been made by Hélie de Brémond d'Ars Migré, *Les Chevaliers du porc-épic ou du camail, 1394-1498* (Macon, 1938); Charles d'Orlac, "Les Chevaliers du porc-épic ou du camail 1394-1498," *Revue historique nobiliaire et biographique*, n.s., 111 (1867) 337-350; G. Demay, "Note sur l'ordre du Camail ou du Porc-Épic," *Bulletin de la Société nationale des antiquaires de France* (1875) 71-75; E. Kovacs, "L'Ordre du camail des ducs d'Orléans," *Acta Historiae Artium, Academiae Scientiarum Hungaricae* 27 (1981) 225-231.

See also the following unpublished manuscript sources: Paris, BN MSS nouv. acq. fr. 20013, 22289, 22290, and Clairambault MS 1241, 1308.

of a ruler or knight and an author. With the aid of the details in the London copy, we can more readily view the figure of Hector as Louis and Othea as Christine.

One other detail, absent in the earlier manuscript, secures the identity of Hector as Louis of Orleans: the falcon perched on Hector's arm. In any book about the training of knights, this bird can refer simply to the sport of falconry, a pastime learned at the appropriate age by any young chevalier such as Hector. But the prominence of the falcon as a contemporary symbol for Louis suggests that it may be present here as a personal attribute rather than a reference to knighthood. In Philippe de Mézière's *Songe du vieil pèlerin,* he uses the textual image of the brown falcon with a white chin to signify Louis, along with a white falcon with a gold beak and feet for Charles VI.[69] Later illustrations of Philippe's text portray the brothers posing with their respective birds perched on their arms exactly as Hector poses in the *Epistre* (Figs. 53, 54).[70] The existence of this later tradition of illustration raises the possibility that an earlier manuscript with similar miniatures once existed and thus could have provided the model for the miniatures in the *Epistre.* Confirmation of this hypothesis is not necessary, however, for us to accept the falcon as an attribute of Louis. Since Christine knew Philippe's text, she could have invented the visual depiction, having already used the same imagery for her allegory in *L'Avision.* In *L'Avision* she identified the beautiful butterflies that were transformed into birds of prey, falcons, as symbols for Louis of Orleans and Charles VI.[71] If this interpretation of the falcon in the *Epistre* is valid, then the identities of Hector and Louis are merged in the London manuscript through the symbol of the brown bird.

To this point we have been considering details in these two pictures that are for the most part either consistent with the tradition of presentation miniatures or called for by the text. However, two additional features in the London copy stand out as exceptional in their deviation both from tradition and from the text, thus suggesting that they were included to emphasize an iconographic point that has not yet been explained.

The first of these details is the careful reproduction of the collar of the Order of the Porcupine worn by Louis and his courtiers in the first miniature. What makes this detail so remarkable is that it constitutes the only accurate contemporary representation of the collar, otherwise known

[69] Philippe de Mézières, *Le Songe,* 1: 110.
[70] See also ch. 4, p. 153.
[71] Christine, *Lavision,* pp. 84-85; and Phillipps MS 128, fol. 6r.

from documents or later portrayals.[72] According to documents the collar consisted of an enamelled image of a porcupine suspended from a necklace composed of eight links of gilded silver chain mail joined together like points of stars. Although it is not possible to discern whether the porcupines in the London miniature once had pigment on them to indicate their enamelling, it is clear that the collar is painted with gold leaf, applied over black brush strokes perhaps to indicate the silver links. Such attention to detail strongly suggests a considerable desire for accuracy even in the face of technical considerations. Later equestrian seals of Louis's descendants display the collar of the porcupine as it is depicted in the miniature, thereby further confirming the accurate portrayal of it in the London manuscript (Fig. 71). One seal belonging to Louis's son Charles includes a corresponding collar with eight points of mail and a dangling bauble.[73] A later seal belonging to Louis's grandson, King Louis XII, includes a reasonable facsimile of the chain mail collar, but without the porcupine.[74] The unique contemporary representation of the collar in the London manuscript is all the more striking since none of the extant portraits of Louis, with the exception of that in the related Paris copy, includes a reproduction of the collar.[75]

Identification of the detail of the collar of the Order of the Porcupine prompts a rereading of the presentation miniature in other respects as well. Louis's blue robe and red hat constitute the livery that all members of the order were to wear along with the collar; missing only is the violet mantle customarily worn over the robe.[76] Although this painstaking attention to details of costume and accessories could be understood just as an attempt to secure the identity of the sitter as Louis of Orleans and of the courtiers as his faithful companions, another interpretation seems more plausible based on further analysis of the miniature. In an apparently

[72] For documents on the collar, see Laborde, *Les Ducs*, 2.3: 251: "Un camail en façon de treliz ... au bout duquel fermeilet pent un porc espy et des huit points dudit camail sont pendans quatre vins huits grosses perles..."; 2.3: 268: "... un collier d'argent d'un camail a un porte espy...." See also the unpublished drawings of the collar done after now-destroyed sculpture from the Château de Blois and the Church of the Célestine: Paris, BN MS Clairambault 1241, fols. 687, 723-724.

[73] L.-C. Douët-d'Arcq, *Collection de sceaux (Inventaires et documents publiés par ordre de l'Empereur sous la direction de M. Le Comte de Laborde)*, 3 vols. (Paris, 1863-1870), no. 944.

[74] *Ibid.*, nos. 951, 951 bis.

[75] For portraits of Louis, see P. Pradel, "Le Visage inconnu de Louis d'Orléans, frère de Charles VI," *La Revue des arts* 2 (1952) 93-98.

[76] Helyot, *Histoire des ordres*, p. 336; and A. Champollion-Figéac, *Louis et Charles ducs d'Orléans, leur influence sur les arts, la littérature et l'esprit de leur siècle* (Paris, 1844), p. 62.

unprecedented deviation from the conventions of the presentation miniature, the man next to Louis conspicuously displays his porcupine ornament with one hand, while he points with his other hand to the book Christine offers the enthroned prince. These unusual gestures, coupled with the presence of the livery and the collar of the order, thus serve to underscore the importance of the order, which in one sense forms the very subject of the miniature.

No less extraordinary is the second detail, a plain gold shield, unadorned with heraldic charges, that hangs from a tree in front of Hector in the lower left corner of the second miniature. The possibilities that this shield once had heraldic designs on it that were scraped off at a later date or that it was meant to be painted but was overlooked by the original team of illuminators can be discounted for two reasons. First, a comparable plain gold shield is also present in the Paris manuscript which was illustrated by a different group of artists. Second, technical examination of the London miniature conducted in the laboratory shows no evidence of abrasion and, further, discloses only underpaint beneath the gold.

What has been overlooked is that the gold shield is, like the porcupine, a symbol of a chivalric order, Louis of Bourbon's Order of the Gold Shield (*Ecu d'or*), founded in 1363.[77] As in the case of the collar of the Order of the Porcupine, depictions of the gold shield are rare, and they do not conform exactly with the description in the chronicle, which notes that the shield was to have two bands of pearls running diagonally through it, on which was written the word, *Allens*. The plain gold shield does appear, however, on the counterseal of Louis of Bourbon, where it is represented suspended from a belt just as it is in the London miniature.[78] It also appears, again without the bands of pearls or the motto, throughout a destroyed manuscript known to us through a copy by Gaignières, the *Hommages du Comté de Clermont*, which recorded the acts of homage to the Duke of Bourbon by different knights belonging to his order (Fig. 72).[79]

[77] On this order, see Helyot, *Histoire des ordres*, pp. 319-335; Favyn, *Theatre of Honour*, pp. 468-491; and especially the near-contemporary account of its founding and description of its livery by the chronicler Jehan Cabaret d'Orville, *La Chronique de bon duc Loys de Bourbon*, ed. A.-M. Chazaud (Paris, 1876), pp. 8-15. See also J.-B. de Vaivre, "Un Document inédit sur le décor héraldique de l'ancien hôtel de Bourbon à Paris," *Archivum Heraldicum* 86 (1972) 2-10.

[78] Described also in Vaivre, pp. 3-4.

[79] Paris, BN MS fr. 20082. The shield appears on nearly every illuminated folio of this manuscript: fols. 135, 171, 209, 251, 295. On this manuscript, see H. Bouchot, *Bibliothèque nationale. Inventaire des dessins exécutés pour Robert de Gaignières et conservés aux Départements des Estampes et des Manuscrits*, 2 vols. (Paris, 1891), 2:

Both the collar and the shield are also included in the comparable miniatures in the Paris manuscript, although the collar is executed with less exactitude, a characteristic that applies as well to details of color and costume (Figs. 7, 8; Pls. C, D). Worn by Louis, the collar of the Order of the Porcupine is composed of links of chain mail, but the mail is joined differently.[80] The porcupine bauble is evident on Louis's collar, but it does not appear on the collars of his attendants. Nor does the attendant make the same gesture toward the book that he makes in the London miniature. Louis wears a green garment instead of the blue and red livery that distinguished members of the order. Absent also are personalizing devices on Louis's and Hector's garments. And the attendants in both miniatures wear plumes of different colors.

In spite of these differences, the same broad conception lies behind the Paris miniatures, associating them more with those in London than with those in the first autograph. Hector wears a green full-length robe, comparable in color and style to that of Louis, a device that helps us to associate these two figures with each other. He holds a brown falcon, an attribute of Louis. And the gold shield hangs from the tree in front of Hector in the Paris miniature as it did in the London miniature. However, Christine wears a pale brown garment, whereas Othea wears a purple one in the same style. Still, in the Paris miniatures it is clear that some effort went into making it easy for the viewer to read the figures of Hector as Louis and Othea as Christine, although the overall program has been worked out less carefully than it was in the London miniatures. Nonetheless, the prominence of the collar of the Order of the Porcupine and the shield of the Order of the Gold Shield in both sets of miniatures strongly suggests that it is necessary to account for these unusual details to understand the opening sequence of pictures.

It might be said that these references to orders of chivalry can simply be explained by the fact that the *Epistre Othéa* is a courtesy book for the training of knights. This could indeed account for the portrayal of Louis of Orleans and his attendants as knights dressed in the costume of the Order of the Porcupine. We can imagine them ready to learn the code of chivalry taught by the text. However, it less readily explains the presence

---

428-432; and C. de Luçay, "Le Comté de Clermont en Beauvoisis," *Revue historique nobiliaire et biographique* 13 (1877) 265-310, 388-427, 467-513, 14 (1877) 42-81, 227-260, 310-358, 376-404.

[80] C. Nordenfalk, quoted by M. Meiss, *French Painting in the Time of Jean de Berry. The Boucicaut Master* (London/New York, 1968), p. 144 n. 32, previously pointed out that Louis wears a porcupine badge in the Paris maniscript.

of the gold shield of the Order of the Gold Shield in the tree in front of Hector. Are we supposed to imagine that Hector is about to learn the code of chivalry necessary to join the Order of the Gold Shield? If so, and this implication seems likely, why is Hector supposed to strive for acceptance in the order of the Duke of Bourbon rather than the order of the Duke of Orleans pictured in the first miniature? Another question also arises when we consider the prominence of these references to orders of chivalry. What does the political allegory, fulfilled through the dynastic figure of Hector of Troy, have to do with such orders?

In order to understand the allusions made in the miniatures, it is necessary to understand the function of these orders. The orders of the Porcupine and the Gold Shield were secular orders of chivalry that differed from earlier forms of knighthood. Originally an individual became a knight to participate in battle. The rites by which the knighting was done might take place in church or on the field, but in either case the job of the knight was the same: it was war. Even when knighthood developed into a special estate for which one qualified through the rights of birth, entering into a kind of brotherhood, the knight remained a soldier. These characteristics do not apply to the secular orders of chivalry that only arose in the fourteenth century.

The objectives of the secular orders were political, whether on a national, domestic, or personal scale.[81] For instance, the first of them, the English Order of the Garter, has been seen as asserting England's claim to the throne of France.[82] Its French counterpart, the Order of the Star, in turn promoted the dynastic supremacy of French monarchs, who ruled by divine right.[83] Thereafter, a series of lesser orders put forward lesser claims. The orders were composed of a limited number of members — often around twenty-four — selected from among the nobility by one individual, usually a duke. A typical order thus consisted of an elite group of men who gathered around the prestige of a ducal house and who formed a sort of political party to defend the partisan interests of their leader. To demonstrate their allegiance to the leader and distinguish themselves from other knights, members wore special clothes or accessories that sometimes held symbolic value.

[81] On the secular orders, see Favine, *Theatre of Honour*; Helyot, *Histoire des ordres*; Philippe Contamine, "Points de vue. La Chevalerie en France à la fin du Moyen Âge," *Francia* 4 (1976) 255-285, 987-988; and the catalogue of the exhibition held in Paris, Musée Monétaire, *Ordres de chevalerie et récompenses nationales* (Paris, 1956).

[82] Y. Renouard, "L'Ordre de la Jarretière et l'Ordre de l'Étoile," *Le Moyen Âge* 55 (1949) 281-300.

[83] *Ibid.*, pp. 296-297. On the depiction of this order in the *Grandes Chroniques*, see Hedeman, "Restructuring the Narrative," pp. 176-178.

Both the Order of the Porcupine and the Order of the Gold Shield had special but different import for contemporary French politics. If we can believe later accounts, the Order of the Porcupine, founded by Louis on the occasion of the baptism of his son, came to signify that the Orleanist party could defend itself against the rival party of John of Burgundy, just like the porcupine that sticks out its quills when attacked.[84] The Order of the Gold Shield had more lofty objectives.[85] It was founded by Louis of Bourbon so that its members could unite to honor one another and God and to acquire honor and defend peace. This order took on the character of its founder. As the uncle of Louis of Orleans and Charles VI, the Duke of Bourbon was the senior statesman of the French princes. He frequently mediated between the various dukes and, since he apparently did not crave power in his own right (and as the brother of the queen, Jeanne de Bourbon, he could never be in line for the throne), he was often relied on to propose and implement an equitable solution when political difficulties arose at the royal court. Of all the secular orders, the Order of the Gold Shield seems to have been least concerned with the rivalries of partisan politics.

With this background in mind, let us return to the subject of the miniatures. In the first miniature, Louis of Orleans is depicted as founder of the Order of the Porcupine and is grouped with members of the order. That is, he is shown as the head of a political party whose aim is to uphold the Orleanist claims over those of Burgundy, and he is accompanied by those who support this objective. For the present, we can read the gestures of the knight who holds out his porcupine and points to the book as having something to do with the relationship between the content of the book and the aims of the order. In the second miniature Hector is shown with the symbol of another order, the Order of the Gold Shield, before him. As mentioned earlier, this suggests that Hector is to strive to follow the precepts of Louis of Bourbon's order. It might seem odd at first that Louis of Bourbon should be used as a model in a book that otherwise has nothing to do with him. But what must be kept in mind is that Christine and Gerson both used Louis of Bourbon as an example of an ideal ruler in other works on the art of government addressed to the king, the dauphin, and the dukes.[86]

---

[84] This is the view given by Helyot, *Histoire des ordres*, pp. 336-337.

[85] See above, n. 77.

[86] Christine, *Le Livre des fais et bonnes meurs*, 1: 153-160; Gerson, *Jean de Gerson*, ed. Thomas, p. 44 n. 1.

When read together, these two miniatures make a political point that reinforces the meaning of the text as an epistolary allegory about government. They make clear that the chivalry learned by the knight in the text is a certain kind of chivalry, the political chivalry of the secular orders. Then they imply that of all the chivalric orders, including that of the Order of the Porcupine, the Duke of Bourbon's Order of the Gold Shield should serve as the model for Hector. By putting forward this model, the miniatures offer counsel through their manipulation of visual symbols. They caution that Hector, the prototype for a ruler and an ideal knight, should not engage in partisan politics. Rather, he should pursue the common objectives of honor and peace, like the Duke of Bourbon. Hector's chivalry is thus meant to serve a national cause; it is not training in social manners.

Thinking back to the gestures of the attendant knight in the first miniature, we can now understand them to point to the theme of the *Epistre Othéa*. These gestures call attention to those very symbols − the collar and the book − that are central to a reading of the *Epistre*. They serve to highlight their equivalents − the shield and the letter − in the second miniatures. They help us to understand that, in the end, the *Epistre Othéa* is an advice-giving book written as a letter about the training of royal knights in a chivalry that entails the practice of nonpartisan politics in the government of France.

THE FOUR CARDINAL VIRTUES AND GOOD GOVERNMENT

The four cardinal virtues that introduce the text of the *Epistre* teach the art of good government to Hector. Christine reminds us in the first gloss that they are "necessary to good policy."[87] We have already seen that at the very beginning of the *Epistre* Hector learns to manage current affairs from Prudence, who is personified as Othea. Next, the sister virtue, Temperance, defined as the demonstration of Prudence, is taught by another female personification. As Fortitude and Justice, two exemplum allegories follow. The labors of Hercules teach fortitude, and Minos, as king of Crete and the underworld, teaches justice.

It has not previously been recognized that the importance of the cardinal virtues, indicated partly by their prominent position in the text, relates the *Epistre* specifically to Mirror of Princes handbooks designed

---

[87] London, BL Harley MS 4431, fol. 96r: "Et commes les iiij. vertus cardinaulz soient neccessaires a bonne pollicie, nous en parlerons ensuivant."

to teach good government at court. Like the *Epistre*, the standard manuals of this genre place the four cardinal virtues at the beginning of the text because, as Aegidius Romanus said, they are "more principal than the others," being those virtues with which "the king and prince ought to be endowed."[88] In these manuals, just as in the *Epistre*, the order of the virtues proceeded from Prudence to Temperance, followed by Fortitude and Justice. Such manuals were popular at the French court, many of them having been translated into French for King Charles v.[89]

Often relying on these earlier examples, contemporaries at the royal court wrote new Mirror of Princes texts that, like the earlier versions, typically began with the four cardinal virtues as a means of emphasizing their importance for kingship. For example, the anonymous author of the *Avis au Roi* stated that these virtues were essential for a good king because all others issued from them.[90] Jean Gerson placed the virtue of Prudence at the beginning of his treatise written for the education of the dauphin.[91] He also stressed the cardinal virtues in his royal sermon, the *Vivat Rex*, in which he said that these virtues, headed by Prudence, must all "live and reign in the king and his realm."[92] This evidence suggests that a revision of earlier views is necessary. Thus, it no longer seems correct to understand the *Epistre* as relating most closely to examples of courtesy literature such as compendia on the virtues and vices. In such compendia, the four cardinal virtues do not stand out, since they are usually intermingled with others, the sum of which was taken to influence good behavior.[93]

The miniatures that accompany the earliest versions of the *Epistre* reinforce the importance of the four cardinal virtues.[94] In fact, the first

---

[88] Egidio Colonna, *Li Livres du gouvernement des rois. A xiiith-Century French Version of Egidio Colonna's Treatise "De Regimine Principium,"* ed. S. P. Molenaer (New York, 1899), pp. 35-36.

[89] Many such books appear in Delisle, *Librairie*, 1: 259-260, 262, 369, 370, and *passim.* Two useful summaries of Mirror of Princes texts of the period are D. Bell, *L'Idéal éthique de la royauté en France au Moyen Âge d'après quelques moralistes de ce temps* (Geneva, 1962); and W. Berges, *Die Fürstenspiegel des hohen und späten Mittelalters*, Schriften der Reichsinstituts für ältere deutsche Geschichtskunde, Monumenta Germaniae Historica, 2 (Leipzig, 1938).

[90] New York, Pierpont Morgan Library MS M.456, fols. 25-38, described in Bell, *L'Idéal éthique*, pp. 61-70.

[91] Gerson, *Jean Gerson*, ed. Thomas, pp. 32-33, 41.

[92] Gerson, *Harangue*, p. 14.

[93] Comparisons with the *Somme le Roi* have been most forcefully advanced by Tuve, *Allegorical Imagery*, pp. 80-134, 286, and *passim.*

[94] On the representations of the virtues, see M. Evans, "Tugenden," in *Lexikon der christlichen Ikonographie*, ed. E. Kirschbaum (Breisgau, 1972), 4: 364-380; A. Katzenellenbogen, *Allegories of the Virtues and Vices in Medieval Art from Early Christian Times*

autograph has pictures only for these four virtues, in addition to a companion fifth virtue, a feature that serves to call attention to the virtues when the *Epistre* is read in manuscript form. In this copy, the two female personifications are paired, as are the two exemplum allegories that follow (Figs. 2, 3). We have already discussed the ways in which Prudence, personified as Othea handing Hector a letter, would have been understood as a visual metaphor for Christine teaching the art of good government to specific individuals at court. Next to this scene is an image of Temperance standing next to a clock, the mechanism of which she adjusts. In rubrics in the later London and Paris copies, Christine explains this imagery: just as each individual must employ reason when dealing with the human body which is composed of multiple parts, so Temperance must adjust a clock, which has many wheels and measures, in order for it to work properly.[95] Christine also reminds her readers that temperance is the demonstration of prudence. In other words, she cautions that knowledge is not enough; an understanding of how to apply it is necessary also.

When considered together in relationship to the meaning of the text of the *Epistre*, these paired images make two points. First, they establish at the outset that Christine believes women to be qualified to teach the virtues that determine behavior with regard to government. Second, they underscore the message of the opening pair of miniatures; specifically, that the prospective ruler should use his knowledge to act temperately, like those knights of the Order of the Gold Shield.

Following Prudence and Temperance are two male models of Fortitude and Justice, who act out these virtues (Fig. 3). Fortitude is indicated by Hercules killing the porter of Hell, Cerberus, and rescuing Proserpina. Christine's choice of Hercules as Fortitude was probably due to the fact that she knew him to be a Greek knight and, thus, a type for the chevalier in her text.[96] He may have served a dual purpose, however, since he was

---

to the Thirteenth Century, Studies of the Warburg Institute, 10 (London, 1939); and E. Gombrich, "Icones symbolicae: Philosophies of Symbolism and their Bearing on Art," in *Symbolic Images: Studies in the Art of the Renaissance* (London, 1972), pp. 123-195.

[95] London, BL Harley MS 4431, fol. 96v. This imagery may derive from Suso's *L'Horloge de Sapience*, see E. Spencer, "L'Horloge de Sapience. Brussels, Bibliothèque Royale, Ms. IV.III," *Scriptorium* 17 (1963) 277-299, Pls. 21-22. See also Willard, "Christine de Pisan's 'Clock of Temperance'," pp. 149-156.

[96] London, BL Harley MS 4431, fol. 97v; Christine, *Epistle of Othea*, tr. Scrope, pp. 11-12.

also presented in royal entries as a model for kingship.[97] The choice of
Minos as Justice is more difficult to explain. In her text Christine indicates
that she knew he was a Greek king who initially ruled in Crete and later
served as judge of the underworld.[98] She credits him with dispensing legal
justice in both capacities. In the miniature he is portrayed as a king before
whom two prisoners have been brought for him to judge. Just as Hercules
probably appealed to Christine because he was a Greek type for the strong
knight, Minos was probably chosen as a Greek type for the just king. The
miniaturist of the Paris autograph has given him the attributes of kingship,
specifically of French kingship: a throne, a crown, and a fleur-de-lis
sceptre. In the London manuscript (Fig. 9), he is even further transformed into a contemporary king through the royal colors of his garment,
painted blue and red, and the canopy of his throne, decorated with an oak
leaf motif commonly used in ceremonial at the royal court.[99] The virtues
of prudence and temperance taught by the female personifications are thus
fulfilled in the male examples of kingship, Hercules and Minos, who
practice fortitude and justice.

The cardinal virtues help to confirm at the outset that the *Epistre Othéa*
is not just an ordinary manual for good conduct but a Mirror of Princes
for rulers. If Hector, the model of a French knight and ruler, learns
prudence and temperance, he can perform virtuous deeds in his role as
a knight, following Hercules, and as a king, following Minos. As we have
seen, the earliest autograph of the *Epistre* makes this program clear
through the inclusion of just five miniatures, which illustrate these four
subjects and a fifth one, fame, depicted as Perseus rescuing Andromeda.
For the royal theoreticians writing over the course of the fifteenth century
the virtue of fame became an essential determinant of good rulership.[100]

---

[97] See M.-Rene. Jung, *Hercule dans la littérature française du XVIe siècle, de l'Hercule
courtois à l'Hercule baroque*, Travaux d'humanisme et renaissance, 79 (Geneva, 1966),
pp. 37-40.

[98] London, BL Harley MS 4431, fols. 98v-99r; Christine, *Epistle of Othea*, tr. Scrope,
p. 13.

[99] Laborde, *Les Ducs de Bourgogne*, 2.1: 67; Evans, *Dress in Mediaeval France*, p. 38.
Oak-leaf decoration was used prolifically at the royal festival in May 1389, according to
documents published by Barroux, *Les Fêtes royales*, p. 37. Similar decoration appears on
the robes worn by the Orleans children in the frontispiece to Sallust's *Jugurtha* (Paris,
BN MS lat. 5747, fol. 1r).

[100] Fame or *Bonne renomée* eventually became equated with *gloire*. See F. Joukovsky-Micha, "La Notion de 'vaine gloire' de Simund de Freine à Martin Le Franc,"
Romania 89 (1968) 1-30, 210-239. *Bonne renomée* was the subject of a tapestry owned
by Philip the Bold, recorded by J. Guiffrey, E. Muntz and A. Pinchart, *Histoire générale
de la tapisserie*, 3 vols. (Paris, 1878-1885), 1: 19.

The implication here is that Hector will acquire fame through his many valiant deeds, which make up his good government, just like Perseus, who rescued Andromeda. Of course, it is by now evident that the letter sent by Othea teaches him these lessons.

THE TROJAN SEQUENCE AND THE FRENCH MONARCHY

With regard to the selection of the subjects of the chapters, two points become apparent as the *Epistre* evolves. First, events involving Hector and his family regularly appear, undoubtedly because he is the recipient of the letter and the hero of the work. For example, stories are related about the advice of his brothers Troilus and Helenus, the prophecies of his sister Cassandra and his wife, Andromache, the revenge by his cousin Memnon, and the activities of his parents, Hecuba and Priam. At this stage the focus on Hector and his family may be understood simply as a desire on the part of Christine to provide a full historical context for her ancient hero. We will see later, however, that the strategy also permits a broader range of contemporary associations with persons in the French royal circle.

The second notable feature of the subject matter of the *Epistre* is the focus on the Trojan war. Nearly one-third of the chapters interspersed throughout the work center around episodes or events that were critical for the outcome of the Trojan war. Over several chapters Christine tells the stories of Jason and Medea, the Judgment of Paris, and Hector and Achilles, among others. Since Hector is both a Trojan prince and a model for contemporary rulers, it is likely that the emphasis on the Trojan war is meant to serve as a lesson about the government of France.

The jumbled order of these stories of Trojan history makes it clear that considerations other than chronology determined their place within the *Epistre*. Most often the placement of the stories was determined by the needs of the allegories. For example, the Amazon queen Penthesilea, who avenged Hector's death, appears early in the work, as the subject of chapter 15, instead of at the end, where she would belong in a historical sequence. She immediately follows the planetary deities that embody the virtues of chivalry and wisdom, of which she herself offers another example. She is, in fact, linked with two pagan goddesses, Minerva and Pallas, who immediately precede her in chapters 13 and 14. Christine uses Minerva and Pallas to represent the theological virtues of Faith and Hope. Penthesilea provides an example of the third theological virtue, Charity, since she allied with the Trojans in an effort to rescue them from the Greeks. Discussion of her at this point allowed Christine to expand further on the theme of wise women, which had been introduced by the figure of Othea-Prudence in the very beginning of the book.

A rapid overview of the subjects of other chapters reveals the existence of certain clusters of episodes whose proximity to one another probably does derive from their place in the Trojan narrative, in spite of the fact that they are out of sequence. For instance, a group of events that focus on Achilles – his death, his battle with Memnon, and his son Pyrrhus's battle with the Trojans – occur in the space of ten chapters (31, 36, and 40). A judgment of Paris sequence that includes the dream of Mercury, the wedding of Peleus and Thetis, and the judgment itself, takes place over thirteen chapters (60, 68, and 73). Such recurrent insertions of Trojan events help to preserve the thread of the narrative, although the placement of the story of Penthesilea is more typical of the inattention to historical sequence that characterizes most of the book.

Given the obvious absence of chronology, the ending of the *Epistre* is one of the most striking characteristics of the work. From chapter 88 on, events most closely linked to the fall of Troy suddenly are narrated in strict chronological order. This sequence serves as a climax to the *Epistre* and concludes abruptly with the fall of Troy. Two final chapters follow, on the deceit of Ino and the appearance of the Cumean sibyl to Augustus, whose presence at the very end of the book is equally anomalous partly since they seem to have little to do with the Trojan narrative that immediately precedes them. In fact, the retelling at this point of the story of Ino planting boiled corn is all the more puzzling because the complete story of Ino has already been told much earlier, in chapter 17. Yet, if we now examine the ending of the work in light of what we have learned about the political content, it becomes apparent that the epistolary allegory is fulfilled in the last section of the *Epistre*.

The closing section of the *Epistre* begins with the vision of Andromache in chapter 88. Hector's wife, Andromache, begs him not to go into battle for she has had a premonition of his death. When Hector ignores her advice, she asks his father, Priam, to intercede, but to no avail (ch. 90). Found without his weapons, Hector is slain by Achilles, an event that is told over two chapters instead of the usual one (91 and 92). Subsequent events include the funeral of Hector, at which Achilles falls in love with Hector's sister, Polixene, thus hastening his own death (ch. 93), the death of Ajax (ch. 94), the betrayal of Troy by Antenor (ch. 95), the ruse of the Trojan horse (ch. 96), and the final burning of Ilion as the event that marks the fall of Troy (ch. 97). Implicit in this sequence is the principal role played by Andromache, since her premonition of Hector's death leads to the destruction of Troy. The text and gloss in chapter 88 urge Hector to listen not only to the counsel of his wife but also to that of all other wise women. Andromache thus assumes a position next to Othea as a prudent woman who recommends correct action. Had Hector followed her advice the downfall of Troy could have been avoided.

Linguistic changes in this chapter and in chapter 90, where Andromache's vision is repeated, place further emphasis on the importance of the vision. Othea customarily speaks in direct discourse in her letter, that is in the four-line verse texts at the beginning of each chapter. She nearly always employs the imperative mode and addresses Hector in the second person familiar, *tu*. For example, in chapter 41: "Never imitate Busiris"; in chapter 60: "Flee the goddess of discord"; and in chapter 77: "Do not despise the counsel of Helenus."[101] However, for the first time in the entire work in chapter 88 and 90, Othea speaks in the first person, "I," and calls Hector by name. In chapter 88 she says: "Also I make mention to you, / the premonition of Andromache...."[102] Then, in chapter 90, she reiterates: "Hector, I must announce your death...."[103] In this chapter, she adds that because King Priam did not believe Andromache's premonition any more than did Hector, he did nothing to stop this disastrous chain of events. Othea's language is insistent. It clearly communicates that doom is imminent and unavoidable, and it is Andromache's vision that foretells this destruction.

How are we to understand the chapters on Andromache in the context of the work as a whole? First of all, Andromache's identity merges with those of Othea and Christine in these chapters. When read in one way, it is Othea who speaks to Hector in these texts, but we have already understood that the form of the epistolary allegory encouraged the reader to understand the fictional and actual writers as one and the same person, that is, to understand Othea as Christine. As Othea and Christine are interchangeable, so too are Othea and Andromache, for what Othea says to Hector in these chapters is precisely what Andromache says to him. She tells him of her premonition. The voice of Andromache thus speaks here through that of Othea, who, we will remember, is also the virtue of Prudence. Though her premonition, Andromache even exercises one of the faculties of Prudence, her ability to see into the future. If we reflect further on the multiple identities of Hector within the allegory, it should

---

[101] London, BL Harley MS 4431, fols. 114r, 122r, 130r: "Ne ressembles mie Busierres"; "Fuis la déesse de discorde"; "Ne desprises pas le conseil Helenus."

[102] *Ibid.*, fol. 135v: "Aussi te fais je mencion / D'Andromacha l'avision...."

[103] *Ibid.*, fol. 136v: "Hector, nonier m'esteut ta mort...."

be clear that Andromache is addressing Hector but that Christine is speaking simultaneously to the present rulers of France. Thus, what is at stake here is the government of France, about which the destruction of Troy serves as an example. Naturally, it is an example to be avoided so that similar destruction will not take place. How can the reader learn to avoid this example? By heeding the contents of the letter, of which the language at this juncture is so insistently direct and, for the first time, so personalized.

The themes of wisdom and government climax in the last two chapters. The stories of Queen Ino and Augustus and the Cumean sibyl are told as antithetical examples of good and evil, of wisdom and ignorance. In chapter 17, Christine had already recounted at considerable length the story of Queen Ino, second wife of King Athamas and jealous stepmother of his children. She described how Ino planted boiled corn that could not grow in order to incur the wrath of the gods against the stepchildren who as a result were subsequently exiled. Because Athamas had consented to this banishment, Juno ordered that serpents be sent to plague him and induce insanity. Insanity provoked Athamas to murder Ino and then to slay his children. Not surprisingly, the entire chapter cautions the knight to avoid the deadly sin of ire.

In chapter 99, however, Christine retells only the beginning of the story, Ino planting boiled corn, using it this time as an example of ignorance. The gloss focuses on the sowing of good corn in bad or unreceptive soil — in ignorant soil — and the allegory is a powerful invective against ignorance.[104] The gloss informs Hector that sound, well-presented reasons and wise authorities should not be told to people of little understanding, because they will only be lost on them. A metaphor from Aristotle follows: just as rain is of no use for corn sown under a stone, so arguments cannot aid the ignorant. Developing the same theme in her allegory, Christine paraphrases Saint Bernard: whoever is ignorant has been too negligent to gather knowledge or too lazy to ask about it or too shameful to inquire into it. There is, she concludes, no excuse for such ignorance.

Used as an obvious contrast to the example on ignorance, the final chapter on Augustus and the Cumean sibyl focuses on wisdom. Christine probably borrowed the story from Jacobus de Voragine's *Golden Le-*

---

[104] London, BL Harley MS 4431, fol. 140v; Christine, *Epistle of Othea*, tr. Scrope, pp. 118-119.

gend.[105] The emperor has sought out the sibyl to ask whether he is the greatest king of all, and she replies that a child has just been born who will be greater than he. Augustus then worships the child, and the golden age begins. Othea's text is again written in direct discourse: "I have written a hundred authorities for you / So do not disdain them / For Augustus learned from a woman / that he should not be worshipped."[106] Read in the context of the epistolary allegory, it is Othea who again speaks, Othea who has written "one hundred authorities." As the reader learned at the beginning of the book that Othea and Christine were one and the same person, here too he understands Othea as the voice of Christine. By alluding to the teaching of wisdom, an activity shared by Christine, Othea, and the sibyl, the chapter may even intentionally merge the roles of all three women. As the sibyl addresses the emperor, Othea addresses Hector, and Christine addresses the present rulers of France. In this context, it is probably no accident that Augustus, like Hector and the kings of France, traced his lineage through the Trojan line.

The *Epistre* thus concludes with a story of a wise woman who teaches a monarch, a story that can be read in many ways. In this particular chapter, Othea teaches the monarch that he is neither the center of a cult nor the world's most powerful king. It is here also that Christine makes an analogy between the appearance of the Cumean sibyl to Augustus and her own letter when she writes that she has written "one hundred authorities." She uses the word "authority" to refer to the entire textual structure she has created, thereby departing from the medieval notion of *auctoritas* as a supporting quotation from another source. On one level she thus presents herself, or Othea, as the authority. This idea is consistent with the use of Othea within the form of the epistle, that is, as a made-up classical authoress with authority comparable to that of Plutarch. The one-hundred authorities of the epistolary allegory culminate in the example of the emperor who, we are told, "learned from a woman." The implication is clear that all those who, like Augustus, "do not disdain" the authorities included in Christine's letter will learn to be good monarchs.

Through the force of the Trojan sequence at the end of the letter, we have come to learn, in general terms, what being a good monarch meant

---

[105] Jacobus de Voragine, *The Golden Legend*, tr. G. Ryan and H. Ripperger (New York, 1941; repr. 1969), p. 49. The story is also in the *Ovide moralisé*, ed. de Boer, XIV. What is puzzling is Christine's departure from her sources which include the Tiburtine (or Roman) sibyl, not the Cumean (or Greek) sibyl.

[106] London, BL Harley MS 4431, fol. 141r: "Cent auctoritez t'ay escriptes; / Si ne soient de toy despites / Car Augustus de femme apprist, / Que d'estre aoure le reprist."

to Christine. She believed that the kingdom of France might falter, as had that of Troy, without the practice of those virtues required for good government. This general message, present in all the textual editions of the *Epistre*, is worked out differently in the various manuscript copies through the miniatures that accompany the text.

2

The Creation of the Miniatures

In the preceding analysis of the text of the *Epistre*, a parallel discussion of selected miniatures reinforced the interpretation of the text as a political allegory written in the form of an epistle. The opening sequences of miniatures, consisting of the presentation images and those of the four cardinal virtues, were shown to be particularly relevant. The presentation miniatures were found to make more concrete the multiple identities offered by the textual allegory and to specify the kind of chivalry referred to in the text. The miniatures of the cardinal virtues were seen to reiterate ideas about wisdom and action in government also present in the text. It is also evident that the relationship between text and image is slightly different in each of the three versions of the *Epistre*. The copy in London emerged as the most carefully planned and executed with respect to the ways in which the miniatures work with the political allegory of the text.

On the basis of these preliminary observations about the close relationship between the meaning of the text and the content of the pictures, it would seem reasonable to offer the hypothesis that Christine had a hand, figuratively speaking, in determining the content of the pictures. It is not possible, however, to conjecture intelligently about the extent of her involvement. Nor can it presently be determined why the miniatures in the three versions differ more in terms of their details than of their general conception. Without further evidence, then, it might just as easily be proposed that the miniaturists undertook the entire task of devising and executing the pictures on the basis of their independent readings of the text and, further, that the differences in detail among copies are due simply to the distinctive workmanship of the various artists who participated in the illustration of the separate copies.

Were this proposal found to be correct, it would not make very much difference with respect to our understanding of the meaning of the text as a political allegory, but it would most certainly affect our understanding of the ideological programs of the individual manuscripts – their text and illustrations – insofar as we might want to know whether the message put forward in the illuminated manuscripts came from Christine or not. Therefore, before proceeding with an extended analysis of the full cycles of illumination in the various versions of the *Epistre* in an attempt to perceive the ideological program of each manuscript, it is important to arrive at an understanding of the relative responsibilities of Christine and her artists in the production of her illuminated manuscripts.

At first this task might seem an easy one, since an unusually complete picture of the production of Christine's manuscripts has emerged over the years. Much evidence has been brought forward to confirm that she supervised the writing of her manuscripts. As we have seen, her activity as a scribe has been well documented.[1] Strictly on the basis of Christine's scribal activity, it has become commonplace to credit her with a substantial role in creating the pictures that decorate some of these manuscripts. It was once even suggested that she was the artist as well as the scribe for her own works.[2] More often, it has been assumed that she planned the pictures in the *Epistre Othéa*, supervising the miniaturists who worked for her just as she oversaw the scribes.[3] Most recently, the following claims have been advanced: the illuminators worked "under Christine's direction," following "Christine's verbal instructions," probably "at the suggestion of Christine," and finally the illuminators received "explicit instructions" from Christine, who "certainly supervised" the illustration.[4]

What is surprising in light of such assertions is that neither the nature nor the extent of Christine's involvement insofar as the miniatures are concerned has ever been adequately clarified. For instance, no one has tried to discover whether she actually selected the subjects, chose the models, or specified the details, and if so, how. Definite answers to these questions are not easily provided since little direct evidence exists; that is, no documents connected with the production of the manuscripts survive, and the manuscripts include no sketches or any written instructions (except the purple rubrics) that were provided to assist the illuminator.

Having pointed out that direct evidence is lacking, we may legitimately ask what sort of information might then be useful. Three different kinds of sources shed light on the problem. First, accumulated evidence about

---

[1] Ouy and Reno, "Identification des autographes," and C. Reno, "The Cursive and Calligraphic Scripts of Christine de Pizan," *Ball State University Forum* 19 (1978) 3-20.

[2] L. Gilissen, *La Librairie de Bourgogne* (Brussels, 1970), p. 10.

[3] First suggested by Campbell, *L'Épître d'Othéa*, p. 19; and Pinet, *Christine de Pisan*, p. 62.

[4] Meiss, *Limbourgs*, 1: 24, 26, 29, 34.

manuscript production in Paris offers some idea of what authors, scribes, and illuminators customarily did and did not do. Such data include records of payment, written programs for use by illuminators, marginal sketches, and model books and sheets.[5] A brief review of this material is worthwhile, because it is probable that neither Christine nor her artists departed very much from the traditional procedures of manuscript production in Paris. Second, and closer to the manuscripts at hand, certain passages in Christine's writings may be interpreted as revealing her views about the status and talents of miniaturists. Since she admits to having had direct contact with illuminators,[6] these passages may be taken as an indication of what the miniaturists who worked for her actually did. Third, a comparison between the picture cycles in Christine's manuscripts of the *Epistre Othéa*, and others in manuscripts of similar contents that were potentially available to her and her artists, shows how they used their visual sources. This third examination will help us to isolate the incidents of borrowing and at the same time elucidate the conditions that led to fresh inventions in the make-up of the picture cycles for the *Epistre*. From the combined evidence found in these sources, we can come to understand more clearly the nature of Christine's role in shaping the pictorial program of her manuscripts.

AUTHORS AND ILLUMINATORS AS BOOKMAKERS

Examples of Parisian manuscript production are drawn from the milieu of the professional illuminator, since his environment is probably most comparable to that in which Christine's artists worked. The Master of the *Cité des dames* who painted the London miniatures worked with a number of assistants and for a wide variety of clients and so cannot have been employed in a court household as an artist working for a single patron.[7] The *Epître* Master and the Saffron Master who painted the miniatures in the Paris book seem to have worked only for Christine, with one exception.[8] Although this phenomenon is a little unusual, it is so unlikely that Christine independently sought, housed, and employed her own illuminators that the logical conclusion remains that they must all

[5] Summarized in Meiss, *Late Fourteenth-Century*, 1: 3-18.

[6] Christine, *City of Ladies*, tr. Richards, p. 85.

[7] Here, and elsewhere, I have used the names Meiss gave to these illuminators. See Meiss, *Limbourgs*, 1: 377-382.

[8] *Ibid.*, 1: 388-389. Collaborating with the *Cité des dames* Master, the *Épitre* Master also did six miniatures in a *Grandes chroniques*, Paris, Bib. Mazarine, MS 2028.

have been professional illuminators working out of a quarter of the city. In studying these examples, we shall consider what the procedure of making books tells us about the artist's participation in that enterprise.

Even a cursory review of the procedure of making a manuscript book suggests that authors or, sometimes, scribes, rather than artists, selected the subjects of the miniatures. By the time an illuminator began work on a manuscript, it had already passed from a bookseller, publisher, or author to the scribe, who had written the text, leaving spaces for the miniatures at junctures that were predetermined. A rubricator, who may or may not have been identical with the scribe, had also written rubrics, which might both describe the contents of a chapter and synopsize the corresponding subject of the miniature. A number of unfinished manuscripts help to confirm that the miniatures were normally completed last, after a variety of other tasks that were undertaken in the following order: ruling, writing, rubricating, and painting initials, line endings, and borders.[9] Unless the illuminator were consulted early in the production process, and it will become clear shortly why this is unlikely, it is difficult to imagine how he could have selected the subjects, since by the time he actually began work on a book he had to put his pictures in preexisting blank spaces that already had descriptive rubrics above or below them. When the illuminator did begin his task of creating the pictures, he could still proceed in several ways. But as we shall see, none of these entailed his selecting the subjects.

Full written programs were sometimes provided for the illuminator. Detailing the contents of all miniatures in a book, these descriptions vary considerably in complexity, although their scarcity makes it difficult to draw any conclusions as to which types were more common. Some, such as the marginal notes in Honoré Bouvet's *Somnium super schismatis*, specify the identity of the figures (e.g., the king of Castille, the duke of Berry), the setting (e.g., a chapel), and a few pictorial details (e.g., the position of a crown or a sceptre).[10] Others, such as those in the margins of a *Grandes chroniques de France*, also include the disposition of the

---

[9] For example, see R. G. Calkins, "Stages of Execution: Procedures of Illumination as Revealed in an Unfinished Book of Hours," *Gesta* 17 (1978) 61-70; and J. D. Farquhar, "The Manuscript as a Book," in Sandra Hindman and J. D. Farquhar, *Pen to Press. Illustrated Manuscripts and Printed Books in the First Century of Printing* (College Park, MD, 1977), pp. 11-99.

[10] Transcribed by G. Ouy, "Une maquette de manuscrit à peintures (Paris, B.N. lat. 14643, fols. 269-283v, Honoré Bouvet, Somnium prioris de Sallono super materia Scismatis, 1394)," in *Mélanges d'histoire du livre et des bibliothèques offerts à M. Frantz Calot*, Bibliothèque elzevirienne, n.s., Études et documents (Paris, 1960), pp. 44-51.

figures within the composition.[11] Still others, like the sheets of instruction by Jean Lebègue for a manuscript of Sallust's *Catalina*, supply nearly every imaginable detail — those of color and heraldry as well as points of interpretation.[12] Further examples include the rubrics on the virtues and vices in Frère Laurent's *Somme le Roi*, the guide to the calendar of the Belleville Breviary, and a set of instructions accompanying the *Chevalier délibéré*.[13]

It is safe to assume that many more written programs must have existed either in the margins of manuscripts from which they were trimmed at the time of binding or as hastily written sheets of instructions which, being neither illuminated nor luxurious, were discarded once they had served their purpose. The authors of these programs, when it is possible to identify them, are found to be educated advisors, not artists. The theologian Gerson penned the instructions to Bouvet's manuscript, perhaps in consultation with the author. The humanist Jean Lebègue wrote the guide to Sallust's text. The important point, though, is that miniaturists invariably followed these guides to the letter. Comparisons between sets of instructions and the corresponding illuminations show that the artists did not improvise much.

A look at socioeconomic conditions of the late Middle Ages also supports this view of the illuminator's limited role — a role that precluded his selecting the subjects or planning the programs. Miniaturists, since they were artisans, entered an apprenticeship to learn their trade and abandoned any formal schooling at an early age.[14] There were exceptions: a master mason, Drouet de Dammartin, sent two sons to study in Paris.[15] Mostly, however, children followed in the footsteps of their parents, as did Drouet's eldest son, who was apprenticed as a mason. Thus, although some artisans might have had a rudimentary knowledge of the vernacular

[11] Valenciennes, Bib. municipale, MS 637, c. 1400-1410, published by J. Mangaert, *Catalogue descriptif et raisonné des manuscrits de la Bibliothèque de Valenciennes* (Paris, 1860), pp. 512-516. I thank Anne D. Hedeman for this reference.

[12] Jean Lebègue, *Les Histoires que l'on peut raisonnablement faire sur les livres de Salluste*, ed. J. Porcher (Paris, 1962).

[13] R. Tuve, "Notes on the Virtues and Vices," JWCI 26 (1963) 264-303; 27 (1964) 42-72; S. Berger and P. Durrieu, "Les Notes pour l'enlumineur dans les manuscrits du moyen âge," *Mémoires. Société des antiquaires de France* 53 (1893) 11-30 [on the *Somme le Roi*]; E. G. Holt, ed., *A Documentary History of Art*, 2 vols. (New York, 1947), 1: 130-134 [on the Belleville Breviary]; and F. Lippmann, *Le Chevalier délibéré by Olivier de la Marche*, Illustrated Monographs, 5 (London, 1898), pp. xiii-xx.

[14] See A. Martindale, *The Rise of the Artist in the Middle Ages and Early Renaissance* (New York, 1972), esp. pp. 9-52.

[15] *Ibid.*, p. 48.

necessary to read or have read to them instructions, they were probably ill equipped to read all but the most elementary texts. To put it simply, they were craftsmen.

When the illuminator did not work from written instructions but rather from manuscript models, he seems also to have exercised little initiative. One example is especially instructive since it is so well documented. A manuscript originally made in Italy of the *Histoire ancienne* was copied twice in Paris around 1400 under the direction of a "Maistre Renaut," probably Regnault de Montet, a professional book-seller.[16] One copy was sold in 1401 to the duke of Berry by the Parisian merchant Bureau de Dampmartin, who must have purchased it from Renault. As Avril has shown, the same duke owned the original. The second copy, executed by a different scribe and different team of illuminators, went to an unidentified owner. Two points are worth noting here; first, the miniatures in all three books are remarkably close in overall composition to those in their model, but they depart from those in the model in many details, including the layout of the architecture, the positions of the figures, the color, and the brushwork.[17] Second, the model was provided by the bookseller or patron, not by the artists. Illuminators, unless, like the Limbourg brothers, they held special positions within court households, rarely would have had extended access to a book. Being from the lower classes, they would not have moved freely in book-owning circles.

It might be objected that this example presents a special case, since the very nature of the commission entailed the making of copies and the illuminators would have failed to fulfill the terms of their contract if they had not faithfully copied their model. It might also be objected that, since all copies were of the same text, it is not especially surprising that the pictures are similar. Yet, even when pictures were devised for new texts or texts that had not previously been illustrated, models for them were often sought in manuscripts of other texts. As we will see, this was what happened with the creation of some of the miniatures in the *Epistre Othéa.*

[16] The original is London, BL Roy. MS 20 D I. The copies are London, BL Stowe MS 54 and Paris, BN MS fr. 301. These are studied by F. Avril, "Trois manuscrits napolitains des collections de Charles V et de Jean de Berry," BEC 127 (1969) 291-328, esp. 300-314. The Royal manuscript has also been published by G. F. Warner and J. P. Gilson, *Catalogue of Western Manuscripts in the Old Royal and Kings Collections in the British Museum*, 4 vols. (London, 1921), 2: 375-377 and 4: Pl. 118; and the Royal and Stowe MSS by F. Saxl, *Verzeichnis astrologischer und mythologischer illustrierter Handschriften des lateinischen Mittelalters*, Pt. 3, *Handschriften in Englischen Bibliotheken*, 2 vols. (London, 1953), 1: 223-242, 268-272. See also Appendix A.

[17] Compare Meiss, *Limbourgs*, 2: Pls. 275-276.

Other times, as in the case of pictures for the *Decameron*, which was illustrated for the first time in Paris around 1400, the miniatures were pastiches that were probably put together from studies in an illuminator's repertory.[18] In other words, the very process of making miniatures, whether for newly composed or preexisting texts, naturally entailed copying.

Illuminators may have enjoyed a bit more freedom when they worked from marginal sketches.[19] Most of these drawings are simple, indicating merely the arrangement of the principal figures and omitting most if not all secondary details. For example, a marginal sketch in a thirteenth-century manuscript of Gratian's *Decretals* indicates with unmistakable clarity the costume, stance, and gesture of the bishop, and it only roughly outlines the presence and arrangement of the other figures in a setting.[20] Only in two instances out of thirty-seven in this manuscript did the illuminator deviate from the sketches, and then only slightly. Similar examples can be found among the early fifteenth-century manuscripts of the Boucicaut Master group.[21] Marginal sketches seem often to have been drawn by one person, who was probably the illuminator in charge. Presumably they were intended as aids to the "lesser" craftsmen. Perhaps their presence in a given book also indicates an effort to ensure some degree of stylistic unity throughout the work. As Martin pointed out long ago, they were nearly always erased or intended to be erased. Thus, although the surviving sketches do not support a view of the creative artist, they do suggest that many miniaturists, working from generalized sketches, exercised a certain latitude in realizing the final product.

Still, from the preceding discussion, it would appear that the illuminator was little more than a rote copyist carrying out someone else's ideas. This view passes over the actual creative autonomy of the illuminator, however, assuming from a modern bias that he cannot have been truly original if he did not fully conceive of as well as execute his product. The evidence of pattern sheets and model books, the "nuts and bolts" of an illuminator's trade, suggests that here was one area in which the late medieval miniaturist really excelled: sketches that were studies after life.[22]

[18] M. Meiss, "The First Fully Illustrated Decameron," in *Essays in the History of Art Presented to Rudolf Wittkower*, ed. D. Fraser, H. Hibbard and M. Lewine (London, 1967), pp. 56-61.

[19] H. Martin, "Les Esquisses des miniatures," *Revue archéologique* 4 (1904) 17-45.

[20] Baltimore, Walters Art Gallery, MS W. 135, published by A. Melnikas, *The Corpus of the Miniatures in the Manuscripts of Decretum Gratiani*, 3 vols. (Rome, 1975), *passim*.

[21] For example, a *Grandes chroniques* in London, BL Cott. MS Nero E. II, discussed by Meiss, *Boucicaut*, pp. 92-95.

[22] R. W. Scheller, *A Survey of Medieval Model Books* (Haarlem, 1963).

The sketchbooks, such as the exquisite set of leaves on boxwood executed around 1390 and housed in the Pierpont Morgan Library, include drawings of extraordinary freshness and vitality.[23] Some of the pages in the Morgan book include bust-length portraits, two of which perhaps even represent the king and queen; others display images of full-length figures posed differently; and one includes a study of an acanthus leaf. Just how important such sketches were to the illuminator may be judged from the fact that the painter John of Holland initiated litigation against Jacquemart de Hesdin, alleging that he stole his patterns.[24]

What we have observed about the process of bookmaking can be summarized in the following way. A learned advisor working with an author might have devised a program of instructions, like that by Jean Lebègue. A publisher or an author or even a patron might have selected a manuscript model, as in the case of the *Histoire ancienne*. A master illuminator might have left sketches as guidelines in the margins, as in Gratian's *Decretals*. The illuminator showed his mettle by the use of his personal sketches, like those contained in the Morgan book, which helped to individualize the picture. Naturally, the production of all books did not proceed in exactly the same way. As might be expected, the different aids to illuminators were used singly or in combination, as befit the task at hand. Thus, in order to understand how any individual book came into being, it is necessary to try to retrace the particular steps taken in its production. Above all else, though, it becomes clear that the role of the illuminator was a practical or manual one, rather than an intellectual one. It was not his job to choose the subjects of miniatures or to formulate their contents, except insofar as he executed their design.

ART AS THE 'APESS' OF NATURE

It is worth considering in some detail a small group of overlooked passages by Christine on the artist, because they can help us to see through the eyes of contemporaries the esteem in which the artist was held and why. These passages offer confirmation of the characterization of the medieval illuminator that has been advanced so far: specifically, that he was a craftsman.

---

[23] Fully reproduced in color with earlier bibliography in A. Châtelet, "Un Artiste à la Cour de Charles VI. À propos d'un carnet d'esquisses du XIVe siècle conservé à la Pierpont Morgan Library," *L'Œil* 216 (1972) 16-21, 62.

[24] Meiss, *Late Fourteenth-Century*, 1: 226.

Much has been made of the mention in the *Cité des dames* of Anastasia, an artisan who, Christine tells us, is so skilled in "painting manuscript borders [*vignettes d'enlumineure*] and miniature backgrounds [*champ-aignes d'istoires*]" and who paints "flowers and details" so delicately that she is better than all others in Paris, "where the best in the world are found."[25] Christine goes on to say that she is personally acquainted with the work of Anastasia since Anastasia has executed ornamental borders for Christine. Preoccupied with the novelty of finding a reference to a contemporary woman artist to whom an identity and an œuvre could be readily attached, scholars have tried without success to retrieve from the Parisian documents other facts about this illuminator. Because of her name, which is unusual in France, Anastasia is thought of as coming from Italy.[26] Her collaboration with Christine has thus been used as testimony of Christine's continuing link with her homeland.

Writers have tried to credit Anastasia with a larger role, perhaps because they have been reluctant to accept that Christine praised so highly someone involved only in the secondary aspects of miniature painting.[27] The Italianate style of certain miniatures in Christine's manuscripts, particularly those by the *Épître* Master, has led some to identify this anonymous illuminator with Anastasia.[28] Others have proposed that the name could even be a sort of anagram for Christine as the artist-scribe.[29] However, a review of the phrasing in contemporary documents supports Martin, who convincingly demonstrated some time ago that the technical terms used by Christine to describe the work done by Anastasia most likely meant "manuscript borders" and "miniature backgrounds."[30] Anastasia was a specialist in borders and backgrounds, not a full-fledged miniaturist.

These previous considerations may miss the point of Christine's discussion of Anastasia in the context in which she appears in the *Cité des*

---

[25] Christine, *City of Ladies*, tr. Richards, p. 85. This passage has been commented on by H. Martin, *Les Miniaturistes français* (Paris, 1906), pp. 85-86, 164-165, 183; *idem, La Miniature française du XIIIe au XVe siècle* (Paris, 1923), pp. 73-76. See also Mombello, *La tradizione manoscritta*, p. 15 n. 3; and Meiss, *Late Fourteenth-Century*, 1: 3 n. 3, and *idem, Limbourgs*, 1: 13-14.

[26] De Winter, "Christine de Pizan, ses enlumineurs," p. 348.

[27] *Ibid.*

[28] Mombello, *La tradizione manoscritta*, pp. 15-16 n. 3, for a summary of opinions about Anastasia's activity as a miniaturist.

[29] De Winter, "Christine de Pizan, ses enlumineurs," p. 348 n. 25.

[30] See, for example, the records of payments to Robin de Fontainnes and Jehan de Jouy in 1398 and 1399, which distinguish between miniatures (*histoires*) and borders (*vignetes*), published by A. Vallet de Viriville, "La Bibliothèque d'Isabeau de Bavière," *Bulletin du bibliophile* 36 (1858) 679-680, 682-683.

dames. The passage on Anastasia occurs at the end of a section devoted to painters in which Christine first extolls the talents of two Greek painters, Thamaris and Irene, and then those of the Roman painter Marcia, all three of whom are cited by Pliny.[31] She got the stories about these three painters from Boccaccio's *Des Cleres femmes*, but she approached these as well as other stories from Boccaccio selectively, as she did all her sources.[32] Whereas Boccaccio treated no modern-day examples and arranged his tales chronologically, with the result that these three painters appear dispersed over ten chapters and separated by other stories, Christine organized her chapters around themes intended to show the worthy contributions of women throughout history in various spheres of life. In her chapter on painters she gathered together a group of female models to demonstrate that women can learn the "speculative sciences ... and likewise the manual arts."[33] To build her argument she understandably omitted much of the information in Boccaccio that she regarded as extraneous.

For our purposes, it is important to look at what she praised these women for: Thamaris had painted an image of the goddess Diana; Irene had displayed such consummate skill that a sculpture of her likeness was made for display; and Marcia had created a realistic self-portrait with the aid of a mirror. Each was associated, thus, with realistic portrayal. It might seem at first that Anastasia shared little with her classical antecedents and that her inclusion here merely shows Christine's desire to update Boccaccio by including an example of an accomplished woman artist from her own time. Yet such an explanation does not account for the fact that Anastasia was a border decorator, whereas other women miniaturists appear in the Paris documents.[34] Rather, Christine's passage on Anastasia could be interpreted as suggesting that she saw no real difference between the skills of painters in Greece and Rome and those of border painters in Paris. To put it another way, just as Marcia was able to paint her self-portrait in a realistic manner, so Anastasia excelled at her specialty, painting flowers and others details, presumably realistically. That she happens to be a border painter, rather than a miniaturist, is irrelevant to

[31] Pliny, *Natural History*, tr. H. Rackham (Cambridge, Mass., 1952), 9: 147.

[32] On Christine's use of Boccaccio, see especially the introduction by E. J. Richards in Christine, *City of Ladies*, pp. xxxiv-xli. For Boccaccio's stories in *De mulieribus claris*, see the translation, *Concerning Famous Women*, tr. G. Guarino (New Brunswick, NJ, 1963), pp. 122, 131, 144.

[33] Christine, *City of Ladies*, tr. Richards, p. 83.

[34] For example, the daughter of the illuminator Jean Le Noir, who was named Bourgot, cited by Meiss, *Late Fourteenth-Century*, 1: 4, 167-168.

Christine, who still finds her worthy of praise. Christine thought of Anastasia as an artisan, like the painters of Greece and Rome. This view of the artist as an artisan may account for the placement of this chapter. It immediately follows those treating women who practiced the crafts of weaving and tapestry.[35]

Another text by Christine, *Le Livre du corps de policie*, also touches on the subject of illuminators and confirms that she valued most their ability to paint after nature.[36] Inspired by John of Salisbury's *Policraticus* and adapted from a French translation of Valerius Maximus's *Facta et dicta memorabilia*, *Le Corps* is a sort of Mirror of Princes. In it, Christine presents the makeup of the state through the well-known metaphor of a human body composed of three parts: the head, arms and hands, and legs and feet, which correspond respectively with the king, the nobles and knights, and the people. In the third part, that devoted to the three estates of the people, she first takes up the calling of the artisans, who are considered along with the tradesmen and laborers, who comprise the third estate. Art historians have called attention to those lines that proclaim Paris to be the capital of the practice of manuscript illumination, a remark that echoes one in Dante's *Divine Comedy*.[37] Christine's colorful lament on the debauched lifestyle of artisans has additionally been cited.[38] She exhorts illuminators, workers who were accustomed to frequenting taverns and brothels, to abandon vice and pursue Christian virtue. Yet, to my knowledge, no one has looked at the chapter to discover why the artisan merited praise in Christine's eyes.

In this passage, Christine asserts that, of all the groups in the third estate, that of the artist is closest to the sciences, especially geometry, because art depends on the science of measurement and proportions. As she develops her argument, she first cites a story from antiquity: when the Greeks wanted to build an altar to Minerva they initially sought advice from the philosopher Plato, who sent them instead to Euclid the mathematician. Thus, "one can see that the manual trades follow science." On the authority of Valerius Maximus, she proceeds to affirm that art must be close to the sciences since, like science, it follows nature. The accomplished painter, she tells her readers, reproduces nature well: "Art seeks to follow nature. This happens when a worker accurately reproduces a thing that nature has made, as when a painter who will be

---

[35] Such as Arachne and Pamphile in Christine, *City of Ladies*, tr. Richards, pp. 81-83.
[36] Christine, *Corps de policie*, ed. Lucas, pp. 194-197.
[37] *Purgatorio*, 11, 80-81; Meiss, *Late Fourteenth-Century*, 1: 3.
[38] *Ibid.*, 1: 3.

so accomplished a worker that he will make a figure of a man or a bird or other beast so much after life and so accurately that everyone will recognize it."[39] This remark recalls her statement in the *Cité des dames* praising Marcia's skill at rendering her self-portrait with the aid of a mirror. The prerequisite task of the artist, according to Christine, is that he imitate reality, an idea that finds more coherent expression in *Le Corps* than in the *Cité des dames*.

Given Christine's interest in realistic portrayal, it is not surprising that she makes use here of the well-known analogy between art and the ape as follows: "... some said that art is, thus, the apess or the ape of nature."[40] It is worth looking in some detail at this part of her passage in its historical context. Throughout the Middle Ages, as Janson has shown, the topos was regarded in a negative light, coming only in the fourteenth century to be seen in a complimentary sense.[41] By seeking to create the illusion of truth, painting was seen as an attempt to deceive the spectator into accepting works of art as works of nature, or God's works. Such deception, it was thought, could lead to idolatry. Then in the fourteenth century, especially in the works of Boccaccio, the practice of imitating nature came to be associated with poetic skills. In the *Genealogy of the Gods*, Boccaccio used the epithet of the poet as "the ape of nature" to imply the poet's ability to set forth in words "the forms, habits, discourses, and actions of all animate things," or the very essence of the reality of the external world.[42] Christine's use of "the ape of nature" as applied to the painter and sculptor in *Le Corps* is in line with this new attitude toward the poet as expressed by Boccaccio.

But there is another, more unusual, feature of her statement that is entirely characteristic of her own thought and, at the same time, quite distinct from tradition. Through her clever use of language, Christine provides the dictum with a feminist twist. She personifies art (*l'art*), a feminine noun, as a female ape (*la singesse*) in her statement that "art is, thus, the apess or the ape of nature," and continues with the same metaphor to point out that "just as the apess follows many of the manners

---

[39] Christine, *Corps de policie*, ed. Lucas, p. 196.

[40] *Ibid.*, p. 196: "dirent aucuns que art est ainsi que la singesse ou le singe de nature, car ainsi comme la singesse ensuit beaucop des manieres de l'omme, suyt art beaucoup des euvres de nature."

[41] H. W. Janson, *Apes and Ape Lore in the Middle Ages and the Renaissance*, Studies of the Warburg Institute, 20 (London, 1952), pp. 287-325, esp. 287-294.

[42] Boccaccio, *Boccaccio on Poetry Being the Preface and the Fourteenth and Fifteenth Books of Boccaccio's 'Genealogia Deorum Gentilium'*, tr. C. G. Osgood (Princeton, NJ, 1930), pp. 78-79.

of man, so art follows many of the works of nature." As such a statement indicates, Christine misses few opportunities to praise women, even when we least expect it and, therefore, are all the more struck by it.

What is most important about this passage in *Le Corps* is that it confirms Christine's own interest in realistic portrayal, that skill for which she praises illuminators. Along this line, it is worth noting that the painters who worked for Christine were unusually accomplished in the reproduction of reality. Because she placed a high premium on this skill, she probably selected artists who were good at it and perhaps even instructed them as to the inclusion of realistic details. In the London "Collected Works," the *Cité des dames* Master, for example, recorded with unprecedented accuracy the moment of presentation, although it is unlikely that he was present (Fig. 4), and, even if he were present, such an occasion would have occurred after the miniature was painted. Every detail – dress, furnishings, and location – can be shown to correspond with documentary descriptions.[43]

Now, we may well ask, if the primary enterprise of the illuminator was the replication of reality, then who was responsible for telling him what to reproduce ? One other text by Christine may shed some light on this question. In the *Livre des fais et bonnes meurs du sage roy Charles v*, she also discusses the artisan, in this case the mason, in a chapter intended to show "how king Charles was a true artist and learned the sciences."[44] It might be objected that this passage is not relevant to our discussion of illuminators. However, in other texts Christine grouped together masons, sculptors, and illuminators as tradesmen, a fact that allows us legitimately to consider her remarks on masons as potentially revealing of her views on illuminators.[45]

This passage is especially interesting, for in it Christine tries to grapple with the distinction between an "artist" and an "artisan." She uses the distinction between knowledge and application to call attention to the involvement of the artist, who has the knowledge, and the artisan, who applies it. *Artiste* was a neologism that apparently made its earliest appearance in the vernacular in a written text by Christine.[46] In *Le Corps*

---

[43] S. Hindman, "The Iconography of Queen Isabeau de Bavière (1410-15): An Essay in Method," *Gazette des Beaux-Arts*, ser. 6, 102 (1983) 102-110.

[44] Christine, *Le Livre des fais et bonnes meurs*, ed. Solente, 2: 33-37.

[45] Christine, *Corps de policie*, ed. Lucas, p. 196.

[46] See L. M. Gay, "On the Language of Christine de Pisan," *Modern Philology* 6 (1908) 69-96, esp. 72; Christine, *City of Ladies*, ed. Richards, p. 1 n. 32; and F. Godefroy, *Dictionnaire de l'ancienne langue française et de tous ses dialectes du IXe au XVe siècle* (Paris, 1895), 8: 195. According to Godefroy, the somewhat earlier *Songe du verger* uses the word in a second sense, as a master of liberal arts.

Christine hints at the novelty of the word, for she introduces it as a word by which clerics identify artisans, a remark that also suggests its Latin roots.[47] Having read Thomas Aquinas's commentary on Aristotle's *Metaphysics*, which she quotes at length both in *Le Corps* and in *Le Livre des fais et bonnes meurs*, she realized, of course, that to be a true artist one must do more than work with one's hands.[48] Quoting Aquinas on the *Metaphysics*, she identifies the chief artist or architect as the individual who knows the causes of the things that are done: "Aristotle says, 'The artist is reputed to be wiser than the expert, in the measure that he best recognizes the reasons why it is necessary that it be thus and the expert does not know any other reasons'."[49] The artist is, thus, distinct from the expert who works with his hands, even though, as Christine says, the expert demonstrates a certain, lesser, grasp of science as he applies himself to the task at hand.

Employing examples from the building trade, Christine differentiates between three levels of operations. At the lowest level is the mason or carpenter, who shapes the stone or cuts the wood. Next is the person who assembles that material to build the final structure. Last is the person who understands the structure and function of the object. Whether he is the artist or in some cases the patron, this last person is the principal. He is, therefore, the true artist. This tripartite hierarchy allows Christine to claim that the wisest person is Charles v, for he had the buildings built, a claim that stands as an interesting early demonstration of the enlightened ruler-patron topos.[50] Most relevant for our purposes, however, is the definition of the artist as distinct from the artisan. According to Christine, he is the individual who possesses "greater science than the expert who works with his hands."[51]

Based on what we have just seen, we can extrapolate from Christine's views in *Le Livre des fais et bonnes meurs* to understand better how she saw the roles of those involved in another craft, bookmaking. At the lowest level, like the individual who cut the timber, would be the craftsmen who ground the pigments or prepared the parchments, for

[47] Christine, *Corps de policie*, ed. Lucas, p. 195.

[48] On her use of the *Metaphysics*, see Christine, *Livre des fais et bonnes meurs*, ed. Solente, 1: lxvi-lxvii.

[49] Christine, *Livre des fais et bonnes meurs*, ed. Solente, 2: 35; compare St. Thomas Aquinas, *Commentary on the Metaphysics of Aristotle*, tr. J. P. Rowan, 2 vols. (Chicago, 1961), 1: 13-14, sections 23-28.

[50] For a preliminary discussion of this *topos*, see E. Kris and O. Kurz, *Die Legende vom Künstler, ein geschichtlicher Versuch* (Vienna, 1934), p. 48 and *passim*.

[51] Christine, *Livre des fais et bonnes meurs*, ed. Solente, 2: 36.

example. Of interest from the standpoint of medieval techniques of bookmaking, they do not concern us here. At the next level might be the illuminators, who assemble the materials into a miniature, or the scribes, who write out the text on the pages. At the highest level is the person who understands the reasons and knows how to do it, such as the author. In other words, assuming that to Christine book production paralleled the other trades, such as architecture, the role of the illuminator was a subordinate one in creating the final work of art. If we can accept Christine's distinction between artist and artisan as accurately reflecting ideas of the time, then neither masons nor illuminators could legitimately be called artists.

One last important piece of evidence, this one from the *Epistre* itself, supports the view that miniaturists had little to do with planning a program of illustrations. An autograph guide to the pictures written in the form of purple rubrics describes the contents of some of the pictures in the *Epistre*.[52] These passages, which would seem to have functioned both as guides to the illuminator and as guides to the reader, constitute the most concrete evidence for Christine's participation in the creation of the picture cycle. Since they display an extraordinary familiarity with the subject matter of the text, with which their language is wholly consonant, there can be little doubt that Christine composed these rubrics. To say that she was inspired to write them by a clever illuminator who had devised the iconography of the miniatures in an earlier manuscript version of the *Epistre*, as one writer has recently suggested,[53] runs counter to what is generally known about how authors and illuminators functioned. Further, as we have just seen, Christine's views on the limited role of the artisan are inconsistent with such an interpretation.

For our purposes, an important distinction between the activities of authors and illuminators is implicit in the first of these rubrics, that prefacing the miniature of Othea:

> So that those who are neither clerics nor poets can understand readily the meaning of the miniatures of this book, namely that throughout where the images are in clouds, it is to be understood that they are the figures of gods or goddesses about whom words follow or the book speaks according to

---

[52] These purple rubrics appear only in the edition written around 1405. They have been discussed by Campbell, *L'Épître d'Othéa*, pp. 143-146; Tuve, "Notes on the Virtues and Vices," esp. pp. 281-282, 289; and Meiss, *Limbourgs*, 1: 24-25.

[53] G. Bumgardner, "Christine de Pizan and the Atelier of the Master of the Coronation," in *Seconda Miscellanea di studi e ricerche sul quattrocento francese*, ed. F. Simone, J. Beck and G. Mombello (Chambéry-Turin, 1981), pp. 35-52, esp. 42-43.

the manner in which the ancient poets speak. And because deity is something spiritual and elevated from earth, the images are pictured in clouds and this first one is the goddess of wisdom.[54]

What Christine expresses in the rubric is that her readers, unless they are clerics or poets, might not understand the pictures. Likewise, if the miniatures express the notions of poetry, as Christine asserts, illuminators, who were not poets but manual workers, can hardly be expected to have invented their iconography.

A similar distinction between the activities of poets and painters can be found in remarks by Boccaccio. In the *Genealogy of the Gods*, he claims merit for poetry and painting alike on the basis of the beauty of their ornament, the one verbal and the other visual.[55] He goes on, however, to distinguish poetry from painting because the poets are really "men of wisdom" who can render "their compositions full of profit to the reader." In other words, poets used their knowledge; painters simply plied a craft.

This view of the medieval illuminator as a technician, a craftsman, suggested by evidence on Parisian manuscript production and confirmed by passages in Christine's writings, should lead us to conclude that as a rule authors, and not illuminators, determined the content of miniatures. We can thus assert with some measure of assurance that Christine played a considerable role in the creation of the pictures in the *Epistre*. Certainly, it now seems unthinkable that the illuminators who worked for her thought up the pictures inspired by her text.

But we still do not know precisely what Christine's role was, for she could have proceeded in several ways when it came to illustrating the text. She could have started from nothing, devising a set of instructions like the purple rubrics for all one hundred pictures. In this way, she could have produced a highly individualized book that was capable of addressing issues that were of special concern to her and closely keyed to the political allegory of the text. We have already indicated, however, that it was more common for new texts to appear with suitable pictures adapted from preexisting texts. Since much of the text of the *Epistre* comes from the *Ovide moralisé* and the *Histoire ancienne*, both of which had been densely

---

[54] London, BL Harley MS 4431, fol. 95v: "Affin que ceulz qui ne sont mie clercs poetes puissent entendre en brief la significacion des histoires de ce livre, est a savoir que par tout ou les ymages sont en nues, c'est a entendre que ce sont les figures des dieux ou deesses de quoy la lettre ensuivant ou livre parle selon la maniere de parler des ancians poetes. Et pour ce que deyté est chose espirituelle et eslevee de terre, sont les ymages figurez en nues et ceste premiere est la deesse de sapience."

[55] Boccaccio, *Boccaccio on Poetry*, tr. Osgood, pp. 103-105.

illuminated, it was not necessary for Christine to go to all the trouble of devising entirely new pictures. Models for most of the subjects were readily available to her. If she simply used these models without much modification, we would be unable to characterize the program of illustrations in the *Epistre* as especially unique with respect to its contents.

PICTORIAL ANTECEDENTS REINTERPRETED

The final area of investigation with regard to the creation of the miniatures is their sources. Without trying to be exhaustive, we shall look at examples from three selected groups of miniatures that are representative of the entire cycle, defined as the set of miniatures found in the *Epistre*. The three groups are: the seven planets, mythological subjects, and Trojan subjects. We shall examine models for miniatures in these groups, an undertaking that permits us to conclude that the pictures in the *Epistre* reveal in the aggregate a heretofore unappreciated originality. The essence of this originality can be shown to be so closely inspired by points in the text that it allows us not only to confirm Christine's considerable role in the creation of the miniatures but also to gain a clearer understanding of the nature of this role. Appendix A presents in greater detail the findings summarized here.

"Children of the Planets" and the French Court

A consideration of the miniatures of the seven planets should be central to an investigation of the pictorial sources of the *Epistre* for two reasons. The first is that a certain amount of evidence internal to the manuscripts suggests the hypothesis that these miniatures were created from the sets of autograph rubrics that describe their contents. Beginning with chapter 6 after the cardinal virtues, each of these miniatures is prefaced by a long rubric written in purple ink; this color sets the rubric off from the other parts of the text, which are penned in the more commonly used colors of black and red. The rubrics prefacing the seven planets are among the first of such passages in the *Epistre*, following two similar, though shorter, descriptions that appear before the opening miniatures of Prudence and Temperance. Shortly after the end of the sequence on the planets, the purple rubrics become much more abbreviated and then cease altogether, the last one occurring before the miniature of Penthesilea in chapter 14.

One additional feature underscores the potential importance of these rubrics for the creation of the miniatures. No sources have been uncovered for the texts of these chapters,[56] whereas nearly every other chapter in the *Epistre* has a clearly identifiable, contemporary textual source, most of which were available at the time in illuminated versions. We can imagine, thus, the following hypothetical situation. Christine had written her text on the seven planets and, having decided to illustrate it, she found no illuminated examples that could serve as suitable models. So she wrote for the illuminators a set of instructions which took the form of these unusual purple rubrics.

The second reason for considering these miniatures of the planets is that, in spite of the existence of the purple rubrics, more pictorial sources have been proposed for them, paradoxically it would seem, than for all the other miniatures in the *Epistre.* These include, first, miniatures from the *Ovide moralisé,*[57] in which the planets appear as mythological divinities and, second, images of the so-called "children of the planets" schema, in which a planetary god rules over his earthbound offspring who are engaged in activities influenced by the planet's inherent makeup.[58] The hypothetical situation just described, which views Christine as the inventor of the iconography of the planets in the *Epistre*, thus runs counter to the suggestion implicit in the literature, which points to the impact on the *Epistre* of earlier traditions of illustrating the planets. Thus, one body of evidence argues for originality that was innovative, the other for copying in accord with tradition.

Before proceeding with the first hypothesis, which holds that the miniatures were created from the purple rubrics that accompany them, it is necessary to show that the pictures do indeed correspond with the rubrics. This can be easily done. The first rubric sets up the general formula for the depiction of the planetary gods that continues unchanged through the subcycle: "And because the seven planets turn in circles that are named zodiacs, they are pictured seated on circles. And because they are seated in the heavens above the clouds, they are depicted against a starry sky and above clouds."[59] In accord with the rubric, each of the

[56] Campbell, *L'Épitre d'Othéa*, p. 154. Campbell does note the borrowings from the *Ovide* in the chapters on the planets.

[57] See especially Meiss, *Limbourgs*, 1: 24-28.

[58] J.Seznec, *The Survival of the Pagan Gods. The Mythological Tradition and Its Place in Renaissance Humanism and Art*, Bollingen Series, 38 (Princeton, NJ, 1972), pp. 71; and E. Panofsky and F. Saxl, "Classical Mythology in Mediaeval Art," *Metropolitan Museum Studies* 4 (1932-1933) 228-280, esp. 246.

[59] London, BL Harley MS 4431, fol. 99r: "Et est a savoir que pour ce que les .vij. planettes ou ciel sont tournans au tour des cercles que on nomme zodiaques, sont les ymages des .vij. planettes ycy figurées assis sur cercles. Et pour ce que elles sont ou

seven miniatures displays a planet seated on a golden arc against a variegated, star-lit blue background (Fig. 10). Clouds at the foot of each god separate him from the space below. The remainder of the first rubric identifies the attribute of the planet and explains the god's "influence" over the group below: "because Jupiter is the planet in the sky who gives influence of sweetness and friendship, this image holds up his hand in a sign of love directed to the men on earth." It concludes: "because the dew of the sky is the cause of fertility and abundance ... he is portrayed pouring dew toward earth." This description accords fully with the depiction of Jupiter, who gestures with one hand and pours water from a jug with the other toward the men seated below. Thus, it would seem that the miniatures do correspond with the rubrics.

A look at the chapter on Apollo (ch. 9) shows that the picture (Fig. 13) with its explanatory rubric makes richer and more vivid the message of the text, which in essence urges Hector to pursue truth, characterized as a chivalric virtue and as a gift of the Holy Spirit. Here the miniature again closely follows the text of the rubric, as follows:

> The sun, which they formerly named Phoebus or Apollo, is the planet which illuminates or clarifies all things that are confused and abstruse and which signifies truth that clarifies all confused and hidden things. And because of this there are men gathered below who make the sign of an oath and take an oath to speak the truth. He holds a harp, which can be taken for beautiful harmony and sweet sound which is part of the virtue of truth. Next to him is a raven, which signifies the first age of the century that was pure and later blackened by the sins of beings.[60]

The divine Apollo, enthroned in the star-lit sky, influences the behavior of mortals, who demonstrate their allegiance to truth by their gestures; they are swearing oaths. No such concrete demonstration is called for in the text. Apollo's symbols, the harp and the raven, further adorn the pictorial allegory. The harp recalls the sweet sounds of truth as practiced

---

firmament assises et au dessus des nues, sont elles cy pourtraites ou ciel estoilé au dessus des nues.... Et pour ce que Jupiter est planette ou ciel qui donne influence de doulceur et amistie, tend ceste ymage en signe d'amour la main aux hommes de terre. Et pour ce que la rosée du ciel est cause de fertilité et habondance, et le doulx air attrempé vient de celle planette, est il ycy pourtrait getant rosée contre val."

[60] *Ibid.*, fols. 100v-101r: "Le souleil, que anciennement ilz nommerent Phebus ou Appollo, est planette qui enlumine ou esclere toutes choses troublés et obscures, qui signifie verité qui esclere toutes choses troublés et muciées. Et pour ce y a gens dessoubz qui font signe jurer et faire serment de dire verité. Il tient une harpe, qui peut estre pris pour bel accort et doulx son qui est en la vertu de verité; il a coste soy un corbel, qui signifie le premier aage du siecle, qui fu net et puis noirci par les pechez des creatures."

in everyday speech, and the raven refers to a time in the history of the world when there was as yet no need to choose between truth and falsehood. Again, neither symbol is present in the text. In fact, because so many details found in the miniature are not present in the text, these miniatures cannot be seen as straightforward explications of any or all parts of the text. Instead it would seem that the pictures portray extra-textual examples. Individuals act out the virtue acquired from the plane-tary god.

Using similarly extensive detail, the remaining purple rubrics describe each of the other miniatures of the planets. They focus on the gestures and attributes of the planets. Occasionally they also explain any deviant features that may characterize the placement and appearance of a given planet and identify more explicitly the "children" below him. An over-view of the cycle finds Venus, goddess of love, directly following Jupiter (Fig. 11). She hands out hearts to a group of male and female lovers. Then comes Saturn, an old man who holds a sickle and presides over a group of wise men and attorneys who read and talk (Fig. 12). Because his location in the heavens is above those of the other planets, he is seated on a configuration of seven arcs instead of a single one, a deviation explained in the rubric. Next, Apollo clasps his harp and is watched over by a white bird; as we have seen, he emanates light and teaches truth. On the same page, the moon, Phoebe, uses her bow and arrow to induce lunacy (specifically, the illnesses of melancholy and frenzy) in the afflicted mortals (Fig. 13). Then, Mars teaches the right use of arms to the chivalric warrior (Figs. 14, 15). Finally, Mercury, dressed in royal garb, holds a flower and wears a money bag as he determines the beautiful language practiced by a group of rhetoricians (Fig. 16).

Although the rubrics help us to understand these pictures, they still do not fully explain them. Two other features characteristic of all the pictures may be understood by saying that they were triggered by a desire to illustrate more completely, although not at all in a literal fashion, the various levels of the text, in addition to the rubrics. In the London copy, the inclusion of one detail can be interpreted as a reference to Hector, the subject of the verse texts. A blond youth reappears from miniature to miniature in the subcycle, mingling with the other "children." He is dressed in a royal blue or sometimes red robe, variously decorated with gold embroidered designs. He thus wears a costume comparable to Hector's in this manuscript's opening miniature, where it was meant to remind us that the Trojan hero could be interpreted as a French prince. The presence of a similarly outfitted figure in these miniatures, therefore, continues to remind the reader that the "good knight" Hector of the text is also a contemporary prince in the royal circle. This detail, then, illustrates the text as it applies to the kingdom of France, and it should be evident that this device reinforces the political reading inherent in the epistolary form.

A second feature of the miniatures in the Paris and London copies ensures that they also illustrate the Christian component of the text conveyed in the allegories. They all conform to a specific compositional model, the representation of Pentecost, at which time the gifts of the Holy Spirit were given to the apostles so that they, in turn, might preach them to mankind. The use of this model was long ago recognized by Panofsky and Saxl, who nevertheless overlooked its importance.[61] The association of the pictures of the planets with scenes of Pentecost is an appropriate reminder that the planetary divinities also teach Christian virtues in the allegories, specifically the seven gifts of the Holy Spirit. Just as the pagan divinities influence the behavior of mortals, including that of Hector, so Christ's emissary, the dove, passes out the Beatitudes to the apostles. Here the planetary divinity occupies the position of the dove and the mortals the positions of the apostles, implying that the planets also teach the gifts of the Holy Spirit. Through what amounts to a clever reworking of a traditional iconographic formula, the schema used for the miniatures of the seven planets thus helps to sustain the religious didacticism of the text.

In a rather exceptional way, then, all three parts of the text of the *Epistre* are served by these pictures. The miniatures illustrate the texts, the glosses, and the allegories from the perspectives of political, secular, and spiritual allegories. My proposal of this triple reading for the miniatures of the planets should come as no surprise to those familiar with Christine's other writings, such as *L'Avision*. In a series of autograph glosses explaining how to interpret *L'Avision*,[62] Christine specifies that it should be read in these same three ways, from a political, a secular, and a spiritual perspective. No other set of miniatures in the *Epistre* so completely fulfills the rich texture of Christine's verbal allegory, nor is any other group accompanied by elaborate instructions. We can conclude that, at least in the case of the planets, the pictures must have been authorially inspired and reveal besides the intervention of an author whose sensibility was highly tuned to visual imagery.

---

[61] Panofsky and Saxl, "Classical Mythology," p. 246, Figs. 31-32; their view was adopted by Seznec, *Survival of the Pagan Gods*, p. 71; and Meiss, *Limbourgs*, 1: 26 and 2: Fig. 90.

[62] Formerly Phillipps MS 128, fol. 3r.

Given the subtle relationship between picture and text which strongly suggests that these miniatures were tailor-made for the *Epistre*, what are we to make of the obvious paradox: the numerous sources proposed for them? An examination of the previously proposed sources quickly shows that the differences between these sources and the *Epistre* far outweigh the similarities. From this examination, a greater sense of the uniqueness of the miniatures of the seven planets also emerges. In addition, the examination sheds light on the thematic concerns that led Christine away from such possible models.

Manuscripts of the *Ovide moralisé* must have provided one possible source for pictures of the planetary divinities. There can be no doubt that Christine knew this text well, since it served as a principal source for much of the mythological material in the *Epistre*.[63] Of course, Christine read the *Ovide* in manuscript form. The text of the *Ovide* remained basically the same from one manuscript copy to another, but Christine could have known two different traditions of illustrations.

Both traditions of illustrating the *Ovide* were popular in late-four-teenth-century Paris.[64] The first tradition consisted of narrative pictures of the myths.[65] The most dense cycles of this type, which contained as many as four hundred miniatures, date from early in the fourteenth century, probably close in time to the composition of the poem between 1316 and 1328, although manuscripts with such narrative cycles continued to be popular throughout the century, one having been produced for the duke of Berry. As we shall see later, Christine used models from these manuscripts for many narrative miniatures in the *Epistre*. The second tradition consisted only of fifteen pictures of the planetary divinities, together with some other famous gods, used as frontispieces to the fifteen books of the text.[66] These pictures were inspired by a mythographic introduction by Pierre Bersuire to the Latin *Ovidius moralizatus*, in which graphic descriptions of the divinities come before the text of the moralized

[63] See Campbell, *L'Épître d'Othéa*, pp. 110-141. Thirty-four chapters of the *Epistre* derive from the *Ovide*.

[64] See E. Panofsky, *Renaissance and Renascences in Western Art*, Figura, Studies edited by the Institute of Art History, University of Uppsala, 10 (Stockholm, 1960), pp. 75-81 n. 2, where he has distinguished four groups (A, B, C, D) of manuscripts that illustrated the *Ovide*. Only two of these, A and D, are relevant here, since the others postdate the material under consideration.

[65] *Ibid.*, p. 80 n. 2; Appendix: Groups A1 and A2. Panofsky was apparently unaware of the earliest and most densely illustrated examples from this group (A1), which have since been studied by C. Lord, "Three Manuscripts of the 'Ovide moralisé'," *Art Bulletin* 57 (1975) 161-175.

[66] Panofsky, *Renaissance and Renascences*, pp. 80-81 n. 2 (Group D).

Ovid.[67] Manuscripts with this type of illustration seem to have been equally popular at the end of the fourteenth century; several can be localized in Paris, one having belonged to the duke of Berry.

It has been convincingly demonstrated that Christine knew one specific copy of the *Ovide* that had miniatures conforming to this second, abridged system of illustration.[68] The miniature of Jupiter is at first glance strikingly similar to its counterpart in the *Epistre* (Fig. 73). Just as in the *Epistre*, in the *Ovide* Jupiter is enthroned on an arc, and a group of mortals is below him. He pours liquid from a jug onto his "children." Here the similarities end, however. Whereas Jupiter in the *Epistre* influences friendship, indicated by the friendly spirit that animates the gathering below him, in the *Ovide* he influences tranquility, suggested by the figures that have collapsed on the ground after having been showered from his jug. Clouds are above him instead of at his feet. And a narrative detail appears in the upper right, where the armor-bearer lifts up the young Idean. In spite of the dissimilarities, the shared features coupled with some other common characteristics not related to the representations of the planets are sufficient to substantiate, as Meiss proposed, that Christine knew this copy, as well as another, of the *Ovide*.[69]

A more thorough comparison shows, however, that all the other miniatures of the planetary divinities in the *Ovide* are more narrative than those in the *Epistre*. For example, in the *Ovide* (Fig. 74), Saturn waves a flame-bearing dragon with one hand and lifts a child to his mouth with the other, as he prepares to devour it, while four of his children, Juno, Jupiter, Neptune, and Pluto, stand two on either side of him, and in the foreground Venus emerges, "born" from his genitalia in the sea.[70] Venus again appears as she cavorts in a pond with the sea geese.[71] Apollo holds a lute — instead of a harp — and a bow and arrow, while he stands over Python, the two-headed monster that he vanquished. Diana, shown as the huntress, portrays the moon,[72] and Mercury is depicted playing his flute

[67] Studied by F. Ghisalberti, "L'Ovidius moralizatus di Pierre Bersuire," *Studi Romanzi* 23 (1933) 5ff; and reproduced in facsimile as Ovid, *Metamorphoses: Lyon, 1518*, The Renaissance of the Gods (New York, 1976).

[68] Paris, BN MS fr. 373, by Meiss, *Limbourgs*, 1: 24-28.

[69] Paris, BN MS fr. 871, fol. 116r, illustrating Apollo, Minerva, Pegasus, and the Muses on Mount Helicon, served as a model for a miniature in the *Chemin de long estude* in, for example, Paris, BN MS 836, fol. 5v; compare Meiss, *Limbourgs*, 2: Figs. 143-144.

[70] Paris, BN MS fr. 373, fol. 1r, reproduced by Meiss, *Limbourgs*, 2: Pl. 80.

[71] Paris, BN MS fr. 373, fol. 207r, and Geneva, Bib. pub. et univ., MS fr. 176, fol. 216r, reproduced by Panofsky, *Renaissance and Renascences*, Figs. 56-57.

[72] Geneva, Bib. pub. et univ., MS fr. 176, fol. 153r, reproduced by B. Gagnebin, "L'Enluminure de Charlemagne à François Ier. Manuscrits de la Bibliothèque publique et universitaire de Genève," *Genava*, n.s., 24 (1976) 5-200, esp. 77.

to enchant the sleeping Argus. Only the identities of Mars are similarly conceived; in the *Ovide* as in the *Epistre* he wears armor befitting the god of war. With the exception of that of Jupiter, these miniatures illustrate events from the lives of the gods instead of the "children of the planets" schema found in the *Epistre*. Therefore, they cannot have been the source for the miniatures in the *Epistre*.

In light of the pervasive differences, as well as the few striking similarities, between the *Ovide* and the *Epistre*, we may conclude that Christine was consciously trying something else when she devised the miniatures of the planets, something different from what she knew well from the *Ovide*. One other observation bears out this hypothesis. Christine's purple rubrics are quite similar both in their general descriptive contents and in their use of language to the mythographic descriptions of the planetary gods by Bersuire. The individual details differ, of course, because Christine's rubrics describe her miniatures, not those in the *Ovide*, which we have already seen are disparate from hers. But her familiarity with Bersuire and with the associated pictures in the *Ovide* may have been what prompted her to write the purple rubrics, which constitute her own mythographic description of the gods and call for a different set of pictures.[73] In doing so, she could be seen as attempting to establish her independent credentials as a mythographer.

It has been suggested that Christine knew Eastern traditions of representing the planetary gods, since some features in the *Epistre* seem to depend on them instead of on the *Ovide*.[74] In particular, the belief that the planets govern man's behavior, which lies behind the "children of the planets" iconography, was an Arabic one.[75] It occurs in Islamic astrological manuscripts, from which it was transmitted to the West in the thirteenth century. There, the idea is encountered most often in astrologi-

---

[73] A different conclusion was reached by Campbell, *L'Épître d'Othéa*, p. 144, who, while recognizing the similarities between these passages by the two authors, believed that because Christine's rubrics are different from Bersuire's passages, she could not have known those by the mythographer, since she would have followed them if she had known them.

[74] Apparently first by Seznec, *Survival of the Pagan Gods*, pp. 69-75. The idea is adopted by Meiss, *Limbourgs*, 1: 25; and C. C. Willard, "Christine de Pizan: the Astrologer's Daughter," in *Mélanges à la mémoire de Franco Simone. France et Italie dans la culture européenne. I. Moyen Âge et Renaissance*, Bibliothèque Franco Simone, 4 (Geneva, 1980), pp. 95-111, esp. 100.

[75] See Seznec, *Survival of the Pagan Gods*, pp. 156-163; F. Saxl, "Beiträge zu einer Geschichte der Planetendarstellungen im Orient und Okzident," *Der Islam* 3 (1912) 51-77; and *idem*, "Probleme der Planetenkinderbilder," *Kunstchronik und Kunstmarkt*, n.s., 30 (1918-1919) 1013-1021.

cal treatises by Michael Scot. Christine's proposed familiarity with this tradition would fit well with the interest in astrology that she is thought to have acquired from her father.[76]

Yet any systematic attempt to evaluate what Christine used from this tradition produces evidence that is at best contradictory. On the one hand, it does seem as if some of the portrayals of the gods and goddesses in the *Epistre* are ultimately derived from Eastern sources, perhaps through their Western intermediaries. For instance, Venus was perceived in the Islamic world as Ishtar, the goddess of pleasure. For this reason, she plays a musical instrument in Islamic depictions and hands out flowers to lovers in miniatures in Scot's manuscripts (Fig. 75). Similarly, as the goddess of love in the *Epistre*, she passes out hearts to lovers. Mercury was thought of as Nebo, the god of writing. As a result, he was frequently portrayed as a scribe,[77] an image that closely parallels his representation in the *Epistre* as a rhetorician who governs scribes. On the other hand, some portrayals are so different that they could not possibly have been sources for the *Epistre*. For example, Jupiter was identified with Marduck, the god of destiny. He therefore holds a scroll to show his control over man's fate.[78] This imagery is at odds with that in the *Epistre*, where we have already seen that he is the god who influences friendship. At the most, then, it could be said that Christine knew the tradition of the Eastern gods and picked freely what she wanted from it.

Even if examples from the Eastern tradition of representing the planetary gods could, in this limited sense, be considered sources for the miniatures in the *Epistre*, they cannot be shown to have supplied actual models for it. Neither the miniatures in Scot's manuscripts nor those in their Islamic antecedents accord either in general features or individual details with those of the planets in the *Epistre*. In particular, none of these examples illustrates the "children of the planets" schema as we have seen it used in the *Epistre*, even when the idea is found in the accompanying texts. In these examples, we find instead that each god occupies an undefined setting where he is pictured engaged in a solitary activity that suggests his character. Without further evidence, then, it cannot be

---

[76] Willard, "Astrologer's Daughter," p. 101. Saxl, "Geschichte der Planetendarstellungen," pp. 175-177, has transcribed Scot's descriptions of the representations of the planetary gods.

[77] Seznec, *Survival of the Pagan Gods*, Fig. 62.

[78] Saxl, "Geschichte der Planetendarstellungen," Fig. 29. In the West, Marduck was transformed into a figure of Jupiter as a monk, holding a chalice and a cross, an imagery that diverges from that in the *Epistre*. See Seznec, *Survival of the Pagan Gods*, Fig. 32.

maintained that these manuscripts offered models for the miniatures in the *Epistre*. Thus a comparison between them and the miniatures in no way challenges the notion of originality that has been advanced so far with regard to the miniatures of the seven planets.

Nor is this notion of originality challenged by examples from the last proposed source: frescoes in the Palazzo della Ragione in Padua, known as the Salone.[79] What is important about this monument in comparison with the *Epistre* is that it preserves the earliest full version of the "children of the planets" schema, one that may predate that in the *Epistre*.[80] The Salone that exists today is restored. A set of paintings attributed to Giotto was destroyed in a fire in 1424 and replaced, presumably accurately, in 1430. More than five hundred frescoes were inspired, Saxl has shown, by astrological manuscripts of Guido Bonatti and Pietro d'Abano.[81] Among many other subjects appear pictures of the planetary deities placed side by side with pictures that show their "children" engaged in various activities. Even this brief description of the frescoes suggests that they cannot have provided Christine with compositional models. The planets and their "children" do not appear within integrated compositions as they do in the *Epistre*. Instead, such scenes are horizontally arranged along the walls. It is unlikely, in any case, that Christine knew firsthand this monument, since she left Italy as a small child and never returned. However, it is still worth comparing the two programs, particularly since the cycle in the Salone preserves the tradition that came to dominate "children of the planets" imagery throughout the fifteenth century.[82]

[79] A. Barzon, *I cieli e la loro influenza negli affreschi del Salone in Padova* (Padova, 1924), with full reproductions; and W. Burges, "La Ragione de Padove," *Annales archéologiques* 18 (1858) 331-343, 19 (1859) 241-251, 26 (1869) 250-271.

[80] There are other fourteenth-century Italian monuments with "children of the planets" schema, which have been put forward as sources for the *Epistre* by Meiss, *Limbourgs*, 1: 25. They include: capitals in the Doge's Palace, Venice; frescoes in the Eremitani, Padua; sculpted reliefs on the Campanile of Santa Maria del Fiore, Florence; and frescoes in the Palazzo Schifanoja, Ferrara. None of these monuments consistently corresponds with the *Epistre*, however. See, for example, A. Warburg, "Italienische Kunst und internationale Astrologie im Palazzo Schifanoja zu Ferrara," in *Gesammelte Schriften*, 2 vols. (Leipzig, 1932), 2: 459-481.

[81] F. Saxl, *Verzeichnis astrologischer*, vol. 2, *Die Handschriften der Nationalbibliothek in Wien*, Sitzungsberichte der Heidelberger Akademie der Wissenschaften, Phil.-hist. Kl., Abhandl. 2 (Heidelberg, 1925-1926).

[82] On the tradition, see the surveys by A. Hauber, *Planetenkinderbilder und Sternbilder. Zur Geschichte des menschlichen Glaubens und Irrens*, Studien zur deutschen Kunstgeschichte, 194 (Strassburg, 1916); and F. Lippmann, *Die sieben Planeten* (Berlin, 1895).

What emerges from such a comparison is this: while some of the occupations influenced by the planets in the Salone are comparable to those in the *Epistre*, the cycle in the Salone has a wider scope. In it, each planet governs a more diversified group of activities. For instance, Jupiter appears next to a knight on horseback in the Salone, suggestive of his role in the *Epistre*, where he influences courtesy and friendship. However, in the Salone he also governs other actions as a result of his high spiritual and secular authority: those of friars and bishops and abbots, scholars and students and pilgrims, as well as acts of charity and compassion.[83] In the Salone as in the *Epistre*, Venus influences lovers; in the Salone they dress up, converse, dance, make music, give flowers, receive garlands.[84] In one instance, a woman even rejects her lover.[85] In both works, Mars governs warriors, but in the Salone he also rules over acts of violence in general, such as homicide, suicide, infanticide, and even quarrelling women.[86] In the frescoes, Mercury protects the liberal arts. Those under his influence engage in activities that stand for rhetoric, arithmetic, geometry, grammar, painting, dialectic, and philosophy.[87] Bankers and merchants are also present. In the *Epistre*, we find only the rhetoricians. Given these many differences, if we are to accept the Salone as a potential source for the *Epistre*, we would have to say that Christine approached this source selectively, just as she did with the Eastern representations of the planets.

Some activities that are included in the *Epistre* are not found in the Salone or in the later cycles that derive from it. For instance, the wise men and lawyers under the sway of Saturn in the *Epistre* do not appear in the Salone. There, Saturn protects those engaged in the manual and mechanical arts: farmers, parchment-makers, cobblers, blacksmiths, ship-builders, and joiners.[88] Likewise, the men who swear oaths to tell the truth as influenced by Apollo in the *Epistre* are absent in the Salone. Instead, Apollo rules varied subjects, especially the occult sciences like magic, conjuring, and necromancy. A hunter, scholar, and prince appear, as well.[89] Finally, the imagery of the moon is also divergent in the two works. The mentally ill, suffering from lunacy in the *Epistre*, are not present in

---

[83] Barzon, *I cieli*, nos. 82B-C, 83B-C, 84A, 84C, 104C, 107C, 108C. The numbers are taken from Barzon's chart of the layout of the Salone, to which his illustrations are also keyed.

[84] *Ibid.*, nos. 11A, 11C, 61B, 64B, 65A, 66B, 67B, 63C.

[85] *Ibid.*, no. 62A.

[86] *Ibid.*, nos. 3A, 4B, 5C, 6C, 7A.

[87] *Ibid.*, nos. 51B-C, 52C, 54B, 55C, 56B-C, 57B-C, 58C.

[88] *Ibid.*, nos. 93A, 97B-C, 98B-C, 99C, 100C, 101C.

[89] *Ibid.*, nos. 43C, 44C, 45C, 46C.

the Salone where subjects of the moon travel, go boating, and swim because Phoebe rules over water-related activities.[90] It would seem, then, that Christine turned elsewhere for some details in her sequence of the planets.

Having pointed out the differences between the miniatures of the planets and their proposed sources, it is time to characterize the unique features in Christine's cycle. It addresses those knights of good disposition who are courteous, a virtue they learn from Jupiter. Like the "good knight" Hector, they take lovers and go to war, influenced by Venus and Mars. According to their bodily temperaments, as influenced by Phoebe, they may occasionally be melancholy or mad, a cause of inconstancy and capriciousness. It is noteworthy that the theme of madness, not normally found as an attribute of the moon in other "children of the planets" cycles, may have held a timely importance at the court of the mad king.[91] But above all else, Christine's knights should be wise, patterning themselves after Apollo and Saturn as lawyers and judges, and guided in truth like Apollo. They can best acquire the virtue of wisdom if they heed the sounds of fine language taught by Mercury, with whom the cycle concludes. In comparison with other cycles, this group of miniatures places unusual emphasis on the theme of wisdom.

By stressing the theme of wisdom, the cycle alters the very notion that lies behind the "children of the planets." In its pure form, such as in the Salone, the sum of the "children of the planets" represents a kind of astrological macrocosm of a world in which all dispositions and occupations have a place. For Christine, who was addressing a special, limited public, only certain dispositions and occupations were relevant. When we reflect on what the patronage of the manuscripts and the meaning of the text suggest about the identity of that public – that it was a royal one in the French court – it should come as no surprise to find that friars, farmers, joiners, and cobblers are not among the "children" in the *Epistre*. When we consider further the emphasis on wisdom at the very beginning of the *Epistre* in the figure of Othea, it should also come as no surprise

---

[90] *Ibid.*, nos. 36c, 37c, 40b-c. It is possible that an unidentified scene from the Salone (no. 33c) is a representation of Melancholy. A woman appears sleeping, with her hand supporting her chin, an image that Barzon suggested has something to do with sleep during the month of July, although the gesture is found in some portrayals of Melancholy, the most famous being Dürer's *Melencolia I, 1514*, discussed by E. Panofsky, *The Life and Art of Albrecht Dürer* (Princeton, NJ, 1955), pp. 156-171, Figs. 209-221.

[91] It is worth recalling that Charles vi's lunacy was characterized by manic-depressive symptoms (frenzy and melancholy). See below, ch. 4, pp. 167-168, and Brachet, *Pathologie mentale*, pp. 622-649.

to encounter wisdom again as a virtue here. Early in the *Epistre* Christine makes clear her belief that wisdom can be acquired through the reading of good books, of which her manuscript containing Othea's letter was an example. With this in mind, we can point to the importance of her characterization of Mercury, in whom the subcycle of the planets culminates; Mercury governs only rhetoric among the liberal arts. What Christine communicates again as she brings to a close the cycle of the seven planets is her hope that her public will heed the words, the rhetoric, contained in her book.

It would seem that, failing to find adequate models for the seven planetary deities in her usual sources, Christine devised a series of rubrics that called for the creation of brand new miniatures. As we have seen, the resulting pictures specially suited the needs of her text, illustrating its several allegorical levels. The pictures were inspired by an assortment of Eastern and Western sources that include astrological and mythographic examples, none of which served as compositional models. Ideas from these sources were incorporated into a compositional model of her own choosing selected from the realm of religious art. Through this process of elimination and substitution, she formulated an original set of miniatures with her special public in mind. For this public, she stressed the theme of wisdom. These miniatures of the seven planets reveal, in the end, a new iconography for which only she could have been responsible, since it is so closely tied to her text.

Mythological Women and Christian Virtues

If we turn now from the miniatures of the planetary deities to those of other mythological subjects, for which there are no purple rubrics, we find that more precise models can be identified. Illuminated manuscripts of two different texts include miniatures with subjects comparable to many of those in the *Epistre*. The first were manuscripts of the *Ovide moralisé*, the availability of which has been discussed. The second were manuscripts of Boccaccio's *De mulieribus claris*.[92] This text relates the lives of one hundred and five famous women from antiquity, thirteen of whom also appear in the *Epistre*. Christine knew Boccaccio's text well by 1405, the year she wrote the *Cité des dames*, and used this text as the principal

---

[92] On the tradition of Boccaccio's text in France, see C. Bozzolo, *Manuscrits des traductions françaises d'œuvres de Boccace, xv* siècle*, Medioevo e umanesimo, 15 (Padua, 1973), pp. 23-24; see also G. Mombello, "I manoscritti di Dante, Petrarca e Boccaccio nelle principali librerie francesi del secolo xv," in *Il Boccaccio nella cultura francese*, ed. C. Pellegrini (Florence, 1971), pp. 81-209.

source for her own work.[93] Around this same time, just a few years before
the London and Paris copies of the *Epistre* were made, several lavishly
illustrated copies of Boccaccio's work, in its new French translation
entitled *Des Cleres femmes*, were produced.[94] It seems likely that Christine was familiar with one of these illuminated copies.

In particular, one unusual feature that characterizes certain miniatures
of mythological subjects in the *Epistre* is found also in the corresponding
miniatures in *Des Cleres femmes*. A peculiarity in the *Epistre* is that the
iconography of the "children of the planets" continues to be used later
in the book for some other gods and goddesses who were not planets. For
example, immediately following the series of pictures of the planets is
Minerva, who is depicted distributing armor to soldiers over whom she
reigns (ch. 13, Figs. 17, 18). Next comes a depiction of Minerva paired
with Pallas; they respectively govern a group of warriors and learned
women (ch. 14, Fig. 19). Later, Bacchus, god of wine, reigns over
drunkards (ch. 21). In manuscripts of *Des Cleres femmes* certain goddesses also preside over their "children." Minerva is enthroned above those
who practice her inventions: the arts of working with wool, crushing
olives to make oil, shaping pipes to form flutes, and making weapons
(Fig. 76). Juno, guardian of marriage and protector of childbirth, governs
pregnant women. Ceres, goddess of agriculture, reigns over farmers
(Fig. 77). In the *Epistre*, the absence of a clear distribution between the
seven planets and those other divinities whose characters could be used
to provide models of behavior may result from the impact on Christine
of the pictures in *Des Cleres femmes*.

Although certain miniatures from *Des Cleres femmes* may thus have
provided the idea for treating a number of gods and goddesses like the
planetary divinities, they were considerably modified before being adapted. In *Des Cleres femmes*, Minerva's "children" are occupied with a
variety of activities. In the *Epistre*, they are concerned only with weapons,
which they do not make but prepare to use. Minerva's appearance also
differs in the *Epistre*, where she sports a long lance and is outfitted in
armor, in contrast to her appearance as a courtly queen dressed in

---

[93] A. Jeanroy, "Boccace et Christine de Pisan, Le 'De claris mulieribus,' principale
source du 'Livre de la Cité des Dames'," *Romania* 48 (1922) 92-105; and Christine, *City
of Ladies*, tr. Richards, pp. xxxiv-xli.

[94] The earliest, Paris, BN MS fr. 12420, was given to Philip the Bold in 1403; the
second, Paris, BN MS fr. 598, was given to the duke of Berry in 1404; closely related to
these two is the third, undated manuscript, Brussels, Bib. Roy., MS 9509 (see Appendix A).

feminine finery in *Des Cleres femmes.* For the present, we can understand these changes to have been brought about because the skills of working with wool, olives, and flutes were considered to be less essential than warfare to the education of the prince.

Distinctly different interpretations of Venus are also presented. She is cast in a positive light as goddess of lovers in the *Epistre,* whereas she is associated with lust in *Des Cleres femmes.* There she possesses such beauty that she can "befuddle with gestures the minds of the fools who looked at her," a description from the text illustrated in the miniature by her arrogant bearing before those who stand in her train.[95] This change may result from Christine's desire throughout the *Epistre,* as in the *Cité des dames,* to present women in a more positive light than had Boccaccio.

Illuminated manuscripts of *Des Cleres femmes* must also have been the source for miniatures of Ceres and Isis in the *Epistre* (chs. 24 and 25), for they appear to have been illustrated nowhere else. In *Des Cleres femmes,* Ceres, who invented the plow,[96] directs the planters, sowers, and plowers working in the field below her (Fig. 77). Isis is generally shown arriving in Egypt (Fig. 78); finding the people to be barbarous and unskilled there, the text informs us, she taught them how to till, seed, and cultivate the land and how to form letters so that they could read and write.[97] Once again, Christine has transformed her sources. She has shown Ceres as goddess of agriculture, herself engaged in planting, and Isis as goddess of grafting, likewise busy with this chore (Fig. 24). She has placed the two miniatures on the same page, whereas stories of Ceres and Isis are separated by three chapters in *Des Cleres femmes* and by four books in the *Ovide,* where they also occur, although without illustrations.[98] This visual pairing allowed her to stress their kinship as goddesses of the land.

Both the changes in the miniatures and their location in the *Epistre* enabled Christine to develop pictorially the interrelated textual allegories. In the allegories Ceres and Isis teach the second and third lines of the Credo: a belief in Jesus Christ as the single Son of God and faith in his conception by the Holy Spirit and birth by the Virgin Mary.[99] In the

---

[95] Boccaccio, *Concerning Famous Women,* p. 16; Brussels, MS 9509, is illustrated in Boccaccio, *Decameron,* ed. V. Branca, 3 vols. (Florence, 1966), 1: 162.

[96] Boccaccio, *Concerning Famous Women,* pp. 11-13.

[97] *Ibid.,* pp. 18-19.

[98] de Boer, ed., *Ovide moralisé,* Bks. 5, 10.

[99] London, BL Harley MS 4431, fols. 107v-108r; Christine, *Epistle of Othea,* tr. Scrope, pp. 36-37.

miniature in the left column, Ceres appears in the clouds, as she scatters seeds on the tilled ground below. A row of wheat stalks rises on the left, while a solitary plow lies abandoned on the ground. The elimination of the laborers, present in *Des Cleres femmes*, and the prominence of the wheat are striking. So, too, is Ceres's changed physical appearance. The blue dress and the crescent shape and position of her kerchief equate her with the Madonna as queen of heaven, an iconographic type used to denote Mary's divine mission and destiny.[100] The wheat, already miraculously grown from the seeds that we see her scattering, serves both to associate her with Mary as mother of Christ and to underscore the function of the eucharist through which worshippers affirm their belief in Jesus Christ. Belief in Jesus Christ is, it should be recalled, the lesson of the textual allegory.

In the right-hand column, Isis's grafting becomes, as Wells demonstrated,[101] a simile for Christ's conception and birth, which is the lesson of the textual allegory for this chapter. Here Christine has probably adapted the text of Guillaume de Digueville's *Pèlerinage de la vie humaine*, where the regenerative function of grafting, by which a new branch was bound to an old, was compared to the dry tree of Jesse which became the green tree of the Virgin and produced the mystic apple, Christ. The miraculous conception and birth of Christ is, thus, implicit in the picture of Isis binding a dry, dead tree. With an unexpected twist, Christine's text further associates Isis's productivity with the knight's edification.[102]

Such miniatures are not only unfounded in tradition, they also seem to have been so obviously and interestingly inspired by ideas in the text that we are led to conclude that Christine must have formulated their iconographies. She transformed miniatures of Ceres from *Des Cleres femmes* to communicate better the textual allegory of the *Epistre*. When no pictorial antecedent existed for the miniature of Isis grafting, Christine probably invented an iconography to elucidate her unusual allegory. Ceres and Isis not only teach Christian theology in text and miniature alike, they contribute to the knight's moral education, for they recommend that he multiply all virtues and eschew all vices. In this way, Ceres and Isis are paired as wise women in the *Cité des dames* as well, where their

---

[100] See L. Réau, *Iconographie de l'art chrétien*, 3 vols. (Paris, 1955-1959), 2: 75ff.

[101] W. Wells, "A Simile in Christine de Pisan for Christ's Conception," JWCI 2 (1938-1939) 68-69.

[102] London, BL Harley MS 4431, fol. 108r; Christine, *Epistle of Othea*, tr. Scrope, p. 37.

knowledge, along with that of Minerva, is said to have brought a civilized, rational existence to savage, uncultivated peoples.[103]

Christine further associated the pair of miniatures of Ceres and Isis with the theme of wise women when she prefaced them in chapter 23 with a unique rendering of Diana (Fig. 23). The miniature, modelled on the "children of the planets" formula, depicts Diana in the sky, where she reads from a book and supervises a gathering of chaste women who also contemplate open books. Diana appears two other times in the *Epistre*, once as goddess of hunting and once with Actaeon (chs. 63 and 69). These miniatures closely follow models found in both versions of the illustrated *Ovide*.[104] But the representation of Diana and her "children" reading has no such antecedent, excepting those miniatures that we have already considered from Boccaccio's *Des Cleres femmes*. Diana does not figure in *Des Cleres femmes*, however. Nor is the imagery supplied in the text of this chapter in the *Epistre*. In the gloss, Diana, goddess of the moon, stands for honesty and chastity, which she recommends to the young knight.[105] In the allegory, she teaches the first article of the Credo: "I believe in God the Father Almighty, creator of heaven and earth."

Yet this miniature of Diana effectively communicates beliefs that we know Christine to have held, that is, a conviction that moral and spiritual virtues can be learned from books. The message to be learned from the miniature is this: if the knight studies this chapter, just as the chaste women read their books, the example of Diana will teach him — as it does them — honesty, chastity, and a belief in God. It is difficult to imagine a miniaturist creating this imagery for Diana. Like the iconography of the seven planets, for which there were instructions, it is entirely extratextual. It is, moreover, self-referential of the author, referring as it does to book-writing and -reading. Rather, having developed her iconography of the planets and being familiar with miniatures in *Des Cleres femmes* where a similar formula was used throughout, Christine adapted the schema to different subjects, such as this one of Diana.

Not all miniatures of mythological subjects in the *Epistre* are as inventive as these. At least a quarter of the miniatures that illustrate myths in the *Epistre* come directly from manuscripts of the *Ovide*. These include miniatures of Diana and Actaeon and Diana as a huntress, as we just

---

[103] Christine, *City of Ladies*, tr. Richards, pp. 76-81.

[104] Compare, for example, the miniature of Diana as a huntress in Geneva, Bib. pub. et univ., MS 176, illustrated in Gagnebin, "L'Enluminure," p. 77.

[105] London, BL Harley MS 4431, fols. 107r-107v; Christine, *Epistle of Othea*, tr. Scrope, pp. 35-36.

indicated, as well as many others, including those of Pyramus and Thisbe, Hero and Leander, Latona and the Frogs, Mercury and Argus (Figs. 26, 79), Alcyon and Ceyx.[106] It can be shown that Christine knew a manuscript like that produced for the duke of Berry late in the century, for the compositions in the *Epistre* and in that manuscript are quite similar, although they are usually reversed.[107] She also must have known a manuscript with a fuller cycle, like those that had been executed earlier in the century, because some subjects included in the *Epistre* are only found in these more densely illustrated versions, where they generally appear in reverse.[108] Details of costume and setting are naturally more elaborate in miniatures in the *Epistre*. Nevertheless, on the basis of many similarities, we are obliged to conclude that Christine had her artists use these earlier miniatures as models.

The fact that some models from the *Ovide* were adapted unchanged, when other miniatures in the *Epistre* are so novel, suggests that Christine considered the former to provide satisfactory illustrations for those particular chapters in the *Epistre*. These miniatures from the *Ovide* function in the *Epistre* as pictorial retellings of the myths, alluded to in the texts and narrated in the glosses. They confirm Christine's abiding interest in the narrative content of the myths which she worked into the framework of a political allegory. What is important is that, having established that some miniatures depend quite closely on their models, we can now more freely suppose the departure from other models to have been the result of conscious choice.

Trojan Stories and the Wisdom of Women

Turning to the final group of subjects in the *Epistre*, the Trojan episodes, we might expect to find that the same situation applies there as with the *Ovide* and the mythological subjects. That is, since Christine used the text of the *Histoire ancienne* as her source for these chapters,[109] we might

---

[106] Illustrations may be found in Lord, "Ovide moralisé"; Seznec, *Survival of the Pagan Gods*, Figs. 34, 82; and Meiss, *Limbourgs*.

[107] Lyons, Bib. mun., MS 742, illustrated in Meiss, *Limbourgs*, 2: Pls. 78, 92; and Seznec, *Survival of the Pagan Gods*, Figs. 33-36.

[108] Such as Rouen, Bib. mun., MS 0.4 or Paris, Bib. de l'Arsenal, MS 5069, discussed and illustrated by Lord, "Ovide moralisé," Figs. 1-22.

[109] Campbell, *L'Épitre d'Othéa*, pp. 80-109, discusses Christine's use of the Trojan material. Thirty-six chapters use material from the *Histoire ancienne*. Campbell has shown that she preferred the second edition of the *Histoire ancienne*, which included an expanded version of the history of Troy based on a prose redaction of Benoit de Sainte-More's *Roman de Troie*. On the versions of the *Histoire ancienne*, see P. Meyer,

assume that she adapted its pictures in much the same way that she adapted those from the *Ovide*. This did not happen, however. Yet, it is probable that Christine had access to an illuminated manuscript of the *Histoire*, such as one of the second edition, which allotted greater space to the Trojan story.[110] Like the *Ovide*, the *Histoire* was extensively illustrated in the century preceding the production of the *Epistre*. Illuminated manuscripts of the *Histoire* and the *Epistre* do, in fact, share a certain number of common subjects: for example, Jason and the dragon, Ulysses playing chess, Paris and Helen, Troilus and Cressida, Hector and Andromache, Hector's funeral, and Priam and his barons. Yet these are usually treated differently. Moreover, other subjects illustrated in the *Epistre* are not illustrated at all in copies of the *Histoire*. These include the advice of Troilus and Helenus, the prayers of Cassandra, the revenge of Memnon, and Jason and Medea.

A look at the miniatures of Jason and Medea in the *Epistre* is particularly instructive of the way in which Christine used her pictorial sources,[111] including the *Histoire*, where the story of Jason and Medea is narrated in the most extensive detail.[112] Christine tells the story of Jason and Medea over two chapters.[113] In chapter 54, she relates that Medea used her charms to teach Jason how to acquire the golden fleece, a strategy that was successful, but that Jason was unappreciative of her good deed and, hence, forsook her. In the gloss to this chapter, the young knight is understandably urged not to emulate Jason's behavior since it is unchivalric. This chapter is prefaced by a miniature of Jason slaying the dragon that has no exceptional features, although it does not bear a direct model-copy relationship with its counterpart in the *Histoire* (Figs. 39, 82).

"Les Premières compilations françaises d'histoire ancienne. 2. Histoire ancienne jusqu'à César," *Romania* 14 (1885) 36-81; and important additions and corrections by B. Woledge, "La Légende de Troie et les débuts de la prose française," in *Mélanges de linguistique et de littérature romanes offerts à Mario Roque*, 4 vols. (Paris, 1952), 2: 313-324.

[110] Such as London, BL Roy. MS 20 D 1; Stowe MS 54; and Paris BN MS fr. 301. See Appendix A.

[111] This miniature has been previously discussed by C. Reno, "Feminist Aspects of Christine de Pizan's 'Epistre d'Othéa à Hector'," *Studi francesi* 71 (1980) 271-276, who came to somewhat different conclusions about its content.

[112] In the absence of a published edition, see the prose *Roman de Troie*, which the *Histoire ancienne* incorporated; Benoît de Sainte-More, *Le Roman de Troie en prose*, ed. L. Constans and E. Faral (Paris, 1922).

[113] London, BL Harley MS 4431, fols. 120r, 122r; Christine, *Epistle of Othea*, tr. Scrope, pp. 66-67, 72.

In chapter 58 Christine continues her account of Medea. She characterizes Medea as one of the most accomplished sorceresses, a sorceress who was so in love with Jason that she compromised her honor, giving herself to him. The gloss teaches Hector not to be too strong-willed, and the allegory cautions him to avoid the temptations of the flesh. The miniature has no apparent relationship to the text, however (Fig. 40). In it, Medea is seated on the edge of the bed, while Jason kneels before her. The hands of both of them touch a small box, a detail that has been interpreted both as Medea receiving gifts from Jason and as Medea offering Jason a coffer.[114]

If we examine the various models of Jason and Medea which Christine knew, it is apparent that her miniature deviates from the traditional representations. Illuminated manuscripts of the *Ovide, Des Cleres femmes*, and *Des Cas des nobles hommes et femmes* all illustrate another episode in the story (Fig. 80). They depict Medea's anger, showing her murdering her own children, which she did in a jealous rage over Jason's rejection of her in favor of another lover.[115] According to these other versions, Medea was a wicked woman, who was ruled irrationally by unbridled passions.

Christine, however, has chosen to illustrate an earlier moment in the narrative, as related in the *Histoire ancienne*.[116] After Medea met and fell passionately in love with Jason, she asked him to visit her in her bedroom late one night. She promised that if he complied, she would be able to help him to realize his ambitions, specifically to capture the golden fleece. On the night of the designated rendezvous Jason attended a banquet that lasted so long that he was almost prevented from seeing Medea, but he came to her finally, just as she had nearly given up hope. At this time, she took out a jewelry box, from which she offered him a charm and a ring, telling him their magic would aid him to capture the golden fleece. The miniatures in the Paris and London books depict this moment when Jason accepts the charm. In the Paris manuscript, the magic ring is visible between the fingers of Medea's left hand. Through the choice of this subject for illustration in the *Epistre*, instead of the usual subject of Medea as murderess, Christine demonstrates her interest in portraying the

---

[114] Reno, "Feminist Aspects," pp. 274-275; and Meiss, *Limbourgs*, 1: 294.

[115] See Meiss, *Limbourgs*, 1: 288; and Boccaccio, *Decameron*, 1: 222. The *Ovide* depicts Medea poisoning a drink given Theseus by Aegeus; see Lord, "Ovide moralisé," p. 173.

[116] Benoît de Sainte-More, *Le Roman de Troie en prose*, ed. Constans and Faral, pp. 14-15.

positive side of Medea's character. For Christine, Medea was another model of a wise woman.

Where did this unusual miniature of Medea come from? We have already seen that the pictorial details cannot come from the text of the *Epistre*, for they are not included there; only the indication that Medea was a sorceress who compromised her honor for Jason is present in the text. Nor is the subject found among the miniatures in those manuscripts of the *Histoire* which Christine might have known.[117] Rather, the miniature was probably inspired by a close reading of the text of the *Histoire*, for all the details are mentioned there. It is evident that this activity, the reading of the text of the *Histoire*, is one in which Christine, not her artists, engaged. It seems implausible, therefore, to assume that anyone but the author determined the content and details of the miniature, which is, besides, completely in line with the textual contents of the *Epistre* in that it seeks to emphasize Medea's virtues rather than her failings.

One final use of models in the *Epistre* is instructive about the procedure by which Christine's artists made miniatures. After working on the *Epistre*, the *Cité des dames* Master went on to participate in the illustration of a number of copies of Boccaccio's *Des Cas des nobles hommes et femmes*.[118] This text has in common with the *Epistre* a small number of subjects. Yet not a single common subject was illustrated with the same model. This observation supports the view presented earlier in this

---

[117] This subject is illustrated, however, in manuscripts of the twelfth-century poem by Benoît de Sainte-More, the *Roman de Troie*. Of special interest is a group of three manuscripts which can be dated in the latter half of the fourteenth century and localized in Bologna: Vienna, ONB, Cod. 2571; Paris, BN MS fr. 782; and Leningrad, Pub. Lib., MS fr. F. v. XI, 3. On this group, see F. Saxl, "The Troy Romance in French and Italian Art," in *Lectures*, 2 vols. (London, 1957), 1: 125-138, esp. 131ff; and H. Buchthal, *Historia Troiana. Studies in the History of Mediaeval Secular Illustration*, Studies of the Warburg Institute, 32 (London, 1971), pp. 14, 39. The subject is found in Leningrad, MS fr. F. v. XIV, 3, fol. 10r, reproduced by Saxl, Pl. 80b. There is no indication that Christine knew any of these manuscripts, since this version of the Troy story was not used for her text and this cycle of miniatures does not share model-copy relationship with the *Epistre*. Besides, this version was not particularly popular in Paris, all the manuscripts coming from Italy. Therefore, we may conclude tentatively that the illustration of the *Epistre* was undertaken independent of illuminated manuscripts of the verse *Roman de Troie*, with which it nevertheless shared some common features. An edition of the text and a listing of the manuscripts is found in Benoît de Sainte-More, *Le Roman de Troie par Benoît de Sainte-More*, ed. L. Constans, 6 vols., SATF (Paris, 1904-1912).

[118] For the manuscripts, see Meiss, *Limbourgs*, 1: 283-287; on the tradition of the text in France, see Bozzolo, *Boccace*, pp. 15-23; a partial translation (Book 1) has been completed by P. M. Gathercole, ed. and tr., *Laurent de Premierfait's 'Des Cas des nobles hommes et femmes'*, University of North Carolina Studies in Romance Language and Literature, 74 (Chapel Hill, NC, 1968).

chapter that miniaturists followed a different set of instructions for each assignment, even when the shared subject matter might have made possible the reuse of pictures. Yet the pictures in *Des Cas* were not put together anew. Models for individual figures and particular settings were reused. For example, in one copy of *Des Cas*, the architectural setting of Priam's throne room in the *Epistre* reappears as the setting for Constantine II.[119] Ulysses's tent is reused as that of Posthumius Albinus.[120] The figure of the doctor Aesculapius recurs as that of the philosopher Callisthenes.[121] Such shared details allow us to confirm the conclusions drawn earlier from evidence of manuscript production in Paris. A picture was a composite put together by the artist from models of individual figures and props. Its content, however, was the responsibility of the author.

By looking at three kinds of evidence – information on manuscript production in Paris, Christine's writings on art, and the sources for the miniatures in the *Epistre Othéa* – we have been able to demonstrate that the premises commonly held about Christine's participation in the production of her manuscripts are, in fact, valid. Specifically, Christine seems to have been involved to a considerable degree in the make-up of the pictorial cycle. The degree of her involvement fully justifies claims that the illuminators worked under Christine's direction, following her verbal instructions. It is clear, moreover, that she gave explicit instructions in the form of the purple rubrics to the illuminators. She certainly supervised the illustration.

Evidence concerning manuscript production in Paris suggests that this sort of involvement on the part of the author may have been common. Christine's own writings on art show her to have been more outspoken in the role of the artist than her contemporaries and, further, to have perceived the artist as an imitator of reality, not an inventor of pictures. A study of the various pictorial sources for the *Epistre* reveals that probably the author, not the miniaturists, studied related illuminated manuscripts and selectively adapted their models to the *Epistre*. In some cases, such as the *Ovide*, these models were close to Christine's ends and

---

[119] Paris, Bib. de l'Arsenal, MS 5193, executed between 1409 and 1419; published by Meiss, *Limbourgs*, 1: 283-287; Bozzolo, *Boccace*, pp. 51-53; and in facsimile by H. Martin, *Le Boccace de Jean sans Peur: Du cas des nobles hommes et femmes* (Brussels, 1911). See Martin, Pl. 34, fig. 130.

[120] Martin, *Boccace*, Pl. 25, fig. 99.

[121] *Ibid.*, pl. 16, fig. 63.

therefore were retained unchanged. In many other cases modifications were introduced so as to express the themes emphasized in the text of the *Epistre.*

When Christine turned away from her models, she often did so in order to emphasize two interrelated themes that were not given sufficient prominence in her sources: namely, the importance of wisdom and the role of women as teachers of wisdom. Her transformations of possible sources for the seven planets, other mythological subjects, and certain Trojan subjects can all be shown to have been derived from an interest in these themes. This emphasis on the wisdom of women develops a theme that we saw at the beginning of the *Epistre* in the miniatures of the double presentation and those of the four cardinal virtues. In the opening miniatures, the theme of the wisdom of women was linked with an interest in good government as practiced by the French princes. As the Trojan cycle develops within the *Epistre* — a picture cycle for which exact sources cannot be found, although the associated texts derive from the *Histoire* — we shall see that the theme of wisdom continues to be mingled with an interest in good government. The theme of good government is one that the very choice of the genre of the epistolary allegory would lead us to expect. It is also one that is worked out differently in the Paris and London manuscripts. We can now turn to these manuscripts, confident that the overall characteristics and the individual details of their particular programs were worked out by Christine, not by her illuminators.

3

The Ideological Programs of the Manuscripts

As we have seen, miniatures in the Paris and London copies of the *Epistre Othéa* were executed under close authorial supervision. The evidence suggests that a great deal of thought went into choosing the most suitable models and then altering them, when necessary, to reflect the themes of the text. This view of the creation of the miniatures argues against a view that might see these copies of the *Epistre* as luxury exemplars that were lavishly illuminated just to be more pleasing to Christine's patrons and, perhaps, therefore to fetch higher prices. Instead, it suggests that the subjects of the miniatures were carefully selected and their details carefully executed in order to convey a concrete message. This view of a program of illustrations as communicating an individualistic message within a given book is in line with what we know to have been common practice in the production of late medieval miniatures.

In the case of the Paris and London copies of the *Epistre*, moreover, three additional observations suggest the presence of conscious ideological programs. First, they are the only two manuscripts that preserve the imagery of the so-called double dedication miniatures discussed earlier. The highly individualized, complex imagery of these opening miniatures thus raises the question of whether the imagery of the remainder of the illustrations develops the theme presented by them. Second, many of the miniatures have been shown to depart significantly from their models. The thematic and compositional originality of pictures in the Paris and London copies of the *Epistre* argues for a program that was tailored to these particular manuscripts. Third, when compared with other contemporary and later manuscripts of the *Epistre*, the cycles in the Paris and London copies can be shown to be exceptional. It would seem, therefore, that the imagery of the pictures in the Paris and London copies was created in response to special requirements, but that this imagery was not appropriate either for the other illustrated contemporary copies or for later copies of the book.

While proceeding with an investigation of the full cycles in these manuscripts in order to define the ideological programs, two other questions must be borne in mind. What were the respective roles of the patrons of the Paris and London books? And what is the importance, if any, of the dedication of the book to Louis of Orleans?

With regard to these questions, it is necessary to review briefly the circumstances of the production of these books. We have seen that the Paris copy may have been begun for Louis of Orleans and completed for Duke John of Berry. The dates that circumscribe its production are, thus, 1406 to 1408. Until a convincing alternative hypothesis is put forward,[1] we can for the time being accept that Berry owned the book. In the absence of additional evidence, however, it remains difficult to speculate about the role of the patron with respect to the Paris book, since the circumstances surrounding its actual production remain clouded. The London copy of the *Epistre* is included in a "Collected Works" for Queen Isabeau of Bavaria, to whom it was certainly given between 1410 and 1415. At one time, however, it existed apart from this compendium to which it was joined through an amazingly complicated, technical procedure.

The new evidence about the composition of the London "Collected Works" forces us to consider very seriously the effect of the queen's patronage on the ideological program in the London manuscript, since it is unlikely that the *Epistre* would have been enlarged for inclusion in the volume, if it were not especially suited for the queen. We have already observed that the London copy, to a greater extent than the one in Paris, includes details that highly contemporize the figures; it alone preserves a more refined version of the double dedication schema, the royal interpretation of King Minos, and the allusions to a royal prince among the children of the planets. Did these details have anything to do with the fact that the manuscript was intended for the queen? This evidence about the manuscript's production has led also to a redating of the London copy, which can now be dated before 1410 to 1415 and perhaps as early as 1408, around the same time as or just a little after the Paris copy. Now that we know the time of the composition of the manuscript, as well as its patron, it is necessary to try to understand it in the context of the historical circumstances of the moment insofar as they involved the queen and were of concern to Christine.

---

[1] De Winter's alternative hypothesis that the manuscript was made for a member of the Villaines family does not seem likely; see below, n. 13.

Another significant feature of the manuscripts is that their completion most likely postdates the life of the person to whom they were dedicated, Louis of Orleans, who was murdered in 1407. Yet the Paris and London copies both include especially elaborate representations of him as the founder of the Order of the Porcupine. Why? It is not unusual, of course, for a manuscript to preserve its original dedication, since this was considered part of the text, and a copy of the dedicatory miniature usually accompanied the dedication. It might be possible, therefore, to understand the inclusion of the dedications and the associated miniatures of Louis of Orleans simply as examples of this common phenomenon. However, since four alternative dedications had been written for the *Epistre*, the inclusion of the one addressed to Louis entailed a deliberate choice. The fact that the choice was made to include a dead prince and to present him so ceremoniously leads to the possibility that the manuscripts in some way use for didactic purposes the image of the murdered duke. Thus Louis of Orleans's presence may be crucial to the message, the point of view, presented in the manuscripts.

In order to determine whether a coherent theme runs through the cycle of miniatures in these manuscripts, it will be necessary to examine a number of different miniatures. It is not necessary to look at all one hundred pictures in each book. Since we now have some idea of the visual models Christine used and, further, of her interpretations of them, we can restrict our study to those miniatures that depart from the models. Two sorts of deviations occur. There are those miniatures whose very subjects are altogether idiosyncratic, not being found in the models, and there are those miniatures that illustrate subjects found in the manuscript models but alter their details. Because we have already been able to differentiate between certain details in miniatures of the same subject in the Paris and London exemplars, it will be necessary to continue to compare miniatures from these copies to determine the full extent of the differences and then, if possible, to try to understand the reasons for them.

Instead of isolating themes of miniatures and treating them as a group, we shall proceed more or less sequentially through the *Epistre*, since the program can thus be seen to evolve. Furthermore, progressing in this fashion simulates the process by which its readers originally perused the manuscript, and it was of course to them that the program was directed.

IMAGES OF THE ROYAL QUARREL

After the first chapter, in which Othea gives Hector her letter, references to Hector and his family are interspersed throughout the work. This is not surprising for a number of reasons. Hector is the hero of the tale, is set up at the beginning as a stand-in for the person to whom the book was dedicated, and is important for the dynastic continuity of the French monarchs descended from the Trojans. Many of these references in the *Epistre* do not involve Hector himself but members of his family. This strategy, on the simplest level, can be understood as filling out the details, the plot, of the narrative by making the principal character more believable. However, since Hector is a model for royalty, members of Hector's family can also be understood as models for the French royal family.

Early in the *Epistre*, Christine supplies Hector with a classical genealogy. She tells us that Mars and Minerva are called the father and mother of Hector (chs. 11 and 13), notwithstanding the fact that Hector's true parents were King Priam and Queen Hecuba.[2] Because the good knight loves arms and uses them wisely, Mars, the god of wars and battles, is his father. Minerva, the maker of armor, is his mother. Christine adds that the love and use of arms is governed by another goddess, Pallas Athena, the goddess of wisdom (ch. 14). In both manuscripts, the miniatures for these two chapters show Mars presiding over a battle and Minerva distributing armor to the knights who prepare for battle (Figs. 14, 15, 17, 18).

In order to appreciate the special features of the miniatures of Mars and Minerva, it is useful to recall their models: the "children of the planets" imagery. We have already seen that as god of war Mars influenced all forms of physical violence, from animal slaughter to one-on-one combat to large-scale warfare. Christine has limited the activities, however, to a single battle in which two principal adversaries fight each other. A third warrior conspicuously occupies the entire foreground, and a legion of anonymous soldiers decorates the background. As we saw earlier, Christine also changed the imagery of Minerva, which she probably adapted from Boccaccio's *Des Cleres femmes*, where the goddess appears supervising the making of wool, flutes, and olives, as well as weapons (Fig. 76). In the *Epistre*, the activities of Minerva, like those of Mars, are limited as she distributes the equipment of war to waiting knights.

In the London copy, details in the miniature of Mars make explicit the father-son relationship between Mars and Hector and simultaneously evoke the milieu of the French court (Fig. 14). The knight on the right is dressed in a costume of the same reddish-orange color that Mars wears,

---

[2] London, BL Harley MS 4431, fols. 101v-102r, 102v; Christine, *Epistle of Othea*, tr. Scrope, pp. 21, 23.

a simple device that serves to connect visually the two figures and thereby encourages the viewer to interpret the knight as Hector, son of Mars. The tunic worn by Mars is adorned with oak leaves, a common motif at the French royal court.[3] The garment worn by Hector is decorated with embroidered gold crowns, a motif that occurred earlier in this manuscript, on Hector's robe in the first miniature. In the first miniature, the motif of crowns helped us to understand the figure of Hector as Louis of Orleans. Coming so soon after the first miniature, the reuse of the motif, coupled with the use of other patterns common at court, may again encourage the visual association between Hector, the knight on the right, and Louis of Orleans. The text of the manuscript thus specifies that Mars is a parent of Hector, and the miniature adds that, if he is a parent of Hector, he is also a parent of Louis of Orleans.

The parentage of Louis by Mars that is implied in the London miniature is consistent with the late medieval practice of marshaling a mythological genealogy for contemporary rulers. For example, Pietro da Castelletto, writing in 1402, supplied a family tree for Gian Galeazzo Visconti, father-in-law of Louis of Orleans.[4] In one manuscript version, illuminators added painted roundels with inscriptions which gave visual form to the text, which traced Gian Galeazzo's lineage through Troy back to the gods Jupiter, Anchises, and Venus.[5] Around the same time, Ambrogio Migli, secretary of Louis of Orleans, wrote two poems that similarly bestowed a divine genealogy on Louis.[6] According to Migli, Louis descended from specific gods and goddesses, from whom he acquired different virtues. Juno gave him wealth, Venus beauty, and Pallas wisdom. It was from Mars, however, that he learned the arts of warfare. Formidable like Mars, Louis is summoned by Migli to decide the outcome of the French war against the English. It should be evident that Migli's imagery anticipates that in the London miniature, where Louis, like Hector, descends from Mars, from whom he learns conduct in battle.

---

[3] Laborde, *Les Ducs de Bourgogne*, 2.1: 67; Evans, *Dress in Mediaeval France*, p. 38. See above, ch. 1, p. 53, n. 99.

[4] Pietro de Castelletto, *Gian Galeazzo Visconti's Funeral Oration* described and illustrated by P. Toesca, "Le Miniature dell'Elogio funebre di Gian Galeazzo Visconti (Parigi, Bib. Nat., Ms. lat. 5888)," *Rassegna d'Arte* 10 (1910) 156-158.

[5] *Ibid.*

[6] G. Ouy, "Humanisme et propagande politique en France au début du xve siècle: Ambrogio Migli et les ambitions impériales de Louis d'Orléans," *Culture et politique en France à l'époque de l'humanisme et de la Renaissance. Atti del convegno internazionale promosso dall'Accademia delle scienzi di Torino, 1971*, ed. F. Simone (Turin, 1974), pp. 13-42. These poems are found in Paris, BN MSS lat. 9684, 7371 and nouv. acq. lat. 1793.

The miniature does not just make a genealogical point; it also shows us a battle. Just as one figure is more prominent on the right, the one we have identified as Hector or Louis, so a single fighting knight stands out on the left. His prominence is emphasized by three details. First, his horse is the only horse apart from Hector's that is covered by a sort of saddle-cloth constructed of chain mail. Second, he is the only knight who sports a plumed helmet; here he wears red and white plumes. Third, he is the only knight to carry a shield with charges on it. His shield displays a gold double-headed eagle that recalls the shield of the Holy Roman Emperor, which it inverts. Since he is thus distinguished from the other warriors in the miniature, it would seem important to determine whether we can learn anything from these details about his meaning. For this purpose, we can eliminate the details of costume, for the accoutrements of the helmet and the horse seem merely to draw attention to him, not to identify him. But the shield is striking in the context of this battle between two combatants. Its presence should make us inquire into the possible meaning of the empire for Louis of Orleans.

We do not need to search far to find that Louis of Orleans had imperial ambitions that may be the subject of this miniature. The French monarchs had long sought the imperial command, and from the time of King Charles V royal propagandists renewed their efforts to justify the king's claim to the empire.[7] Some precedent also existed for the assignment of the imperial throne to a son of a French king.[8] Then, early in the fifteenth century, Ambrogio Migli argued directly for Louis's right to the imperial crown.[9] He referred to Louis and Charles VI as twins of the fleur-de-lis, analogous to the constellations Castor and Pollux, and concluded that, while Charles VI ruled France, Louis must assume his rightful position as head of the empire that was his by virtue of his Trojan blood. Migli ended by acclaiming Louis to be the new Caesar of a forthcoming golden age. Interpreted against the background of Migli's writings, the miniature shows Louis, who shares a descent with the Trojan Hector, trying to wrest the imperial shield from the knight on the left.

But, does the miniature present a point of view? We may well ask whether Christine, who instructed her miniaturists, concurred with Migli

---

[7] See especially G. Zeller, "Les Rois de France candidats à l'empire. Essai sur l'idéologie impériale en France," *Revue historique* 173 (1934) 273-311, 497-534; and R. Folz, *L'Idée d'Empire en Occident du Ve au XIVe siècle* (Paris, 1953).

[8] Zeller, "Les Rois de France," p. 279, discusses chroniclers of the thirteenth century who celebrated in the birth of Louis VIII, son of Isabelle of Hainaut and Philip Augustus, the return of the crown of France to the line of Charlemagne.

[9] Ouy, "Ambrogio Migli," p. 40.

that the imperial throne belonged to Louis, or whether the miniature simply refers to the imperial aspirations of the person to whom it is dedicated, as though to historical fact, without commenting further on them. Another detail in the London miniature helps us answer this question. More conspicuous than any of the other warriors is a third knight whose body, along with that of his horse, stretches across the whole of the immediate foreground. The horse is fully covered with a pink cloth, and thus is distinguished from all the other mounts in the miniature. The knight is unidentifiable; his face and body are completely concealed by a chain-mail hauberk. From their positions, it is not entirely clear whether rider and horse have fallen or whether the knight has freely dismounted. What is apparent, however, is that the knight reaches for a plain gold shield that lies on the ground in the left-hand corner. The horse's mouth almost touches the shield, a detail that emphasizes its importance. This plain gold shield is identical with that in the first miniature. It is the shield of the Order of the Gold Shield. Recalling that the aim of the Order of the Gold Shield was the pursuit of peace, to which Christine alludes in the first miniature when she presents the order as a model one for Hector, the message here is probably also one of moderation. Specifically, the shield reminds viewers that moderation should be the preferred course for all warring knights and that the best end of all war is peace.

Before leaving the London miniature of Mars, we should compare it with its counterpart in the Paris copy (Fig. 15). There the shields and banners are merely fantasies, composed of a gold rampant lion on a blue ground, a red double-headed eagle on a gold ground, and a red cross on a green ground. These charges still call forth associations in turn with the shields of Hector (a lion), the empire (an eagle), and the oriflamme (a red banner). But, the genealogical link between Mars and Hector, the identity of Hector as Louis, and the allusion to the imperial ambitions of Louis are absent.

If we consider now the miniatures of Minerva, Hector's mother, we find that the Paris manuscript includes contemporary references in the form of identifiable shields of actual persons (Fig. 18). On the far left, one knight has received the standard of the Coucy family, while the knight in the center reaches up to grasp another shield.[10] The arms of the Coucy

---

[10] J. B. Rietstap, *Armorial général précedé d'un dictionnaire des termes du blason*, 2nd ed., 2 vols. (Gouda, 1884-1887), 1: 447 (Coucy: *fascé de vair et de gueules*). I am extremely grateful to François Avril, Conservateur des manuscrits, BN, Michel Pastoureau, Conservateur des médailles, BN, and Mme H. Loyau, Section héraldique, CNRS, for

family can only be a reference to Louis of Orleans, who purchased the chateau of this great family from its last heir, Marie de Coucy.[11] Her father, Enguerrand VII of Coucy, had been count of Soissons, captain general of Guyenne, and lieutenant general for the duke of Orleans.[12] At the time of his purchase, Louis took over the seigniory of Coucy and with it the family heraldry, becoming sire of Coucy as well as duke of Orleans. The central shield has been identified as that of the Villaines family, a family whose connections with Louis of Orleans and Christine are documented, but actually the charges could refer to any of five families prominent at the time.[13] There seems thus to be no way of determining exactly to which family the central shield might point, and the third one is too abraded to be read.[14]

We can still ask, however, why the representation of Minerva has been transformed in this unusual way in order to highlight an activity related to warfare, specifically to a battle for which she prepares Louis of Orleans and his companions. In this context, we should recall that forging weapons, rather than distributing them, was but one of Minerva's many tasks in Boccaccio's *Des Cleres femmes*. It seems reasonable to offer the hypothesis that the miniature in the *Epistre* refers to a struggle, a battle, in which Louis of Orleans figured. The most obvious struggle, one that at the time was foremost in the thoughts of many connected with the royal circle, was the Burgundian-Orleanist controversy. Read in this way, the miniature shows Minerva outfitting Louis for his struggle against John the Fearless, duke of Burgundy.

suggesting, checking, and confirming heraldic details. For an alternate identification of these shields see de Winter, "Christine de Pizan, ses enlumineurs," pp. 370-371 n. 54. In consultation with Michel Pastoureau, I have confirmed that de Winter's identification of what I have called the Coucy shield as that of Jacques de Châtillon-Dampierre (*écartelé aux 1 et 4 de gueules à 3 pals de vair au chef d'or; au 2 et 3 de gueules à 2 lions léopardes d'or*) is not sustained by the visual evidence.

[11] See Nordberg, *Les Ducs*, pp. 14, 16.

[12] On Enguerrand, see E. de Lépinois, *Histoire de la Ville et des Sires de Coucy* (Paris, 1859); and the popular account by B. Tuchman, *A Distant Mirror. The Calamitous 14th Century* (New York, 1978).

[13] De Winter, "Christine de Pizan, ses enlumineurs," pp. 370-371, and n. 54. According to Pastoureau, the Villaines shield (*d'argent à trois lions de sable posés 2 et 1*) was the same as those of the following families: Abancourt, Beaucorroy, Berlettes, DuHamel, Fouilloy, and Proisy.

[14] An examination of the miniature under magnification and ultraviolet does not sustain the identification of this shield as that of [Jehannequin d'] Esquaquélon (*de gueules à 3 fasces d'or*) suggested by de Winter, "Christine de Pizan, ses enlumineurs," pp. 353, 370-371 n. 54.

The comparable miniature in the London book also makes specific references, but not in the form of shields (Fig. 17). In it, the shields are probably fantasies, since all attempts to identify them with those of actual families have been unsuccessful. However, a knight on the left wears a costume decorated with emblems that can be associated with a specific individual in the French court. The embroidered decoration consists of sun rays, an emblem of King Charles VI that was taken over by his young son the dauphin, Louis of Guyenne.[15] The sun rays are a probable reference to the early Christian motif of the Sun of Justice, indicating the ruler's function of upholding justice in his realm and perhaps identifying Charles VI, and then Louis of Guyenne, with Constantine, for whom the emblem had been used.[16] The sun rays help to establish that the knight on the left is not just an ordinary soldier, but a contemporary ruler. At the same time, we know that the knight must be Hector, whom the text addresses. Thus, this miniature merges the identity of Hector with that of another individual, Louis of Guyenne.

These probable references to the Burgundian-Orleanist controversy in the Paris manuscript and to the dauphin in the London copy, both within the context of warfare, require explanation. In order to understand them, it is necessary to review the history of the conflict between the houses of Orleans and Burgundy.[17] Spurred by Charles VI's recurring illness, the conflict was largely motivated by a power struggle over the control of the regency. The quarrel took place in three stages between three sets of antagonists: Louis of Orleans and Philip of Burgundy until 1404, Louis of Orleans and John of Burgundy until 1407, and Charles of Orleans or

[15] Sun rays are mixed with other emblems on standards recorded in documents published by L. C. Douët-d'Arcq, *Choix de pièces inédites relatives au règne de Charles VI*, 2 vols., SHF, 119, 122 (Paris, 1863-1864), 2: 397. See also J.-B. de Vaivre, "À Propos des devises de Charles VI," *Bulletin monumental* 141 (1983) 92-95. They appeared also as emblems of King Richard II, decorating the sails of his fleet, in Jean Creton's *Histoire de Richart II* (London, BL Harley MS 1319, fol. 18r). See E. M. Thompson, "A Contemporary Account of the Fall of Richard II," *Burlington Magazine* 5 (1904) 160-172, 267, 270, Pl. 4.

[16] See E. H. Kantorowicz, "Oriens Augusti: lever du roi," *Dumbarton Oaks Papers* 17 (1963) 117-177; and C. Ligota, "L'Influence de Macrobe pendant la Renaissance," in *Le Soleil à la Renaissance: sciences et mythes* (Brussels, 1965), pp. 465-482. Sun rays were used as an emblem by later Valois kings especially Charles VIII, as discussed by R. W. Scheller, "Imperial Themes in Art and Literature of the Early French Renaissance: the Period of Charles VIII," *Simiolus* 12 (1981-1982) 5-69.

[17] On this period, see Nordberg, *Les Ducs*; A. Coville, "Les Premiers Valois et la Guerre de Cent Ans (1328-1422)," in *Histoire de France depuis les origines jusqu'à la Révolution*, ed. E. Lavisse, 11 vols. (Paris, 1901-1911), 4: 1-441; and *idem, Les Cabochiens et l'ordonnance de 1413* (Paris, 1888); and Famiglietti, *Royal Intrigue*.

his allies and John of Burgundy until 1419. Only the period up to 1412 through 1415, at which time the London book was given to the queen, concerns us here.

The first stage of the troubles must be seen against the background of the ordinances passed under Charles v and reaffirmed by Charles vi and his council.[18] As we have seen, these ordinances established the order of succession and regulated the interim guardianship and tutelage of the heir before his age of majority, which was declared to be fourteen. Before the dauphin's majority, his guardianship and tutelage were to be jointly managed by the queen and the dukes. Should the king die without a legitimate male heir, the succession was to pass to his brothers according to the order of seniority. In 1380, when he was only twelve, Charles vi had come to the throne and was immediately crowned. But his repeated illnesses dating from 1392 attached considerable importance to the question of succession; until the birth of a dauphin, succession would have favored, first, Louis of Orleans as the only brother and, second, Philip of Burgundy. Even the production of a legitimate heir remained problematic: the first, born in 1386, died one month later; the second, born in 1392, died in 1401; and the third and fourth, born respectively in 1397 and 1398, were unhealthy.[19]

The discord between Louis of Orleans and Philip of Burgundy was marked by recurring disturbances from 1392 to 1401. This period ended in 1401 and 1402 with an overt crisis of major proportions.[20] During the last decade of the century Philip was annoyed by the power Louis exercised over the king and queen. The situation worsened in October, 1401, however, when Philip wrote a letter to the parliament expressing dismay and disapproval at certain events in the kingdom. What he probably objected to was the appointment of Louis's allies to the parliament. In any event, Philip was so enraged that he traveled to Paris, arriving in November of the same year accompanied by an army of his vassals. Efforts by the queen and the dukes of Bourbon and Berry eventually appeased the quarrelling dukes, who jointly signed a letter in 1402 in which they promised to safeguard future peace and to submit to the arbitrating judgment of the queen, the king of Naples, and the dukes of Bourbon and Berry.

Peace was not kept, however, and, fearing Louis's power, Philip issued in 1403 a series of decrees designed to weaken the power of Louis of

[18] See above, Intro. p. 7.
[19] On the royal children, see Grandeau, "Les enfants de Charles vi."
[20] See especially Nordberg, *Les Ducs*, pp. 65-70.

Orleans.[21] The first decree stated that, in the event of the king's death, the dauphin would immediately become king. The second proposed that, in case of the king's inability to rule, the queen, dukes, constable, chancellor, and counsel would govern jointly. A final decree upheld Louis of Guyenne, then only five, as the natural heir. A letter by Charles VI written in May of the same year countermanded these ordinances. Then, in 1404 Philip's death concluded this first stage of the quarrel.

John the Fearless, whom historians have characterized as both ruthless and clever, succeeded his father, Philip, as duke of Burgundy.[23] Like his father, he resented Louis's control of the government, a resentment perhaps aggravated by Queen Isabeau's manifest dislike of John and by her growing friendship with Louis. A crisis occurred in 1405 when, ostensibly fearing John's army of one thousand, Louis and Isabeau left Paris for Melun and Chartres, ordering the dauphin, Louis, to follow them. John overtook the dauphin and triumphantly escorted him back to Paris, where both were praised and welcomed, doubtless in part a response to Burgundian propaganda that the queen and Louis had attempted to kidnap the dauphin.[23]

Minor skirmishes interspersed with public reconciliations marked the next few years. During a celebrated rapprochement in 1406 on the occasion of a double wedding of the Burgundian and Orleanist children, the dukes wore each other's badges: a blunt stick or club was Louis's symbol and a carpenter's plane was John's.[24] Then, in November, 1407, at a reconciliatory dinner at the Hôtel de Nesles, Louis gave John his collar of the Order of the Porcupine as a token of peace between the two houses.[25] Yet, during the same month, apparently without any immediate provocation, assassins hired by the duke of Burgundy murdered Louis of Orleans as he left the queen's house.[26]

The final stage of the quarrel witnessed first the unquestioned ascendancy of John and then his ultimate fall from power.[27] Although royal ordinances of 1407 and 1408 implicitly excluded John from the govern-

---

[21] *Ibid.*, pp. 61-65.

[22] See especially R. Vaughan, *John the Fearless. The Growth of Burgundian Power* (New York, 1966).

[23] L. Mirot, "L'Enlèvement du dauphin et le premier conflit entre Jean sans Peur et Louis d'Orléans (juillet-octobre 1405)," *Revue des questions historiques*, n.s., 51 (1914) 329-335, 52 (1914) 47-68, 369-419; and Famiglietti, *Royal Intrigue.*

[24] Vaughan, *John the Fearless*, p. 38.

[25] Favyn, *Theatre of Honour*, p. 465.

[26] L. Mirot, "Raoul d'Anquetonville et le prix de l'assassinat du duc d'Orléans," BEC 72 (1911) 445-458.

[27] Vaughan, *John the Fearless*, pp. 70ff; and Coville, *Les Cabochiens.*

ment, this exclusion proved short-lived. John openly confessed to the murder of Louis and he effectively turned the assassination into a tool of political propaganda. In 1408 he commissioned Jean Petit, a lawyer and theologian, to draw up a justification for the crime in the form of an elaborate syllogism that sanctioned homicide when it was committed to prevent crimes against the king and state.[28] The justification was publicly delivered and widely accepted as the truth, for when John of Burgundy entered Paris with the king and queen in 1409 he was greeted as a victor. The same year brought the signing of an alliance between Queen Isabeau, John, and members of the House of Bavaria. This alliance, coupled with an ordinance that delegated John as surrogate guardian of Louis of Guyenne,[29] marked John's personal ascendancy over the queen as titular ruler of France. For the next four years, John was nearly always in the company of the king, the queen, and the dauphin, as Louis of Orleans had been in the 1390s.

By 1410, however, the other princes had roused considerable opposition to John through an alliance led by Louis's son, Charles of Orleans, and Bernard VII, count of Armagnac, jointly with the dukes of Berry and Bourbon.[30] Louis of Bourbon was, in fact, one of the principal defenders of Valentine of Orleans and her children's demands for justice until his death in 1410; thereafter John of Bourbon continued to offer support that included armed reinforcements of knights and squires in his service.[31] A civil war in 1411 and 1412 between the Armagnacs and Burgundians resulted, nonetheless, in victory for the Burgundians. During this period much of John's support came from his influence over the dauphin, Louis of Guyenne, who in 1412 was fifteen and married to John's eldest daughter, Margaret of Burgundy.

John's subsequent loss of power, likewise, came from his worsening relationship with the young Louis, who more and more asserted his independence from his father-in-law and surrounded himself with Orleanist sympathizers. Finally, in 1413, the Cabochian revolt resulted in the violent deaths of numerous Parisians, including Burgundians and Orleanists, although John escaped harm.[32] Shortly thereafter, in the summer of 1413, John, waylaid during an abortive attempt to abduct the mad king,

---

[28] A. Coville, *Jean Petit, La question du tyrannicide au commencement du XVe siècle* (Paris, 1932).

[29] Vaughan, *John the Fearless*, p. 81; for a revised reading of the sources, see Famiglietti, *Royal Intrigue*.

[30] Vaughan, *John the Fearless*, and Jacques d'Avout, *La Querelle des Armagnacs et des Bourguignons* (Paris, 1945), pp. 129-159.

[31] Jean Cabernet d'Orville, *Loys de Bourbon*, ed. Chazaud, pp. 309-317.

[32] Coville, *Les Cabochiens*; d'Avout, *La Querelle*, pp. 160-222.

fled to his northern territories. Although he claimed, in the name of the queen, the regency of France in 1418, he did not enjoy his power for long, and was finally assassinated in 1419 on the bridge of Montereau.

A troubled monarchy increasingly beset by internal political difficulties provides a context within which to interpret the pictorial programs of the London and Paris manuscripts. The first step is to try to determine where the Paris and London manuscripts fit in the chronology of these events. Because of the relatively imprecise time span in which they must be dated, it is not possible to place them at an exact moment. But it is probable that both were executed at the climax of the second stage of the Burgundian-Orleanist controversy.

If the Paris manuscript was begun for Louis of Orleans, as Meiss thought, it could even date from the time of the reconciliation, when membership in the Order of the Porcupine was offered as a gesture of peace to the rival duke of Burgundy. In any case, the period from 1406 to 1408, which encompasses the execution of the Paris book, is the interval that includes the climax of events involving these two dukes: the reconciliation, the assassination, and the justification. The London book, produced at the end of this period and still thought timely when it was incorporated into the compendium between 1410 and 1415, was probably done during the aftermath of the assassination, that is, during the third stage of the quarrel. It was during this time that John of Burgundy attempted to press his claims to the throne, partly through his control over the dauphin, who in 1408 was already eleven years old. In 1410, when the London copy could have been inserted in the "Collected Works," the dauphin was thirteen and within one year of the age of majority established for French monarchs.

If we reconsider the London and Paris miniatures of Mars and Minerva within the context of this chronology, their special features, as well as the differences between them, begin to make sense. We should recall that the miniatures alter their models in a fundamental sense. Christine has gone out of her way to emphasize warfare in these illuminations, even in the face of alternative traditions. We may now understand this as reflecting her concern with the discord within the realm, discord in which members of the royal family were directly engaged. Her concern was worked out differently in the individual manuscripts. In the Paris copy, she presented the warring factions in the miniature of Minerva. In the London copy, she underscored the ambitions of the dead duke, Louis of Orleans, in the miniature of Mars, urged the pursuit of peace, and then presented the dauphin, Louis of Guyenne, as an individual who could learn from Minerva, his mother, as she hands out the instruments of war. If this interpretation of the London book is valid, then the dead Louis of Orleans is used there as an example for the future king, Louis of Guyenne. At the beginning of the manuscript, the dedication miniature with its lavish ornamentation helps to insure that the memory of the duke of Orleans pervades the reading of the book.

FRENCH AND TROJAN HISTORY COMMINGLED

Immediately following the planetary deities, to whom Minerva is linked, the Trojan events begin. The first of these, occurring in chapter 14, focuses on Penthesilea, Queen of the Amazons, who because of her fondness for Hector avenged his death. Penthesilea was known for her passion for war, and hence, is depicted riding into battle with her army of female warriors (Figs. 20, 21). From the general similarity of the compositions and the specific parallels in the stances of the horses, we can conclude that a miniature in Boccaccio's *Des Cleres femmes* provided the model for both the Paris and London miniatures in the *Epistre* (Fig. 81). However, in the *Epistre* the miniatures are filled with heraldry, which does not appear in *Des Cleres femmes*. Much of this heraldry is that which was invented for Penthesilea, as can be seen in another manuscript on which Christine's artists worked, *Le Chevalier errant.*[33] Exactly as it appears in *Le Chevalier errant*, Penthesilea's charge — three crowned female heads on a blue ground — is used liberally on the horse, banner, and shield in both copies of the *Epistre*.

Two other shields, which refer to an actual person, are mixed with this fictional heraldry in the London copy (Fig. 20). A black lion rampant on a gold ground appears on a shield held by a woman on Penthesilea's left, and again on a banner directly above her. This was the shield of the count of Flanders, a title that the duke of Burgundy also held.[34] The black lion rampant on a gold ground reappears in the London manuscript fifteen chapters later, in chapter 31, in the miniature that shows Pyrrhus avenging his father's, Achilles's, death by slaying Penthesilea (Fig. 27). It appears nowhere else in the London copy and never appears in the Paris copy (Fig. 28).

What are we to make of these references to the duke of Burgundy? Two factors contribute significantly to the interpretation of the shields. First,

---

[33] Paris, BN MS fr. 12559, reproduced in Meiss, *Limbourgs*, Fig. 48.

[34] Paul Adam-Even, *L'Armorial universel du héraut Gelre* (Archives héraldiques suisses, 1971), Pl. 15.

the shields occur only in the London manuscript, which as we have already noted, postdates the death of Louis of Orleans, an event that led to the ascendancy of the duke of Burgundy. Second, they appear only in miniatures that depict episodes occurring after the death of Hector but intimately related to it. We have already understood that the model of Hector can be identified with Louis of Orleans. The miniatures in the London copy thus can be seen as referring to the duke of Burgundy's rise to power which was brought about by Louis's death.

A little later in the *Epistre*, in chapter 34, the unusual image of Atropos functions partly as a reference to the French monarchy (Figs. 30, 31). Atropos, whom Christine says "the poets call death," reminds Hector of his own mortality.[35] One reason for looking closely at these illuminations in both the Paris and London books is that Atropos does not occur in Christine's usual sources, such as *Ovide moralisé* or the *Histoire ancienne.* It has been shown that Christine turned to an Italian tradition of depicting death as Atropos who was one of the three fates, although death was depicted more commonly in the northern tradition as a skeleton.[36] Following Italian representations, her illuminators portrayed Atropos with disheveled hair, darkened skin, and a bare hanging breast. This depiction accords closely with a description of Atropos given in another of Christine's works, the *Mutacion de fortune*, in which Atropos is guardian of one of the gates leading to the castle of Fortune.[37]

Not only did Christine transform the customary imagery of death into a humanist portrayal of Atropos, she also departed from the standard imagery of Atropos. In the *Epistre* she represents Atropos in the clouds, according to the model she set up for all the gods and goddesses which begins with the first miniature of Othea. Further, she uses a variation on the "children of the planets" imagery, in which those individuals at whom Atropos aims her darts are shown below her as though influenced by her. What we see is indeed a distinguished company. A king, a pope, two princes, and a cardinal are apt illustrations of Christine's characterization of Atropos who "smites and spares no one."[38] Once again, the visual imagery is reminiscent of a passage in the *Mutacion* where Christine says that individuals of all ranks — kings, princes, "all creatures born" — come

---

[35] London, BL Harley MS 4431, fol. 111; Christine, *Epistle of Othea,* tr. Scrope, p. 45.

[36] M. Meiss, "Atropos-Mors; Observations on a Rare Early Humanist Image," in *Florilegium Historiale. Essays Presented to Wallace K. Ferguson,* ed. J. G. Rowe and W. H. Stockdale (Toronto, 1971), pp. 152-159.

[37] Christine, *Mutacion de fortune,* ed. Solente, 1: 103-104.

[38] London, BL Harley MS 4431, fol. 111; Christine *Epistle of Othea,* tr. Scrope, p. 45. Only the figure of the king is correctly identified by Willard, *Christine de Pizan,* p. 96.

under her power at the time of their deaths.[39] The king and the pope on the far right stand out in the miniature, particularly since the other figures have fallen and only they remain kneeling upright beneath the figure of death.

In the London manuscript, the miniature of Atropos is the first, apart from the dedication miniature, to portray individuals who can be read unambiguously as actual persons: the king and the pope (Fig. 30). Situated on the far right, the king wears the fleur-de-lis crown and a blue mantle decorated with gold embroidered designs over a scarlet robe. This is the costume worn by French kings at state occasions and other ceremonious events; it appears on Charles VI in the second dedication miniature of Pierre Salmon's *Demandes et lamentations.*[40] It seems likely, therefore, that this king is meant to represent King Charles VI. Next to him kneels a pope, whose office is clearly indicated by the papal tiara. Over a white robe he wears an orange-red mantle that is decorated with a cone-like plant. The same garment is worn by Pope Alexander V as he is portrayed in Salmon's *Demandes*, so that it is probable that Alexander is depicted in the *Epistre* as well (Fig. 83).

These details of costume are sufficient to associate the king and pope with King Charles VI and Alexander V, but some portrait-like features strengthen the identifications. Charles VI was blond, with a pronounced nose, high cheekbones, and square jaw, as he is shown here.[41] Pope Alexander V, the Greek-born Petros Philigari, was dark with a swarthy complexion, round face and black hair, as he appears in this miniature, as well as in that in Salmon's manuscript.[42]

If this reading is valid, how are we to understand the presence of King Charles VI and Pope Alexander V in the London miniature? On the simplest level, the London miniature is a rather inventive variation of the *memento mori* iconography designed to prompt viewers to reflect on

---

[39] Christine, *Mutacion de fortune*, 1: 105.

[40] Paris, BN MS fr. 23279, illustrated in Meiss, *Boucicaut*, Fig. 67.

[41] On these and other images of Charles VI, see C. Maumené and L. d'Harcourt, *Iconographie des rois de France*, Pt. 1, *De Louis IX à Louis XIII, Archives de l'art français* 15 (Paris, 1928; rept. 1973) 59-64. Reproductions appear in B. de Montfaucon, *Les Monumens de la monarchie françoise*, 5 vols. (Paris, 1729-1733), 3: 180, Pl. 26; catalogued by Bouchot, *Inventaire des dessins*, 1: 53 and 226; see also Joseph Guibert, *Les Dessins d'archéologie de Roger de Gaignières*, 3 vols. in 15 (Paris, 1912-1913), ser. 1, *Les tombeaux*, and L. Magne, *Le Palais de justice de Poitiers, étude sur l'art français au XIVe et au XVe siècles* (Paris, 1904), Pls. 3 and 6.

[42] See above, n. 40, and N. Valois, *La France et le grand schisme d'Occident*, 4 vols. (Paris, 1886-1902), 4: 109-112.

death in order to motivate pious behavior.[43] It makes clear that death in the person of Atropos eventually reaches out for everyone, even the reigning king and pope. Seen in this way, the London miniature presents a somewhat more personalized form of the *memento mori* type, referring as it does to specific individuals.

But given that the *Epistre* was written for a French prince who was being trained to rule, the London miniature may also have served to evoke for the dauphin associations at the thought of the actual deaths of King Charles VI and Pope Alexander V. During the last years of the decade, Charles VI was increasingly unwell.[44] His repeated relapses of madness left him virtually unable to rule, and as a result the government was increasingly turned over to the young dauphin. Recalling that the earlier miniature of Mars seemed to address the dauphin, here too perhaps the dauphin was being warned of the death of his father, an event that would offcially place the reins of state in his hands.

The simultaneous reference to Alexander V could allude to the similarly precarious state of the papacy during the time of the schism.[45] Elected in 1409 by the Council of Pisa, Alexander V was declared by the council to be the official pope. According to the terms of his election, he thus replaced the two reigning popes, Benedict XIII and Gregory XII, who were accused at the same time of being heretics. This strategy was unsuccessful, however. Instead of ending the schism, it inaugurated a three-fold division: the popes Benedict XIII and Gregory XII resided in Avignon and Rome respectively, and Alexander was lodged in Pisa. Yet Alexander was the French favorite, in whom hopes of Church unity rested. His proposed inclusion here may have been meant to warn that his death, which occurred in 1410, might prolong the schism. If this identification is valid, then it would also serve to date the London copy more precisely, specifically to after 1409.

In the Paris version of the same subject, such particularizing details are absent (Fig. 31). Neither the royal nor the papal costumes are clearly delineated. Nor do the facial types correspond with those of the king or the pope. Two historical circumstances may explain these differences. First, Alexander's election, which brought to a head the crisis within the

---

[43] On this iconography, see E. Mâle, *L'Art religieux de la fin du moyen âge en France*, 5th ed. (Paris, 1949), pp. 347-389; Raimond van Marle, *Iconographie de l'art profane au Moyen-Âge et à la Renaissance*, 2 vols. (The Hague, 1932), 2: 361-414.

[44] Brachet, *Pathologie mentale*, pp. 637-646.

[45] On the schism during these years, see Valois, *La France et le grand schisme*, 4: 75-157.

Church, occurred after the manuscript was produced. And second, Charles VI's illness was more serious, and therefore more of an issue later in the decade than it had been at the time of the execution of the Paris book.

In the Paris and London copies a more direct allusion to the health of Charles VI may have been made only five chapters later, in chapter 39. The examples of Aesculapius, the Greek physician, and Circe, the Greek enchantress, are used in the text and gloss to contrast the virtues of medicine with the hazards of sorcery.[46] Then, in the allegory, they teach the fifth commandment, "Thou shalt not kill." In this way, the chapter is made to fit in a series of examples of the Ten Commandments, such as the abduction of Helen in chapter 43 which understandably teaches the ninth commandment, "Thou shalt not covet thy neighbor's wife." Tuve puzzled over the allegory to chapter 39, however, wondering what could have prompted Christine to associate medicine and sorcery with killing, an association for which Tuve could find no precedent.[47]

Other features of this chapter also seem peculiar, although Tuve did not comment further on it. After offering the fifth commandment as a lesson, the allegory goes on to say that it is defensible for princes or judges to execute wrong-doers, but only when they have authority to act in this way. As an explication of the fifth commandment, this line of reasoning seems odd, since it concentrates on the punishment of evil-doers rather than on evil deeds themselves, such as murder. The very combination of Aesculapius and Circe is also exceptional. Both are treated in the *Ovide*, from which Christine took her information, but the accounts are separated by twelve books rather than joined in one passage.[48] Moreover, manuscripts of the *Ovide* do not usually include an illustration of Aesculapius, although one of Circe is consistently present. In a departure from tradition, the two individuals appear together in the *Epistre*, where Aesculapius examines a flask used to test urine, while Circe collects toads from a nearby stream (Fig. 34). Another, unidentified, woman stands beside Aesculapius. What all of this suggests is that Christine went out of her way in both text and image to contrast medicine with sorcery, a contrast that brought up for her associations with killing and, further, triggered thoughts about the execution of wrong-doers.

---

[46] London, BL Harley MS 4431, fol. 113v; Christine, *Epistle of Othea*, tr. Scrope, pp. 51-52.

[47] Tuve, *Allegorical Imagery*.

[48] *Ovide moralisé*, ed. de Boer, Bks. 2: 2426-2429; 14: 2355-2562.

All of its peculiarities are understandable if we see this chapter as being inspired by contemporary events. Shortly after the king's first episode of madness in 1392, attempts were initiated to cure him.[49] Throughout this decade those closest to the court were unsure about the cause of his illness, however. The suspicion that he was being slowly poisoned, and therefore was not mad at all, was a recurring sentiment. As a result, in 1393 a doctor who was a specialist in poisons was called in. But the most notorious of these ministrations, and the one to which the text and picture may refer, involved two monks, who were likewise brought in to cure the king. In 1397 they prescribed a series of dietary restrictions from which Charles VI seemed initially to improve. Then in 1398 his condition again worsened. When the monks were unable this time to restore his health, they accused Louis of Orleans of practicing sorcery on the king. This accusation was taken very seriously. For example, it even prompted Deschamps to write a treatise to Louis on the harms of sorcery.[50] Louis, in turn, had the monks accused, tried, and convicted on the charges of practicing black magic or sorcery. The suspicion that Louis of Orleans was an accomplice, along with his wife, Valentine, in attempts to poison the king was an enduring one. It was entertained again in 1408, when it was offered as a justification for Louis's murder.[51]

Returning to the content of the chapter on Aesculapius and Circe, then, it seems likely that these two individuals were discussed together because the practice of medicine versus the use of sorcery had been a serious and persistent issue with regard to Charles VI's health. It was an issue that, moreover, directly involved Louis of Orleans, to whom the *Epistre* is dedicated. The reference to the fifth commandment may now be seen to have been inspired by fears that the use of sorcery might even kill the king. And the accompanying commentary about the execution of evil-doers would seem to justify Louis's execution of the monks.

All of this should be seen in the context of Christine's own grave concern over the problem of Charles VI's illness. When writing the *Mutacion* between 1400 and 1403, she expressed her wish that Fortune would intervene to cure the king.[52] In 1405, in *Le Corps*, she elaborated on the metaphor of the state as a human body, the head of which was the

---

[49] A summary of these events is found in Brachet, *Pathologie mentale*, pp. 628ff, and below ch. 4, pp. 167-169.

[50] Deschamps, *Démonstracions contre sortileges*, in *Œuvres* 7: 192-199 and 11: 148-155.

[51] A. Coville, *Jean Petit.*

[52] Christine, *Mutacion de fortune*, ed. Solente.

ruler. She expressed the belief that the head of state must be in good health, sane, because if he is ill the effects will be felt by all.[53] We have also seen her concern with insanity in the *Epistre*, where the planetary goddess Phoebe influenced madness by imparting melancholy or frenzy to her children. Then, in chapter 39, Christine cautions that only doctors, not those who use spells, charms, or magic, can cure the sick.

Within the sequence of chapters on the Ten Commandments, a number of other subjects may be understood to refer to actual individuals or concrete events. One of these is chapter 36 on Memnon who was a king of Ethiopia and son of Eos and Tithonus. Christine's text signals Memnon's importance in relation to Hector, when it informs the reader three times in twenty-five lines that Memnon and Hector were cousins.[54] Her gloss explains that as a loyal cousin Memnon often came to Hector's aid, and on one occasion wounded Hector's archenemy, Achilles. The gloss continues to urge all princes and knights to follow Memnon's model; they should love their relatives, support their endeavors, and be loyal to them. Oddly, the allegory is on the second commandment, "Thou shalt not take the name of God in vain." It makes special reference to bearing false witness, perjury, and blasphemy.

As an illustration of this chapter, the miniature of Memnon in the London manuscript is initially puzzling. A fully armored warrior bearing a sword prepares to attack a prince whose red garment is decorated in gold with the royal emblem, the broom flower (Fig. 32).[55] The prince also wears a necklace composed of links that resemble broom pods. In the face of imminent calamity, the calm outfitting of the apparently anonymous knight in the foreground appears secondary. The importance of the background action is emphasized further by the considerably greater scale of these individuals when compared with those in the foreground. The identities of Memnon and Achilles, the subjects of the chapter, are not made clear in the illustration.

Instead of illustrating literally the combat between Memnon and Achilles, the background incident may be meant to recall the treacherous assassination of Louis of Orleans by his cousin John of Burgundy. The chief reason for advancing this interpretation is the design on the costume

[53] Christine, *Le Corps de policie*, ed. Lucas, pp. 4-5.

[54] London, BL Harley MS 4431, fol. 112; Christine, *Epistle of Othea*, tr. Scrope, p. 47.

[55] Broom was the most common emblem of Charles VI who had garments, tapestries, standards, banners, and saddles all decorated with it. See Douët-d'Arcq, *Pièces inédites*, 2: 395-399; *idem, Compte de l'Argenterie*, pp. 161, 196, 198, 306, *passim*, and below, ch. 4, pp. 176-178.

of the prince dressed in red. Louis would have been the only person, apart from the king and the dauphin, suited to wear the broom flower and pod as they appear here. If we recall that Louis and John were cousins, like Hector and Memnon, the advice of the text acquires special force when read with the miniature. The miniature becomes a kind of counter-example to the message of the text, which dwells on the virtues of family ties. By engaging in internecine quarrels, neither cousin took the advice in Christine's gloss. Moreover, in his defense of Louis's murder, John had been accused of bearing false witness and of perjury.[56] That is, he violated the second commandment referred to in the allegory. The details of the Paris miniature do not evoke such specific associations (Fig. 33).

Still within the sequence of the Ten Commandments, one other chapter places Louis of Orleans and John of Burgundy in the context of Trojan history. In chapter 43, the Greek messengers come before King Priam and Helen, asking the king to return Helen to the Greeks. In the case of this subject, miniatures in the Paris and London versions make different contemporary references that help us to define further the changed concerns in the programs of the two books.

In the Paris copy, King Priam is enthroned on the right beneath a red and white canopy on a green ground (Fig. 37). Two figures at the king's left look toward the Greek messengers who stand in the doorway. It would appear that the messengers have just requested the king to allow Helen to return with them. It would seem further that Priam, who raises his right hand toward them while he engages in conversation with Helen, has refused. Two details specify the contemporary reference. First, the white, red, and green colors of the cloth of honor are those of *Bourgogne moderne*.[57] Second, the Greek knight on the left wears a collar of mail that closely resembles the collar of the Order of the Porcupine, although it lacks the suspended porcupine. If we try to understand the meaning of these details within the context of the subject of the miniature, it would seem that the conflict between the Greeks and the Trojans is presented as the conflict between the houses of Orleans and Burgundy.

A number of details have been changed in the London copy (Fig. 36). References to Burgundy have been made even more explicit. Not only is the cloth of honor decorated with the Burgundian colors of white, red, and green, but the garment of the prince on the right of Priam suggests Burgundy. This prince wears a tunic of green cloth, the favorite color of

---

[56] Coville, *Jean Petit*.

[57] Laborde, *Les Ducs*, 2.1: 67, 73, 76, and *passim*. I thank Michel Pastoureau for his identification of the Burgundian colors in this miniature.

the duke of Burgundy.[58] It is decorated with oak leaves, a device used by many different princes at the royal court, but associated here with Burgundy because of its simultaneous appearance on the cloth of honor, which is decorated with his colors.[59] At the same time, references to Orleans have been omitted altogether. The messenger on the left no longer wears a collar of mail, and no other particularizing details have taken the place of this one. One additional emblematic detail suggests a reference to yet another individual, however. The plain gold and white floor tiles, comparable to those in the Paris miniature, are inset in the London picture with clusters of other tiles composed of the four colors of the king: red, white, black, and green.[60] The sum of these changed details suggests that the London miniature is in some way about the kingdom of France and the house of Burgundy instead of the houses of Orleans and Burgundy.

A few other minor compositional changes suggest that the London miniature presents a slightly altered version of the story which may help us to understand the changes in emblematic details. In the London picture, Priam no longer seems to gesture negatively. The subtle change in the position of his hand now implies an animated discussion with Helen. Instead, the prince who wears the Burgundian costume and stands next to Priam holds up his hand to tell the Greek messengers that Helen will not return with them. In the Paris version, this prince plays a passive role; both hands hang limp at his side and his costume is undistinguished. In other words, a prince of Troy instead of King Priam makes this important decision about the return of Helen. Returning now to a consideration of the emblems in the miniature, we should understand that this prince may be taken for the duke of Burgundy and the king for the king of France. The miniature thus presents the chamber of the king under the influence of the duke, a message that corresponds with the reality of royal and ducal power during the years immediately following the assassination. It should be added that in the miniature the duke, rather than the king, makes the wrong decision, since the failure to return Helen to the Greeks hastened the downfall of Troy.

[58] On John the Fearless's love of green, see the documents in Laborde, *Les Ducs*, 2.1: 67, 73, 76, 77, and *passim*; and Evans, *Dress in Mediaeval France*, p. 38. He wears green trimmed in red in Salmon's *Demandes*, Paris, BN MS fr. 23279, fol. 53, reproduced in Meiss, *Boucicaut*, Fig. 67.

[59] See above, pp. 54 and 104.

[60] On the king's colors, see Jal, *Dictionnaire critique de biographie et d'histoire*, 2nd ed. (Paris, 1872), p. 364, and G. Desjardins, *Recherches sur les drapeaux français. Oriflamme, bannière de France, marques nationales, couleurs du roi, drapeaux de l'armée, pavillons de la marine* (Paris, 1874), pp. 23-24.

Sometimes the miniatures make points about the nature of government without including such concrete references. For example, in chapters 40 and 41, which immediately precede the chapter on the Greek messengers' approach to Priam, come two miniatures illustrating the stories of Paris slaying Achilles and Busiris's human sacrifices (Fig. 35). The placement of the miniatures on the same page and their parallel settings (each show temples adorned with statues of pagan gods) establish an interrelationship between them that is not so explicit in the text. The glosses for these two chapters counsel the knight in relatively general terms to beware his enemies and to moderate his behavior by following good examples.[61] The allegories teach the sixth and seventh commandments: "Thou shalt not commit adultery" and "Thou shalt not steal." In each picture, a ruler oversees a murder. On the left, Queen Hecuba watches as Paris slays Achilles at her command. On the right, King Busiris, not content with mere slaughter, delights also in making sacrifices to the gods. Viewing the miniatures together leads us to read this page as a lesson on bad government or, more specifically, on bad queenship juxtaposed to bad kingship. The fact that this page immediately precedes the chapter concerning Priam and Helen gives it an added impact. If the ruler learns to govern well, he will be able to exercise the proper judgment needed to make important decisions that affect the fate of his kingdom.

Shortly thereafter in the Paris copy of the *Epistre*, another, relatively frivolous reference to Charles VI occurs. Charles appears at the beginning of chapter 47 in the guise of a heavenly Cupid who greets a young courtier (Fig. 38). Cupid's green garment is decorated with a white fleur-de-lis design. His wings are composed of peacock feathers. In order to view this miniature as a representation of Charles VI as Cupid, it is necessary to realize, as contemporary viewers would have, that the king as the God of Love was head of a society called the *Cour d'amours*.[62] Instituted in 1401 in the presence of the king, this society was composed of several hundred members who together resolved to promote the writing of love poetry. Emphasizing Charles VI's nominal patronage of the society, a manuscript of its founding charter was prefaced by the fleur-de-lis arms shown above

---

[61] London, BL Harley MS 4431, fol. 114r-114v; Christine, *Epistle of Othea*, tr. Scrope, pp. 52-53.

[62] On the court of love, see O. LeMaire, "La Cour amoureuse de Paris, fondée en 1401 et ses armoriaux," *Le Blason. Revue mensuelle belge de généalogie, d'héraldique et de sigillographie* 10 (1956) 66-78; F. Diez, *Essai sur les cours d'amour* (Paris, 1842); A. Piaget, "Un Manuscrit de la Cour amoureuse," *Romania* 31 (1902) 597-603; and *idem*, "La Cour amoureuse dite de Charles VI," *Romania* 20 (1891) 417-454.

a ground strewn with his royal emblems, which include peacock feathers, broom sprays, and peapods (Fig. 84).[63] Two of Charles's symbols, the peacock and the lion, flank the shield on left and right. What argues in favor of an identification of Cupid as Charles is, thus, the portrayal of the figure of Cupid as a crowned king whose costume is decorated with Charles's emblems, specifically the fleur-de-lis and the peacock feathers.[64]

It might be objected that in representing Cupid as a crowned figure of princely status, Christine's illuminators were merely following the well-established tradition of picturing the God of Love after his description in the *Roman de la Rose*.[65] According to the celebrated poem, he is supposed to be crowned, winged, finely attired, and armed with arrows as his weapons of love. Since this description is fully in line with Cupid's portrayal in the Paris book, it might be said that he is not Charles VI but only the princely Cupid. But if we compare the Paris miniature with others that represent the God of Love, we find that there are a few differences. For example, the London "Collected Works" includes a copy of Christine's *Epistre au dieu d'amours*,[66] which is prefaced by a frontispiece of Cupid as the God of Love in which Cupid is depicted according to his description in the *Roman* (Fig. 85). But he does not wear a fleur-de-lis robe or have peacock-feather wings. Nor is he depicted with these special features in the London copy of the *Epistre Othéa*. It would seem then that these two details have been added to the customary iconography of Cupid only in the Paris miniature. Their addition transforms the more usual portrayal of Cupid to suggest Charles VI's position as God of Love in the society of the *Cour d'amours*.

GOOD GOVERNMENT AND THE ROLE OF FORTUNE

The reader never reads very far in the *Epistre* without encountering a commentary on government. The next explicit one occurs in the miniature that prefaces chapter 60 in both the Paris and London copies (Figs.

[63] Discussed by C. Nordenfalk, "Hatred, Hunting, and Love: Three Themes Relative to Some Manuscripts of Jean sans Peur," in *Late Medieval and Renaissance Painting in Honor of Millard Meiss*, ed. I. Lavin and J. Plummer (New York, 1977), pp. 324-341.

[64] On the peacock feather as an emblem of Charles, see the documents published by Douët-d'Arcq, *Pièces inédites*, 2: 397; the costume decorated with peacock feathers worn by Charles in the Geneva version of Salmon's *Demandes*, reproduced in Meiss, *Boucicaut*, Figs. 69, 72; and Vaivre, "À Propos des devises," pp. 94-95.

[65] This iconography has been aptly elucidated by E. Panofsky, *Studies in Iconology, Humanistic Themes in the Art of the Renaissance* (New York, 1939), pp. 95-128, esp. 101-102.

[66] This poem has been studied by Willard, "A New Look," pp. 73-92.

41, 42). These miniatures illustrate the wedding of Peleus and Thetis, a subject that was discussed in the *Ovide* and alluded to in the *Histoire*.[67] It was not usually illustrated in the *Ovide*, although it was pictured in the *Histoire*, but in an entirely different fashion.[68] The imagery of the *Epistre* thus appears to be unprecedented. Here, the wedding is a royal feast at which the tables have been arranged in three tiers. The highest members of the court attend, including three French kings and an emperor seated at the upper tier. Queens occupy the middle and lower levels. Semele, goddess of discord, has entered and stands in the lower right. She places the apple on the table in front of her. However, at the upper table the emperor already holds an apple, while three kings seem to covet it, if we can interpret their expressions and gestures in this way.

Two features of the chapter, in addition to the unusual composition of the wedding as a French royal banquet, encourage us to interpret this miniature as a political allegory. The first is pictorial and the second textual. First, the presence of two apples in the miniature is odd, since it departs entirely from the story, which specifies only one. When we look closely we realize, furthermore, that neither apple is painted naturalistically; both are rendered in gold leaf. This depiction transforms the apple from an ordinary fruit into the orb of rule, which is depicted in this same way in Salmon's *Demandes* where the orb is referred to figuratively as a golden apple.[69] The fact that in the *Epistre* one of these golden apples is held by the emperor at the uppermost table further confirms this interpretation of it as an orb of rule.

Second, the allegory of the text is strongly worded and would appear to have nothing to do with the subject of the wedding itself. It cautions the knight to avoid strife and riots: "for to strive against peace is madness, to strive against one's sovereign is insanity, and to strive against one's subjects is great villany."[70] Thus the conflict over the orb of rule that takes

[67] *Ovide moralisé*, ed. de Boer, Bk. 11: 1242-1315; for the relevant passage in the *Histoire* see Paris, BN MS fr. 301, fol. 36.

[68] For example, Paris, BN MS fr. 301, fol. 35v, where three women appear seated at a table.

[69] Paris, BN MS fr. 23279, fol. 9v: "[the king must] ... tenir ... en la senestre main un pomme ou semblance ronde ... Et par la pomme ou semblance ronde qu'il tient en sa main senestre nous est montré qu'il doit entendre et considérer devement et faire droitare: c'est assavoir refraindre les mauvais et soustenir les bons en leur droit." This text is partially transcribed in P. Salmon, *Les Demandes faites par le Roi Charles VI touchant son état et le gouvernement de sa personne, avec les réponses de Pierre Salmon*, ed. C. Crapelet (Paris, 1833), p. 23.

[70] London, BL Harley MS 4431, fol. 122v-123r; Christine, *Epistle of Othea*, tr. Scrope, p. 75.

place at the upper table between the kings and emperor has a parallel in the conflict described in the text. If we now read all of this according to the contemporary context established for the manuscripts, that is, with the knowledge that they are dedicated to Louis of Orleans, we can surmise that this chapter warns against the duke's rivalry with his brother for the throne, with his cousin John of Burgundy for the regency, and with the emperor for the empire.

Later miniatures in the London and Paris manuscripts make an equally pointed reference to the government of France, one that is important for our understanding of the political allegory. In chapter 74, the goddess Fortune cautions Hector to trust not in the promises of Fortune because even the highest personages sometimes fall from her favor.[71] As an illustration to this chapter, the blindfolded goddess, dressed in a blue robe, turns the Wheel of Fortune to which six persons, including one king, cling (Figs. 43, 44). The rather general account of Fortune's activities in the *Epistre* could have come from a number of textual sources used by Christine in which Fortune appeared, including Boethius's *Consolation of Philosophy* and Dante's *Divine Comedy*.[72] She returned again and again to the role of Fortune, even writing between 1400 and 1403 a long allegorical poem, the *Mutacion de fortune*, in which Fortune is the principal subject. Miniatures in the *Mutacion* depict the dwelling place of Fortune, her appearance, and her brothers, Eur and Meseur, personae who came to stand for the two sides of Fortune's character.[73] The very fact that the depictions of Fortune are so different in the *Mutacion* and in the *Epistre* leads us to look carefully at the imagery in the *Epistre* in an attempt to ascertain whether it fulfills special demands of the ideological program.

If we compare the miniature of the Wheel of Fortune in the *Epistre* with those in the *Histoire ancienne*, its probable source, we see that they display a similar iconography of the wheel (Fig. 86).[74] A king appears astride the top of the wheel, and various other figures are positioned around its circumference. The goddess Fortune stands on one side,

---

[71] London, BL Harley MS 4431, fol. 129r; Christine, *Epistle of Othea*, tr. Scrope, p. 91.

[72] On Christine's use of these texts, see Campbell, *L'Épitre d'Othéa*, pp. 64, 120, 152, 185.

[73] The illustrations to various manuscripts of the *Mutacion* are discussed and reproduced in Meiss, *Limbourgs*, 2: Figs. 1, 2, 14-16, 19-34.

[74] On the iconography of Fortune in the *Histoire ancienne*, see Buchthal, *Historia Troiana*, pp. 18-19. Other standard studies include A. Doren, "Fortuna im Mittelalter und in der Renaissance," *Vorträge der Bibliothek Warburg* 2 (1922-1923) 71-144; and H. R. Patch, *The Goddess Fortuna in Mediaeval Literature* (Cambridge, Mass., 1927).

turning the wheel by means of a handle that she rotates in the *Histoire* and by pushing down (or pulling up) on a spoke in the *Epistre*. This composition expresses the idea that Fortune controls the destinies of all figures, including rulers.

What distinguishes the miniature in the *Epistre* from those in the *Histoire* (and from all others that I know of) is the representation of the individuals placed on the wheel. In the *Histoire*, the individuals who occupy four different positions around the circumference of the wheel are accompanied by inscriptions. A king sits upright at the highest position, and next to him an inscription states "I reign." On the right, another individual, who in some examples is also a king, faces downward as he descends the wheel and illustrates "I have reigned." On the left, a third individual, again frequently a king, ascends the wheel as an illustration of the words "I will reign." Finally, at the lowest position on the wheel is an individual whose inscription states "I am without reign." In some examples from the *Histoire* it is the image of King Priam that is repeated at different locations around the wheel.[75] Such miniatures convey the precarious nature of rulership.

A look at the equivalent figures in the *Epistre* suggests that Christine has modified the iconography of the Wheel of Fortune known to her from the *Histoire*. Using six instead of four figures, she has created a link between the three uppermost figures by representing all of them seated upright, as though enthroned, instead of showing the lateral figures clinging to the wheel, one in an ascending and the other in a descending posture. The two individuals on either side of the king seem to be given more prominence in this new iconography. Instead of interpreting one as a previous and the other as a future king, the viewer can more readily understand each as a potential ruler. In other words, the sense of the inevitable, everchanging destiny of a particular reign, as communicated in the traditional iconography in the *Histoire*, has been altered. The fact that we can no longer so easily imagine the wheel rotating in the *Epistre*, since all three figures seem to be stable at its top, contributes to our different perception of the Wheel of Fortune.

The portrayal in the *Epistre* of the two individuals seated alongside the king departs in other ways from that in the *Histoire* and encourages us to read the entire miniature of the Wheel of Fortune as a contemporary allusion. In the *Epistre*, these two figures are princes, not kings. By their costume, they may even be intended to be interpreted as specific princes.

[75] Buchthal, *Historia Troiana*, p. 18, pl. 17b-17c.

In the London and Paris versions, the prince on the right is dressed in a pale purple robe and wears a square black hat with a jewel pinned to it. This is the style of hat much favored by Louis of Orleans, who wears it as an accessory to his costume in the dedication miniature in the first autograph of the *Epistre* (Fig. 1).[76] Additional support for the interpretation of this figure as Louis comes from another manuscript, Salmon's *Demandes*. Executed by the same artists who painted the London *Epistre*, miniatures in Salmon's book repeatedly portray Louis wearing a black hat identical to this one, as well as a pale purple robe.[77]

If we can accept the figure on the right as Louis, then who is the figure on the left who seems to have an equal status? Given the similar status, only two possibilities are plausible. He could be John the Fearless, duke of Burgundy, or Louis of Guyenne, the dauphin of France. Both these princes were fair, and both preferred green,[78] the color worn by the figure in the London book, so the details of the portrayal assist little in our identification of this figure. Yet, the fact that the prince on the left seems youthful, coupled with the facts that in the Paris book he wears a necklace whose parts resemble broom pods and holds a baton normally carried by rulers, may support the view that this figure is meant to be the duke of Guyenne.

Christine has still preserved the general correspondence between parts of the wheel and the fate of rulers, by using a model from the *Histoire*. Viewers familiar with this model would thus understand the person portrayed on the right has reigned while the one on the left will reign. This interpretation of the miniature is confirmed by our knowledge that Louis of Orleans, the figure on the right, was in fact dead at the time of its execution. The adolescent Louis of Guyenne is shown next in line for the throne. His placement face to face with his murdered uncle thus underscores the idea that Louis of Orleans is meant to serve as a model here, as in the dedication miniature, for the duke of Guyenne. It is surely no accident that the pictorial model for King Charles VI at the top is the Trojan king Priam, since this reinforces the idea of the Trojan story as a lesson for the rulers of the present day.

Coming at this place in the *Epistre*, the miniature of Fortune is a critical one for the development of the Trojan story. Its placement on the page with the miniature of Paris embracing Helen emphasizes its importance.

---

[76] See above, ch. 1, n. 64.

[77] Paris, BN MS fr. 23279, fol. 70r.

[78] On the dauphin's preference for green, see L. Pannier, "Les Joyaux du duc de Guyenne. Recherches sur les goûts artistiques et la vie privée du dauphin Louis, fils de Charles VI," *Revue archéologique*, 2ᵉ série, 26 (1873) 218-219.

The text of this next chapter hints that if only Paris had been as thoroughly conditioned for warfare as he was interested in love, Troy might not have fallen.[79] The fact that another key event in the history of Troy, the judgment of Paris, immediately precedes the chapter on Fortune further highlights Fortune's role in the events that are to come. Those episodes that are most critical to the outcome of the Trojan war are concentrated in the last quarter of the book; some of the most important appear soon after the chapter on Fortune.

Sandwiched between two critical events and preceding a narrative in which the Trojan story evolves at a rapid pace, the chapter on Fortune is of obvious significance. It seems important, then, to find out how Christine understood the role of Fortune in order to understand further the function of Fortune at this point in the *Epistre*. To do this, we can most easily turn to the *Mutacion*, since it was written around the same time as the *Epistre*. Fortune is not always cruel, does not always exert a negative influence. For example, in the beginning of the *Mutacion*, Christine constructs an allegory in which she and her beloved husband are sailing when he is taken and drowned by Fortune.[80] His premature death is attributed to Fortune's cruel wiles. Afterward, however, Fortune again intervenes, this time to help Christine, whom she turns into a man in order to teach her how to navigate her own ship. Unlike Atropos, Fortune's wishes are not always inevitable; she does not always exercise a will against which mankind is powerless. Later in the *Mutacion*, when Christine discusses the rulers who have succumbed to Fortune's will, she particularly admonishes John the Fearless for being too easily lured by what Fortune offers – that is, by honor and riches.[81] An antidote to Fortune's wishes is put forward, however: wisdom.[82]

Christine's belief in the value of wisdom that brings about good judgment in the face of Fortune – not in the power of Fortune – stands behind the *Mutacion*. It also helps to explain Fortune's portrayal in the *Epistre*, where, even as the goddess Fortune blindly spins her wheel, she offers the example of Louis of Orleans to Louis of Guyenne in the hope that the latter will learn to rule well.

---

[79] London, BL Harley MS 4431, fol. 129v; Christine, *Epistle of Othea*, tr. Scrope, p. 92.

[80] Christine, *Mutacion de fortune*, ed. Solente, 1: 46-53.

[81] *Ibid.*

[82] *Ibid.* For Christine's view of history in the *Mutacion*, see also Nadja Margolis, "The Poetics of History: An Analysis of Christine de Pizan's *Livre de la Mutacion de Fortune*," Unpublished doctoral dissertation, Stanford University, 1977.

HISTORICAL EXEMPLA AS MODELS OF ADVICE

Wisdom that influences judgment, specifically with respect to the course of the Trojan war, is the subject of chapters 77 and 80, which focus on Hector's brothers, Helenus and Troilus (Figs. 45, 46). Helenus and Troilus advised Paris and Priam respectively. The older brother, Helenus, offered judicious advice but was ignored. The younger one, Troilus, gave bad advice that was contrary to the prophecies but nevertheless overruled the advice of the wiser counselors. Neither subject is illustrated in manuscripts of the *Histoire*, Christine's source for the information in these chapters. As her model for the miniatures of these brothers, she turned instead to a Bible or a Book of Hours, appropriately adapting a miniature of Christ among the doctors,[83] the theme of which is also wisdom. The common theme of these chapters in the *Epistre* is thus reinforced by this reference to a well-known model. We are led to understand from text and image alike that the fall of Troy could have been avoided, since the wisdom necessary to proceed along the correct course existed, but that good judgment was lacking.

The glosses and allegories of these two chapters reinforce this idea by focusing on the opposition between wisdom and ignorance.[84] In chapter 77, Christine urges the knight to heed the counsel of wise authorities. Then, in the gloss for chapter 80, she cites a quotation from Augustine: "the land is miserable when the prince is a child." In a regime increasingly dependent on an adolescent dauphin, Louis of Guyenne, such a quotation, however commonplace, must have struck with special force. Using exceptionally forceful language in the allegory, she elaborates by teaching that ignorance is an evil mother whose two daughters could be called deviousness and suspicion. While the first is merely naughty and vicious, the second is wretched and still more disagreeable. Ignorance, she says, can only be abolished by wisdom, of which Othea is, of course, the goddess.

Helenus and Troilus are respectively wise and foolish, but mostly it is women who are wise in the *Epistre*.[85] We have already encountered many of these models of wise women, beginning with Othea, or Prudence, and Temperance. Then comes Pallas Athena, holding a book as a personifi-

---

[83] Such as that in Paris, BN MS nouv. acq. lat. 3093, reproduced in Meiss, *Late Fourteenth-Century*, 2: Fig. 11.

[84] London, BL Harley MS 4431, fols. 130r-130v; 131v-132r; Christine, *Epistle of Othea*, tr. Scrope, pp. 94, 97-98.

[85] Some of these examples are discussed by Reno, "Feminist Aspects," pp. 271-276.

cation of wisdom (Fig. 19). Next, in chapter 29, Io as the founder of Egyptian letters directs a scriptorium (Fig. 25). She provides an opportunity for Christine, in the accompanying allegory, to urge the knight to listen to and read letters, scriptures, and histories in which he will find examples that may be valuable to him. In the very next chapter, Io again appears, this time in her more customary guise as a cow (Fig. 26). Christine even transforms Io the cow into a model of wisdom by comparing the nourishment that comes from the milk of a cow to the understanding that comes from the reading of good books. Immediately after Io comes Hector's sister, Cassandra, in chapter 32 (Fig. 29). She is wise because she spoke only the truth when she predicted the tragic outcome of the Trojan war. In chapter 79 yet another wise woman, the queen Alcyon, foresees danger, when she cautions her husband Ceyx against undertaking a dangerous ocean voyage. He ignores her advice and drowns at sea. Ceres, Isis, Diana, and Medea are among the other wise women in the *Epistre*. In short, these many models of wise women are interspersed throughout the work. At periodic intervals they return, reminding readers to heed the recommendations of women who, like Othea, combine the virtues of memory, intelligence, and foresight.

These models of the wise woman all culminate in Andromache, Hector's wife, who is the subject of chapters 88 and 90. The importance of these two chapters for an understanding of the text was discussed earlier, but we should now consider the miniatures in the Paris and London versions as they contribute to the differing ideologies of the books. Let us consider first how both miniatures illustrate the narrative (Figs. 47, 48).

Although the narrative of this moment is not fully told in the *Epistre*, Christine does tell the story in the *Cité des dames*, which provides the general outline for these pictures.[86] Andromache's vision of Hector's death, "which was no dream but a true prophecy" so frightened her that she begged him not to go into battle. Christine says further that Andromache went before him "holding their two beautiful children in her arms." In the Paris miniature Hector prepares to mount his horse, while Andromache speaks to him, pointing toward one of two children who stand before her. The single major difference in the London miniature is that only one child accompanies Andromache. It is evident that this detail is at odds with the story as Christine recounts it in the *Cité des dames*.

---

[86] Christine, *City of Ladies*, tr. Richards, p. 139.

Before attempting to account for this difference, it is important to observe that other differences in the depictions of Hector and Andromache also distinguish the two miniatures without altering the narrative. The identity of Hector is made more explicit in the London miniature, where his horse is covered with a blanket emblazoned with his heraldry. In the absence of such heraldry in the Paris miniature, we have to read the text in order to realize that the knight is surely Hector. The portrayals of Andromache also differ, since she wears altogether different outfits in the Paris and London miniatures. In the Paris book, her dress is a *cotte* with a *surcotte* over it.[87] These garments were common everyday dress; Christine wears them when she appears in the dedication miniatures. As a head-covering Andromache wears a scarf-like hood comparable to that worn by Othea in the first miniature and the sibyl in the last miniature. She has thus been costumed like a woman of antiquity, a goddess or a sibyl, a characterization that is in line not only with her identity in the Trojan story but also with her function as a prophetess. In the London miniature, Andromache wears a *houppelande*, made out of pink cloth and lined with ermine. Instead of the hood, she wears a pointed hat called a *potences*.[88] Thus she is no longer dressed like a classical woman but, rather, like a lady of the French court.

Recalling that throughout the *Epistre* Christine has encouraged the reader to interpret Hector as signifying different actual persons, we should examine the possibility that she has done the same with Andromache and her children. Two observations increase the credibility of this hypothesis. First, the device of using a courtly costume to suggest other identities for a fictional person is one that we have seen Christine use in other miniatures, so that when she had Andromache outfitted like a French princess she may have intended her to serve as a model for an actual person at court. Second, the fact that Andromache is Hector's wife and therefore plays a key role in the dynastic continuity of the Trojans, from whom the French descended, suggests that Christine might mean to use her identity in a way similar to the way that she uses Hector's, that is, as a model for present-day rulership. In fact, royal readers of the *Epistre*, who knew that a son of Hector named Francio founded France, must have understood a miniature that portrayed Hector's children as a reference to their own noble lineage.

---

[87] On these garments, see Gay, *Glossaire archéologique*, 1: 449-452; 2: 362-363; and Evans, *Dress in Mediaeval France*, pp. 52-53, 57-58.
[88] On these details of costume, see Gay, *Glossaire archéologique*, 2: 264.

The meaning of this important chapter in the context of the *Epistre* as a whole, coupled with the changes in the costume of Andromache and the number of her children in the London manuscript, leads us to suggest that this miniature in the London manuscript carries a specific message to its readers. I believe that it asks Isabeau of Bavaria to practice good queenship, while it puts forward her son, Louis of Guyenne, as a future ruler. The miniature communicates this message partly by dressing Andromache like a queen of the court and by emphasizing her one male descendant. Such an interpretation is consistent with the ideological program of the manuscript as we have presented it, since we have seen that the theme of the wisdom of women is coupled with the theme of good government with regard to the kingdom of France. As part of this program, Louis of Orleans is repeatedly offered as an example to Louis of Guyenne. Moreover, such an interpretation is in line with what we know about the circumstances of the production of the London copy, which was altered to conform with the dimensions of a volume of works collected for the queen.

In order to judge further the validity of this suggestion, it is necessary to consider it for a moment in light of the historical circumstances as they involved Louis of Guyenne, Isabeau, and Christine. We should look more closely at the lives of those persons in the period from around 1407 and 1408, the earliest date at which the London copy could have been made, to between 1410 and 1415, when it was enlarged for insertion into a volume of other works.

Let us consider first Louis of Guyenne who was born in 1397.[89] These years between his tenth and fifteenth birthdays were important ones for Louis. Because of the king's madness, the source of so much rivalry over the government of the kingdom, and the firmly established pattern of dynastic succession which determined that Louis would succeed Charles vi, Louis enjoyed a degree of attention that was perhaps somewhat unusual, even for a dauphin. Further, in 1408 a royal ordinance gave him special powers.[90] By its terms, in the absence of the king and queen, Louis was to make all decisions of state with the help of the princes of the blood and the council. He was only eleven years old at the time, still three years from the age of majority.

---

[89] A biography of Louis is included in Famiglietti, *Royal Intrigue*; see also Pannier, "Les Joyaux du duc de Guyenne."

[90] Douët-d'Arcq, *Pièces inédites*, 1: 312-313.

Determined to gain control of the government in the aftermath of the assassination of the duke of Orleans, John of Burgundy sought at this time to exercise control over his son-in-law Louis of Guyenne. As time went on, however, Louis seems to have chosen a more moderate course, seeking peace between the rival factions. In 1412 he was instrumental in concluding the peace at Auxerre, by which the Burgundians and the Armagnacs agreed to end the civil war.[91] This brief background, without outlining his actual role in affairs of state year by year, is sufficient to show that Louis was an important force in the government of France during this period. As acting regent he was, moreover, someone for whom models of rulership would have been particularly appropriate.

As Louis of Guyenne's role was an unusually important one for a dauphin, so too Isabeau of Bavaria's position was more important than that of most earlier French queens had been.[92] She was one of only five French queens through to the end of the seventeenth century who were designated to take an official role in government.[93] According to ordinances of 1393, the guardianship and tutelage of the royal children, particularly the dauphin, were jointly conferred on the dukes and the queen. Then, in 1403 and 1407, two other ordinances gave Isabeau special power: she was given the care of the sovereign until he became of age and the control of the government with the assistance of the dukes of Burgundy, Berry, Orleans, and the council. Only in the thirteenth century had a queen before Isabeau, Blanche of Castille, mother of Saint Louis, enjoyed similar powers.[94] But in some respects Isabeau's powers far exceeded those of Blanche. For example, Isabeau was the first French queen to have accounts separate from those of the king; it had been customary for the queen's accounts to be part of the king's general accounts.[95] In 1393 Isabeau's own account for luxury goods was set up, and then in 1409 a separate treasury was established for her. Such unprecedented measures came about so that Isabeau could take full charge of the finances of the dauphin. In any case, they serve to highlight further

---

[91] On this, see Christine, *Livre de la Paix*, ed. Willard, pp. 23-24.

[92] See especially M. Thibault, *Isabeau de Bavière, reine de France. La jeunesse, 1370-1405* (Paris, 1903); and H. Kimm, *Isabeau de Bavière, reine de France 1370-1435. Beitrag zur Geschichte einer bayerischen Herzogstochter und des französischen Königshauses*, Miscellanea Bavarica Monacensia, 13 (Munich, 1969).

[93] F. Barry, *Les Droits de la reine sous la monarchie française jusqu'en 1789* (Paris, 1932), pp. 152-153.

[94] *Ibid.*, p. 132.

[95] M. Rey, *Les Finances royales sous Charles VI. Les Causes du déficit (1388-1413)* (Paris, 1965), pp. 176-187.

the weakness of the king and the compensatory power of the queen during this period.

The years around the time of the execution of the London *Epistre* and the presentation to her of the "Collected Works" — that is, between 1408 and 1415 — mark one of the high points of Isabeau's power. A series of events led her to a manœuver for a separate treasury.[96] In 1408 an ordinance had given her power to establish peace between the dukes of Burgundy and Orleans. Yet in the same year her financial advisers refused to cooperate as executors to approve her will. In the next year her favored counselor, John of Montaigu, was arrested and then executed, despite her efforts to free him. So, as a gesture of protest Isabeau took the dauphin and retreated to the country, a move which brought to a halt the machinery of government, because during the king's nearly perpetual convalescence her approval, along with that of the dauphin, was needed for official items of business. The end result was that she was awarded her own treasury, an action that somewhat curtailed the power of John the Fearless. Thus, although Isabeau has often been dismissed as a positive force in the government of France under Charles VI, because contemporaries criticized her morals, it is clear that the special contingencies of the reign were such that she acquired and exercised a certain amount of power.

Over these years, Christine took an interest in Louis's and Isabeau's roles. With regard to Louis, she thought of him as a prospective ruler at least by around 1407, when she wrote the *Corps de policie*. Although she dedicated this Mirror of Princes book to Charles VI and the French princes, in reality she wrote it with the young dauphin in mind.[97] In 1412 she presented him with another work, the now-lost *Avision du Coq*. Christine tells us that this work was about the problems of the French realm, with special reference to the evils of covetousness.[98] When Christine wrote about covetousness, she was no doubt thinking of the quarrels among the princes for control of the monarchy. In 1412 she also dedicated to Louis the *Livre de la Paix*, the title of which celebrated his role in concluding the peace at Auxerre.[99] In the *Livre de la Paix*, Christine mixed praise and criticism, hoping to instill in Louis the

---

[96] Rey, *Les Finances*, pp. 183-186.

[97] Christine herself tells us this in her *Livre de la Paix*, ed. Willard, p. 174.

[98] *Ibid.*, p. 152. On this lost work, see Solente, "Christine de Pizan," p. 409; and K. Sneyders de Vogel, "Une Œuvre inconnue de Christine de Pisan," in *Mélanges de philologie romane et de littérature médiévale offerts à Ernest Hoepffner par ses élèves et ses amis* (Paris, 1949), pp. 369-370.

[99] Christine, *Livre de la Paix*, ed. Willard.

qualities necessary for good rulership. In all these works, Christine can be seen to be pursuing a single idea.[100] She hoped that the princes would prepare Louis of Guyenne for rulership, while taking over the government during the periods of Charles VI's madness.

Christine knew that the proper training of the dauphin also required the queen's help. French queens traditionally were in charge of preparing the royal princes and princesses for their adult responsibilities.[101] We have already seen that new ordinances reiterated Isabeau's responsibilities with regard to these duties. Christine must have had in mind Isabeau's role when she wrote to the duke of Berry in 1410 a work entitled *Lamentacion sur les maux de la France*, in which she referred to Isabeau as "mother of the noble heirs" and asked her to remember the "balance of heredity of the noble children."[102] At this time she also requested the queen's aid in stopping dissension within the realm, calling on all those who were wise to come with the queen and serve the kingdom. Earlier in her famous 1405 letter to Isabeau she had also reminded her that during the minority of her son she could exercise her authority to persuade the quarrelling princes to stop dissension amongst themselves.[103] She cited examples of good and bad queenship, ending with Queen Blanche, who, Christine says, was able to bring about peace in France, despite the fact that Blanche's son, Saint Louis, like Louis of Guyenne, had not yet reached his majority. In the same year Christine added Isabeau to Boccaccio's roster of famous women when she included her in the *Cité des dames.*[104]

Taken together, these writings make clear that, whatever the historical personality of Isabeau (and much work needs to be done on Isabeau's role in the institution of French monarchy before we can confidently separate myth from reality), Christine understood Isabeau, by virtue of the very fact that she was queen of France and mother of the royal children, to have an important role to play in the scheme of the future of the monarchy. In particular, she called on the queen to insure that the dauphin had

[100] This view is shared by Krynen, *Idéal du prince*, pp. 141-142.

[101] Discussed by Sherman, *Portraits of Charles V*, pp. 29-30.

[102] Edited twice, by R. Thomassy, *Essai sur les écrits politiques de Christine de Pisan, suivi d'une notice littéraire et de pièces inédites* (Paris, 1838), pp. 141-149; and Christine de Pizan, "La Lamentacion sur les maux de la France de Christine de Pisan," ed. A. J. Kennedy, in *Mélanges de langue et littérature françaises du Moyen Âge et de la Renaissance offerts à Monsieur Charles Foulon par ses collègues, ses élèves et ses amis* (Rennes, 1980), pp. 176-185, esp. 181.

[103] In *Écrits politiques*, ed. Thomassy, pp. 133-140, esp. 137; and in *Anglo-Norman Letters and Petitions from All Souls Ms. 182*, ed. M. D. Legge, Anglo-Norman Text Society, 3 (Oxford, 1941), pp. 144-150.

[104] Christine, *City of Ladies*, tr. Richards, p. 212.

sufficient training to undertake the difficult task of kingship that lay before him.

When we return now to the final two chapters in the *Epistre*, those on Queen Ino and Emperor Augustus, they make more sense in light of the contemporary context (Figs. 49, 50). Might it not be possible to see Ino, the ignorant queen, who is dressed in a regal blue robe and wears a gold crown in the London book, as a model for Isabeau, a model that she should shun rather than emulate? It may be more than coincidental that Ino, like Isabeau, was the wife of a mad king. In support of this hypothesis, we should point out that no pictorial source has been uncovered for the miniature of Ino sowing boiled corn. Further, we should note that the earlier portrayal of Ino in the *Epistre*, in chapter 17, focused on the theme of the king's madness, an emphasis unusual in representations of this story (Fig. 22). If we can thus accept Ino as a negative model for Isabeau, surely we should see Augustus, the wise emperor, as a positive model for Charles VI, the dauphin, and Louis of Orleans, that is, as an ideal French monarch. Through this striking visual pairing of the miniatures, arranged on facing pages, at the conclusion of her manuscripts, Christine expresses her conviction that an era of ignorance will be concluded by a future ruler who, like Augustus, will inaugurate a golden age.

The interpretation of the *Epistre* presented here prompts us to reconsider the question of Christine's feminism since, because of the role the *Epistre* projects for the queen, it emerges as a work concerned, like so many of Christine's works, with the equality of the sexes even when it comes to the government of France. We need to ask whether Christine's stance on the political power of queens in the *Epistre* is in line with and expresses institutional values or whether it is wholly individualistic. Concrete evidence (already presented) on Isabeau's power during the period could have led Christine to imagine an active political role for the queen. Moreover, even were Christine unaware of the specifics found in individual royal ordinances, her own biography might have prompted her to envision Isabeau as a potential force in the government. But the question is not so readily answered, for Isabeau emerges as a somewhat anachronistic figure when considered in the broader context of late medieval French queenship.

A brief survey of late medieval queenship suggests that, at the very most, the monarchy as an institution might, by the time Christine was writing, have allowed for the view of the queen found in the *Epistre*; having said this, what is exceptional, of course, is that this view is found spelled out nowhere else but in the *Epistre*. It has been successfully demonstrated that as the institution of French monarchy was strengthened, gaining under the Capetian rulers in sacerdotal and political authority, the role of the queen was simultaneously weakened as she became relegated to the ceremonial and symbolic spheres of office.[105] Thus, by the thirteenth century, the queen cannot be said to count for much in concrete political terms. Then, through the fourteenth century, the queen's institutional powers were even further undermined in an attempt to counter, using all available means, the English claim to the throne, which was pressed through the right of the female line to rule; if such a right could be shown to be not only suspect but altogether invalid, the English claim understandably lost considerable ground.[106] Paradoxically, French queens in the fourteenth century, especially Jeanne de Bourbon (wife of King Charles V and mother of Charles VI) seem to have achieved increased importance in other spheres, particularly as mothers and teachers. That these changes with respect to the queen's role were not inconsequential is reflected in the altered coronation ceremony for the queen, which legitimized her role in ensuring dynastic continuity, and in frontispieces to Aristotle's *Ethics*, which depict her role in educating the royal offspring.[107] What all of this suggests is that, when Christine portrays Isabeau in the *Epistre* as the royal mother and teacher, she is drawing on an accepted view of the queen that had evolved by the end of the fourteenth century.

Yet the novelty of Christine's portrayal of Isabeau should not be understimated. For Christine, Isabeau, like other female examples in the *Epistre*, is not only someone who bears and nurtures the dauphin; she is someone, like Andromache, Cassandra, Medea, and Othea, who is capable of actively intervening in political life, of changing the course of history. This view of the queen's heightened engagement with government is an unusual one. It was fostered by the particular political circumstances of the day, and it was stimulated further by Christine's own unusual role as a woman author who through her writings attempts to influence politics. In the end, the *Epistre* thus shows Christine to be a feminist of a slightly different stripe than in her other "feminist" works, like the *Cité*

---

[105] See especially M. F. Facinger, "A Study of Medieval Queenship: Capetian France, 987-1237," *Studies in Medieval and Renaissance History* 5 (1968) 3-48.

[106] For the French side, which evoked the Salic law, see R. E. Giesey, *The Juristic Basis of Dynastic Right to the French Throne*, Transactions of the American Philosophical Society, n.s. 51, pt. 5 (Philadelphia, 1961).

[107] See Sherman, "The Queen," pp. 291-293; and *idem*, "Some Visual Definitions," p. 322, Fig. 2.

des dames, where she rewrites history to include women. Here, she shows how women — queens and authors — can rewrite history. In this sense, Isabeau, I would argue, is a projection of Christine herself.

THE *EPISTRE* ADAPTED

Even a quick overview of all the manuscripts of the *Epistre* shows that it was an extraordinarily popular book, one that retained its popularity for a century in France, Flanders, and England. In France, luxurious, as well as routine, manuscript copies continued to be made.[108] Early printers in Paris and Rouen published the *Epistre* seven times, a phenomenon that suggests the considerable extent of its public.[109] In the milieu of the Burgundian court, at least eight luxury copies of the *Epistre* were produced in the last half of the fifteenth century. Translations of the text were undertaken in England, where it was later printed. In light of the interpretation of the ideological programs presented here for the London and Paris copies, the later popularity of the *Epistre* calls for some explanation. It seems initially implausible that a book that can be shown to have been such a timely response to a set of specific circumstances and individuals would attract a broad public. It is important to point out that none of these later manuscript copies or printed editions reflects the ideological programs of the Paris and London copies, so that we must account for the popularity of the *Epistre* in another way.

In order to understand its popularity, we should try to understand how it was regarded. One way of determining how a work was thought of is to see what others it was gathered with when editors compiled into one volume, called a miscellany, works on related subjects. When we examine the heterogeneous Burgundian copies of the *Epistre*, we find that it was understood either as a chivalric handbook, a treatise on the virtues, or a compendium of ancient classics. Editors gathered with the *Epistre* works about chivalry like the *Ordre de chevalerie* or the *Chemin de vaillance*, treatises on the virtues such as Jean Courtecuisse's *Livre des quatre vertus*, and mythological works like the *Metamorphoses*.[110]

---

[108] On the diffusion of the *Epistre* see especially Mombello, *La tradizione manoscritta*, pp. 328-342.

[109] *Ibid.*, pp. 359-370.

[110] For example, London, BL Roy. MSS 14 E II and 17 E IV, the first with the *Chemin*, the *Ordre de chevallerie* and other texts, and the second with the *Metamorphoses*, both catalogued by Warner and Gilson, *Catalogue of Western Manuscripts*, 2: 139-140, 259; and described by Mombello, *La tradizione manoscritta*, pp. 210-221. The *Livre des quatre vertus* prefaces Oxford, Bod. Lib., MS Laud. misc. 570.

Another way of determining how a work was understood is to consider whether and in what ways its text was changed. One Burgundian copy of the *Epistre* expanded Christine's original version to include an elaborate index that functioned as a table of contents and itemized those subjects found in the text: chivalric duties, virtues, vices, and historical events and persons.[111] In this instance the *Epistre* had become a kind of *summa* on contemporary manners and ancient history. Another copy, that by Jean Miélot commissioned by Duke Philip of Burgundy, radically transformed the text of the *Epistre* by introducing an additional gloss, whose contents were taken from Boccaccio's *De Genealogia Deorum*, Virgil's *Aeneid*, Ovid's *Metamorphoses*, and "many other poets, philosophers and ora-tors."[112] Miélot wrote that two considerations had prompted him to execute the changes: first, the obscurity of the subjects, which were presented too briefly in Christine's texts; and second, the disparity of the lengths of the original chapters, which he wished to dispose uniformly on facing pages.[113] In this example the *Epistre* became a kind of source book of quotations by classical authors on mythographic and historical subjects. Such evidence leads us to confirm that the text of the *Epistre* was regarded in several ways, but that it was not understood in Burgundy as providing a political allegory.

In fifteenth-century England, translators of the *Epistre* thought of it primarily as a handbook of chivalry. Even though Stephen Scrope in his mid-fifteenth-century translation for Sir John Falstaff closely followed Christine's text, his prologue repeatedly refers to the *Epistre* as "this seyde Boke off Cheuallry," which he titled *The Boke of Knyghthode*.[114] When Anthony Babyngton translated the *Epistre* around the turn of the century, he added a proem that called the book the "lytle bibell" of one of the three "estats of humanitie," that is, "knyghthod" or the "estat of noble chyvallrye."[115] It is this late fifteenth-century English interpretation of the *Epistre* that has survived in modern scholarship, resulting in its classification as a chivalry manual.

---

[111] Cologny-Geneva, Bib. Bodmeriana, MS 49, fols. 1r-6v; catalogued by F. Vielliard, *Manuscrits français du Moyen Âge*, Biblioteca Bodmeriana Catalogues, 2 (Cologny-Geneva, 1975) 146-149, Pl. 15; and Mombello, *La tradizione manoscritta*, pp. 280-283.

[112] *Ibid.*, pp. 147-153; Doutrepont, *La littérature française*, pp. 307-309, 488, 492; and J. van den Gheyn, *Christine de Pisan. Épître d'Othéa, Déesse de la Prudence à Hector, Chef des Troyens. Reproduction des 100 Miniatures du Manuscrit 9392 de Jean Miélot* (Brussels, 1913).

[113] Van den Gheyn, *Christine de Pisan*, pp. 5-6.

[114] Christine, *Epistle of Othea*, tr. Scrope, pp. 121-124.

[115] Christine, *Epistle of Othea*, tr. Babyngton, ed. J. Gordon, pp. 1, 2.

A final way of understanding these later versions of the *Epistre*, many of which are extensively illustrated, involves an examination of their picture cycles. An overview indicates that the picture cycles in later manuscripts changed more than the texts. For example, the double presentation miniatures in later versions consistently lack those features that contribute to the special political significance of these pictures in the Paris and London manuscripts. Hector and Louis (or the later patron) are represented differently in the first and second miniatures, thus eliminating the link between them.[116] The absence of Christine, for whom Miélot substituted himself in his own presentation miniature, altered radically the original meaning of Christine's text by removing her identity with Othea.[117] With one exception, all other versions omit Hector's progeny in the miniature of Andromache and Hector (Figs. 87, 93). By this change, they suppress the dynastic reference to the line of French kings descended through Hector's children.

Christine's most idiosyncratic pictorial versions of Ovidian myth and Trojan history were also changed in later versions. Later miniatures of the wedding of Peleus and Thetis omit the rulers who hold a second golden apple in the London and Paris copies.[118] Instead, they focus on the three goddesses to whom Semele offers the apple, thereby more accurately rendering the Ovidian narrative. One miniature presents a novel reinterpretation of this mythological story (Fig. 88). It portrays the goddess of discord as the female-headed serpent from the garden of Eden, adopting the model from Hugo van der Goes's *Temptation* panel.[119] Miniatures of Atropos substitute a skeletal personification of Death for Christine's figure of the female fate (Fig. 89).[120] The company that Death keeps is changed as well, for the monarch and the pope are eliminated. Such changes were probably made because the political commentaries, which the earlier miniatures offered, were no longer timely.

Alterations to the picture cycles were sometimes incorporated as responses to the demands of a reedited text of the *Epistre*. A few pictures

---

[116] See, for example, van den Gheyn, *Christine de Pisan*, Pls. 1, 2; and L. M. J. Delaissé, J. Marrow and J. de Wit, *The James A. Rothschild Collection at Waddesdon Manor. Illuminated Manuscripts* (Fribourg, 1977), Figs. 19-20.

[117] Van den Gheyn, *Christine de Pisan*, Pl. 1.

[118] For example, van den Gheyn, *Christine de Pisan*, Pl. 61; and Biblioteca Bodmeriana MS 49, fol. 91.

[119] Compare M. J. Friedländer, *Early Netherlandish Painting*, vol. 4, *Hugo van der Goes* (New York, 1969), Pl. 4.

[120] These are illustrated in Meiss, "Atropos-Mors."

in Miélot's reedited version, for example, followed his glosses instead of Christine's narrative, such as the miniature of Saturn devouring his children, a detail supplied by Miélot although it conflicts with Christine's gloss and allegory (Fig. 90). For Christine, we should recall, the wise Saturn, who taught deliberation, good counsel, and considered judgment, presided over assembled lawyers and judges (Fig. 12). Many other changed pictorial details would deserve careful study as responses to a different cultural and historical milieu, but that is outside the scope of this study.

A study of text and image in these later French, Burgundian, and English examples thus appears to sustain the conclusion that the Paris and London manuscripts preserve unique cycles that were appropriate at specific moments for royal readers. A brief look at one other manuscript, this one contemporary with these early copies, adds another dimension to the question of meaning in the *Epistre*. Until now, this version in Cambridge has been largely ignored partly because it was thought to date later in the century and partly because it is not especially lavish.[121] Since the Cambridge manuscript can now be shown to have been produced in Paris early in the century, either under Christine's supervision or following a copy prepared by her, it acquires considerable importance for what it might suggest when compared with the Paris and London copies. For example, we might want to know whether there are any reflections of the ideological programs of these royal manuscripts in the Cambridge manuscript.

It is evident immediately that the Cambridge manuscript includes a picture cycle in which the special features of the Paris and London copies are absent. The unusual iconography of the "children of the planets" group is lacking. Miniatures of Mars, Minerva, Atropos, Fortune, and the wedding of Peleus and Thetis are also different, including none of the particularizing features that the Paris and London pictures display (Fig. 92). The double dedication sequence is also absent, because there is no dedication miniature. In the opening miniature, Hector is dressed in a less princely costume, as are other characters in the remaining miniatures (Fig. 91). Along with the differing portrayal of Hector, the absence of Andromache's children helps to suppress a political reading (Fig. 93).

---

[121] See Mombello, *La tradizione manoscritta*, pp. 242-245; Henry Yates Thompson, *A Descriptive Catalogue of Twenty Illuminated Manuscripts Nos. LXXV to XCIV (Replacing twenty discarded from the original number) in the Collection of Henry Yates Thompson* (Cambridge, 1907), pp. 33-38; and Seymour de Ricci, "Les Manuscrits de la collection Henry Yates Thompson," SFRMP, *Bulletin* 10 (1926) 42-72, esp. 65.

What all of this may indicate is that there was, contemporary with the royal exemplars of the *Epistre*, another solution to the illustration of the *Epistre*, one that was more suited to a general public since it omitted those allusions to persons in the royal circle. The absence of a dedication in the Cambridge manuscript, the inclusion of costumes worn by individuals outside the court, and the more routine execution of the manuscript support this suggestion.

To understand these two ways of perceiving the *Epistre Othéa*, as a moralizing manual and as a political commentary, we can say that it had two purposes and two publics. First, the work had a generalized purpose that did, in fact, make it accessible to a large public. Christine wanted to teach as much as she could about classical mythology, Trojan history, the Bible, and the writings of the Church Fathers. She also wished to stress the importance of the cardinal and theological virtues, the seven gifts of the Holy Ghost, the seven deadly sins, the Credo, and the Ten Commandments for the training of young knights. These concerns appear throughout the text in its glosses, its allegories, and its general structure. Many of the miniatures function simply as picture guides to the myths. Many of the manuscripts, such as the early Cambridge copy and nearly all the later copies, must have satisfied this large public by presenting such a variety of material in a readable form.

Second, the *Epistre* had a highly individualized purpose, which was suited to a limited public. Christine put herself forward as a political advisor in an epistolary allegory, which cautioned Louis of Orleans, Charles VI, Isabeau of Bavaria, and Louis of Guyenne on bad kingship, kingship that Christine feared would bring about the ruin of France as it had Troy. She adorned her epistolary allegory with pictures which, partly through the use of costume, heraldry, emblems, and colors, helped to make her allusions to certain individuals more specific. Through their idiosyncratic interpretations of Trojan events and Ovidian myths, the pictures also allude to concrete events. Taken together, the pictures and texts of the Paris and London copies thereby present coherent ideological documents, ones built on a belief in the continuity between the past and the present and embellished with the language of allegory, thought to be especially appropriate for advice-giving works devised to shape the future.

On this second level the *Epistre* involves one author speaking to a small and particularized group of readers in the court. The *Epistre Othéa* is not just a chivalric handbook. It is an epistle, a letter. It is an individual communication from one writer, Christine, to selected recipients. Through it, she hoped to inspire others to act wisely, especially regarding France, which was threatened with destruction by forces both inside and outside the kingdom.

The Context of the *Epistre Othéa*

Certain illuminated manuscripts of the *Epistre Othéa*, the Paris and London copies, have been seen as standing out, because they are exceptional within the tradition of illustrating this text. I have interpreted the message in these copies as one that would have been appropriate only for certain high-ranking individuals in the royal court, who, in Christine's view, merited such attention since they were in positions to act in accord with her hopes and beliefs. Thus, I have proposed that these copies were created in response to an exceptional set of historical circumstances. I have found, moreover, the views presented in the *Epistre* to be consistent, in a number of respects, with Christine's perspective on the contemporary situation as expressed in her other writings. If we were to go no further with this investigation, the *Epistre* might be understood finally as a rather unusual document, one that had few precedents in late medieval French art production. This view of the *Epistre* would fit well with the many anomalies in Christine's life and works, but, as we shall see, it is a misleading view.

It has not previously been shown that a historical context for Christine's *Epistre* can be provided through illuminated manuscripts of works by her contemporaries, specifically Philippe de Mézières and Honoré Bouvet. These two authors used literary genres similar to those employed by Christine, such as the epistolary and dream allegories, to offer advice about contemporary issues to individuals at court. Some of the subjects treated by these authors are among those to which we have found references in the *Epistre*, for example, the quarrel between the Burgundians and Orleanists, the regency of France, the insanity of Charles VI, the division within the Church. Others, such as the Hundred Years' War and the Crusade of Nicopolis, although not mentioned in the *Epistre*, were no less timely. In addition to these illuminated works by Philippe and Bouvet, many others at the court of Charles VI addressed these and other issues inspired by events of the time. But what justifies the isolation of Philippe and Bouvet as part of this inquiry is their close connection with Christine; both can be shown to have been her mentors.

In turning, finally, to another illuminated work by Christine, the *Chemin de long estude*, we find that it too shares characteristics with the *Epistre*, as well as with works by Philippe and Bouvet. This entire body of works by Christine, Philippe, and Bouvet can be shown to reflect political thought during the reign of Charles VI. Christine is better understood, in the end, as belonging to a tradition of writing and painting at the court of Charles VI than she is as an idiosyncratic author ahead of, or out of step with, her time.

PHILIPPE DE MÉZIÈRES, KINGSHIP, AND A CRUSADE

We have already suggested that Christine knew the works of Philippe de Mézières, whose epistolary allegories were proposed as a source of inspiration for the *Epistre Othéa*.[1] Evidence of a business transaction confirms Christine's direct contact with Philippe.[2] In 1392, she sold him the castle and lands of Mimorant which she had acquired from her father. An examination of three illuminated works by Philippe reveals the nature of his politics, and indicates more fully the extent of Christine's debt to this author. These three works are the *Songe du vieil pèlerin*, the *Epistre au roi Richart*, and the *Chevalerie de l'Ordre de la Passion*. In the *Songe*, a Mirror of Princes book for the young king, Philippe sets forth his vision of French kingship in a work that simultaneously exalts and advises the king. In his *Epistre* and the *Chevalerie*, he pursues his favorite project, a crusade to the Holy Land led by the French king along with other European rulers.

The *Songe du vieil pèlerin*[3] was written between 1385 and 1389 for King Charles VI, whose tutor Philippe had been. Its full title is: *Le Songe du vieil pèlerin addressant au blanc faucon pèlerin couronné au bec et piés dorés* ("The dream of the old pilgrim addressing the crowned white peregrine falcon with a gold beak and feet"). Composed in the form of a dream allegory, which Philippe explains in the prologue, his *Songe* is a work that "speaks morally, a vision, a consideration, an imagination."[4]

---

[1] See above, ch. 1, pp. 29-32.

[2] Iorga, *Philippe de Mézières*, p. 510 n. 5.

[3] Philippe, *Le Songe*, 2 vols., ed. G. W. Coopland (Cambridge, 1969). See also the study by Dora M. Bell, *Étude sur le Songe du vieil pèlerin de Philippe de Mézières (1327-1405) d'après le ms. fr. B.N. 22542. Document historique et moral du règne de Charles VI* (Geneva: E. Droz, 1955). Both studies rely on MS fr. 22542, executed around 1450, rather than the earlier autograph, Paris, Bib. de l'Arsenal, MSS 2682-2683, so that a diplomatic edition based on all the extant manuscripts is still needed.

[4] Philippe, *Le Songe*, ed. Coopland, 1: 89.

For Philippe, supported by statements of medieval authorities on dream literature, dreams forecast truth. In the prologue, Philippe also makes clear that the principal allegorical figures, the Old Pilgrim and the peregrine falcon, represent himself and Charles VI as the author and the recipient of the work. Parenthetically, Philippe's suitability as advisor to the young king derived in part from his earlier position at court as Charles's tutor.

The agenda put forward in the *Songe* must be read through an intricate allegory, which evolves in the three books that make up the work. At the beginning of the work, the Old Pilgrim, having fallen asleep in the Chapel of the Celestines, has a dream. In the dream the virtues of Charity, Truth, and Justice have either departed from the world or are about to depart, dismayed at finding the world so full of sin. In order to evaluate the extent of this erosion of goodness in the world, two figures who stand for Philippe, namely Ardent Desire and Good Hope, are led by Queen Truth on a journey through Christendom, which constitutes Book I. Finding most of Christendom wanting, they turn to an examination of the kingdom of France, which is presented as the most praiseworthy, the subject of Book II. The subject of Book III is the king, his duties and responsibilities with regard to domestic and foreign affairs. At the conclusion of the work, the Old Pilgrim awakens, finding himself again in the Chapel of the Celestines. He comes face to face with Divine Providence, who assures him of a happy ending. Encouraged by the words of Divine Providence, the Old Pilgrim expresses confidence that with God's help the young French king will negotiate peace between France and England, form a union of the European states, and, with the aid of this union, lead a successful conquest of the infidel to achieve harmony within the Church.

When Philippe urges Charles VI to undertake this mission, he indicates his familiarity with the so-called "second Charlemagne" prophecy which was current from the early years of Charles's reign.[5] According to this prophecy, a king named Charles, son of Charles, of a large stature, with a high forehead, large eyes, and an aquiline nose, would assume the throne of France at the age of fourteen. Between his fourteenth and twenty-fourth year he would subjugate the English, Spanish, Aragonese, Lombards, and Italians. He would then go on to be crowned emperor in

---

[5] The text of the prophecy has been published and studied both by M. Chaumé, "Une prophétie relative à Charles VI," *Revue du Moyen Âge Latin* 3 (1947) 27-42; and M. Reeves, *The Influence of Prophecy in the Later Middle Ages. A Study in Joachism* (Oxford, 1969), pp. 328-331.

Rome and lead a crusade to Jerusalem. Favored by God, he would eventually lay down his crown at Mount Olive, having reigned a total of thirty-one years. It should be pointed out that this topos dominates Philippe's writings. In the presentation copy of the *Epistre au roi Richart* the crowns, heraldry, and devices of the kings of France and England, which are juxtaposed to the crown of thorns, give visual form to the idea of a union of France and England for the purpose of a crusade (Fig. 56). It is worth noting that the second Charlemagne asks to be crowned with the crown of thorns, as it is shown here. In manuscripts of the *Chevalerie de la Passion* those knights to be recruited for the crusade are portrayed wearing the costumes and carrying the banner of the proposed order (Figs. 59-61).

Among the many allegorical figures introduced in the text of the *Songe*, only those that stand for Charles VI and Philippe are illustrated, and they are depicted as symbols who stand alone rather than as figures who participate in the story line of the allegory. A glossary introduces all the figures in the work, so that "the reader will better understand the book," Philippe writes.[6] Philippe identifies himself as the Old Pilgrim, Ardent Desire, and Good Hope, who stand for "all those who desire reform of the world, Christianity, and France." He presents a series of figures to be understood as Charles VI: "the crowned flying stag, the young peregrine falcon with a gold beak and feet, the great keeper of the large park [France], the gardener of the large garden full of white gilded flowers [fleur-de-lis], the grand master of the rivers and forests of France, the head banker, and finally the young crowned Moses."

An examination of the illuminated manuscripts of the *Songe* indicates that allegorical images of kingship were highlighted in the program of illustrations. Only one of the many extant illuminated versions of this text can be dated during the reign of Charles VI, but it is an important one, since it bears numerous autograph corrections that lead us to suppose that Philippe supervised its production.[7] Sparsely illustrated with one full-page

---

[6] Philippe, *Le Songe*, ed. Coopland, 1: 106-114. In the Bib. de l'Arsenal, MSS 2682-2683, the table is rubricated as follows: "La table morale des divers noms des persones et sentences oyseaux et bestes vertus et vices prins en figure parlant moralement en cestui livre appelé le songe du viel pelerin pour mieulx entendre au lisant cestui livre les figures proposées."

[7] Paris, Bib. de l'Arsenal, MSS 2682-2683. See H. Martin, *Catalogue des manuscrits de la Bibliothèque de l'Arsenal*, 6 vols. (Paris, 1885-1889), 3: 74-75. I am indebted to Gilbert Ouy for his confirmation that the notes in MSS 2682-2683 are autograph.

miniature and two historiated initials, this copy bears no indication of the original owner's identity, so we cannot know whether it was the presentation copy for Charles VI. Nevertheless, the fact that Philippe oversaw the transcription of the manuscript, coupled with the close correspondence between the text and the pictures, gives this copy considerable interest as one that preserves a textual and pictorial program that probably reflects the wishes of its author.

The two historiated initials portray the figures in the title and the glossary. The first, prefacing the prologue, depicts the white peregrine falcon according to the description of this bird in the rubric that accompanies the picture (Fig. 51). The falcon, wearing a crown, is painted white with golden flecks among his feathers and has a gold beak and feet. The second historiated initial, occurring at the beginning of the first chapter, again depicts the falcon, who is perched high in a tree along with the pilgrim, who is shown as an old, white-haired man (Fig. 55). Stooped and kneeling, supported by his cane, the old man is dressed in a simple blue robe and carries a green purse around his neck. Although the pilgrim's — or Philippe's — physical appearance is not described in the text of the *Songe*, the depiction here does conform closely with a passage in the *Chevalerie*, in which he describes himself as doubled over with age in the last quarter of his life, holding a tattered book and asking Divine Providence to relieve him of his duties.[8] The representation is consistent, moreover, with all of Philippe's metaphors for himself which refer repeatedly to his advanced age and solitary life. He is the Poor Pilgrim in a lost work called the *Songe du povre pèlerin*, the Old Writer in the *Chevalerie*, and the Old Solitary in the *Epistre au roi Richart*.[9] The miniature thus gives visual form to the title of the work by depicting "the old pilgrim addressing the crowned white peregrine falcon."

If the meaning of the pilgrim is clearly dictated by Philippe's perception of himself, the meaning of the peregrine falcon as a figure for Charles VI is more difficult to interpret. In the prologue, Philippe offers a significance for each of the bird's physical characteristics, as depicted in the initial. Its white color signifies Charles's innocence and purity and testifies to the fact that he has exercised no tyranny over his subjects. Its gold beak shows that the king's speech is gilded and attractive — sweet, courteous, full of

---

[8] Philippe, "Philippe de Mézières and the New Order of the Passion," ed. Abdel H. Hamdy, *Bulletin of the Faculty of Arts, Alexandria University* 18 (1964) 8.

[9] See Iorga, *Philippe de Mézières*, pp. 466-467; *Letter to King Richard II*, ed. Coopland.

love, charity, and humility. Its gold feet indicate that the monarch's political goals are good and are blessed by God, with whose help he will deliver the French nation from servitude. The many gold flecks among its white feathers stand for the numerous virtues that Charles possesses. The peregrine falcon is thus a rich image of royal sovereignty, one that expresses confidence in the king as the perfect prince.

Yet this explanation of the bird's individual attributes still does not account for the choice of the peregrine falcon, which remains an unusual one among the other animal images for rulers (e.g., the lion, the leopard, the eagle, and the peacock).[10] To understand this choice, we must examine the multiple associations that the imagery evokes. Above all, the falcon is an accoutrement of chivalry, since every knight must possess his falcon for use during the hunt. Indeed, Philippe praises Charles VI as the most perfect knight who practises the true chivalry; for such an individual the falcon is a reasonable attribute. But the falcon is not just a property of chivalry. According to Bartholomeus Anglicus's *Livre des propriétés des choses*, a work which was widely read during the era, the falcon is also a royal bird. It is more endowed with temerity than its relative, the vulture, and, although small in build, its considerable audacity and courage make up for its size.[11] In the prologue, Philippe makes use of the bird's combative function, when he compares the military successes of Charles VI, who as a youth was victorious in five or six battles, to the high, swift flight of the peregrine falcon, which he identifies as a bird of prey trained to hunt and kill small animals.[12] Might it not be possible thus to think of the royal peregrine falcon as an alternative to the imperial eagle, which was also a symbol of military prowess? With this in mind, we should recall that Philippe envisioned for Charles VI a reconquest of the Holy Land, an expedition which would require a considerable militia.

Philippe's conception of imperial kingship as expressed in the *Songe* acquires more force through the work's most prominent illustration, a full-page frontispiece of the flying stag (*cerf volant*) that precedes the first chapter (Fig. 52). This figure is the first among the many listed in the prologue that stand for Charles VI. As depicted in this miniature, the graceful stag rises rampant on a hilly, soft-green mound which cuts

---

[10] See H. S. London, *Royal Beasts* (East Knoyle, Wilts, 1956); and M. Pastoureau, *Traité d'héraldique* (Paris, 1979).

[11] Bartholomeus Anglicus, *Le Livre des propriétés des choses*, BN MS fr. 9141, fol. 186: "Le faucon est un oysel royal qui est plus arme de hardiesse que de vugles et ce que nature ne lui donne en grandeur de corps elle lui recompanse en hardiesse et en grant couraige...."

[12] Philippe, *Le Songe*, ed. Coopland, 1: 97.

diagonally across the miniature. The curving shapes of his wings cross each other in the upper right corner, while the gentle arcs formed by his long antlers occupy the upper left corner of the space. The contours of the body are delicately drawn and convincingly modelled in tones of brown and beige. In fact, the execution of the miniature displays a remarkably subtle balance between naturalism and abstraction, the realistic and the iconic. Gently embellished with delicate clusters of daisies, the pale green ground is sharply set off against the bright flat red background. Framed by a fleur-de-lis border and given wings and a crown, the material body of a stag has been transformed into a royal symbol.

Although we know from the prologue that the flying stag is a figure for Charles VI, this information alone does not seem sufficient to account for the prominence of the miniature in the *Songe*, especially since the flying stag appears only infrequently in Philippe's text. When the image of the stag does appear in the *Songe*, it merely replaces the peregrine falcon which remains the dominant image throughout the text. We can assume, therefore, first, that Philippe did not invent the figure of the stag, since he probably would have explained it as he did the falcon, and, second, that the image was so well known that Philippe considered it unnecessary to enlighten his readers about its symbolic significance. In the light of these assumptions, it would be instructive to try to understand from other sources what meaning the flying stag had during the reign of Charles VI in order to clarify its meaning in the *Songe*.

The earliest written accounts that fix the stag as a symbol of French kingship are two chronicles from the reign of Charles VI. According to the first account, Juvenal des Ursins's *Histoire de Charles VI*, the young Charles was hunting one day in 1380 in the forests around Senlis when he spotted a stag.[13] The stag could not be captured without being killed, a feat accomplished by no king before Charles. Charles, however, was able to kill the animal, at which time he discovered that it wore around its neck a gilded leather chain with the words "Caesar gave this to me" (*Caesar hoc mihi donavit*) imprinted on it. Juvenal des Ursins explains that the king henceforth wore the device of the flying stag with a gold crown at its neck and that whenever the arms of France appeared they were supported by two flying stags. This account is based on medieval

---

[13] Jean Juvenal des Ursins, *Histoire de Charles VI*, ed. J. F. Michaud and J. J. F. Poujoulat (Paris, 1936), pp. 343-344. On the stag as a device, see also: C. Beaune, "Costume et pouvoir en France à la fin du Moyen Âge: Les devises royales vers 1400," *Revue des sciences humaines* 55 (1981) 125-146; and J.-B. de Vaivre, "Les Cerfs ailés et la tapisserie de Rouen," *Gazette des Beaux-Arts*, 6ᵉ sér., 100 (1982) 93-108.

legend, which depends on classical sources, that held that Julius Caesar had fastened a golden collar to the neck of a stag that subsequently lived a miraculously long time.[14] The image carried the meaning that the French monarch, superior to all other rulers who were unable to capture the stag, was heir to the imperial command.

Although this account explains the crowned stag as a royal emblem, it does not explain the fact that the stag is winged in all representations, including that in the *Songe*. For an explanation of this feature, we must turn to the second account, found in Froissart's *Chroniques*, where Froissart recounts a dream of Charles VI.[15] In 1382 the count of Flanders had given the young king a peregrine falcon that had flown away. In the dream, a winged stag miraculously appeared and bore Charles aloft, enabling him to retrieve his falcon. Froissart proceeds to attribute military success to the power of the image of the flying stag when it is worn. He asserts that its use by the armies of the king when they intervened to quell the Flemish insurrections in 1382 assured victory. This fiction is similar to the idea of the victory eagle, which hovered over the battlefield and designated, by its presence over one group, the victor.[16] Like the victory eagle, the heavenly stag was invented as a sign that served to define further the sacred, imperial character of French kingship. Added to the stock of royal myths, the stag affirmed the divine right to imperial rule on the part of Charles VI.

These two accounts combine the ideas of divinity (the stag had lived more than 700 years) with victory, which are those very properties of the stag that account for its endurance as a royal symbol. Colette Beaune has shown that other textual associations for the stag, both Christian and secular, are coupled with the accounts in the chronicles.[17] According to the bestiaries, which interpreted biblical passages from the Books of Job and Psalms, the stag was a symbol for Christ: like Christ, it was blessed with eternal life (it resuscitated itself every 32 years); it had recourse to the waters of purification; and it fought against the powers of evil. According to French historiography, which added to the myths surrounding the divine stag, the stag appeared miraculously to Charles just as it had

---

[14] The legend has been traced by Michael Bath, "The Legend of Caesar's Deer," *Medievalia et Humanistica*, n.s., 9 (1979) 53-66.

[15] Froissart, *Œuvres*, 10: 69-71.

[16] See E. Kornemann, "Adler und Doppeladler im Wappen des alten Reiches," *Das Reich – Idee und Gestalt* (Stuttgart, 1940), pp. 45-69; and K. Schwarzenberg, *Adler und Drache. Der Weltherrschaftsgedanke* (Vienna, 1958).

[17] Beaune, "Costume et pouvoir."

appeared to his saintly ancestors, for example, to Charlemagne, whom it enabled to ford a river and to find his path in the forest. And according to chivalric romances, the stag led Lancelot and his companions to the holy grail. Finally, according to medical treatises, the horns, skin, and cartilage around the heart of the stag were thought to be antidotes for poison, frenzy, and madness. These curative powers of the stag may have had special meaning for Charles VI after 1392, when he experienced his first fit of insanity. During a reign of a mad king, it must have become increasingly important to distinguish between the mortal king, who was vulnerable, and the office of the king, which, like Caesar's stag, never dies. At a time when France was beset by threats from Flanders, England, and the Empire, it must have been important likewise to advance a symbol of military invincibility, like the stag as Christ militant.

Turning to other appearances of the stag, we find that these diverse associations are bound up in its many visual manifestations. One document even testifies to the presence of an actual "royal" stag. According to the household accounts, a special branding iron with a fleur-de-lis insignia was wrought in 1381 to brand an actual stag.[18] This was accomplished in the stable at the leper colony at Choisy before the animal was allowed to return to the forest at Compiègne. By this action, the royal court could be seen to emulate Caesar's act of placing a collar on a stag, thereby fortifying the myth as it had come to be associated with Charles VI.

The stag appeared frequently at court in its symbolic form as an image of powerful rule. One such representation had been painted on the walls of the palace during the reign of Charles V.[19] Then, in 1389, on the occasion of Queen Isabeau's entry into Paris before her coronation, a giant artificial stag was made out of wood to the dimensions of the painting in the palace.[20] Painted white, with gilded antlers and a gold crown around its neck, the stag had a fleur-de-lis shield suspended from its collar. Every part of its body was hinged, a feature of its construction that enabled its eyes to roll and its antlers, mouth, and legs, to move. Those who stood at the Châtelet during the queen's entry were well

[18] Douët-d'Arcq, *Comptes*, p. 182.
[19] See Philippe Henwood, "Jean d'Orléans peintre des Rois Jean II, Charles V et Charles VI (1361-1407)," *Gazette des Beaux-Arts*, 6ᵉ sér., 95 (1980) 137; tapestries belonging to Charles V are cited by G. Desjardins, *Recherches sur les drapeaux français* (Paris, 1874), p. 23.
[20] Jean Juvenal des Ursins, *Histoire de Charles VI*, p. 378; Froissart, *Œuvres*, 14: 11.

placed to witness the animation of the stag. The same stag participated in a *tableau vivant*. It was placed next to the king's *lit de justice*, which it valiantly defended from attacks by an eagle and a lion by swinging to and fro a huge sword. Twelve young girls, also armed with swords, advanced to protect it. A symbol of French rule, the stag thus displayed its prowess by safeguarding the state from assaults by the empire (the eagle) and Flanders (the lion).

That the flying stag conveyed the military prowess of the kingdom is suggested by records of payment that describe its use as an emblem. A large number of these documents describe the accoutrements of warfare as being decorated with stags.[21] For example, red horse blankets and red satin standards were both embellished with stags. These references not only suggest a source of inspiration for the background coloring of the miniature, which was executed on a red ground, they also remind us that the flying stag was regarded as especially effective in combat, like the imperial eagle, surely because it was thought to remind enemies of the superior powers of the French monarchy, equal even to those of the empire.

Philippe thus had portrayed in the *Songe* potent images of royalty. The peregrine falcon offers a symbol of Charles as the perfect, victorious prince, and the flying stag combines the idea of the divine status of kingship with that of imperial might. An allegorical presentation miniature shows a figure for Philippe, the pilgrim, before a figure for Charles, the falcon. This last device calls attention to the work as an allegory of advice.

A later manuscript copy of the *Songe* is less concerned with highlighting symbols of kingship than it is with presenting the full range of allegorical figures found in the text of the *Songe*.[22] The miniature illustrating Book II depicts a scene in a barrel-vaulted room, the blue walls of which are covered with a fleur-de-lis pattern to indicate that the location is France (Fig. 53). Book II, in fact, narrates Philippe's journey through France. Within the room, three queens — of justice, truth, and mercy

---

[21] Douët-d'Arcq, *Pièces inédites*, 2: 394, 397, 398, 401; Gay, *Glossaire archéologique*, 1: 299. In these examples, the stag often appears with the broom, another emblem of the king.

[22] Vienna, Österreichische Nationalbibliothek, Cod. 2551, described by Otto Paecht and Dagmar Thoss, *Die illuminierten Handschriften und Inkunabeln der Österreichischen Nationalbibliothek, Französische Schüle I*, 2 vols., Österreichische Akademie der Wissenschaften, Philosophisch-historische Klasse, Denkschriften, vol. 118 (Vienna, 1974), 1: 89-91, 2: Figs. 157-159.

— preside over a parliament of virtues. Ardent Desire and Good Hope (figures for Philippe) approach from the far end of the room, while on the left and right are arranged four hierarchies of French society. Seated side by side and both dressed in fleur-de-lis mantles trimmed with ermine, Charles VI and Louis of Orleans rule over France from their thrones which are placed against the right wall. Charles's flying stag rises at the side of his throne. What is important to note, however, is that the brothers are identified by their respective falcons. Charles VI holds the white peregrine falcon, while Louis of Orleans holds a brown falcon. This is the figure for Louis provided in Philippe's glossary and in which he appears throughout the text. As we have already seen, it is one that Christine, familiar with Philippe's text and perhaps with a cycle of illustrations such as this one, used to identify Louis in the *Epistre*.

The miniature introducing Book III focuses on the king (Fig. 54). Once again, the action takes place within a room patterned with the fleur-de-lis. The kneeling author, shown as Ardent Desire accompanied by Good Hope, presents his book to Charles VI. Charles is portrayed surrounded by his symbols. He holds the peregrine falcon in one hand, while in the other he clasps the tablets of the law to show that he is also "the young crowned Moses." A chessboard is situated beneath his chin because an allegory of the game of chess as the government of France dominates the third book. The flying stag appears at the side of his throne. Facing Charles on the opposite side of the room sits Louis of Orleans, who is shown once again holding his brown falcon. For the next decade, after writing the *Songe*, Philippe continued to address the king and his court, but usually in works of a more topical nature.

Philippe's *Epistre au roi Richart* is an epistolary letter written in 1395 for presentation from the king of France to the king of England.[23] The letter was discussed earlier with regard to its twofold aim of, first, promoting peace between France and England through the forthcoming marriage of Richard II and the young French princess Isabel and, second, furthering peace throughout Christendom through a projected Anglo-French crusade.[24] The illuminated presentation copy of the *Epistre au roi Richart* still exists.[25] This copy enables us to study the way in which the miniatures enhance the message of the text, since we know that it was ordered and executed for Charles VI to give to Richard II.

---

[23] Philippe, *Letter to King Richard II*, ed. Coopland.
[24] See above, ch. 1, pp. 30-31.
[25] London, BL Roy. MS 20 B VI, described by Warner and Gilson, *Catalogue of Western Manuscripts*, 2: 363-364.

The lavish frontispiece illumination underscores the second of the two aims: namely, an alliance between the kings of England and France in pursuit of the common objective of peace in Christendom.[26] Composed almost entirely of abstract forms, the frontispiece communicates its message primarily through a juxtaposition of heraldic and emblematic symbols (Fig. 56). In the upper register appear three crowns set under flamboyant gothic arches. Over each crown the name of a king is written, and under each is inscribed his motto. In the upper left Charles VI's crown of France appears with his motto "in goodness" (*en bien*). In the opposite corner is the crown of England with Richard's motto, "it cannot be divided" (*sans départir*). Between these two crowns on a black field covered with tears appears a third, the crown of thorns, painted so as to suggest that it radiates beams of gold toward each of the crowns. Above and below this last crown are written the words "Jesus king of peace" (*Jesus roy de paix*) and "peace to you" (*pax vobis*). In the lower register, beneath the crowns appears the abbreviation for "Jesus" (*ysu*) written over blue and red heraldic fields made up respectively of the gold fleur-de-lis of France and the gold leopard of England. As stated above, this miniature gives visual form to the idea that the combined efforts of the kingdoms of France and England can bring about peace in the Holy Land, the subject of the third of seven chapters in the *Epistre au roi Richart.*

Only two other miniatures decorate the *Epistre au roi Richart,* and both confirm that the primary concern of the letter was the conquest of the Holy Land. Represented in each of these miniatures is the banner of a chivalric order, the Order of Chivalry of the Passion of Jesus Christ, founded by Philippe as early as 1355 so as to recruit knights for a projected crusade. A small miniature of the banner introduces the third subject in Philippe's *Epistre* (Fig. 58). In the miniature, the banner is composed of the cross of St. George, that is, a red cross on a white ground, on which a black ground sets off a gold *Agnus Dei* carrying another banner. A description of the banner cannot be found in this *Epistre.* Rather, its depiction conforms exactly with its description in another text by Philippe, the *Chevalerie de la Passion,* in which he also explains its symbolism.[27] In a passage reminiscent of the one on the

---

[26] Discussed by Iorga, *Philippe de Mézières,* pp. 482-487; M. V. Clarke, "The Wilton Diptych," in *Fourteenth Century Studies by Maude Violet Clarke,* ed. L. S. Sutherland and M. McKisack (Oxford, 1937; repr. Freeport, NY, 1967), pp. 272-292; and Paul Durrieu, "L'Union des couleurs nationales de la France et de l'Angleterre au XIVᵉ siècle en vue de la conquête de Jérusalem," *La Revue hebdomadaire* 27, no. 19 (11 May 1918) 166-176.

[27] Philippe, "A New Order of the Passion," ed. A. Hamdy, p. 86.

peregrine falcon, Philippe informs us that each of the parts of the banner is symbolic. The black color represents the sorrow of the Passion, the gold of the *Agnus Dei* the glory of Christ resurrected. He tells us further that the banner is to be carried only by the prince when he leads his army in great battles. This last statement probably accounts for Philippe's presentation of the banner, along with his book, to Richard II in the presentation miniature (Fig. 57).[28]

The illustrations Philippe planned thus show him to have been concerned primarily with the third subject — the crusade — presented in his text, in spite of the fact that Charles's main interest as communicated in the text lay in the marriage plans between his daughter Isabel and the English king, the subject of the fourth chapter, which had significant political ramifications for the balance of power between France and England.[29] By using the stunning heraldic frontispiece, Philippe hoped to draw Richard's attention to the prospect of a crusade.

Philippe's commitment to the idea of a crusade had led him to found a new order, the subject of his *La Chevalerie de la Passion de Jhésu Crist*. The text for this work was rewritten three times between 1369 and 1396.[30] The version which concerns us is the second one, the only one that was illustrated, which was composed between 1389 and 1394. This intermediate version contains only the rule of the order which Philippe intended to have duplicated and sent to various European princes. We can get some idea of what these presentation copies were supposed to look like by the single manuscript of it that survives from the period.[31] A badly damaged and inadequately restored copy is thought to have been the one sent by Philippe to the earl of Huntington. In it, six miniatures depict the

[28] This frontispiece repeats an earlier composition, to which it adds the author and the banner, the frontispiece to Jean Cuvelier's *Life of Bertrand Duguesclin*, London, BL Yates Thompson MS 35, fol. 1, described and illustrated by Henry Yates Thompson, *Illustrations from the Life of Bertrand Duguesclin by Jean Cuvelier from a Manuscript of about 1400 A.D. in the Library of Henry Yates Thompson. No. C* (London, 1909).

[29] The view that the letter was intended to facilitate these plans is argued by J. J. N. Palmer, "The Background to Richard II's Marriage to Isabel of France (1396)," *Bulletin of the Institute of Historical Research* 44 (1971) 1-17, esp. 12. Special gold rubrication prefacing the section on the marriage helps to support Palmer's claim.

[30] The various editions have been studied by A. Molinier, "Description de deux manuscrits contenant la règle de la 'Militia Passionis Jhesu Christi' de Philippe de Mézières," *Archives de l'Orient Latin* 1 (1899) 335-364. Autograph manuscripts are extant of the first and third editions: Paris, Bib. Mazarine, MS 1943 and Bib. de l'Arsenal, MS 2551. See A. Molinier, *Catalogue des manuscrits de la Bibliothèque Mazarine*, 4 vols. (Paris, 1885-1892), 2: 289 (no. 1943); H. Martin, *Catalogue*, 2: 457-458.

[31] Oxford, Bodleian Library, Ashmole MS 813, ed. by A. Hamdy, "A New Order of the Passion." Ashmole MS 813 was copied in the seventeenth century in Ashmole MS 865.

costumes to be worn by members of the order and the banner and shield (Figs. 59-61). The execution in multiple copies sent to powerful princes suggests that an important purpose of these illuminated manuscripts was to persuade such princes to recruit knights willing to participate in a crusade.

The special emphasis on a crusade in the programs of these illuminated manuscripts can be better understood against the background of Philippe's involvement with the crusades of the fourteenth century.[32] In 1365, four years before Philippe wrote the first draft of his *Chevalerie*, he had been present at the Sack of Alexandria. From the moment of this triumph against the Saracens, he urged further expeditions. Possibly his propaganda helped foster preparations for the Crusade of Nicopolis, a project masterminded by the duke of Burgundy. Led by John of Burgundy, then count of Nevers, the Crusade of Nicopolis began in the summer of 1396.[33] Nearly one hundred thousand knights from the countries of Italy, Hungary, France, and England were matched by an army of similar size formed of the Sultan's men. The outcome for the West was disastrous; most of its army was massacred. Nobles like John of Nevers who were captured were saved only by the intervention of princes back home who paid enormous ransoms for their release. Philippe's last work, the *Epistre lamentable* discussed in a previous chapter,[34] urged the duke of Burgundy to consider additional expeditions, despite the heavy losses he had suffered on this one. But a resumption of hostilities between France and England, the continuing schism in the Church, and civil war in France thwarted further deliberations over any crusade. Philippe fell silent, perhaps disillusioned with conditions of the monarchy and the Church. He died in 1405.

HONORÉ BOUVET, ROYAL POWER, AND INTRIGUE

Christine acknowledged Honoré Bouvet as her "sweet master" in 1410 when she wrote the *Livre des fais d'armes et de chevalerie*,[35] a work

---

[32] See Iorga, *Philippe de Mézières, passim*; A. S. Atiya, *The Crusade in the Later Middle Ages* (London, 1938), pp. 128-154; and Kenneth M. Setton, *The Papacy and the Levant*, 2 vols., Memoirs of the American Philosophical Society, 114, 127 (Philadelphia, 1976, 1978), 1: 236-238, 241-244, 259-261, and *passim*.

[33] A. S. Atiya, *The Crusade of Nicopolis* (London, 1934), pp. 33-34; Setton, *The Papacy and the Levant*, 1: 342-367.

[34] See above, ch. 1, p. 31. Edited in Froissart, *Œuvres*, 16: 444-523. Brussels, Bib. Roy. MS 10486 contains within a decorated border the arms of Philip the Bold (fol. 2v) for whom the manuscript was made and to whom it is dedicated.

[35] As quoted by A. Coville, *La Vie intellectuelle*, p. 240. On Christine's treatise, see

indebted to his *Arbre des batailles*.[36] Even without this direct reference, we might suppose that the two authors knew each other. Bouvet worked for the court from 1386, the year of his first work, to 1399, the year of his last.[37] He cultivated a patronage with the duke of Orleans, whom Christine also addressed during those years, and collaborated at one point with Jean Gerson, with whom Christine was also acquainted. Bouvet and Christine thus shared a circle of acquaintances, which may have put them in direct contact with each other, and, as we shall see, they took an interest in some of the same contemporary issues, which they treated in similar forms of literature. Before 1389, Bouvet had had a career in the Church, serving Pope Urban VI and holding the position of prior at Selonnet in Provence. This accounts for some of his interests that differ from Christine's, especially a concern with the fate of the Church.

Three illuminated works by Bouvet are of particular interest here: the *Arbre des batailles*, the *Somnium super materia Schismatis*, and the *Apparicion Maistre Jehan de Meun*. In the first, the *Arbre des batailles*, he presented a political platform for the new French king, who was portrayed as a powerful European monarch capable of influencing world-wide peace. In the second, the *Somnium*, Bouvet continued to address the idea of the French king's authority, this time with regard to the king's sway over the papacy. In the third work, the *Apparicion*, Bouvet turned to other individuals at court in order to urge their participation in reform on numerous issues.

Bouvet dedicated the *Arbre des batailles* to Charles VI sometime between 1386 and 1389.[38] Divided into four parts, the *Arbre* treats, first, the tribulations of the Church throughout its history; second, the destruction of four ancient kingdoms (Babylon, Carthage, Macedonia, and

---

C. C. Willard, "Christine de Pisan's Treatise on the Art of Medieval Warfare," in *Essays in Honour of Louis Francis Solano*, University of North Carolina Studies in Romance Languages, 92 (Chapel Hill, 1970), pp. 179-191.

[36] Honoré Bouvet, *The Tree of Battles*, ed. G. W. Coopland (Cambridge, Mass., 1949); *idem, L'Arbre des batailles d'Honoré Bonet*, ed. E. Nys (Brussels and Leipzig, 1883).

[37] On Bouvet's life and work, see A. Coville, *La Vie intellectuelle*, pp. 215-318, with important corrections by Gilbert Ouy, who noted that the name is not Bonet but Bouvet (meaning "ox" or "bullock"); see G. Ouy, "Honoré Bouvet (appelé à tort Bonet), prieur de Selonnet," *Romania* 80 (1959) 255-259. Further confirmation of Ouy's proposal occurs in the *Tree of Battles*, ed. Coopland, p. 204: "My father, by his own wish has adopted as arms a cow *gules* with three stars above it," a shield which conforms exactly with that for the Bouvet family identified by Ouy.

[38] Two early editions can be singled out, one between 1386 and 1387 and the other between 1387 and 1389, as indicated by Coville, *La Vie intellectuelle*, pp. 256-257.

Rome); third, war in general; and fourth, battles in particular. A few manuscripts also preserve a historical interpolation that chronicles European history between 1139 and 1354.[39] This popular work was copied and recopied more than fifty times through the end of the fifteenth century, probably because it acquired a wide appeal as a handbook on various aspects of war.[40] Included are easy-to-follow practical discussions on the "do's and don'ts of battle" — what to wear, how much to pay soldiers, what to do with prisoners, how to collect ransoms, and so forth.

The first half of the work, however, is more didactic than practical, offering historical exempla to the rulers of the present who, Honoré hopes, will be able to bring to an end widespread dissension. Dating from the same time as the *Songe du vieil pèlerin*, that is, at the beginning of the reign of Charles VI, the *Arbre* may be seen as asking a specific ruler, Charles, to prepare for combat so as to hasten peace. Only if the king acts in this way can France avoid the destruction experienced by Babylon, Carthage, Macedonia, and Rome. Indeed, Bouvet gives one of his reasons for writing the work in the prologue where he refers to "recent glosses" on the ancient prophecies which claim that "a member of the high lineage of France" (Charles VI) will bring healing to an age full of great evils.[41] The *Arbre*, like the *Songe*, is thus a work that offers advice to and at the same time expresses hope in a new monarch, a "second Charlemagne."

A study of the frontispieces in the earliest manuscript copies confirms this interpretation of the *Arbre des batailles*. These frontispieces were meant to be read as an integral part of the text, for Bouvet incorporated into the prologue and the first chapter comments on their composition and explanations of their meaning. In the prologue he states: "I make a Tree of Mourning at the beginning of my book, on which you may see, first, at the head, the governors of Holy Church in such tribulation as never was before.... Next, you may see the great dissension which is today among Christian princes and kings, and afterwards you may see the great grief and discord which exist among the communities."[42] In the first chapter he amplifies this description: "Now, since you see that the Tree of Suffering has two branches, between which are many great discords, and great war against the Holy Papacy of Rome, and further, you see that

---

[39] See Bouvet, *The Tree of Battles*, ed. Coopland, p. 80.
[40] See especially N. A. R. Wright, "The Tree of Battles of Honoré Bouvet and the Laws of War," in *War, Literature, and Politics in the Late Middle Ages*, ed. C. T. Allmand (New York, 1976), pp. 12-31.
[41] Bouvet, *The Tree of Battles*, ed. Coopland, p. 79.
[42] *Ibid.*, p. 79.

among the kings, princes, and earthly lords, there are many dissensions, and again, you see the great commotion and very fierce misdeeds of nobles and communities...."[43] These passages describe a tree of "mourning" or "suffering," divided in two parts, which provides a setting for various battles called "discords" or "dissensions."

The frontispiece in the earliest extant manuscript, which probably dates around 1389, closely follows this description (Fig. 62).[44] The branches of a tree divide the space into eight compartments on four levels, and armies are engaged in battles at each of the levels. At the highest level, the armies of the papacy confront each other; then come those of the kings and dukes; and finally, at the lowest level, the commoners do battle. At the apex of the tree, a figure of Fortune stands behind a wheel. Her presence corresponds to the active role assigned Fortune in the text, where she is repeatedly held responsible for the conflicts that result in war.[45]

Other details suggest that Bouvet had in mind specific conflicts when he planned this frontispiece. References to concrete events and individual persons not mentioned in the text are made through the inclusion of heraldry, which was first identified by Warner and Gilson, who did not seek to explain it further.[46] Shields identify the popes as Clement VII on the upper left and Urban VI on the right. The presence of Urban helps to fix this representation before 1389, the year of his death. This, then, is a reference to the world torn asunder by the papal schism.

On the next level at the left, shields identify the armies of France (fleur-de-lis) and England (a leopard). The representation of these two armies fighting each other is certainly an allusion to the ongoing Hundred Years' War, caused by the English claim to the French throne. The fact that the English banner is charged only with leopards, and not with the accompanying fleur-de-lis that the English had by this time incorporated, serves visually to deny this claim.[47] On this same level at the right, the

---

[43] *Ibid.*, p. 8

[44] London, BL Roy. MS 20 C VIII. See Warner and Gilson, *Catalogue of Western Manuscripts*, 2: 374-375. This copy includes the Duke of Berry's arms and a portrait of the duke in the dedication miniature, but it does not correspond with the description in the inventory. A manuscript from the Phillipp's Collection corresponds with the inventory reference. See Bibliotheca Phillippica, N.S., Pt. X, *Catalogue of Manuscripts on Papyrus, Vellum, and Paper* (London, Sotheby's, 26 November 1975), pp. 43-47, no. 80, pl. 15.

[45] Bouvet, *The Tree of Battles*, ed. Coopland, pp. 97, 113.

[46] Warner and Gilson, *Catalogue of Western Manuscripts*, 2: 374-375.

[47] Under the reign of Edward III (ruled 1327-1377), who first called himself "King of England and France," the arms of England were quartered with the arms of France. It was Edward III who gave the Black Prince, Edward, the principality of Acquitaine

armies of Louis of Anjou and Philip of Burgundy confront each other. This depiction may allude to the Anjevin-Burgundian conflicts over the regency of France which had occurred at the beginning of Charles VI's reign between 1380 and 1383.[48] The conflict was resolved only when Louis shifted his focus of attention to Italy where he settled and died, in 1384. Below on the left, the armies of the king of Castille and Leon face those of the king of Portugal, a probable allusion to the struggle between these half-brothers, both named John, for the throne of Portugal after the death of Ferdinand of Castille in 1383. On the right, Emperor Charles VI battles his archrival, Lewis the Great, king of Hungary, probably for control of Italy. At the lowest level are some of the victims of war, the prisoners awaiting torture and execution, who appear amidst the masses fighting among themselves.

In order to interpret this frontispiece as bearing directly on the meaning of the text as Bouvet thought of it, we should try to find out more about the manuscript in question. There is no certain evidence that this is the presentation copy the author offered to Charles VI in 1389. Still, a series of observations makes it likely that this copy, if not the actual one offered to the king, accurately reflects the presentation copy. First, this frontispiece is the most elaborate, with regard to the kinds of references it makes, of all extant frontispieces to the text. Second, these references would have been appropriate only for the king or a person in the royal circle, for whom they would have been both recognizable and provocative. Third, with only a few exceptions which are less carefully worked out, the other frontispieces to the *Arbre* are illustrated with a picture less appropriate for a presentation copy. And fourth, the sorts of references included in this frontispiece are consistent with those in illustrations for other manuscripts known to have been executed under Bouvet's supervision. On the weight of this evidence, we can put forward the hypothesis — but it must remain only a hypothesis — that this frontispiece reflects Bouvet's concerns when he wrote the book for presentation to the king in 1389.

In any case, we can view the frontispiece as presenting a political platform for a new regime. In the picture, Bouvet suggests that the monarch should work to conclude the schism and the Hundred Years' War, by upholding one pope and denying English claims to the throne.

---

formalized in a charter where both Edwards are pictured in armor quartered with the fleur-de-lis and the leopard. See London, BL Cotton Nero MS D VI, reproduced in Joseph Strutt, *The Regal and Ecclesiastical Antiquities of England: Containing the Representations of All the English Monarchs* (London, 1842), pp. 29-30, pl. xv.

[48] See Nordberg, *Les Ducs*, pp. 62-64.

He cautions him to guard against internal disputes that might affect the monarchy, reminding him of the conflict that had transpired between the Angevins and the Burgundians and prophetically anticipating the quarrel between the Orleanists and the Burgundians. He further suggests that the king pay close attention to international affairs, particularly those in Portugal and Italy, thus guarding against a shift in the balance of European power that might adversely affect France. Finally, he indicates that the monarch should be watchful of uprisings within his realm. When attention is paid to its picture as well as its text, the *Arbre des batailles* can be seen to be not so much a treatise on warfare as a guide to a specific prince on how to use warfare effectively to bring about peace within his kingdom and the world. In this way, he may be able to fulfill the ancient prophecies mentioned in the prologue. Although Charles's attack of insanity in 1392 prevented him from implementing much of Bouvet's advice, the king was nevertheless pleased with the book, for he gave the author a yearly pension as a gesture of his appreciation.[49]

A brief examination of the other frontispieces confirms the view that this one is unique. In fact, only two other frontispieces follow the schema used in the earliest one, but they include altered details.[50] In each, the shield of Clement VII has been replaced by that of Peter de Lune as Benedict XIII, a white crescent on a red ground (Figs. 63, 64).[51] The French favorite, Benedict XIII was elected in 1394. In order to indicate that he is the legitimate pope, he is depicted holding the papal cross right side up, while that of the antipope points toward the ground. The shields on the second level seem to repeat their counterparts in the earlier version. Those on the third level have been defaced. On the basis of the inclusion of Benedict XIII, these frontispieces can be dated between 1394 and 1399; they address a changed situation within the papacy. It is not surprising that all later manuscripts, even those executed around 1400 – within only a decade of the original – omit the original frontispiece, which had been fragmentarily preserved in these two manuscripts.[52] The earliest copy of the frontispiece had offered its viewers a pictorial

---

[49] Ouy, "Honoré Bouvet," has published a seventeenth-century copy (Paris, BN MS fr. 21145) of a payment in 1398 of the pension, initially awarded in 1392.

[50] New York, Pierpont Morgan Library, M. 907; Paris, BN MS fr. 1262; both unpublished.

[51] He was commonly called "le Pappe de la lune"; on his heraldry, see D. L. Galbreath, *Papal Heraldry* (London, 1972; repr.).

[52] For example, Paris, BN MS fr. 17183, illustrated in Bouvet, *The Tree of Battles*, ed. Coopland, frontispiece.

commentary that was only appropriate at a single moment during the reign of Charles VI.

Bouvet's *Somnium super materia schismatis*[53] focuses on the subject of the papal schism which had already concerned him in the *Arbre*. Precisely dated between June and September 1394, the *Somnium* was inspired by the rival claims of Clement VII and Urban VI to the papacy.[54] The French generally favored the Avignon pope Clement VII, while other countries supported the Roman claimant Urban VI. One letter by Bouvet tells us that King Charles VI had requested his "humble opinion" on the schism, and his *petit livre* is the result.[55] In it Bouvet sought a compromise. He envisioned King Charles VI, to whom he dedicated the work, as the arbitrator of this compromise which was to be resolved peacefully by all rulers throughout Christendom.

Like the *Songe du vieil pèlerin*, the *Somnium* is a dream allegory. Asleep in the garden of his house just outside Paris, Bouvet dreams of a beautiful woman whom he calls the Church (*Eglise*). He sees that her once-elegant garment is shredded and torn, exposing her back, which is infested with vermin and pus. When asked to account for the decomposition from which she suffers, she blames those who, she says, live in a certain palace. Bouvet gallantly promises to aid her. Represented as Sweet Language (*Doux langage*), he visits the palace, crossing the Bridge-without-Humanity that covers the moat of Blind Ignorance and that is guarded by figures of War and Fame.

Once he has gained entrance to the palace, Bouvet as Sweet Language visits twelve kings and princes, each of whom inhabits a different floor. He seeks audiences in turn with the European kings of Navarre, Portugal, Scotland, Castille, Cyprus, Hungary, Sicily, England, and then with the French dukes of Berry, Burgundy, Orleans, and Bourbon. Finally, he confronts the king of France. He presents arguments in favor of unity within the Church to each ruler, but each refuses to offer assistance. For example, the king of Scotland declares himself powerless, weakened by continual invasions from England. Some do not even offer excuses, like

---

[53] Honoré Bouvet, *L'Apparicion Maistre Jehan de Meun et le Somnium super materia schismatis d'Honoré Bouvet*, ed. I. Arnold (London, 1926), pp. 69-110; also studied by N. Valois, "Un Ouvrage inédit d'Honoré Bonet, prieur de Salon," *Annuaire-Bulletin de la Société de l'Histoire de France* 27 (1890) 193-228.

[54] *Ibid.*, p. 196. On the papacy during these years, see N. Valois, *La France et le grand schisme*, 3: *passim*, 4: 1-107; and H. Kaminsky, *Simon de Cramaud and the Great Schism* (New Brunswick, NJ, 1983).

[55] Published by Valois, "Un Ouvrage," pp. 193-228.

the king of Castille, who merely asks to be left in peace. Even the pious duke of Berry, whom Bouvet praises for his zealous work to end the schism, asserts only that he will act in accord with the wishes of the French king and his council. Each commands Bouvet to "climb higher," that is, to go to the next floor, which is occupied by another ruler.

Bouvet finally concludes that only Charles VI can end the schism. Approaching the king, he proposes a concrete course of action to him. Charles VI should neither engage in war to support his candidate nor urge the abdication of the candidate of his opponents. Instead, he should write letters to all the kings and princes of Christendom, divided for so long, to effect a reconciliation in favor of the Avignon pope, who would be universally recognized by the Church.

No illuminated manuscripts of the *Somnium* have survived, but thirteen miniatures were originally designed to accompany the text.[56] Contemporary with the writing of the text, a *maquette* or manuscript model preserves instructions to the illuminators.[57] These marginal notes were penned by Gerson, who must have worked in collaboration with Bouvet to design the luxury copies. Extant letters of dedication lead us to surmise that such luxury copies would have been offered to Charles VI as well as to Pope Benedict XIII, who became pope at the end of 1394, following the death of Clement VII.[58] In addition, the inventories of the duke of Berry mention three copies of the *Somnium*.[59] The fact that copies of this manuscript were offered to Berry is consistent with the flattering picture presented of him not only in the text but, as we shall see, also in the accompanying miniature. The unexpected death of Clement VII and the immediate election of Benedict XIII at the end of 1394 may have made the text of the *Somnium* obsolete, thereby frustrating plans for multiple luxury copies. Although hopes ran high that Benedict would be able to heal the split, he proved to be as intransigent as his predecessor, and in response to the continued impasse a movement developed that aimed at healing the rift by withdrawing support from both popes.

Whatever the reasons might have been for the thwarted project, the existence of the manuscript model allows us to reconstruct the program of illustrations and then to determine how the miniatures were meant to work with the text. Following a miniature portraying the figures of the

---

[56] Two unillustrated manuscripts have survived: Paris, BN MS lat. 14643; Rome, Vatican Archives, Armarium LIX, fol. XXI, fols. 73-90.

[57] Published by G. Ouy, "Une maquette de manuscrit à peintures."

[58] Both letters are included in Paris, BN MS lat. 14643.

[59] Delisle, *Librairie*, 2: 259, nos. 223, 224, 225, none of which has survived.

sleeping author and the decaying Church, twelve pictures would have constituted a series in which Bouvet appears before a ruler. The image of Bouvet was to have been repeated from picture to picture; those of the rulers were to have been carefully differentiated. Each description identifies the person and describes the setting and costume.[60] For example, the instructions indicate that the duke of Berry was to have been portrayed surrounded by jewels, reliquaries, and ornaments, and seated at Mass in an oratory that displays a magnificence outshining that of any foreign prince. Some descriptions elaborate, specifying the age and appearance of the ruler, perhaps when such details were likely to be unknown to the illuminators. For example, the King of Cyprus is described as "small and old," and the king of Spain is described as a child playing with a hoop while his crown rests on a pillow next to him, presumably to indicate his minority.

As a group, the miniatures present a series of dedication miniatures that are strung together, united by the textual allegory, which they use as a point of reference. This clever strategy would have provided Bouvet with the opportunity of presenting his book to a number of different patrons without changing its cycle of illustration, since each prospective patron was already represented in it, although Charles VI, who commissioned the work, is clearly singled out for special treatment. Because the rulers are carefully differentiated, the miniatures constitute a kind of portrait gallery of kingship within Europe at the end of the fourteenth century. By also including a picture of each French duke, the cycle reflects the division of power within France. In fact, the program was designed to have the same kind of specificity that we have already encountered in the frontispiece of the *Arbre des batailles*, with which the king was well pleased. We can imagine what the monarch's pleasure might have been at seeing himself portrayed as the wisest, most influential king among the world's most powerful rulers.

Bouvet's *Apparicion Maistre Jehan de Meun*[61] no longer addresses the king, who by the time it was written in 1398 must have been seen as less capable of discharging the responsibilities the author had earlier delegated to him. Instead, extant manuscripts bear four successive dedications to other individuals at the royal court, Louis and Valentine of Orleans, John

---

[60] These descriptions are fully published by G. Ouy, "Une maquette de manuscrit à peintures," pp. 49-51.

[61] Bouvet, *L'Apparicion Maistre Jehan de Meun*, ed. Arnold; and *idem, L'Apparition de Jean de Meun, ou, Le Songe du Prieur de Salon par Honoré Bonet*, ed. J. Pichon (Paris, 1845).

of Montaigu, and Philip of Burgundy.[62] A reading of the text of the *Apparicion* suggests that the author was interested in a wide range of political issues, about which he expressed considerable anger and frustration characteristic of the time. An examination of the cycle of illustrations allows us to pinpoint one subject among the many in the text as that which may have inspired the production of these particular manuscripts for the individuals to whom they were dedicated. Like the other works by Bouvet, the *Apparicion* emerges as a work that was concerned with the contingencies of the moment insofar as they affected the extended royal family.

The *Apparicion* is a dream allegory that presents a forceful censure of those aspects of European society which are seen as causing pervasive vice. At the beginning of the work, Bouvet is sleeping in the garden of his house, La Tournelle, which had formerly belonged to Jehan de Meun. This fact of ownership inspired the fiction of the peculiar dream and the resulting title of the work, in which Jehan de Meun appears to the author. Four other individuals – a Jew in disguise, a physician, a Saracen (described as "black as coal"), and a Jacobin – also appear and are interviewed in turn by Jehan de Meun. Bouvet chooses controversial, even rejected figures in French society to voice opinions that are in fact his own. Each voices potent criticism on specific matters. The Jew objects to the banishment of the Jews from Paris, brought about by an ordinance passed in 1394. He then inveighs against Christian money-lenders who secretly practice their usury and therefore get away with it. The physician censures charlatans and sorcerers, observing that they pretend to cure but by their fraudulent practices damage the reputation of legitimate physicians. The Saracen criticizes the French preference for creature comforts, which he sees as a cause of the failure of the Crusade of Nicopolis. He goes on to lament the indifference shown toward prisoners of the crusade and ends by reproving the papacy for its extravagant display of wealth. The emphasis throughout is on the creation of scapegoats and failure to recognize the actual causes of social ills.

---

[62] Paris, BN MSS fr. 810 (for John of Montaigu), 811 (for Valentine); London, BL Landesdowne MS 214, fols. 201r-216v (for the Duke of Burgundy); and Rome, Bib. Vat., Reg. 183. The Paris books are discussed in the editions cited above, n. 61. On the unillustrated Rome and London copies, see E. Langlois, "Notices des manuscrits français et provençaux de Rome antérieurs au XVIe siècle," *Notices et extraits des manuscrits de la Bibliothèque Nationale et autres bibliothèques* 33 (1889) 1-346, esp. 211-216; and Sir Henry Ellis and Francis Douce, *A Catalogue of the Landsdowne Manuscripts in the British Museum* (London, 1819), p. 80.

The Jacobin ("a good and wise man"), the last to be interviewed, reinforces the denunciations made by the others against the charlatans, the papacy, and the rest. The Jacobin's speech has been understood as best reflecting the views of Bouvet, who says in his prologue that he wishes to encourage "remedies" that would bring about a "noble reformation."[63] Mindful of the strength of his criticism, Bouvet apologizes for his frankness, but adds that an author who hopes to exert an influence must write "the truth without flattery."[64]

Two of the four surviving manuscripts of the *Apparicion* are exceptionally important. Not only are they the only two that are illustrated, but they preserve autograph marginal glosses, whose presence allows us to assume that Bouvet oversaw the execution of the manuscripts.[65] Prefaced by a frontispiece depicting Bouvet presenting his book, the first of the two copies is one that was made for Valentine of Orleans, wife of Louis of Orleans (Fig. 66). The second was made for John of Montaigu, an employee in the king's chamber. Text and illustrations differ somewhat in the two copies, which suggests that they were personally tailored to suit these recipients. A precise date of execution of late 1398 can be established on the basis of the marginal glosses, which refer to specific events.[66]

With one notable exception, the illumination in both manuscripts is routine, consisting of depictions of Jehan de Meun facing either the Jew, the physician, the Saracen, or the Jacobin (Fig. 65).[67] The exceptional miniature is in the copy made for Valentine. Unlike the remainder of the pictures, which are inserted within single columns of text, this one occupies half a page (Fig. 67). Interpolated into the textual section of the *Apparicion* in which the physician appears to Jehan de Meun and criticizes quackery, the miniature depicts a physician addressing Valentine, who appears with an attendant. The picture is unexplained by the text of the *Apparicion*, which it does not illustrate in any literal sense, since Valentine is not mentioned in the text. Realizing that the miniature could not be understood from the text alone, Bouvet had additional text inscribed in and below the picture. Red rubrics identify the figures. Black rubrics

---

[63] Bouvet, *L'Apparicion*, ed. Arnold, p. x.

[64] *Ibid.*, p. 4.

[65] Paris, BN MSS fr. 810-811. Identification of the glosses as autograph occurs in Bouvet, *L'Apparicion*, ed. Arnold, p. xxxvi. I thank G. Ouy for his assistance with these paleographic details.

[66] *Ibid.*, p. x.

[67] A partial facsimile of the miniatures in both copies in Paris is included in Bouvet, *L'Apparicion*, ed. Pichon.

address Valentine, asking her to pay attention to Bouvet's poem. Using the scriptural example of Susanna and the Elders, the poem inveighs against lies and liars.

> Beautiful Susanna by her great holiness
> Was accused without any truth
> And condemned by very false judgment
> To suffer death so villanously
> But God in heaven who issues true judgments
> Turned death on the false accusers.
> Therefore, all who are wise ought to bear peacefully
> Lies and their false deffamations
> Because lies do not last long:
> They are nothing but dreams, or scripture lies.
> This is truth, true conclusion
> That all embrace, especially loyalty
> [Very great lady, listen to my song,
> After winter, summer will come again].[68]

Given the placement of the picture within the text, in order to understand the miniature we would need to look for a link between Valentine and the practice of false medicine, a practice that led to "false" accusations against her, like Susanna.

The interpolated miniature with its associated text was inspired by a series of events in which Valentine played a prominent and notorious role. To understand the public stir these events had caused by 1398 it is necessary to reconsider in some detail the circumstances of Charles VI's fits of insanity and the attempts to cure him in the 1390s. Eyewitness accounts of the first fit in 1392 report that the king, suddenly overcome by a loss of his senses, had attempted to kill his brother, Louis of Orleans.[69] This widely accepted version of what happened may have fed rumors that the king was not insane at all but that he had been poisoned by Louis of Orleans.[70] According to such rumors, the king, knowing Louis to be a traitor, turned on him. Indeed, modern research has found a number of the king's symptoms to be consistent with poisoning.[71] What is important, however, is that some of the king's contemporaries whole-

---

[68] Bouvet, *L'Apparicion*, ed. Arnold, pp. 67-68.

[69] Le Religieux de Saint-Denis, *Chronique du religieux de Saint-Denis*, 6 vols. (Paris, 1839-1852), 2: 19. The same account, quoting Jean Petit, appears in Enguerrand de Monstrelet, *The Chronicles of Enguerrand de Monstrelet*, ed. and tr. T. Johnes, 2 vols. (London, 1867), 2: 227.

[70] This version is given by Froissart, *Œuvres*, 15: 44-45.

[71] See especially, Brachet, *Pathologie mentale*, pp. 621-650.

heartedly believed that Louis of Orleans, with the assistance of Valentine, was plotting to poison the king.

Confirmation of Valentine's complicity was sought in a series of subsequent events.[72] After the king's second attack in 1393, she ministered to him daily; in fact, she was the only person he would allow near him apart from those who were brought in to cure him, including, as we have seen, a doctor from Lyon who specialized in poisons and two monks who were apparently expert at prescribing dietary remedies.[73] In spite of such attention the king's condition worsened, with the result that Valentine became an easy target for those who propounded the theory of a plot to poison the king. Chroniclers present contradictory views of Valentine, but those who accepted her complicity believed her to be an envious, ambitious duchess who yearned to be queen.[74] In the event that both the king and the ailing infant dauphin were to die, her husband would of course inherit the throne.

Subsequent events involved Valentine even more directly and must have led to her inclusion in the *Apparicion*. During the king's third and most prolonged relapse in 1395, the dauphin was playing one day with Valentine's son. When her son died after eating an apple given him by his nursemaid, Valentine's enemies claimed that the apple, which was believed to have been poisoned, had been intended for the dauphin and was mistakenly given to the wrong child.[75] This accusation resulted in her banishment from Paris in this same year, first to Asnière-sur-Oise and then, because she was thought to be too close, to the more distant Neufchâtel-sur-Loire.[76] She was permitted to return to Paris only in 1408, following the assassination of her husband, whose memory she defended during the inquiry about his murder.

Shortly after Valentine's exile, the two monks who had been serving as physicians to the king began to lose their credibility as they grew more interested in whoring and gambling than in medicine.[77] When the king's

---

[72] Summaries of Valentine's role may be found in E. Collas, *Valentine de Milan, duchesse d'Orléans*, 2nd ed. (Paris, 1911), pp. 187-227, and Coville, *Jean Petit*, pp. 306-310, 328-336.

[73] On the doctor, see the *Chronique des quatre premiers Valois (1327-1393)*, ed. S. Luce (Paris, 1862), p. 336; and on the two monks, see Le Religieux de Saint-Denis, *Chronique*, 2: 662-666, and E. de Monstrelet, *Chronicle*, 2: 78.

[74] This is the view presented by Froissart, *Œuvres*, 15: 260. She is seen in a more favorable light by Le Religieux de Saint-Denis, *Chronique*, 2: 89.

[75] Froissart, *Œuvres*, 15: 260. E. de Monstrelet, quoting Jean Petit, suggests that the duke was responsible; see his *Chronicle*, 1: 80.

[76] Froissart, *Œuvres*, 15: 353-354.

[77] On these events, see Le Religieux and Monstrelet, as cited in n. 69.

condition continued unchanged, their effectiveness was questioned and they, in turn, accused Louis of Orleans of practicing sorcery and black magic on the king. He countered, apparently effectively since the monks were tried, convicted, and executed in 1398.

Viewed against the background of these episodes, the miniature of Valentine standing with a physician in the *Apparicion* may now be better understood. The picture and the associated poem attempt to absolve Valentine of complicity in plots to poison the king. In the short poem, Bouvet argues that she was wrongly accused, like Susanna. He implies further that she has been vindicated, perhaps by the trial and execution of the two monks, the "false physicians," an event that is mentioned in a marginal note in the text.[78] Bouvet's condemnation of lies and liars must be seen as directed toward those who had originally accused Valentine, and then pressed for her exile from Paris. The picture serves as a visual acquittal of Valentine, by juxtaposing her with a physician who regards a specimen in a glass. As one of the "legitimate" physicians referred to in the text, he would seem to give expert testimony in support of Valentine's innocence.

In conclusion, we should ask what purposes these manuscripts would have served. They certainly were not instruments of propaganda designed to prevent Valentine's banishment from Paris, for she had already endured three years of exile when the book was written. In fact, the timing of the manuscripts seems initially puzzling until one recalls that the two monks were executed around the very time the book was written. Their execution must have been seen by Bouvet as sufficient to vindicate the duchess. He actually may have believed that Valentine might be allowed to return to Paris the next spring, if we can interpret literally the author's concluding recommendation to her in the poem that she await the spring. We can surmise that the picture included in her own copy was intended to solace her. But the poem, appended also to the end of John of Montaigu's copy, may have been intended to spur those in positions of power to press for her pardon.

CHRISTINE DE PIZAN AND UNIVERSAL MONARCHY

Another work, this one by Christine herself, is of interest here because it focuses on a theme that was of central importance to the notions of Valois

---

[78] The marginal notes, which are as yet unedited, are discussed in Bouvet, *L'Apparicion*, ed. Arnold, p. 15 n. 1.

kingship, that of a universal monarchy headed by the French king. Written between October 1402 and March 1403, the *Chemin de long estude* is a dream allegory.[79] In Christine's dream, she is approached by a sibyl who takes her on a journey, "the path of long study" after which the work is titled. They go first to the Fountain of Wisdom where the muses bathe and then up a ladder, called Speculation, to the heavens where, together they look out upon the planets, stars, sun, and moon. In another part of the sky they encounter four queens who rule the world and who are called Wisdom, Nobility, Chivalry, and Wealth. At the moment that Christine and the sibyl arrive, the queens have convened as a parliament, presided over by Reason, to determine who should govern mankind. Christine and the sibyl stop to listen. Each queen argues in turn that the ruler should possess her own attributes. Finally, Reason judges France to be the kingdom from which the ruler will be chosen by a jury of the French princes. She appoints Christine as her messenger, sending her back to earth to await the decision. With the sibyl, Christine returns to earth, but the next thing she knows is that her mother is knocking at her door to awaken her because she has overslept. The *Chemin* ends abruptly at this point.

Even though Christine awakens before the name of the universal emperor is revealed to her, there can be little doubt that she had Charles vi in mind for this role. The dedication of the work first to Charles vi and then to the French dukes makes this assumption likely. Other evidence, as we shall see, makes it virtually indisputable. The idea of a universal monarch being chosen to rule the world had a longstanding place in medieval political thought.[80] We have seen it already in Philippe's *Songe du vieil pèlerin* and Bouvet's *Arbre des batailles*, where it was expressed in less explicit terms. The *Chemin de long estude* thus fits into a tradition of thought, known also to Philippe, Bouvet, Froissart, and others, which saw Charles vi as the universal monarch predicted in the "second Charlemagne" prophecy.[81]

Within this tradition the *Chemin* is somewhat peculiar, however, because it does not actually divulge the name of the universal monarch, even if this person could have been none other than Charles vi. By using

---

[79] On the extant manuscripts and their dates, see Solente, "Christine de Pisan," pp. 361-363.

[80] See Folz, *L'Idée d'Empire*, and Zeller, "Les Rois de France."

[81] See Bouvet, *The Tree of Battles*, ed. Coopland, p. 80; Froissart, *Œuvres*, 21: 365; and A. Leroux, "La Royauté française et le Saint-Empire au moyen âge (843-1493)," *Revue historique* 49 (1892) 241-288, esp. 280-281, where he cites three letters in which other European rulers accuse Charles vi of coveting the imperial crown.

the fiction that the identity is unknown, Christine creates an opportunity to outline those qualities of rulership that, in her opinion, should ideally characterize the universal monarch. In this way, she transforms the doctrine of prophecy into a literature of advice.

More than two-thirds of the *Chemin* is devoted to the proceedings of the parliament of queens during which those virtues necessary for a good ruler are spelled out. Personifications of wisdom, nobility, chivalry, and wealth speak in turn, each favoring the attributes for which they stand. It has been suggested that each was meant to represent a different European ruler.[82] However, it seems more likely that the first three, taken together, stand for those virtues required for a good ruler, whereas the last stands for a vice. Three different sorts of evidence support this view. First, there is historiographic evidence that provides information on the usual interpretation of these virtues; second, there is evidence within the text of the *Chemin*; and third, there is the evidence of the illuminations that decorate the London copy of the *Chemin*. A review of the meanings of these virtues leads to a reinterpretation of the *Chemin* as a work concerned specifically with the ruling French monarchy.

In the first category of evidence, works of French historiography include those in which wisdom and chivalry figure prominently as special virtues, ones particular to French kingship. For instance, in the thirteenth century, in one of the earliest attempts to provide a symbolic interpretation for the heraldic fleur-de-lis, Guillaume de Nangis explains in the *Vita Ludovici regis francorum* that the "double part of the lily's leaves signify wisdom and chivalry, which ... watch over and defend faith, for faith is governed and ruled by wisdom, and defended by chivalry."[83] He goes on to interpret wisdom and chivalry, along with faith, as signs of divine favor of French kingship. Associated with the very symbol of the French king, the fleur-de-lis, the prized virtues of wisdom and chivalry continued through the fifteenth century to distinguish French monarchs from all others.[84] As such, we can readily accept that they were considered by

---

[82] C. B. Petitot, *Collection des mémoires relatifs à l'histoire de France, depuis le règne de Philippe-Auguste jusqu'au commencement du dix-septième siècle avec des notices sur chaque auteur, et des observations sur chaque ouvrage*, ser. 1, 52 vols. (Paris, 1819-1829), 5: 235; and P. A. Becker, "Christine de Pizan," *Zeitschrift fur französische Sprache und Literatur* 54 (1931) 9-164. G. Mombello, however, doubts the specificity of the proposed identifications in "Quelques aspects de la pensée politique de Christine de Pizan," p. 96.

[83] Guillaume de Nangis, *Vita sancti Ludovici*, in *Recueil des historiens des Gaules et de la France*, eds. P. C. F. Daunou and J. Naudet, 24 vols. (Paris, 1840), 20: 320.

[84] S. Hindman and G. M. Spiegel, "The Fleur-de-lis Frontispieces to Guillaume de Nangis's 'Chronique abrégée': Political Iconography in Late Fifteenth-Century France," *Viator* 12 (1981) 381-407.

Christine to be virtues essential for the universal monarch if the monarch were also a French king.

If we turn to the second area of investigation, the text of the *Chemin*, we find confirmation that Christine thought of wisdom and chivalry, along with nobility, as prerequisite virtues for the universal monarch, in contrast to wealth which was to be despised. In support of the virtue of wisdom, she brings up the example of Charles v because he loved knowledge, prudence, science, and astronomy.[85] Christine was to use Charles v as a model for French rulers in the *Livre des fais et bonnes meurs*, so it seems likely that here she is implying that Charles v should serve as an example for the universal monarch.[86] For the virtue of chivalry, she draws on the *Policraticus*, which holds the knight responsible for "guarding the catholic faith, the people and the public good, orphans, woman, and widowed women."[87] Clearly, this is also behavior to be sought after. To these virtues of wisdom and chivalry Christine adds nobility. She makes clear that nobility is a virtue to be prized in part by focusing on the dynastic ties of the European monarchs with the Trojans.[88] This discussion enables her to point out that the French monarch, like the imperial Alexander the Great and Julius Caesar before him, is the most noble because he can trace his lineage directly back to Priam through Hector. In marked opposition to these virtues is wealth, which is called the "duchess of pride" and compared to the deadly sin of avarice.[89] Christine summons numerous classical and exegetical authorities, including Seneca, Valerius Maximus, the Gospels, and Saint Augustine, to show that the monarch ought to disdain worldly goods.[90]

The particular arrangement of the virtues in the sky is one other feature of the text of the *Chemin* that indicates how Christine viewed these virtues, most notably wealth and wisdom. Probably inspired by Philippe de Mézières's *Songe du vieil pèlerin*, she adopted a spatial orientation for the virtues that corresponds with the points on the compass.[91] Wealth is situated in the West, opposite wisdom in the East. Nobility and chivalry are found in the North and South respectively. Philippe used the points

---

[85] Christine, *Le Chemin de long estude*, ed. Püschel, p. 213.

[86] Christine, *Le Livre des fais et bonnes meurs*, ed. Solente. In this text, Charles is praised for his interest in astronomy (pp. 15-19).

[87] Christine, *Le Chemin de long estude*, ed. Püschel, p. 183.

[88] *Ibid.*, pp. 151-156.

[89] *Ibid.*, pp. 195-197.

[90] *Ibid.*, pp. 195-209.

[91] *Ibid.*, pp. 98-105.

of the compass to present an allegory of France under Charles VI as a ship buffeted by the four winds.[92] For Philippe, the West wind was the most cruel. When it blew, the ship was led toward the Three Terrible Things — pride, avarice, and lust — that lead inevitably to death. The East wind blew the fairest. It came from Paradise, was graced by the Holy Spirit, and led the ship out of death, away from vice, and toward the city of Jerusalem in the East. If Christine was using Philippe's allegory, as seems likely, her placement of wealth in the West suggests that, like the cruel West wind, it encourages the proliferation of vice. Her placement of wisdom in the East suggests that she saw it as the most positive virtue for the universal monarch. If we recall that the mission of the universal monarch was to take him ultimately to the city of Jerusalem, the equation between the virtue of wisdom and the East acquires further significance in the *Chemin*.

An examination of the illuminations suggests that Christine used the pictures to gloss further the text of the *Chemin* and, in particular, to put forward specific individuals as models of rulership for Charles VI. Having established in the text that wisdom is the most highly sought after virtue, whereas wealth is a dangerous vice, Christine proceeds in the pictures to equate actual persons with wisdom and wealth. In the London copy of the *Chemin*, three miniatures depict the parliament of the queens. In each miniature in the upper left, a personification of wisdom holds a book (Fig. 69). This attribute accords with the description of Wisdom in the text.[93] At her feet rests another object, an armillary sphere, which is not called for by the text but which suggests an interest in astronomy. As the only one of the queens dressed in a mantle and robe, in red and blue, a costume more fitting to a king than a queen, this figure may be taken to stand for Charles V. Although not specifically called for by the text, this allusion is fully consistent with Christine's reference to Charles V as a wise ruler. The presence of the armillary sphere may be understood to refer to his interest in astronomy, which is also mentioned in the text. In this case the miniature works to define one model as an appropriate one for the universal monarch, "Charles, son of Charles."

If we consider next the attributes of wealth, we can suggest that the personification of wealth also stands for a specific individual. According to the text, Wealth is very richly dressed in a gold garment studded with

---

[92] Philippe, *Le Songe*, ed. Coopland, 1: 108. I thank Anne D. Hedeman for pointing this out.

[93] Christine, *Le Chemin de long estude*, ed. Püschel, pp. 99-101.

garnets and wears an enormous garnet on a broach at her neck.[94] She holds in her right hand a hammer and has at her feet other tools that the text identifies only as those that can be used in the building trade.[95] Christine's description of the sumptuous costume seems a reasonable invention for the imagery of wealth. But the details of the tools seem peculiar, especially since they are not explained in the text. Yet in the miniatures, the Queen of Wealth is characterized not by her dress, which is no more lavish than that of the others and is devoid of jewels besides, but by her attributes: a hammer, a plane, and a saw. This suggests that these attributes are important for our understanding of wealth, but since they are not explained in the text, we must seek their meaning elsewhere.

Numerous documents and chronicles of the period inform us that the plane was a well-known emblem of John the Fearless, duke of Burgundy. He used it everywhere, having it embroidered onto his garments, painted into the backgrounds of his miniatures, and gilded onto cups, chandeliers, and ships.[96] As an emblem, the plane was intended to show his superiority over his rival, Louis of Orleans, since if could be understood metaphorically as shaving off the blunt stick that was Louis's emblem. To convey this notion, the duke of Burgundy even had real carpenter's planes made out of gold and sent them along with bags of gold shavings to his allies.[97] The prevalence of the imagery of the carpenter's plane, always associated with John the Fearless, leads us to propose that the attribute is used in the *Chemin* to identify the figure of wealth with this particular duke. The use of the hammer provides additional confirmation for this identity. Less well documented as an emblem of John the Fearless, it appears nevertheless in several portraits of him and therefore must have been one of his emblems, probably conveying the same political significance as did the plane.[98] Additional support for the identification of wealth with John the Fearless comes from miniatures that illustrate the *Mutacion*; in the *Mutacion*, wealth guards the château of Fortune, in front of whose doors she sits. But the fact that she is not depicted with any attributes in the *Mutacion* suggests that those peculiar attributes that appear in the *Chemin* need to be explained by the special requirements of its ideological

[94]   *Ibid.*, pp. 103-105.
[95]   *Ibid.*, p. 105: "... pluseurs outilz appuiez / De quoy on fait divers ouvrages."
[96]   Evans, *Dress in Mediaeval France*, p. 41; and Laborde, *Les Ducs de Bourgogne*, 2.1: 28, 40, 58, 84, 242, 252, and *passim*.
[97]   Vaughan, *John the Fearless*, pp. 234-235.
[98]   See for example the presumed portrait of John in Salmon's *Demandes*, Geneva, Bib. pub. et univ., MS fr. 165, fol. 4, reproduced by Meiss, *Boucicaut*, Fig. 72.

program.[99] Given the characterization of wealth in the text of the *Chemin*, coupled with its placement in the West, it thus seems probable that as a personification of wealth John the Fearless was included as a negative model to the king, one to shun rather than to emulate.

It is not immediately clear, however, how John the Fearless came to be associated with wealth in miniatures of the *Chemin*, nor why he is presented as a negative model of rulership. His association with wealth could have been inspired by Burgundian political policy on taxation. Following in the footsteps of his father, Philip the Bold, John advocated a decrease in the taxes that were being so heavily levied on the French citizens.[100] Indeed, Christine puts into the mouth of the personification of wealth a similar position when she has her declare that a ruler who is rich enough himself does not need to use taxation as a means of raising money.[101] Although this might seem at first to suggest that John is a positive rather than a negative model, Christine could hardly have looked kindly on the obvious extravagance displayed by the mass production of gold planes and shavings. In fact, we know from other texts, like the *Mutacion*, that she regarded the vice of wealth as responsible for world problems such as the schism.[102] It is possible, therefore, that she has taken this opportunity in the *Chemin* to point out the inadequacy of the Burgundian political stance if it is not tempered by the practice of virtues like moderation, along with wisdom, chivalry, and nobility.

If we consider all the manuscripts of the *Chemin*, another explanation can be suggested for the use of John the Fearless as a negative model. Although the hammer is present as an attribute in all copies, the planes figure most prominently in the London manuscript.[103] The London copy thus firmly establishes the connection between the duke and wealth. This copy is, moreover, the only one in which the miniatures preserve the East-West orientation of the figures standing for wisdom and wealth; comparison with the Paris copy reveals the distinctiveness of the London one (Fig. 70). Now, if we recall that the London copy of the *Chemin* occurs in the same volume of "Collected Works," the one dedicated to

---

[99] Meiss, *Limbourgs*, 2: Fig. 1.

[100] Vaughan, *John the Fearless*, p. 31.

[101] Christine, *Le Chemin de long estude*, ed. Püschel, p. 143.

[102] Christine, *La Mutacion de fortune*, ed. Solente, 1: 76-82.

[103] Earlier manuscripts of this text were illustrated with only three or four miniatures, the entire cycle of the parliament of queens being devised for the later Paris and London copies. The four earlier copies of the text are: Paris, BN MS fr. 1188; Chantilly, Musée Condé, MSS 492-493; and Brussels, Bib. Roy., MSS 10982, 10983.

Queen Isabeau, which also includes the most carefully worked out version of the *Epistre*, the possibility arises that once again Christine is directing a message to the queen. In the text of the *Chemin*, she is recalling the prophecy which declared Isabeau's husband, Charles VI, to be the universal monarch. In the pictures she suggests that his father, Charles V, possessed those virtues which are most desirable for this mission, whereas John the Fearless manifests that vice which is most despised. The message was a timely one around 1410 to 1415 when the "Collected Works" was compiled and presented to the queen. At that moment, John of Burgundy was enjoying an increase of power, the result partly of attention from the queen and partly of his influence over the dauphin.[104]

The dedication miniatures of the *Chemin* contribute an additional gloss on the text, confirming the main theme of the work, Charles VI's supremacy as a ruler (Fig. 68). In these miniatures, a detail of costume is conspicuous: the inclusion of the necklace of the so-called Order of the Broom Pod worn by Charles VI. As depicted in the London copy, this necklace is composed of interlocking gold flowers with two dangling gold broom pods that look very much like pea pods because the broom plant is a shrub belonging to the pea family. Two factors suggest the importance of this detail. First, the necklace does not normally appear in portraits of Charles VI, of which there are many.[105] Second, the necklace is included in the dedication miniatures in every manuscript copy of the *Chemin*, even the earlier, less carefully executed copies.[106] These observations suggest that the presence of the necklace here may be intended to make a point that is in some way related to the ideological program of the *Chemin* (as the inclusion of the collar of the porcupine makes a point in manuscripts of the *Epistre*).

To understand what this point might be, we should attempt to find out what the Order of the Broom Pod signified. Unlike the Order of the Porcupine, the Order of the Broom Pod does not seem to have been an actual order of chivalry with an established membership of knights and a specific rule.[107] Nor was it merely an emblem, part of the livery of the king, like the carpenter's plane of John of Burgundy. Rather, the Order of the

---

[104] See above, ch. 3, p. 111.

[105] It does appear in the miniatures in Salmon's *Demandes*, in two copies in Paris, BN MS fr. 23279, and Geneva, Bib. pub. et univ., MS fr. 165, illustrated in Meiss, *Boucicaut*, Fig. 69.

[106] For example, in those copies cited above, n. 103.

[107] On the Order of the Broom Pod, see A. Favyn, *The Theatre of Honour*, pp. 349-354; P. Helyot, *Histoire des ordres*, 8: 276-279; and F. Steenackers, *Histoire des ordres de chevalerie*, pp. 145-147.

Broom Pod seems to have functioned a little like an order and a little like an emblem, without being exclusively either. It was conferred on blood nobility, as an order would have been. However, presents made up of broom were also given to members of Charles vi's household, as well as to knights, ladies, and rulers abroad who for reasons of social status, sex, or nationality could not normally have belonged to a secular order of chivalry.[108] The broom flower and broom pod were also used extensively at court as emblems of the king; they were embroidered onto his garments and onto tapestries in his chambers, and they were worn as accessories, as shown in the miniature.[109]

The significance of all this lies in the symbolic meaning of the broom plant. Documents from the royal accounts show us that the broom plant, called in Latin the *planta genesta*, was usually depicted with the king's device, *Jamais*, with which it alternated.[110] Thus, on necklaces, belts, and tapestries the letters of the king's device *Jamais* are followed by a representation of the broom, a pairing that was repeated over and over to form a kind of chain. A pun was communicated through this imagery: *Jamais planta genesta*. This pun could be read in two ways, as either "I have loved the broom flower" or "Never Plantagenet." When read in the first way, it communicated a whimsical preference on the part of the king for a certain type of flower or plant. When read in the second, more important, way, it made a political point. "Never Plantagenet" was a forceful response to persistent English claims to the French throne.[111]

---

[108] The order was conferred on John ɪ of Aragon in 1389 who, in turn, sent Charles the Order of the Eagle, according to a document published by L. Mirot and J. Viellard, "Inventaire des lettres des rois d'Aragon à Charles vi et à la cour de France conservées aux archives de la couronne d'Aragon à Barcelone," ʙᴇᴄ 103 (1942) 99-150, esp. 119; on the duchesses of Lancaster and Gloucester, the countess of Huntington, and Johanna, daughter of the Duke of Lancaster, in 1396, according to the contemporary account of the meeting preliminary to Richard ɪɪ's and Isabelle's wedding, in P. Meyer, "L'Entrevue d'Ardres, 1396," *Annuaire-Bulletin de la Société de l'histoire de France* 18 (1881) 219; and on Charles vi's herald, Robert of Mauny, in 1406, according to the document published by Douët-d'Arcq, *Choix de pièces*, 1: 287.

[109] See Meyer, "L'Entrevue d'Ardres," p. 219; Gay, *Glossaire archéologique*, 1: 36-37 and *passim*. Many of the documents refer to the broom pod as the king's livery.

[110] See, for example, the document published by Gay, *Glossaire archéologique*, 1: 412.

[111] On the use of Plantagenet as a surname and its heraldic associations, see J. Nichols, "Observations on the Heraldic Devices Discovered on the Effigies of Richard the Second and His Queen in Westminster Abbey, and upon the Mode in Which Those Ornaments Were Executed; Including Some Remarks on the Surname Plantagenet and the Ostrich Feathers of the Prince of Wales," *Archaeologia* 29 (1852) 32-59; and the analyses of E. W. Tristram, "The Wilton Diptych," *The Month*, n.s., 1 (1949) 379-390, 2 (1949) 18-36. Although this is not the place to pursue the meaning of the Wilton Diptych in which the broom pods also appear, worn by Richard ɪɪ, it would seem that

Widely distributed as a token, the broom flower thus carried with it connotations of the French king's supremacy over England, in much the same way that John of Burgundy's carpenter's plane expressed his domination over his rival, the duke of Orleans. The fact that the broom was often represented without its associated device probably matters little. Once the meaning of the imagery was fixed, it would have communicated this meaning in any form, just as the image of the carpenter's plane was understood even though it was commonly represented without the blunt stick or the gold shavings that contributed to its original significance.

If we return now to the *Chemin*, we can propose that the inclusion of the necklace of the broom pod in the dedication miniature enriches the meaning of the book. We have already seen that the text focuses on those qualities that the universal emperor ideally ought to possess, whereas the miniatures of the parliament of queens propose specific models of rulership to the universal emperor, ones that he should avoid as well as emulate. We can now suggest that the dedication miniature highlights an international concern of considerable importance to the quest for a universal empire, namely, the supremacy of the French kingdom. We should recall that, by the terms of the prophecy, Charles VI was to subjugate England, along with all other European countries, before going on to become emperor, under which title he was to lead the crusade. Yet the resumption of hostilities of the Hundred Years' War in the first decade of the fifteenth century, which brought with it renewed claims to the throne of France on the part of the English king, must have seemed to threaten the fulfillment of the prophecy.

How could a king whose own right to rule was being questioned become the universal emperor? Christine alludes briefly to this question in the text when she points out that the English kings are only indirectly descended from King Priam of Troy and therefore are not as noble as the French royalty, which descended through Hector.[112] The implication, of course, is that the English kings are unsuited for the imperial charge. The dedication miniature more aggressively counters the English claim by referring to the rallying cry of the French against the English, "Never Plantagenet." In this way, the *Chemin* implies that one important

---

the adoption of the broom pod, without the word "never" might have functioned as a sort of challenge to the French on the part of the English. The consistent juxtaposition of the broom with the word *jamais* in Salmon's *Demandes* surely carries the meaning of French supremacy, since a section of this manuscript is devoted to the relationship between France and England.

[112] Christine, *Le Chemin de long estude*, ed. Püschel, p. 156.

obstacle, the English claim to the French throne, on the course toward establishing a universal empire will be easily eliminated.

POLITICAL THOUGHT AND THE ILLUMINATED MANUSCRIPT

This chapter should enable us to see the *Epistre Othéa* from two different perspectives. First, because of the similarities of these works, we can now accept the *Epistre* as one example among others that, taken together, constitute a coherent body of political writings at the court of Charles VI. Second, because of the differences that emerge more clearly when these works are studied as a group, we can understand better where the *Epistre* fits in the reign of Charles VI or, to put it another way, how Christine, writing toward the middle instead of at the beginning of his reign, responded to a different set of circumstances, while holding fast to many of the political beliefs found in works by Philippe and Bouvet.

In many senses (except perhaps its feminism), the *Epistre Othéa* is a work fully consistent with contemporary political thought. As Krynen has shown, works of the period manifest a solid monarchical loyalism that was centered on a certain image of the king and the state and that was inspired in part by various crises of power that characterize the reign of Charles VI.[113] Two crises, the Hundred Years' War and the king's illness, were particularly important because they both seemed to threaten the position of the French king as head of state. Continued fighting served to remind the French that the English claimed their throne. Yet the French king's illnesses left him incapable of actively directing a strong government that could counter such a claim. His weakness led at the same time to internal fighting for control of the government. Writing during a period of crisis, Christine, Philippe, and Bouvet exalted French kingship in order to shape a better state. For these authors, the ideal government that they envisioned was not a faraway utopia with a fictional ruler; it was contemporary France under Charles VI.

The image of the king that emerges in works by these authors may initially seem to be at odds with the reality of a mad king whose very title was being disputed. Christine, Philippe, and Bouvet present a king who is powerful and venerated at home and abroad. His power derives in part from the genealogical myth of his succession from the Trojans, a myth that also made it unthinkable that another could rule in his stead. Among these authors, it is Christine who was most interested in the idea of dynastic

---

[113] J. Krynen, *Idéal du Prince*, pp. 42-46.

perpetuity which finds its fullest expression in the *Epistre*, although it is also a secondary theme in the *Chemin*, where it is used to support the notion of the French king as the universal emperor.

It is this idea of the French monarch as the universal emperor that in various guises permeates much of the writing of the period. This image of the monarch underlies the whole of Philippe's *Songe du vieil pèlerin*, in which the imperial imagery of the peregrine falcon and the flying stag is developed. The idea of the king as emperor underlies other works as well, such as Bouvet's *Arbre* and *Somnium* and Philippe's *Epistre au roi Richart* and *Chevalerie*. In them, Charles is presented as a king who will fulfill the terms of the prophecy, that is, who will establish world peace in the *Arbre*, end the schism in the *Somnium*, and conquer the Holy Land in the *Epistre au roi Richart* and the *Chevalerie*. At first, the *Apparicion* seems somewhat idiosyncratic among these works, because it reveals a weak rather than a strong image of Charles as a ruler preyed upon by those who plot against his life. Yet this work and the circumstances that led to its creation suggest the considerable extent to which contemporaries were unwilling to accept that the king was incurably ill. In the face of the reality of such a situation, the image of a strong monarchy put forward in all these works should be seen as propaganda. The fiction of the powerful, imperial king functioned as a substitute for the unfortunate, but nevertheless inalterable, reality of a weak but well-liked monarch.

Although they all share a view of the state and the monarch, Christine's illuminated manuscripts stand apart from those of Philippe and Bouvet partially because they come at different moments during the reign of Charles VI. When Philippe and Bouvet began to write at the beginning of the reign, they were faced with a new monarch; they had every reason to believe he would live up to his father, the wise king Charles V, whom they had also served. Neither Philippe nor Bouvet wrote after the year 1400, so that neither discussed the quarrel between the dukes of Orleans and Burgundy that only flared up after that year. Likewise, neither was concerned with the training of the dauphin, Louis, who was not even born until 1397, nor with the dauphin Charles, who was born in 1392. Since these were momentous issues during the first decade of the fifteenth century they preoccupied Christine and were present in the manuscripts by her that can be dated during those years, such as the Paris and London copies of the *Epistre*.

These events did not much change the content of political thought with regard to the image of the monarchy as it had come to be defined under Charles VI. Rather, they altered the tone of the writings. In place of the confident optimism communicated with relative detachment which characterizes earlier writings at the court of Charles VI, those by Christine are cautionary pleas, as she herself seems to be at the point of despair over the state of the monarchy. One way of thinking about Christine's position within this group of writers is to see her as picking up where the others left off, incorporating their political ideas and using their literary forms to manifest a staunch loyalty to the monarchy.

Christine was not the only writer to carry on the ideas of Philippe and Bouvet in the first decade of the fifteenth century. Their political ideas are consistent with those of other writers who held a variety of positions during this time: Jean Gerson, Jean Lebègue, Nicolas of Clamanges, Jean of Montreuil, Pierre d'Ailly, Jean Courtecuisse, and Jacques Legrand.[114] A concern with the continuity of the state and its future development led many of these authors to write about the moral education of the king and his offspring.[115] They also strove to define the relationship between royal power and the state.[116] But these writers did not embellish their manuscripts with pictures. Following Philippe and Bouvet, it was Christine who used pictures as well as words to continue the discourse about the monarchy into the fifteenth century.

---

[114] *Ibid., passim* and the various articles by G. Ouy, "L'Humanisme et les mutations politiques et sociales en France aux XIVe et XVe siècles," in *14e Stage international d'études humanistes, Tours. L'Humanisme français au début de la Renaissance* (Paris, 1973), pp. 13-42; and "Paris, l'un des principaux foyers de l'Humanisme en Europe au début du XVe siècle," *Bulletin de la Société de l'Histoire de Paris et de l'Île de France* (Paris, 1970), pp. 71-98.

[115] For example, Jean Gerson's treatise for the education of the dauphin, A. Thomas, ed., *Jean de Gerson*; Jacques LeGrand's sermons discussed by E. Beltran, "Un Sermon français inédit attribuable à Jacques Legrand," *Romania* 93 (1972) 462-478; and works by Jean Courtecuisse, *L'Œuvre oratoire française de Jean Courtecuisse*, ed. G. di Stefano (Torino, 1969).

[116] Especially Jean Gerson, *Harangue, passim*.

Epilogue

A Historical Legacy

Since the focus has been on providing a historical context for Christine's manuscripts, our task would be incomplete if we did not follow through, explaining what happened next, after around 1410 to 1415 when Queen Isabeau's volume of the collected writings was compiled. Christine wrote very little after 1410 and produced no work that was designed for illuminations. Her relative silence was perhaps due to her perceptions of a changed political climate.

Written in 1410 for the duke of Berry, the *Lamentacion Christine de Pizan* provides a glimpse of what she thought in that year.[1] In this powerful work, she lamented the current state of France which she referred to as the "formerly glorious realm" where the "brothers, cousins, and relatives kill each other like dogs motivated by false envy and covetousness."[2] Her favorite duke, Louis of Bourbon, had died that year, and she turned to John of Berry as the "most noble uncle who is living today" and asked him to intervene to stop the warring armies of his nephews, the king and the duke of Burgundy.[3] She promised that if he did intervene he would be acclaimed as the "father of the reign, conservator of the crown and of the noble lily, custodian of the high lineage."[4] Christine feared, however, that she was but a "poor voice crying out in this realm, desirous of peace and of good for all of you," the phrase with which she signed her work.[5] Inspired by the promise of peace offered by the Treaty of Auxerre, she wrote in 1412 and 1413 her only major composition of this decade, the *Livre de la Paix*, in which she pinned her hope for the peaceful continuity of the monarchy on the dauphin Louis of Guyenne.[6]

[1] Thomassy, ed., *Écrits politiques*, pp. 141-149; and Christine, "La Lamentacion."
[2] Christine, "La Lamentacion," pp. 181-182.
[3] *Ibid.*, p. 182.
[4] *Ibid.*, p. 184.
[5] *Ibid.*, p. 185.
[6] See above, ch. 3, pp. 127-128, 134-135.

Peace did not last, and the situation worsened. In 1413, three thousand butchers headed an uprising in Paris which resulted in an ordinance that promulgated massive reform of the royal administration, now largely in the hands of Louis.[7] Next, the defeat of the French by the English at the Battle of Agincourt in 1415 devastated France. Then, in 1417, John the Fearless entered Paris to preside over a new government set up in the name of the queen.[8] He ordered mass executions and expelled the Armagnacs including the new dauphin, Charles. Charles's brother, Louis of Guyenne, had died prematurely, some said by poisoning, in 1415.[9] During this decade, the ambitions of the duke of Burgundy are also reflected in illuminated works of propaganda, manuscripts that should be studied as a first manifestation of Burgundy's own perception of itself vis-à-vis the state of France.[10] The threat of Burgundian rule led many supporters of the monarchy, like Christine, to flee Paris in 1418. Christine retired to a cloister, probably Poissy. During the remaining decade of her life she virtually ceased to write; only a short devotional work can be dated during these years.[11]

From Christine's perspective, there was probably little to write about. In 1419, on the bridge of Montereau, John the Fearless was murdered as an act of revenge for his assassination of Louis of Orleans. The dauphin Charles was alleged to be partly responsible for the murder, an allegation that lost him considerable public support.[12] In the next year, the humiliating terms of the Treaty of Troyes disinherited and banished the dauphin and granted the English Henry v the hand in marriage of Catherine, daughter of Charles vi. Henry v, who was considered to be "heir and regent of France," presided at official functions with Charles vi and resided in the Louvre. The one-year-old English Henry vi succeeded him as king of France and England in 1422, also the year of Charles vi's death. During the 1420s, John of Monmouth, duke of Bedford, acted as regent of Paris. England ruled France for nearly a decade, a historical

---

[7] Coville, *Les Cabochiens.*

[8] Vaughan, *John the Fearless,* p. 263.

[9] Pannier, "Les Joyaux," p. 210 n. 1.

[10] See, for example, A. Coville, "Le Véritable texte de la 'Justification du duc de Bourgogne' par Jean Petit (8 Mars 1408)," BEC 72 (1911) 57-91; C. C. Willard, "The Manuscripts of Jean Petit's 'Justification'. Some Burgundian Propaganda of the Early Fifteenth Century," *Studi francesi* 13 (1969) 271-280; and C. Nordenfalk, "Hatred, Hunting, and Love," pp. 324-341.

[11] The unedited *Heures de contemplacion sur la Passion de Nostre Seigneur* written c. 1420 to be found in Paris, BN MS nouv. acq. fr. 10059, fols. 114-145.

[12] See M. Vale, *Charles VII* (Berkeley, 1974), p. 31.

circumstance reflected in another group of illuminated manuscripts that put forward a forceful campaign of Anglo-French propaganda.[13]

Then, in 1429, something happened that seemed like a miracle to Christine: a woman, Joan of Arc, led the French troops to victory over the English army at the siege of Orleans. Subsequently, Joan escorted Charles VII to Reims where he was crowned king of France. Christine, having "cried for eleven years within an abbey," broke her long silence to write one last poem, this one in honor of the maid.[14] In the *Ditié de Jeanne d'Arc*, she rejoiced in the return of the crown to the legitimate, divinely chosen king. She recalled the prophecies that saw Charles VI as the universal emperor and related them to Charles VII. He became for her "Charles, son of Charles ... surnamed the Flying Stag" who "ought to be emperor."[15] She further envisioned the new king as vanquishing the English and conquering the Saracens.[16] Given Christine's longstanding interest in the role of women in politics, it is not surprising that she took up this subject along with that of the restoration of the monarchy. She called Joan "a credit to the feminine sex," compared her to the biblical heroines Esther, Judith, and Deborah who also freed their peoples, and declared her fortitude to be greater even than that of Hector.[17]

The central theme of Christine's earlier writings, such as the *Epistre* and the *Chemin*, thus reverberated in the *Ditié*. Joan, sent by God, was seen as bringing peace and liberating France from the ruin into which it had fallen. Christine's special vision was of good government in a privileged kingdom that is ruled over by a powerful monarch who is influenced by wise women.

Christine de Pizan probably died in 1430, fortunately ignorant of Joan's fate. But certain of her ideas about politics, along with those of

[13] See, for example, B. J. H. Rowe, "Henry VI's Claim to France in Picture and Poem," *The Library*, 4th ser., 13 (1932-1933) 77-88; J. W. McKenna, "Henry VI of England and the Dual Monarchy: Aspects of Royal Political Propaganda, 1422-1432," JWCI 28 (1965) 145-162; B. J. H. Rowe, "Notes on the Clovis Miniature and the Bedford Portrait," *Journal of the British Archaeological Association*, 3rd ser., 25 (1962) 56-65; and J. Backhouse, "A Reappraisal of the Bedford Hours," *The British Library Journal* 7 (1981) 47-69.

[14] Christine, "Ditié de Jehanne d'Arc," ed. A. J. Kennedy and K. Varty, *Nottingham Medieval Studies* 18 (1974), 19 (1975); and *idem, Ditié de Jehanne d'Arc*, ed. A. J. Kennedy and K. Varty, Medium Aevum Monographs, 9 (Oxford, 1977). The poem opens "Je, Christine qui ay plouré / XI ans en abbaye close...." See the study on Christine's view of Joan of Arc by D. Fraoili, "The Literary Image of Joan of Arc: Prior Influences," *Speculum* 56 (1981) 811-830.

[15] Christine, *Ditié de Jehanne d'Arc* (1974), p. 41.

[16] *Ibid.*, p. 46.

[17] *Ibid.*, pp. 43, 44.

Philippe and Bouvet, outlived her. Although together these authors had created an image of monarchy that was a timely response to the tragic circumstances of a particular regime, the image they formulated was to serve later rulers as well. Later Valois kings, having emerged triumphant from the period of the Hundred Years' War, sought to regenerate national self-esteem. To this end, they mounted a campaign of propaganda for which they refined many of those royal myths used during the reign of Charles VI.

One of the most striking forms that this propaganda took was the royal entry, a public spectacle that celebrated kingship on the occasion of the king's entry into a city or town.[18] At intervals along the route, raised platforms were built for the staging of allegorical dramas, called living pictures (*tableaux vivants*) or mystery plays (*mystères*) and written and performed by the townspeople. Props of various sorts — painted backdrops, woven tapestries, and sculpted objects — further enlivened the spectacles. Over the course of the fifteenth century, the entries became more elaborate. The idea of the power and prestige of the king provided the focus for the dramas, which dealt with themes and used symbols that date from the reign of Charles VI. For example, to enhance the monarch's power and prestige the dramas treated themes such as the dynastic continuity of the monarchy, the imperial rights of the king, and the good government of the realm. Symbols like the flying stag continued to stand for the monarch, while emblems like the radiant sun and the broom plant continued to convey notions about royal rule.[19]

Entries during the reign of Charles VIII (reigned 1483 to 1498) portrayed him in various guises, as a universal emperor like Constantine, a tenth worthy like Hector, and a victorious warrior like Hercules. When Charles entered Rouen in 1485, he encountered a drama that presented him as the new Constantine.[20] As Scheller has shown, royal and imperial imagery, such as the fleur-de-lis and the double-headed eagle, the single- and triple-tiered crown, and the radiant sun were intermingled to identify Charles with the emperor.[21] In this way, the terms of the old prophecy concerning Charles VI, which had been rewritten so as to apply to Charles VIII,[22] were confirmed. Another drama put on in Rouen welcomed

[18] Contemporary descriptions and documents have been collected by B. Guenée and F. Lehoux, *Les Entrées royales françaises de 1328 à 1515* (Paris, 1968).

[19] *Ibid.*, pp. 73 (1437: broom), 132 (1498: flying stag and radiant sun), 162 (1449: flying stag).

[20] *Ibid.*, pp. 257-261.

[21] Scheller, "Imperial Themes," pp. 15-17.

[22] *Ibid.*, p. 28; Chaumé, "Une Prophétie," pp. 31-35; and Reeves, *The Influence of Prophecy*, pp. 325-331.

him as a worthy, son of Solomon, son of David, thus exploiting the dynastic properties of the topos of the worthies.[23]

When Charles entered Vienne in 1490, he was greeted by a series of dramas, in which he was represented as Hercules, the conquering hero.[24] Compared to such epic heros as Charlemagne and Roland, Hercules appeared in the first drama ready to guard the realm against threats from England (the leopards), Flanders (the lions), and Brittany (the ermines). Well armed in the second drama, he faced a choice between vice and virtue, choosing virtue. His powers were then tested in the fourth and fifth dramas. In the fourth drama he was shown to be helpless before Atlas, who carried the world. Then, Othea the goddess of Prudences intervened, recommending that he choose his aids and counselors wisely. In the final and fifth drama staged in the garden of Atlas, which symbolized the realm of France, Othea's advice empowered Hercules to slay the dragon, liberate the maidens, and pluck the golden apples symbolic of the orb of rulership. This theatrical encounter between Othea, a wise woman, and Hercules, a prototype for the king, shows that the theme of the wisdom of women, communicated through Christine's Othea, was still mingled with that of good government for King Charles VIII at the end of the century.

A new, though familiar, image of royalty was borne of the succeeding reign. The grandson of duke Louis of Orleans, Louis XII (reigned 1498 to 1515), inherited the throne, since Charles VIII died without a direct male heir, leaving the Valois line extinct, and the closest descendant was from the cadet branch of Charles V's family.[25] King Louis XII revived his grandfather's emblem, the porcupine, which appeared in royal entries from the beginning of his reign. In 1498, when Louis entered Paris, he was met by a mechanical porcupine led on a leash.[26] It was adorned with a chain mail collar, like that worn by the knights of the Order of the Porcupine, and was further decorated with crowned, interlaced "L's," standing for Louis, and with gold suns, recalling the imperial charge. The apparatus hidden in the porcupine could be operated so that the animal thrust out its quills and then drew them back into its body, a trick that was done for the king when he passed the spot where it stood.

---

[23] Scheller, "Imperial Themes," p. 16; Guenée and Lehoux, *Les Entrées*, pp. 253-257.

[24] Guenée and Lehoux, *Les Entrées*, pp. 295-306; Jung, *Hercule dans la littérature française*, pp. 37-40.

[25] On Louis XII, see P. Lacroix, *Louis XII et Anne de Bretagne* (Paris, 1882).

[26] Guenée and Lehoux, *Les Entrées*, p. 127. On the entries and devices of Louis XII, see also R. W. Scheller, "Ensigns of Authority: French Royal Symbolism in the Age of Louis XII," *Simiolus* 13 (1983) 75-141.

Like the ducal porcupine on which it depended, the royal porcupine was an emblem both of peace and warfare, since its quills promised safety to the humble and threatened death to the arrogant.[27] It was used as a symbol of military power for a new regime, during which Louis embarked on a series of wars with Italy, in Milan, Naples, and Genoa, in a further quest for the universal empire. It evoked at the same time the memory of the past, by commemorating duke Louis of Orleans whose own bid for the throne was vindicated by the accession of his descendant. Perhaps Louis xii's motto, which accompanied the porcupine, was intended to evoke the past glory of the house of Orleans along with the promise of the future glory of France; over the image of King Louis's crowned porcupine, with its quills extended, was written "Having avenged the ancestors of Troy" (Fig. 94).

The legacy of the *Epistre Othéa* lies in these later, inflated expressions of monarchy, especially in the royal entries, which mixed verbal and visual imagery to communicate political thought. The *Epistre* belongs to an early stage in the processes of forging and celebrating ideas about statehood that were to last through the Old Regime. Throughout this period, the state was embodied in the king who remained, in sickness and in health, the very "blood of France."[28]

---

[27] Claude Paradin, *Les Devises héroïques* (Antwerp, 1563), fol. 14v, states that the following verse appeared engraved under a stone porcupine at Blois, the Orleans château: "Spicula sunt humili pax haec, sed bella superbo: / Et salus ex nostro vulnere, nexque venit." (Quills are this kind of peace for the humble animal but wars for the arrogant: / Both safety and death come from our wound).

[28] For the use of this phrase in royal entries, see Guenée and Lehoux, *Les Entrées*, pp. 246-247.

Appendix

A Concordance of the Subjects of Miniatures in the *Epistre Othéa* and their Antecedents

The descriptions that follow are of manuscripts, most of which are discussed in chapter 2, that could have served as sources for the *Epistre Othéa*. Because the emphasis is on manuscripts which Christine or her artists could realistically have known, I have not included all illuminated copies of a given text. Rather I have followed three criteria in selecting manuscripts for inclusion: 1. the manuscripts must have been produced in Paris around 1400 or 2. known to have been located in Parisian libraries of the period or 3. suspected to contain a cycle of illustration that reflects one that was employed around 1400.

The primary purpose of the descriptions is to introduce those manuscripts which share specific subjects with the *Epistre* as indicated in the Table that follows. From this table, an impression of the originality in the selection and treatment of subjects for illustration in the *Epistre* emerges. It can be seen, first, that the miniatures in the *Epistre* were compiled from diverse sources and, second, that the subjects of many of the idiosyncratic miniatures in the *Epistre* — those that put forward the political program — are not to be found among the antecedents. In addition, this Table provides a tool by which comparisons can be readily made between given miniatures in the *Epistre* and those of related subjects in other manuscripts. The Table also includes a concordance of plates illustrating the London and Paris copies of the *Epistre* that are included in this book.

In the descriptions, owners or patrons contemporary with Christine are given, when known; others are omitted. Only the number of the miniatures is included; their subjects, when they correspond with those found also in the *Epistre* appear in the table with the appropriate folio numbers. The identities of miniaturists are included only when relevant, for example, when an artist also worked on Christine's manuscripts or is thought to have had contact with her illuminators. Basic bibliography, where further information can be found, is included.

Ovide moralisé (Group A1: dates from 1316-1328, when the *Ovide moralisé* in verse was written; apparently unknown to Panofsky)
    Rouen, Bibliothèque municipale, MS O.4
        Date: c. 1316-1328
        Owner: unknown, court patron likely

Mins.: 454

Sel. bib.: Lord, "Ovide moralisé," pp. 162-163; J. Dupic, "Ovide moralisé, Ms. du xıvᵉ siècle," *Précis analytique des travaux de l'Académie des Sciences, Belles-Lettres et Arts de Rouen ... 1945 à 1950* (Rouen, 1952), pp. 67-77.

Paris, Bibliothèque de l'Arsenal, MS 5069

Date: c. 1325-1350

Owner: unknown

Mins.: 302

Sel. bib.: Lord, "Ovide moralisé," pp. 163-169; H. Martin, *Catalogue des manuscrits de la Bibliothèque de l'Arsenal* (Paris, 1889), 5: 35ff.

Ovide moralisé (Group A2 [Panofsky A]: comprises a group of manuscripts all from the end of the fourteenth century with essentially the same text as that in A1 but with a greatly reduced narrative cycle of miniatures)

Lyons, Bibliothèque municipale, MS 742

Date: c. 1390

Owner: signature of the Duke of Berry

Mins.: 53

Sel. bib.: Panofsky, *Renaissance and Renascences*, p. 80 n. 2; Lord, "Ovide moralisé," pp. 169-170; Seznec, *Survival of the Pagan Gods*, p. 109, Figs. 33-36; Meiss, *Late Fourteenth Century*, p. 311.

Paris, Bibliothèque nationale, MS fr. 871

Date: c. 1400

Owner: unknown

Mins.: 5

Sel. bib.: Panofsky, *Renaissance and Renascences*, p. 80, n. 2; Meiss, *Limbourgs*, p. 38, Fig. 143.

London, British Library, Add. MS 10324

Date: c. 1400

Owner: unknown

Mins.: 1

Sel. bib.: Panofsky, *Renaissance and Renascences*, p. 80, n. 2.

Ovide moralisé (Group D: group of manuscripts with the same text as that in A1 and A2 but with a different cycle of miniatures, one that replaces the narrative cycle with a set of mythographic images, used as frontispieces to the fifteen books of the text and influenced by Bersuire; thus, invented after 1340-1342, when Bersuire's *Ovidius moralizatus*, a Latin prose version, was composed)

Geneva, Bibliothèque publique et universitaire, MS fr. 1176

Date: c. 1390

Owner: unknown

Mins.: 15

Sel. bib.: Panofsky, *Renaissance and Renascences*, pp. 81ff; Gagnebin, "L'Enluminure," *Genava*, pp. 76-77.

Rome, Vatican Library, cod. Reg. lat. 1480
   Date: c. 1390
   Owner: unknown
   Mins.: 15
   Sel. bib.: Panofsky, *Renaissance and Renascences*, pp. 81ff.; Saxl and
   Meier, *Verzeichnis*, 1: 68-69, Fig. 36.
Paris, Bibliothèque nationale, MS fr. 373
   Date: c. 1440
   Owner: Duke of Berry
   Mins.: 15
   Sel. bib.: Panofsky, *Renaissance and Renascences*, pp. 81ff; Meiss, *Late
   Fourteenth Century*, pp. 288, 313; *idem, Limbourgs*, pp. 24-29, 60, 62,
   Figs. 79, 80, 104, 249.
London, British Library, Cott. Julius MS F VII
   Date: c. 1400
   Owner: unknown, English provenance
   Mins.: 15, but rearranged
   Sel. bib.: Panofsky, *Renaissance and Renascences*, p. 81; and Saxl and
   Meier, *Verzeichnis*, 3: 115-117, Fig. 21.

Boccaccio, 'Des Cleres femmes' (translation of *De mulieribus claris* by an
   anonymous translator who is sometimes identified as Laurent de Premier-
   fait; completed in September 1401)
Paris, Bibliothèque nationale, MS fr. 12420
   Date: 1403
   Owner: given 1 January to Philip the Bold by Jacques Raponde
   Mins.: 107 by the Coronation Master
   Sel. bib.: Meiss, *Limbourgs*, pp. 287-290; Bozzolo, *Boccace*, pp. 96-98.
Paris, Bibliothèque nationale, MS fr. 598
   Date: 1404
   Owner: given February 1404 to John of Berry from Jean de la Barre
   Mins.: 107 by the *Cleres femmes* Master
   Sel. bib.: Meiss, *Limbourgs*, pp. 287-290; Bozzolo, *Boccace*, pp. 92-93.
Brussels, Bibliothèque Royale, MS 9509
   Date: c. 1401-1410
   Owner: unknown
   Mins.: 33 by a follower of the *Cleres femmes* Master
   Sel. bib.: Meiss, *Limbourgs*, p. 373; Bozzolo, *Boccace*, pp. 150-151;
   C. Gaspar and F. Lyna, "Les principaux manuscrits de la Bibliothèque
   Royale de Belgique," *Bulletin de la Société française pour la reproduction
   des manuscrits à peintures*, 1 (1937) 459-461, Pl. CXIIb; V. Branca, ed.,
   Decameron, passim (extensively reproduced in color).

Boccaccio, 'Des Cas des nobles hommes et femmes' (first translation of *De casibus*
   finished in 1400 by Laurent de Premierfait; sparsely illustrated with a

maximum of 10 miniatures; only one extant manuscript dates early in the century, Paris, Bibliothèque nationale, MS fr. 24289, which has only one miniature, a presentation scene)

Boccaccio, 'Des Cas des nobles hommes et femmes' (second translation of *De casibus* completed 15 April 1409 by Laurent de Premierfait for John of Berry; apparently more densely illustrated than manuscripts of the first translation with many miniatures by or in collaboration with the *Cité des dames* Master)

Geneva, Bibliothèque universitaire et publique, MS fr. 190
   Date: 1411
   Owner: given to John of Berry in January 1411 by Martin Gouge
   Mins.: 143 by the Luçon Master
   Sel. bib.: Meiss, *Boucicaut*, p. 283; Bozzolo, *Boccace*, pp. 145-147; B. Gagnebin, "L'Enluminure," *Genava*, and *idem*, "Le Boccace du duc de Berry," *Genava* 5 (1957) 129-148.

Paris, Bibliothèque de l'Arsenal, MS 5193
   Date: c. 1409-1419
   Owner: John the Fearless
   Mins.: 148 by the *Cité des dames* Master and the Luçon Master
   Sel. bib.: Meiss, *Limbourgs*, pp. 283-287; Bozzolo, *Boccace*, pp. 52-53; H. Martin, *Le Boccace de Jean sans Peur. Des cas des nobles hommes et femmes* (Brussels, 1911).

Vienna, Österreichisches Nationalbibliothek, cod. 12766
   Date: c. 1409-1425
   Owner: unknown
   Mins.: 98 by the *Cité des dames* workshop
   Sel. bib.: Bozzolo, *Boccace*, pp. 128-129; Pächt and Thoss, *Die illuminierten Handschriften und Inkunabeln der Österreichischen Nationalbibliothek, Französische Schüle I* (Vienna, 1974), pp. 131-136.

Histoire ancienne jusqu'à César (second edition, composed in the mid-fourteenth century and including a history of Thebes, a history of the Minotaurs, Amazons, and Hercules, a history of Aeneas, a history of Rome, and a history of Troy, the latter taken from the lengthy prose version of Benoît de Sainte-More's *Roman de Troie*, with passages from Ovid's *Heroïdes*)

London, British Library, Royal MS 20 D I
   Date: c. 1340
   Owner: member of the Anjou court, perhaps Robert of Anjou, later King Charles V, then John of Berry
   Mins.: 300
   Sel. bib.: Avril, "Trois manuscrits napolitains," BEC; Buchthal, *Historia Troiana*, pp. 6ff; Saxl and Meier, *Verzeichnis*, 3.1: 223-242; Warner and Gilson, *Catalogue of Western Manuscripts*, 2: 375-377 and 4: Pl. 118.

London, British Library, Stowe MS 54
  Date: c. 1400
  Owner: Louis of Sancerre (?)
  Mins.: 36
  Sel. bib.: Avril, "Trois manuscrits napolitains," BEC and Saxl and Meier, *Verzeichnis*, 3.1: 268-272; Meiss, *Limbourgs*, p. 433.
Paris, Bibliothèque nationale, MS fr. 301
  Date: c. 1400
  Owner: arms of John of Berry
  Mins.: 228 by Remiet, the Orosius Master and an assistant
  Sel. bib.: Avril, "Trois manuscrits napolitains," BEC; Meiss, *Limbourgs*, pp. 7, 42, 62, 398.

Concordance of the Subjects of Miniatures

Ch.	Subject	*Epistre Othéa* London fol. (Fig.)	Paris fol. (Fig.)	*Ovide moralisé* (A)
	Christine and Louis	95r (5)	1r (7)	
1	Othea and Hector	95v (6)	1v (8)	
2	Temperance adjusting a clock	96v	2v	
3	Hercules fighting two lions	97r	3r	
4	King Minos as judge	98r (9)		
5	Perseus and Andromeda	98v	4v	Rouen, fol. 129r Arsenal, fol. 62v Lyon, fol. 8r
6	Jupiter	99v	5v (10)	Rouen, fol. 21r Lyons, fol. 8r
7	Venus	100r (11)	6r	
8	Saturn	100v (12)	6v	
9	Apollo	101r	7r (13)	
10	Phoebe	101r	7r (13)	
11	Mars	101v (14)	7v (15)	
12	Mercury	102r	8r (16)	
13	Minerva	102v (17)	8v (18)	
14	Minerva and Pallas	103r (19)	9r	
15	Penthesilea and her army	103v (20)	9v (21)	
16	Narcissus regarding himself	104r	10r	Rouen, fol. 81v Arsenal, fol. 33r Lyons, fol. 48r
17	Athamas and Ino	104r (22)	10r	Rouen, fol. 112v Arsenal, fol. 53v

in the *Epistre Othéa* and Their Antecedents

Ch.	*Ovide moralisé* (D)	*Des Cleres femmes*	*Des cas des nobles hommes et femmes*	*Histoire ancienne*
1				
2				
3	Geneva, fol. 197r Rome, fol. 199r Paris, fol. 189r			
4				
5				
6	Geneva, fol. 24v Rome, fol. 56r Paris, fol. 24r			
7	Geneva, fol. 216r Rome, fol. 218v Paris, fol. 207v	fr. 12420, fol. 15 fr. 598, fol. 15v Brussels, fol. 16v		
8	Geneva, fol. 1r Rome, fol. 5r Paris, fol. 1r		Geneva, fol. 11v Arsenal, fol. 13r	
9	Geneva, fol. 288v Rome, fol. 290r Paris, fol. 277r			
10				
11	Geneva, fol. 261v Rome, fol. 263r Paris, fol. 241v			
12	Geneva, fol. 239r Rome, fol. 241r Paris, fol. 229r			
13		fr. 12420, fol. 13v fr. 598, fol. 13r Brussels, fol. 15r		
14	Geneva, fol. 130r Rome, fol. 133r Paris, fol. 126v			
15		fr. 12420, fol. 46r fr. 598, fol. 46r		Royal, fol. 157v Paris, fols. 135v, 136r, 136v, 137r, 138r
16				
17				

Ch.	Subject	*Epistre Othéa* London fol. (Fig.)	Paris fol. (Fig.)	*Ovide moralisé* (A)
18	Mercury and Aglauros	104v	10v	Rouen, fol. 64v
19	Ulysses and the Cyclops	105r	11r	
20	Latona and the Frogs	105v	11v	Rouen, fol. 165v Arsenal, fol. 83v
21	Bacchus as god of drink	106r	12r	
22	Pygmalion and Venus	106v	12v	Rouen, fol. 252r, 252v Lyons, fol. 169r
23	Diana reading	107r	13r (23)	
24	Ceres sowing	107v	13v (24)	
25	Isis grafting	107v	13v (24)	
26	Midas, Pan and Apollo in contest	108r	14r	Rouen, fol. 275r Arsenal, fol. 147v
27	Theseus and Pirithous, Hercules and Cerberus	108v	14v	
28	Cadmus kills serpent, Building of Thebes	109r (29)	15r	Rouen, fol. 72v Arsenal, fol. 28r Lyons, fol. 41r (Cadmus and serpent)
29	Io directing a scriptorium	109r	15r (25)	
30	Mercury, Argus, and Io	109v	15v (26)	Rouen, fol. 38r Arsenal, fol. 7r Lyons, fol. 7r
31	Pyrrhus avenging the death of Achilles	110r (27)	16r (28)	
32	Cassandra praying	110v	16v (29)	
33	Neptune guiding a ship	110v	16v (29)	
34	Atropos-Mors	111r (30)	17r (31)	
35	Bellerophon and his stepmother	111v	17v	Rouen, fol. 124v Arsenal, fol. 60r
36	Memnon and Hector	112r (32)	18r (33)	
37	Laomedon threatens Hercules, Jason	112v	18v	
38	Pyramus and Thisbe	112v	18v	Rouen, fol. 96v Arsenal, fol. 42v Lyons, fol. 59v

Ch.	Ovide moralisé (D)	Des Cleres femmes	Des cas des nobles hommes et femmes	Histoire ancienne
18				
19				
20				
21	Geneva, fol. 173r Rome, fol. 176r Paris, fol. 166v			
22				
23				
24		fr. 12420, fol. 12r fr. 598, fol. 16v		
25		fr. 12420, fol. 16r fr. 598, fol. 16v		
26				
27				Royal, fols. 25r, 26r Stowe, fols. 28v, 30r Paris, fol. 24
28			Geneva, fol. 14v Arsenal, fol. 16v Vienna, fol. 9r (Building of Thebes)	
29				
30				
31				Royal, fol. 156r
32		fr. 12420, fol. 48v fr. 598, fol. 48v (Cassandra's death)		
33	Geneva, fol. 314r Rome, fol. 315v Paris, fol. 301v			
34				
35				
36				Royal, fol. 144v Paris, fol. 126v (Memnon fights Achilles)
37				Royal, fol. 34v Paris, fols. 31v, 32v
38		fr. 12420, fol. 20r fr. 598, fol. 20v Brussels, fol. 21v		

Ch.	Subject	*Epistre Othéa* London fol. (Fig.)	Paris fol. (Fig.)	*Ovide moralisé* (A)
39	Aesculapius and Circe	113v (34)	19v	
40	Paris kills Achilles, Hecuba watches	114r (35)	20r	Rouen, fol. 322r Arsenal, fol. 178r Lyons, fol. 222v
41	Busiris's human sacrifices	114r (35)	20r	
42	Hero saves Leander	114v	20v	Rouen, fol. 109r Arsenal, fol. 50v Lyons, fol. 69v
43	Greek messengers asking Priam for Helen	115r (36)	21r (37)	
44	Aurora bringing dawn	115v	21v	
45	Pasiphaë and the bull	116r	22v	Rouen, fol. 204 Arsenal, fol. 108v
46	Thydeus and Polinices, fight, Adrastus sleeps	116v	22v	Rouen, fol. 225r (without Adrastus)
47	Cupid and a young knight	117r	23r (38)	Lyons, fol. 16r (Cupid and Phebus)
48	Apollo shoots Corinus	117v	23v	Rouen, fol. 56r Arsenal, fol. 18r Lyons, fol. 32v
49	Juno as goddess of wealth	118r	24r	
50	Adrastus and his army go to Thebes	118v	24v	
51	Saturn advising silence	118v	24v	
52	A white raven and a black crow	119r	25r	
53	Apollo kills Ganymede	119v	25v	
54	Jason fighting a dragon	120r	26r (39)	
55	Perseus killing the gorgon	120v	26v	Rouen, fol. 126r Arsenal, fol. 59r
56	Apollo; Mars and Venus in bed; Vulcan chaining them	121r	27r	Rouen, fol. 97r Arsenal, fol. 43v
57	Thamyris supervising killings	121v	27v	
58	Medea handing a casket to Jason	122r	28r (40)	

Ch.	Ovide moralisé (D)	Des Cleres femmes	Des cas des nobles hommes et femmes	Histoire ancienne
39				
40		fr. 12420, fol. 47v fr. 598, fol. 47v (Hecuba watches slaughter of Priam's children)	Arsenal, fol. 37r (Hecuba watches slaughter of child)	Royal, fol. 148r Stowe, fol. 178r Paris, fol. 128v (without Hecuba)
41				
42				
43				Royal, fol. 89v Paris, fol. 55r
44				
45				
46				Royal, fol. 6r Stowe, fol. 8r Paris, fol. 18v
47				
48				
49	Geneva, fol. 53r Rome, fol. 56r Paris, fol. 51r			
50				Royal, fol. 16v Stowe, fol. 19v
51				
52				
53				
54				Royal, fol. 33v Stowe, fol. 38v Paris, fol. 30v
55				
56				
57		fr. 12420, fol. 74v fr. 598, fol. 74v	Geneva, fol. 77r Arsenal, fol. 81v Vienna, fol. 65r	Paris, fol. 218v
58		fr. 12420, fol. 26v fr. 598, fol. 27v Brussels, fol. 27v (Medea killing child)	Vienna, fol. 10r (Medea kills child)	Royal, fol. 37v Stowe, fol. 44r (Medea kills child; Jason's grief)

Ch.	Subject	Epistre Othéa London fol. (Fig.)	Paris fol. (Fig.)	Ovide moralisé (A)
59	Polyphemus surprising Acis and Galatea	122r	28r	
60	Wedding of Peleus and Thetis	122v (41)	28v (42)	
61	The Greeks kill Laomedon	123r	29r	
62	Juno advising Semele	123v	29v	Rouen, fol. 76v Arsenal, fol. 29v (Jupiter and Semele)
63	Diana hunting a stag	124r	30r	
64	Arachne at her loom with Pallas	124r	30r	Rouen, fols. 155-157 Arsenal, fols. 77-78
65	Adonis killed by a boar	124v	30v	Rouen, fol. 261r (Venus warns Adonis)
66	Armies of Laomedon, Hercules, and Telamon	125r	31r	
67	Orpheus playing his lyre	125v	31v	Rouen, fol. 261v Lyons, fol. 167r fr. 871, fol. 196r
68	Mercury bringing apple to Paris; Juno, Venus and Minerva	125v	31v	Rouen, fol. 281v Arsenal, fol. 150v Lyons, fol. 186v
69	Actaeon surprising Diana; stag	126r	32r	Rouen, fol. 74v Arsenal, fol. 29r
70	Orpheus and Eurydice	126v	32v	Rouen, fol. 247r Arsenal, fol. 132v Lyons, fol. 166v fr. 871, fol. 196r
71	Ulysses discovers Achilles	127v	33v	
72	Atalante racing Hippomenes	128r	34r	Arsenal, fol. 138r
73	Judgment of Paris	128v	34v	Rouen, fols. 279v-281v Lyons, fol. 187r
74	Fortune turning her wheel	129r (43)	35r (44)	Rouen, fol. 74r
75	Paris embracing Helen	129r (43)	35r	Rouen, fol. 300r Arsenal, fol. 162v
76	Cephalus killing Procris	129v	35v	Arsenal, fol. 104r
77	Helenus advising Paris	130r	36r (45)	
78	Morpheus bringing sleep	130v	36v	
79	Ceyx taking leave of Alycon	131r	37r	Lyons, fol. 193v
80	Troilus advising Priam	131v	37v (46)	
81	Calchas talking to Achilles	132r	38r	
82	Hermaphrodite and Salmacis bathing	132v	38v	Rouen, fol. 102v Arsenal, fol. 47v

Ch.	Ovide moralisé (D)	Des Cleres femmes	Des cas des nobles hommes et femmes	Histoire ancienne
59				
60				Paris, fol. 35v
61				Royal, fol. 35v
62				
63	Geneva, fol. 153r Rome, fol. 156r Paris, fol. 149r			
64		fr. 12420, fol. 28r fr. 598, fol. 29r (Suicide of Arachne)		
65				
66				Royal, fol. 36r Stowe, fol. 42r
67				
68				Paris, fol. 35v (Juno, Venus, Minerva)
69				
70				
71				
72				
73				Paris, fol. 35r
74				Royal, fol. 163r Stowe, fol. 197r
75				Royal, fol. 53r Paris, fol. 47v
76				
77				
78				
79				
80				
81				Paris, fol. 118v
82				

Ch.	Subject	Epistre Othéa London fol. (Fig.)	Paris fol. (Fig.)	Ovide moralisé (A)
83	Ulysses playing chess	133r	39r	
84	Briseis and Diomedes with Cupid	133v	39v	
85	Hector killing Patroclus	134r	40r	Rouen, fol. 316r Arsenal, fol. 173v
86	Narcissus and Echo	134r	40r	Rouen, fol. 81v Arsenal, fol. 33r Lyons, fol. 48r
87	Apollo and Daphne	134v	40v	Rouen, fol. 33r Arsenal, fol. 4r
88	Andromache warning Hector	135r (47)	41r (48)	
89	Ninus besieging Babylon	135v	41v	
90	Priam asking Hector not to fight	136r	42r	
91	Hector's death	136v	42v	Rouen, fol. 319v Arsenal, fol. 176r
92	Achilles spearing Hector, while Hector reaches for Polybetes's armor	137r	42v	
93	Hector's funeral	137v	43r	
94	Death of Ajax	138r	43r	Rouen, fol. 331v Arsenal, fol. 184r (Suicide of Ajax)
95	Antenor's betrayal of Troy	138v	44r	
96	Strategy of the Trojan horse	139r	44v	
97	Burning of Ilion	139v	45r	Rouen, fol. 339v Arsenal, fol. 189r
98	Circe changing Ulysses and his men into swine	140r	45r	Rouen, fol. 364v Arsenal, fol. 204v
99	Ino sowing boiled corn	140v	45v (49)	
100	Augustus and the Cumean sibyl	141r	46r (50)	

Ch.	Ovide moralisé (D)	Des Cleres femmes	Des cas des nobles hommes et femmes	Histoire ancienne
83				Paris, fol. 111v (Achilles)
84				Royal, fol. 136r Paris, fol. 88r
85				Royal, fol. 72v
86				
87				
88				Royal, fol. 110v Paris, fol. 95v
89				
90				Royal, fol. 110v
91				Royal, fol. 113v Stowe, fol. 137v
92				Royal, fol. 113r Paris, fol. 98v
93				Royal, fol. 114v Paris, fol. 105r
94				Royal, fol. 174r Paris, fol. 131r
95				Royal, fol. 162r Paris, fol. 141r
96				Royal, fol. 167v Stowe, fol. 201v Paris, fol. 145v
97				Royal, fol. 169r Stowe, fol. 203r Paris, fol. 146r
98		fr. 12420, fol. 54r fr. 598, fol. 54r		
99				
100				

Bibliography

A. Primary Sources

Benoît de Sainte-More. *Le Roman de Troie en Prose.* Ed. L. Constans and E. Faral. Paris: E. Champion, 1922.

————. *Le Roman de Troie par Benoît de Sainte-Maure.* Ed. L. Constans. 6 vols. SATF. Paris: Firmin Didot et Cie, 1904-1912.

Bersuire, Pierre. "L'Ovidius moralizatus di Pierre Bersuire," ed. Fausto Ghisalberti. *Studi Romanzi* 23 (1933) 5-134.

Boccaccio, Giovanni. *Boccaccio on Poetry Being the Preface and the Fourteenth and Fifteenth Books of Boccaccio's 'Genealogia Deorum Gentilium.'* Trans. C. G. Osgood. Princeton, N.J.: Princeton University Press, 1930.

————. *Concerning Famous Women.* Trans. G. Guarino. New Brunswick, N.J.: Rutgers University Press, 1963.

————. *Decameron.* Ed. V. Branca. 3 vols. Florence: Sadea/Sansoni, 1966.

————. *Laurent de Premierfait's 'Des Cas des nobles hommes et femmes.'* Ed. and trans. P. M. Gathercole. University of North Carolina Studies in Romance Languages and Literature, 74. Chapel Hill, N.C.: University of North Carolina Press, 1968.

Bouvet, Honoré. *L'Apparicion Maistre Jehan de Meun et le Somnium super materia schismatis d'Honoré Bonet.* Ed. Ivor Arnold. Publications de la Faculté des lettres de l'Université de Strasbourg, 28. London/New York: Oxford University Press, 1926.

————. *L'Apparition de Jean de Meun, ou, Le Songe du Prieur de Salon par Honoré Bonet.* Ed. Jérôme Pichon. Paris: Silvestre, 1845.

————. *L'Arbre des batailles d'Honoré Bonet.* Ed. E. Nys. Brussels and Leipzig: Librairie européenne C. Muquardt, 1883.

————. *The Tree of Battles.* Ed. G. W. Coopland. Cambridge, Mass.: Harvard University Press, 1949.

Budé, Guillaume. *Institution du Prince.* Ed. C. Bontems, L.-P. Raybaud and J.-P. Brancourt, *Le Prince dans la France des XVIᵉ et XVIIᵉ siècles.* Travaux et recherches de la Faculté de droit et des sciences économiques de Paris. Série sciences historiques, 7. Paris: Presses Universitaires de France, 1965.

Christine de Pizan. *Lavision-Christine, Introduction and Text.* Ed. Sister Mary Louise Towner. Washington, D.C.: Catholic University of America, 1932.

————. *The Book of the City of Ladies.* Trans. Earl Jeffrey Richards and forew. Marina Warner. New York: Persea Books, 1982.

————. "Christine de Pisan to Isabelle of Bavaria, Paris, October 5, 1405," ed.

M. D. Legge. In *Anglo-Norman Letters and Petitions from All Souls Ms. 182*, pp. 144-150. Anglo-Norman Text Society, 3. Oxford: Blackwells, 1941.

————. "Christine de Pisan's 'Ditié de Jehanne d'Arc'," ed. A. J. Kennedy and K. Varty. *Nottingham Medieval Studies* 18 (1974) 29-55, 19 (1975) 53-76.

————. *Ditié de Jehanne d'Arc.* Ed. A. J. Kennedy and K. Varty. Medium Aevum Monographs, 9. Oxford: Society for the Study of Mediaeval Languages and Literature, 1977.

————. *The Epistle of Othea.* Trans. Stephen Scrope. Ed. C. F. Bühler. Early English Text Society, 264. London: Oxford University Press, 1970.

————. *The Epistle of Othea to Hector: a 'lytil bibill of knyghthod.'* Trans. Anthony Babyngton. Ed. James D. Gordon. Philadelphia: n.p., 1942.

————. *The Epistle of Othea to Hector, or The boke of knyghthode.* Trans. Stephen Scrope. Ed. George F. Warner. London: J. B. Nichols and Sons, 1904.

————. "La Lamentacion sur les maux de la France de Christine de Pisan," ed. A. J. Kennedy. In *Mélanges de langue et littérature françaises du Moyen Âge et de la Renaissance offerts à Monsieur Charles Foulon par ses collègues, ses élèves et ses amis*, pp. 177-185. Rennes: Institut de français, Université de Haute-Bretagne, 1980.

————. *Le Livre de la Mutacion de Fortune.* Ed. S. Solente. 3 vols. SATF. Paris: A. and J. Picard, 1955.

————. *The "Livre de la Paix" of Christine de Pisan. A Critical Edition with Introduction and Notes.* Ed. C. C. Willard. The Hague: Mouton and Co., 1958.

————. *Le Livre des fais et bonnes meurs du sage roy Charles V.* Ed. S. Solente. 2 vols. SHF, 437, 444. Paris: Honoré Champion, 1936-1940.

————. *Le Livre du chemin de long estude.* Ed. R. Püschel. Berlin: R. Damköhler, 1881.

————. *Le Livre du Corps de policie.* Ed. R. H. Lucas. Geneva: Librairie Droz, 1967.

————. *Œuvres poétiques de Christine de Pisan.* Ed. Maurice Roy. 3 vols. SATF. Paris: Firmin Didot et Cie., 1886-1896.

————. *"La Querelle de la Rose": Letters and Documents.* Ed. J. L. Baird and J. R. Kane. North Carolina Studies in the Romance Languages and Literatures, 199. Chapel Hill, N.C.: University of North Carolina Dept. of Romance Languages, 1978.

————. *Les Sept psaumes allégorisés of Christine of Pisan, a Critical Edition From the Brussels and Paris Manuscripts.* Ed. Ruth Ringland Rains. Washington, D.C.: Catholic University of America Press, 1965.

————. See also Secondary Sources: R. Thomassy.

Chronique des quatre premiers Valois (1327-1393). Ed. S. Luce. Paris: V. J. Renouard, 1862.

Colonna, Egidio. *Li Livres du gouvernement des rois. A XIIIth Century French Version of Egidio Colonna's Treatise "De Regimine Principum."* Ed. S. P. Molenaer. New York: Macmillan Company, 1899; rpr. New York: AMS Press, 1966.

Courtecuisse, Jean. *L'Œuvre oratoire française de Jean Courtecuisse*. Ed. G. di Stefano. Torino: G. Giappichelli, 1969.

Deschamps, Eustache. *Œuvres complètes*. Ed. A. de Queux de Saint-Hilaire and Gaston Raynaud. 11 vols. Paris: Librairie de Firmin Didot et Cie., 1878-1903.

Douët d'Arcq, Louis-Claude, ed. *Choix de pièces inédites relatives au règne de Charles VI*. 2 vols. SHF, 119, 122. Paris: Renouard, 1863-1864.

————. *Collection de sceaux (Inventaires et documents publiés par ordre de l'Empereur sous la direction de M. le Comte de Laborde)*. 3 vols. Paris: H. Plon, 1863-1868.

————. *Comptes de l'argenterie des rois de France au XIVe siècle*. SHF, 64. Paris: Renouard, 1851.

————. *Comptes de l'hôtel des rois de France aux XIVe et XVe siècles*. SHF, 130. Paris: Renouard, 1865.

————. *Nouveau recueil de comptes de l'argenterie des rois de France*. SHF, 170. Paris: Renouard, 1874.

Froissart, Jean. *Œuvres*. Ed. Henri Kervyn de Lettenhove. 25 vols. Brussels: V. Devaux, 1867-1877; repr. Osnabruck, 1967.

Gerson, Jean. *Jean de Gerson et l'éducation des dauphins de France. Étude critique suivie du texte de deux de ses opuscules et de documents inédits sur Jean Majoris précepteur de Louis XI*. Ed. A. Thomas. Paris: Librairie Droz, 1930.

————. *Harangue faicte au nom de l'Université de Paris devant le Roy Charles sixiesme, et tout le conseil, en 1405*. 3rd ed. Paris: Chez Debeausseaux, 1824.

Les Grandes chroniques de France. Ed. Jules Viard. 10 vols. SHF, Publications in Octavo, 395, 401, 415, 418, 425, 429, 435, 438, 457. Paris: Librairie C. Klincksieck, 1920-1937.

Guillaume de Nangis. *Vita sancti Ludovici*. In *Recueil des historiens des Gaules et de la France*, eds. P. C. F. Daunou and J. Naudet, 20: 310-465. Paris: L'Imprimerie Royale, 1840.

Jacobus de Voragine. *The Golden Legend*. Trans. G. Ryan and H. Ripperger. New York: Longmans, Green and Co., 1941; repr. New York: Arno Press, 1969.

John of Salisbury. *The Statesman's Book ... Fourth, Fifth, and Sixth Books and Selections from the Seventh and Eighth Books of the Policraticus*. Trans. J. Dickinson. New York: A. Knopf, 1927.

Juvenal des Ursins, Jean. *Histoire de Charles VI, Roy de France*. Ed. J. F. Michaud and J. J. F. Poujoulat. Nouvelle collection des mémoires pour servir à l'histoire de France, première série, 2. Paris: Didier, 1936.

Lebègue, Jean. *Les Histoires que l'on peut raisonnablement faire sur les livres de Salluste*. Ed. J. Porcher. Paris: Librairie Giraud-Badin, 1962.

Legrand, Jacques. "Un Sermon français inédit attribuable à Jacques Legrand," ed. E. Beltran. *Romania* 93 (1972) 462-478.

Macrobius. *Commentary on the Dream of Scipio*. Trans. W. H. Stahl. Records of Civilization, Sources and Studies, 48. New York: Columbia University Press, 1952.

Meyer, Paul. "L'Entrevue d'Ardres, 1396." *Annuaire-Bulletin de la Société de l'histoire de France* 18 (1881) 209-224.

Monstrelet, Enguerrand de. *The Chronicles of Enguerrand de Monstrelet.* Ed. and trans. T. Johnes. 2 vols. London/New York: J. Routledge and Sons, 1867; repr. Kraus, 1975.

————. *La Chronique d'Enguerrand de Monstrelet.* Ed. L.-C. Douët d'Arcq. 6 vols. SHF, 91, 93, 99, 105, 108, 113. Paris: Renouard, 1857-1862.

Oresme, Nicole. "Le Livre des politiques d'Aristote [ed. by] Nicole Oresme," ed. A. D. Menut. *Transactions of the American Philosophical Society,* n.s., 60, pt. 6. Philadelphia: American Philosophical Society, 1970.

Orville, Jean Cabaret d'. *La Chronique du bon duc Loys de Bourbon.* Ed. A.-M. Chazaud. SHF, 175. Paris: Librairie Renouard, 1876.

Ovide moralisé. Ed. Cornelius de Boer. 5 vols. Verhandelingen der Koninklijke Akademie van Wetenschappen te Amsterdam, Afdeling letterkunde, nieuwe reeks, 15, 21, 30, 37, 43. Wiesbaden: Martin Sandig, 1966-1968.

Paradin, Claude. *Les Devises héroïques.* Antwerp: Chez la vefve de Iean Stelsius, 1563.

Philippe de Mézières. "Epistre lamentable et consolatoire sur le fait de la desconfiture lacrimable du noble et vaillant roy de Honguerie par les turcs devant la ville de Nichopoli." In Jean Froissart, *Œuvres,* ed. Henri Kervyn de Lettenhove, 16: 444-523. Brussels: V. Devaux, 1867-1877; repr. Osnabruck, 1967.

————. *Letter to King Richard II. A Plea Made in 1395 For Peace Between England and France.* Ed. and trans. G. W. Coopland. Liverpool: University Press, 1965.

————. "Philippe de Mézières and the New Order of the Passion," ed. Abdel Hamid Hamdy. *Bulletin of the Faculty of Arts, Alexandria University* 17 (1963) 45-54, 18 (1964) 1-105 [*Chevalerie de l'ordre de la Passion*].

————. *Le Songe du vieil pèlerin.* Ed. G. W. Coopland. 2 vols. Cambridge: University Press, 1969.

Pliny the Elder. *Natural History.* 10 vols. Trans H. Rackham. Cambridge, Mass.: Harvard University Press, 1938-1963.

Le Religieux de Saint-Denis. *Chronique du religieux de Saint-Denys, contenant le règne de Charles VI, de 1380 à 1422.* Ed. L. F. Bellaguet. 6 vols. Collection de documents inédits sur l'histoire de France. Paris: BN, 1839-1852.

Rigord. *Gesta Philippi Augusti Francorum regis, descripta a magistro Rigordo.* In *Recueil des historiens des Gaules et de France,* ed. M. Bouquet, 17: 1-62. Paris: Victor Palmé, 1878.

Salmon, Pierre. *Les Demandes faites par le Roi Charles VI touchant son état et le gouvernement de sa personne, avec les réponses de Pierre Salmon.* Ed. C. Crapelet. Paris: Imprimerie de Crapelet, 1833.

Thomas Aquinas, Saint. *Commentary on the Metaphysics of Aristotle.* Trans. J. P. Rowan. 2 vols. Chicago: H. Regnery Co., 1961.

B. Secondary Sources

Adam-Even, Paul. *L'Armorial universel du héraut Gelre.* Archives héraldiques suisses, 1971.

Atiya, Aziz S. *The Crusade in the Later Middle Ages.* London: Methuen and Co., 1938.

————. *The Crusade of Nicopolis.* London: Methuen and Co., 1934.

Avout, Jacques d'. *La Querelle des Armagnacs et des Bourguignons.* Paris: Librairie Gallimard, 1945.

Avril, François. "Trois manuscrits napolitains des collections de Charles V et de Jean de Berry." BEC 127 (1969) 291-328.

Backhouse, Janet. "A Reappraisal of the Bedford Hours." *The British Library Journal* 7 (1981) 47-69.

Barroux, Maurice. *Les Fêtes royales de Saint-Denis.* Paris: Les Amis de Saint-Denys, 1936.

Barry, Françoise. *Les Droits de la reine sous la monarchie française jusqu'en 1789.* Paris: F. Loviton et Cie, 1932.

Barzon, Antonio. *I cieli e la loro influenza negli affreschi del Salone in Padova.* Padua: Tip. Seminario, 1924.

Bath, Michael. "The Legend of Caesar's Deer." *Medievalia et Humanistica,* n.s., 9 (1979) 53-66.

Beaune, Colette. "Costume et pouvoir en France à la fin du Moyen Âge: Les devises royales vers 1400." *Revue des sciences humaines* 55 (1981) 125-146.

Becker, Philippe A. "Christine de Pizan." *Zeitschrift für französische Sprache und Literatur* 54 (1931) 129-164.

Bell, Dora M. *Étude sur le Songe du vieil pèlerin de Philippe de Mézières (1327-1405) d'après le ms. fr. B.N. 22542. Document historique et moral du règne de Charles VI.* Geneva: E. Droz, 1955.

————. *L'Idéal éthique de la royauté en France au Moyen Âge d'après quelques moralistes de ce temps.* Geneva: E. Droz, 1962.

Berger, Samuel and Paul Durrieu. "Les Notes pour l'enlumineur dans les manuscrits du moyen âge." *Mémoires. Société des antiquaires de France* 53 (1893) 11-30.

Berges, Wilhelm. *Die Fürstenspiegel des hohen und späten Mittelalters.* Schriften der Reichsinstituts für ältere deutsche Geschichtskunde, Monumenta Germaniae Historica, 2. Leipzig: K. W. Hiersemann, 1938.

Bornstein, Diane. *Mirrors of Courtesy.* Hamden, Conn.: Archon Books, 1975.

Bouchot, Henri. *Bibliothèque Nationale. Inventaire des dessins exécutés pour Robert de Gaignières et conservés aux Départements des Estampes et des Manuscrits.* 2 vols. Paris: E. Plon, Nourrit et Cie, 1891.

Bozzolo, Carla. *Manuscrits des traductions françaises d'œuvres de Boccace, XVᵉ siècle.* Medioevo e umanesimo, 15. Padua: Antenore, 1973.

Brachet, Auguste. *Pathologie mentale des rois de France. Louis XI et ses ascendants. Une Vie humaine étudiée à travers six siècles d'hérédité. 852-1483.* Paris: Hachette, 1903.

Brémond d'Ars Migré, Hélie de. *Les Chevaliers du porc-épic ou du camail, 1394-1498.* Macon: Imprimerie Protat Frères, 1938.

Buchthal, Hugo. *Historia Troiana. Studies in the History of Mediaeval Secular Illustration.* Studies of the Warburg Institute, 32. London: Warburg Institute, 1971.

Bumgardner, George H. "Christine de Pizan and the Atelier of the Master of Coronation." In *Seconda Miscellanea di studi e richerche sul quattrocento francesi,* ed. F. Simone, J. Beck and G. Mombello, pp. 35-52. Chambéry-Torino: Centre d'Études Franco-Italien, 1981.

Burges, William. "La Ragione de Padove." *Annales archéologiques* 18 (1858) 331-343, 19 (1859) 241-251, 26 (1869) 250-271.

Calkins, Robert G. "Stages of Execution: Procedures of Illumination as Revealed in an Unfinished Book of Hours." *Gesta* 17 (1978) 61-70.

Campbell, Percy G. C. *L'Épître d'Othéa. Étude sur les sources de Christine de Pisan.* Paris: Honoré Champion, 1924.

Cazelles, Raymond. *La Société politique et la crise de la royauté sous Philippe de Valois.* Bibliothèque elzévirienne. Nouvelle série. Études et documents. Paris: Librairie d'Argences, 1958.

—————. *Société politique, noblesse et couronne sous Jean le Bon et Charles V.* Mémoires et documents publiés par la Société de l'École des Chartes, 28. Geneva: Droz, 1982.

Champollion-Figéac, Aimé L. *Louis et Charles duc d'Orléans, leur influence sur les arts, la littérature et l'esprit de leur siècle.* Paris: Comptoir des imprimeurs unis, 1844.

Châtelet, Albert. "Un Artiste à la Cour de Charles VI. À propos d'un carnet d'esquisses du XIV⁰ siècle conservé à la Pierpont Morgan Library." *L'Œil* 216 (1972) 16-21, 62.

Chaumé, M. "Une Prophétie relative à Charles VI." *Revue du moyen âge latin* 3 (1947) 27-42.

Clarke, Maude V. "The Wilton Diptych." In *Fourteenth Century Studies by Maude Violet Clarke,* ed. L. S. Sutherland and M. McKisack, pp. 272-292. Oxford: Clarendon Press, 1937; repr., N.Y.: Books for Libraries Press, 1967.

Collas, Émile. *Valentine de Milan, duchesse d'Orléans.* 2nd ed. Paris: Plon-Nourrit, 1911.

Contamine, Philippe. "Points de vue. La Chevalerie en France à la fin du Moyen Âge." *Francia* 4 (1976) 255-285, 987-988.

Coville, Alfred. *Les Cabochiens et l'ordonnance de 1413.* Paris: Hachette, 1888; repr. Geneva, 1974.

—————. *Jean Petit, La question du tyrannicide au commencement du XV⁰ siècle.* Paris: A. Picard, 1932.

—————. "Les Premiers Valois et la Guerre de Cent Ans (1328-1422)." In *Histoire de France depuis les origines jusqu'à la Révolution,* ed. E. Lavisse. 4: 1-441. Paris: Hachette, 1900-1911.

————. "Le Véritable texte de la 'Justification du duc de Bourgogne' par Jean Petit (8 Mars 1408)." *Bibliothèque de l'École des Chartes* 72 (1911) 57-91.

————. *La Vie intellectuelle dans les domaines d'Anjou-Provence, 1380 à 1435.* Paris: E. Droz, 1941.

Culler, Jonathan. *On Deconstruction. Theory and Criticism after Structuralism.* Ithaca, N.Y.: Cornell University Press, 1982.

Delachenal, Roland. *Histoire de Charles V.* 5 vols. Paris: A. Picard et fils, 1909-1931.

Delaissé, Léon M. J., James Marrow and John de Wit. *The James A. Rothschild Collection at Waddesdon Manor. Illuminated Manuscripts.* Fribourg: Office du Livre for the National Trust, 1977.

Delisle, Léopold. *Le Cabinet des manuscrits de la Bibliothèque impériale.* 3 vols. Paris: Bibliothèque impériale, 1868-1881.

————. *Recherches sur la librairie de Charles V.* 2 vols. Paris: Honoré Champion, 1907.

Demay, Germain. "Note sur l'ordre du Camail ou du Porc-Épic." *Bulletin de la Société nationale des antiquaires de France* (1875) 71-75.

Denieul-Cormier, Anne. *Wise and Foolish Kings. The First House of Valois. 1328-1498.* Garden City, N.Y.: Doubleday and Co., 1980.

Desjardins, Gustave. *Recherches sur les drapeaux français. Oriflamme, bannière de France, marques nationales, couleurs du roi, drapeaux de l'armée, pavillons de la marine.* Paris: Vᵉ A. Morel et Cie, 1874.

Diez, Friedrich. *Essai sur les cours d'amour.* Paris: J. Labitte, 1842.

Dodu, G. "La Folie de Charles VI." *La Revue historique* 150 (1925) 161-189.

Doren, A. "Fortuna im Mittelalter und in der Renaissance." *Vorträge der Bibliothek Warburg* 2 (1922-1923) 71-144.

Dougherty, David. "Political Literature in France during the Reigns of Charles V and Charles VI." Unpublished doctoral dissertation, Harvard University, 1932.

Doutrepont, Georges. *Inventaire de la 'librairie' de Philippe le Bon (1420).* Académie royale des sciences, des lettres et des beaux-arts de Belgique. Commission royale d'histoire. Publications in octavo, 27. Brussels: Kiessling et Cie, 1906.

————. *La Littérature française à la cour des Ducs de Bourgogne, Philippe le Hardi—Jean sans Peur—Philippe le Bon—Charles le Téméraire.* Bibliothèque du XVᵉ siècle, 8. Paris: Champion, 1909.

Dronke, Peter. *Women Writers of the Middle Ages, A Critical Study of Texts from Perpetua (†203) to Marguerite Porete (†1310).* Cambridge, Eng.: Cambridge University Press, 1984.

Durrieu, Paul. "L'Union des couleurs nationales de la France et de l'Angleterre au XIVᵉ siècle en vue de la conquête de Jérusalem." *La Revue hebdomadaire* 27, no. 19 (11 May 1918) 166-176.

Ellis, Sir Henry and Francis Douce. *A Catalogue of the Landsdowne Manuscripts in the British Museum.* London: R. and A. Taylor, 1819.

Evans, Joan. *Dress in Mediaeval France.* Oxford: Clarendon Press, 1952.

Evans, Michael. "Tugenden." In *Lexikon der christlichen Ikonographie*, ed. E. Kirschbaum, 4: 364-380. Breisgau: Verlag Herder, 1972.

Facinger, M. F. "A Study of Medieval Queenship: Capetian France, 987-1237." *Studies in Medieval and Renaissance History* 5 (1968) 3-48.

Famiglietti, R. C. *Royal Intrigue: Crisis at the Court of Charles VI, 1392-1420.* New York: AMS Press, 1986.

Faral, Edmond. *La Légende Arthurienne, études et documents.* Première partie: *Les plus anciens textes.* 3 vols. Bibliothèque de l'École des Hautes Études, Sciences historiques et philologiques, 255-257. Paris: Honoré Champion, 1929.

Farquhar, James D. "The Manuscript as a Book." In Sandra Hindman and James D. Farquhar, *Pen to Press: Illustrated Manuscripts and Printed Books in the First Century of Printing*, pp. 11-99. College Park, Md.: Art Department, University of Maryland, 1977.

Favyn, André. *The Theatre of Honour and Knighthood. Or a Compendious Chronicle and Historie of the Whole Christian World.* London: W. Iaggard, 1623.

Fetterly, Judith. *The Resisting Reader. A Feminist Approach to American Fiction.* Bloomington, In.: Indiana University Press, 1978.

Fleming, John. *The 'Roman de la Rose': A Study in Allegory and Iconography.* Princeton, N.J.: Princeton University Press, 1967.

Folz, Robert. *L'Idée d'Empire en Occident du V. au XIV. siècle.* Paris: Aubier, 1953.

Fraoili, Deborah. "The Literary Image of Joan of Arc: Prior Influences." *Speculum* 56 (1981) 811-830.

Friedländer, Max J. *Early Netherlandish Painting.* 14 vols. in 16. New York: Praeger, 1967-1976.

Gagnebin, Bernard. "Le Boccace du duc de Berry." *Genava* 5 (1957) 129-148.

—————. "L'Enluminure de Charlemagne à François Ier. Manuscrits de la Bibliothèque publique et universitaire de Genève." *Geneva*, n.s., 24 (1976) 5-200.

Galbreath, Donald L. *Papal Heraldry.* London: "Heraldry Today," 1972.

Gautier, Léon. *Chivalry.* Trans. D. C. Dunning. New York: Barnes and Noble, 1959.

Gauvard, Claude. "Christine de Pisan a-t-elle eu une pensée politique? À propos d'ouvrages récents." *Revue historique* 250 (1973) 417-430.

Gay, Lucy M. "On the Language of Christine de Pisan." *Modern Philology* 6 (1908) 69-96.

Gay, Victor. *Glossaire archéologique du Moyen Âge et de la Renaissance.* 2 vols. Paris: Librairie de la Société bibliographique, 1887.

Gheyn, Joseph van den. *Christine de Pisan. Épître d'Othéa, Déesse de la Prudence, à Hector, Chef des Troyens. Reproduction des 100 miniatures du manuscrit 9392 de Jean Miélot.* Brussels: Vromant and Co., 1913.

Ghisalberti, F. "L'Ovidius moralizatus di Pierre Bersuire." *Studi Romanzi* 23 (1933) 15ff.

Giesey, R. F. *The Juristic Basis of Dynastic Right to the French Throne.* Transactions of the American Philosophical Society, n.s., 51, pt. 5. Philadelphia: American Philosophical Society, 1961.

Gilissen, Léon. *La Librairie de Bourgogne.* L'Art en Belgique, 10. Brussels: Cultura, 1970.

Godefroy, Frédéric. *Dictionnaire de l'ancienne langue française et de tous ses dialectes du IXᵉ au XVᵉ siècle.* 10 vols. Paris: F. Vieweg, 1881-1902.

Gombrich, Ernst. "Icones symbolicae: Philosophies of Symbolism and their Bearing on Art." In *Symbolic Images: Studies in the Art of the Renaissance,* pp. 123-195. London: Phaidon, 1972.

Grandeau, Yann. "Les Enfants de Charles VI, essai sur la vie privée des princes et des princesses de la maison de France à la fin du Moyen Âge." *Bulletin philologique et historique (jusqu'en 1610) du Comité des travaux historiques et scientifiques* 2 (1967) 809-849.

Grévy-Pons, Nicole. "Propagande et sentiment national pendant le règne de Charles VI: L'Exemple de Jean de Montreuil." *Francia* 8 (1980) 127-145.

Guenée, Bernard and Lehoux, Françoise. *Les Entrées royales françaises de 1328 à 1515.* Sources d'histoire médiévale, 5. Paris: Éditions du CNRS, 1968.

Guibert, Joseph. *Les Dessins d'archéologie de Roger de Gaignières.* 3 vols. Paris: Catala frères, 1912-1913.

Guiffrey, Jules. *Inventaires de Jean duc de Berry (1401-1416).* 2 vols. Paris: E. Leroux, 1894-1896.

————, Eugène Muntz and Alexandre Pinchart. *Histoire générale de la tapisserie.* 3 vols. Paris: Société anonyme de publications périodiques, 1878-1885.

Hauber, Anton. *Planetenkinderbilder und Sternbilder. Zur Geschichte des menschlichen Glaubens und Irrens.* Studien zur deutschen Kunstgeschichte, 194. Strassburg: Heitz, 1916.

Hedeman, Anne Dawson. "The Illustrations of the *Grandes Chroniques de France* from 1274 to 1422." Unpublished doctoral dissertation, The Johns Hopkins University, 1984.

————. "Restructuring the Narrative: The Function of Ceremonial in Charles V's *Grandes Chroniques de France.*" *Studies in the History of Art* 16 (1985) 171-181.

————. "Valois Legitimacy: Editorial Changes in Charles V's *Grandes Chroniques de France.*" *Art Bulletin* 66 (1984) 97-117.

Helyot, Pierre. *Histoire des ordres monastiques, religieux et militaires, et des congrégations séculières de l'un et de l'autre sexe, qui ont été établies jusqu'à présent....* 8 vols. Paris: N. Gosselin, 1714-1719.

Henwood, Philippe. "Jean d'Orléans peintre des Rois Jean II, Charles V et Charles VI (1361-1407)." *Gazette des Beaux-Arts,* ser. 6, 95 (1980) 137-140.

Hindman, Sandra. "The Composition of the Manuscript of Christine de Pizan's Collected Works in the British Library: A Reassessment." *British Library Journal* 9 (1983) 93-123.

————. "The Iconography of Queen Isabeau de Bavière (1410-1415): An Essay in Method." *Gazette des Beaux-Arts,* ser. 6, 102 (1983) 102-110.

—————. "With Ink and Mortar: Christine de Pizan's *Cité des Dames* (An Art Essay)." *Feminist Studies* 10 (1984) 457-483.

—————— and Gabrielle M. Spiegel. "The Fleur-de-lis Frontispieces to Guillaume de Nangis's 'Chronique abrégée': Political Iconography in Late Fifteenth-Century France." *Viator* 12 (1981) 381-407.

Huot, Sylvia. "Seduction and Sublimation: Christine de Pizan, Jean de Meun, and Dante." *Romance Notes* 25 (1985) 361-375.

Ignatius, Mary Ann. "Christine de Pizan's 'Epistre Othéa': An Experiment in Literary Form." *Medievalia et Humanistica*, n.s., 9 (1979) 127-142.

Iorga, Nicolae. *Philippe de Mézières, 1327-1405, et la croisade au XIVe siècle.* Bibliothèque de l'École des Hautes Études, Sciences philologiques et histo-riques, 110. Paris, E. Bouillon, 1896.

Jal, Auguste. *Dictionnaire critique de biographie et d'histoire.* 2nd ed. Paris: H. Plon, 1872.

Janson, Horst W. *Apes and Ape Lore in the Middle Ages and the Renaissance.* Studies of the Warburg Institute, 20. London: Warburg Institute, 1952.

Jarry, Eugène. *La Vie de Louis de France, duc d'Orléans, 1372-1407.* 2 vols. Paris: A. Picard, 1889.

Jeanroy, Alfred. "Boccace et Christine de Pisan, Le 'De claris mulieribus,' principale source du 'Livre de la Cité des Dames'." *Romania* 48 (1922) 93-105.

Joukovsky-Micha, Françoise. "La Notion de 'vaine gloire' de Simund de Freine à Martin le Franc." *Romania* 89 (1968) 1-30, 210-239.

Jung, Marc R. *Hercule dans la littérature française du XVIe siècle. De l'Hercule courtois à l'Hercule baroque.* Geneva: Librairie Droz, 1966.

Kantorowicz, Ernst H. "Oriens Augusti: lever du roi." *Dumbarton Oaks Papers* 17 (1963) 117-177.

Katzenellenbogen, Adolf. *Allegories of the Virtues and Vices in Medieval Art from Early Christian Times to the Thirteenth Century.* Studies of the Warburg Institute, 10. London: Warburg Institute, 1939.

Kelly, Joan. *Women, History and Theory: The Essays of Joan Kelly.* Chicago: University of Chicago Press, 1984.

Kelly-Gadol, Joan. "Early Feminist Theory and the *Querelle des femmes,* 1400-1789." *Signs* 8 (1982) 4-28.

Kimm, Heidrun. *Isabeau de Bavière, reine de France 1370-1435. Beitrag zur Geschichte einer bayerischen Herzogstochter und des französischen Konigshau-ses.* Miscellanea Bavarica Monacensis, 13. Munich: Neue Schriftenreihe des Stadtsarchivs, 1969.

Kornemann, E. "Adler und Doppeladler im Wappen des alten Reiches." In *Das Reich—Idee und Gestalt. Festschrift für Johannes Haller zu seinem 75. Geburtstag,* ed. H. Dannenbauer and F. Ernst. Stuttgart: Cotta, 1940.

Kovacs, Eva. "L'Ordre du camail des ducs d'Orléans." *Acta Historiae Artium, Academiae Scientiarum Hungaricae* 27 (1981) 225-231.

Kris, Ernst and Otto Kurz. *Die Legende vom Kunstler, ein geschichtlicher Versuch.* Vienna: Krystall-Verlag, 1934.

Krynen, Jacques. *Idéal du prince et pouvoir royal en France à la fin du Moyen Âge (1380-1440). Étude de la littérature politique du temps.* Paris: A. et J. Picard, 1982.

Laborde, Léon E. de. *Les Ducs de Bourgogne: études sur les lettres, les arts et les industries pendant le XVᵉ siècle.* Pt. II, *Preuves.* 3 vols. Paris: Plon, 1849-1852.

Lacroix, Paul. *Louis XII et Anne de Bretagne.* Paris: G. Hurtrel, 1882.

Laidlaw, James C. "Christine de Pizan—An Author's Progress." *The Modern Language Review* 78 (1983) 532-550.

————. "Christine de Pizan, the Earl of Salisbury and Henry IV." *French Studies* 36 (1982) 129-143.

Langlois, E. "Notices des manuscrits français et provencaux de Rome antérieurs au XVIᵉ siècle." *Notices et extraits des manuscrits de la Bibliothèque Nationale et autres bibliothèques* 33 (1889) 1-346.

Lecoy, F. "Note sur quelques ballades de Christine de Pisan." In *Fin du Moyen Âge et Renaissance. Mélanges de philologie française offerts à Robert Guiette,* pp. 107-117. Antwerp: De Nederlandsche Boekhandel, 1961.

Lehoux, Françoise. *Jean de France, Duc de Berri, sa vie, son action politique (1340-1416).* 4 vols. Paris: A. et J. Picard, 1966-1968.

LeMaire, O. "La Cour amoureuse de Paris, fondée en 1401 et ses armoriaux." *Le Blason. Revue mensuelle belge de généalogie, d'héraldique et de sigillographie* 10 (1956) 66-78.

Lépinois, Ernest de. *Histoire de la ville et des sires de Coucy.* Paris: Dumoulin, 1859.

Leroux, Alfred. *Nouvelles recherches critiques sur les relations politiques de la France avec l'Allemagne de 1378 à 1461.* Paris: E. Bouillon, 1892.

————. "La Royauté française et le Saint-Empire au moyen âge (843-1493)." *Revue historique* 49 (1892) 241-288.

Lewis, Peter S. *Later Medieval France: the Polity.* New York: St. Martin's Press, 1968.

Liebeschutz, H. "John of Salisbury and Pseudo-Plutarch." JWCI 6 (1943) 33-39.

Ligota, C. "L'Influence de Macrobe pendant la Renaissance." In *Le Soleil à la Renaissance: sciences et mythes,* pp. 465-482. Brussels: Presses Universitaires de Bruxelles, 1965.

Lippmann, Friedrich. *Le Chevalier délibéré by Olivier de la Marche.* Illustrated Monographs, 5. London: Printed for the Bibliographical Society, 1898.

————. *Die sieben Planeten.* Berlin: Amsler & Ruthardt, 1895.

London, H. Stanford. *Royal Beasts.* East Knoyle, Wilts: The Heraldry Society, 1956.

Lord, Carla. "Three Manuscripts of the 'Ovide moralisé'." *Art Bulletin* 57 (1975) 161-175.

Lottin, Odon. *Psychologie et morale aux XIIᵉ et XIIIᵉ siècles.* Vol. 3: *Problèmes de morale.* Louvain: Abbaye du Mont-César, 1949.

Loukopoulos, Halina D. "Classical Mythology in the Works of Christine de Pisan with an Edition of *L'Epistre Othéa* from the Manuscript Harley 4431." Unpublished doctoral dissertation, Wayne State University, 1977.

Luçay, Comte de. "Le Comte de Clermont en Beauvoisis." *Revue historique nobiliaire et biographique* 13 (1876) 265-310, 388-427, 467-513; 14 (1877) 42-81, 227-260, 310-358, 376-404.

McKenna, J. W. "Henry VI of England and the Dual Monarchy: Aspects of Royal Political Propaganda, 1422-1432." JWCI 28 (1965) 145-162.

McLeod, Enid. *The Order of the Rose. The Life and Ideas of Christine de Pizan.* Totowa, N.J.: Rowman and Littlefield, 1976.

Magne, Lucien. *Le Palais de justice de Poitiers, étude sur l'art français au XIVe et au XVe siècles.* Paris: Librairie Centrale des Beaux-Arts, 1904.

Mâle, Émile. *L'Art religieux de la fin du moyen âge en France*, 5th ed. Paris: A. Colin, 1949.

Margolis, Nadja. "The Poetics of History: An Analysis of Christine de Pizan's *Livre de la Mutacion de Fortune.*" Unpublished doctoral dissertation, Stanford University, 1977.

Marle, Raimond van. *Iconographie de l'art profane au Moyen-Âge et à la Renaissance.* 2 vols. The Hague: M. Nijhoff, 1931-1932.

Martin, Henry. *Le Boccace de Jean sans Peur: Du cas des nobles hommes et femmes.* Brussels: G. van Oest et Cie, 1911.

——————. *Catalogue des manuscrits de la Bibliothèque de l'Arsenal.* 9 vols. Paris: E. Plon, Nourrit et Cie, 1885-1899.

——————. "Les Esquisses des miniatures." *Revue archéologique* 4 (1904) 17-45.

——————. *La Miniature française du XIIIe au XVe siècle.* Paris: G. van Oest et Cie, 1923.

——————. *Les Miniaturistes français.* Paris: H. Leclerc, 1906.

Martindale, Andrew. *The Rise of the Artist in the Middle Ages and Early Renaissance.* New York: McGraw-Hill, 1972.

Maumené, Charles and Louis d'Harcourt. *Iconographie des rois de France.* Pt. 1: *De Louis IX à Louis XIII.* Archives de l'art français, 15. Paris: A. Colin, 1928; repr. 1973.

Meiss, Millard, "Atropos-Mors; Observations on a Rare Early Humanist Image." In *Florilegium Historiale. Essays Presented to Wallace K. Ferguson*, ed. J. G. Rowe and W. H. Stockdale, pp. 152-159. Toronto: University of Toronto Press, 1971.

——————. "The First Fully Illustrated Decameron." In *Essays in the History of Art Presented to Rudolf Wittkower*, ed. D. Fraser, H. Hibbard and M. Lewine, pp. 56-61. London: Phaidon, 1967.

——————. *French Painting in the Time of Jean de Berry. The Boucicaut Master.* London/New York: Phaidon Press, 1968.

——————. *French Painting in the Time of Jean de Berry. The Late Fourteenth Century and the Patronage of the Duke.* 2 vols. London: Phaidon Press, 1967.

——————. *French Painting in the Time of Jean de Berry. The Limbourgs and their Contemporaries.* 2 vols. London: Thames and Hudson, 1974.

————— and Sharon Off. "The Bookkeeping of Robinet d'Estampes and the Chronology of Jean de Berry's Manuscripts." *Art Bulletin* 53 (1971) 225-235.

Melnikas, Anthony. *The Corpus of the Miniatures in the Manuscripts of Decretum Gratiani.* 3 vols. Rome: Libreria Athenea Salesiano, 1975.

Meyer, Paul. "L'Entrevue d'Ardres, 1396." *Annuaire-Bulletin de la Société de l'histoire de France* 18 (1881) 209-224.

—————. "Les Premières compilations françaises d'histoire ancienne. 2. Histoire ancienne jusqu'à César." *Romania* 14 (1885) 36-81.

Mirot, Léon. "L'Enlèvement du dauphin et le premier conflit entre Jean sans Peur et Louis d'Orléans (juillet-octobre 1405)." *Revue des questions historiques,* n.s., 51 (1914) 329-355; 52 (1914) 47-68, 369-419.

—————. "Raoul d'Anquetonville et le prix de l'assassinat du duc d'Orléans." BEC 72 (1911) 445-458.

————— and J. Viellard. "Inventaire des lettres des rois d'Aragon à Charles VI et à la cour de France conservées aux archives de la couronne d'Aragon à Barcelone." BEC 103 (1942) 99-150.

Molinier, Auguste. *Catalogue des manuscrits de la Bibliothèque Mazarine.* 4 vols. Paris: E. Plon, Nourrit et Cie, 1885-1891.

—————. "Description de deux manuscrits contenant la règle de la 'Militia Passionis Jhesu Christi' de Philippe de Mézières." *Archives de l'Orient Latin* 1 (1899) 335-364, 719.

Mombello, Gianni. "Per un'edizione critica dell'Epistre Othéa di Christine de Pizan." *Studi francesi* 8 (1964) 401-417, 9 (1965) 1-12.

—————. "I manoscritti di Dante, Petrarca e Boccaccio nelle principali librerie francesi del secolo XV." In *Il Boccaccio nella cultura francese,* ed. C. Pellegrini, pp. 81-209. Florence: L. S. Olschki, 1971.

—————. "Quelques aspects de la pensée politique de Christine de Pizan d'après ses œuvres publiées." In *Culture et politique en France à l'époque de l'humanisme et de la Renaissance. Atti del convegno internazionale promosso dall'Accademia delle scienze di Torino, 1971,* ed. F. Simone, pp. 43-153. Torino: Accademia delle Scienze, 1974.

—————. "Recherches sur l'origine du nom de la Déesse Othéa." *Atti della Accademia delle Scienze di Torino, Classe di scienze morali, storiche e filologiche* 103 (1968-1969) 343-375.

—————. *La tradizione manoscritta dell'"Epistre Othéa" di Christine de Pizan. Prolegomeni all'edizione del testo.* Memorie dell'Accademia delle Scienze di Torino, Classi di scienze morali, storiche e filologiche, series 4, 15. Torino: Accademia delle Scienze, 1967.

Momigliano, Arnaldo. "Notes on Petrarch, John of Salisbury and the 'Instituto Traiani'." JWCI 12 (1949) 189-190.

Monfrin, Jacques. "Humanisme et traduction au Moyen Âge." *Journal des Savants* (1963) 161-190.

—————. "Les Traducteurs et leur public en France au Moyen Âge." *Journal des Savants* (1964) 5-20.

Montfaucon, Bernard de. *Les Monumens de la monarchie françoise.* 5 vols. Paris: J. M. Gandouin 1729-1733.

Newman, Francis X. "*Somnium,* Medieval Theories of Dreaming and the Form of Vision Poetry." Unpublished doctoral dissertation, Princeton University, 1962.

Nicholas, John G. "Observations on the Heraldic Devices Discovered on the Effigies of Richard the Second and His Queen in Westminster Abbey, and upon the Mode in Which Those Ornaments Were Executed; Including Some Remarks on the Surname Plantagenet and the Ostrich Feathers of the Prince of Wales." *Archaeologia* 29 (1852) 32-59.

Nordberg, Michael. *Les Ducs et la royauté. Études sur la rivalité des ducs d'Orléans et de Bourgogne 1392-1407.* Studia historica upsaliensia, 12. Stockholm: Svenska bokförlaget/Norstedts, 1964.

Nordenfalk, Carl, "Hatred, Hunting, and Love: Three Themes Relative to Some Manuscripts of Jean sans Peur." In *Late Medieval and Renaissance Painting in Honor of Millard Meiss,* ed. I. Lavin and J. Plummer, pp. 324-341. New York: New York University Press, 1977.

Orlac, Charles d'. "Les Chevaliers du porc-épic ou du camail 1394-1498." *Revue historique nobiliaire et biographique,* n.s., 111 (1867) 337-350.

Ouy, Gilbert. "Honoré Bouvet (appelé à tort Bonet), prieur de Selonnet." *Romania* 80 (1959) 255-259.

————. "L'Humanisme et les mutations politiques et sociales en France aux XIVe et XVe siècles." In *14e Stage international d'études humanistes, Tours. L'Humanisme français au début de la Renaissance,* pp. 13-42. Paris: J. Vrin, 1973.

————. "Humanisme et propagande politique en France au début du XVe siècle: Ambrogio Migli et les ambitions impériales de Louis d'Orléans." In *Culture et politique en France à l'époque de l'humanisme et de la Renaissance. Atti del Convegno internazionale promosso dall'Accademia delle scienze di Torino, 1971,* ed. F. Simone, pp. 13-42. Torino: Accademia delle Scienze, 1974.

————. "Une maquette de manuscrit à peintures (Paris, B.N. lat. 14643, ff. 269-283v, Honoré Bouvet, Somnium prioris de Sallono super materia Scismatis, 1394)." In *Mélanges d'histoire du livre et des bibliothèques offerts à M. Frantz Calot,* pp. 44-51. Bibliothèque elzévirienne, n.s., Études et documents. Paris: Librairie d'Argences, 1960.

————. "Paris, l'un des principaux foyers de l'Humanisme en Europe au début du XVe siècle." *Bulletin de la Société de l'Histoire de Paris et de l'Île de France* (1967-1968) 71-98. Paris, 1970.

———— and Christine Reno. "Identification des autographes de Christine de Pizan." *Scriptorium* 34 (1980) 221-238.

Paecht, Otto and Dagmar Thoss. *Die illuminierten Handschriften und Inkunabeln der Österreichischen Nationalbibliothek, Französische Schüle I.* 2 vols. Österreichische Akademie der Wissenschaften, Philosophisch-historische Klasse, Denkschriften, vol. 118. Vienna: Verlag der Österreichische Akademie der Wissenschaften, 1974.

Palermo, Joseph. "Les Armoires d'Hector dans la tradition médiévale." In *Jean Misrahi Memorial Volume. Studies in Medieval Literature*, ed. H. R. Runte, H. Niedzielski and W. Hendrickson, pp. 88-99. Columbia, S.C.: French Literature Publications Co., 1977.

Palmer, John J. N. "The Background to Richard II's Marriage to Isabel of France (1396)." *Bulletin of the Institute of Historical Research* 44 (1971) 1-17.

—————. *England, France and Christendom, 1377-1399*. London: Routledge and Kegan Paul, 1972.

Pannier, Léopold. "Les Joyaux du duc de Guyenne, recherches sur les goûts artistiques et la vie privée du dauphin Louis, fils de Charles VI." *Revue archéologique*, n.s., 26 (1873) 158-170, 209-225, 306-320, 384-395; 27 (1874) 31-42.

Panofsky, Erwin. "Classical Mythology in Mediaeval Art." *Metropolitan Museum Studies* 4 (1932-1933) 228-280.

—————. *The Life and Art of Albrecht Dürer*. Princeton: Princeton University Press, 1955.

—————. *Renaissance and Renascences in Western Art*. Figura, Studies edited by the Institute of Art History, University of Uppsala, 10. Stockholm: Almquist and Wiksell, 1960.

—————. *Studies in Iconology, Humanistic Themes in the Art of the Renaissance*. New York: Oxford University Press, 1939.

Paris, Bibliothèque Nationale. *La Librairie de Charles V*. Paris, 1968.

Paris, Musée Monétaire. *Ordres de chevalerie et récompenses nationales*. Paris: Administration des monnaies et médailles, 1956.

Pastoureau, Michel. *Traité d'héraldique*. Paris: Picard, 1979.

Patch, Howard R. *The Goddess Fortuna in Mediaeval Literature*. Cambridge, Mass.: Harvard University Press, 1927.

Pernoud, Régine. *Christine de Pisan*. Paris: Calmann-Levy, 1982.

Petitot, Claude B. *Collection complète des mémoires relatifs à l'histoire de France, depuis le règne de Philippe-Auguste jusqu'au commencement du dix-septième siècle, avec des notices sur chaque auteur, et des observations sur chaque ouvrage*. Ser. 1, 52 vols. Paris: Foucault, 1819-1826.

Piaget, Arthur. "La Cour amoureuse dite de Charles VI." *Romania* 20 (1891) 417-454.

—————. "Un Manuscrit de la Cour amoureuse." *Romania* 31 (1902) 597-603.

Pinet, Marie-Josèphe. *Christine de Pisan 1364-1430. Étude biographique et littéraire*. Bibliothèque du XVe siècle, 35. Paris: H. Champion, 1927.

Pradel, Pierre. "Le Visage inconnu de Louis d'Orléans, frère de Charles VI." *La Revue des arts* 2 (1952) 93-98.

Quillet, Jeannine. "Songes et songeries dans l'art de la politique au XIVe siècle." *Les Études philosophiques* 30 (1975) 327-349.

Réau, Louis. *Iconographie de l'art chrétien.* 3 vols. Paris: Presses Universitaires de France, 1955-1959.

Reeves, Marjorie. *The Influence of Prophecy in the Later Middle Ages: A Study of Joachism.* Oxford: Clarendon Press, 1969.

Reno, Christine. "The Cursive and Calligraphic Scripts of Christine de Pizan." *Ball State University Forum* 19 (1978) 3-20.

──────. "Feminist Aspects of Christine de Pizan's 'Epistre d'Othéa à Hector'." *Studi francesi* 71 (1980) 271-276.

Renouard, Y. "L'Ordre de la Jarretière et l'Ordre de l'Étoile." *Le Moyen Âge* 55 (1949) 281-300.

Rey, Maurice. *Les Finances royales sous Charles VI. Les Causes du déficit (1388-1413).* Paris: S.E.V.P.E.N., 1965.

Ricci, Seymour de. "Les Manuscrits de la collection Henry Yates Thompson." SFRMF, *Bulletin* 10 (1926) 42-72.

Richards, Earl Jeffrey. "Christine de Pizan and the Question of Feminist Rhetoric." *Modern Language Association Conference* 22 (1983) 15-24.

Richardson, Lula M. *The Forerunners of Feminism in French Literature of the Renaissance.* Part I. *From Christine de Pizan to Marie de Gourmay.* Baltimore: Johns Hopkins University Press, 1929.

Rietstap, Johannes B. *Armorial général précédé d'un dictionnaire des termes du blason.* 2nd ed. 2 vols. Gouda: G. B. van Goor zonen, 1884-1887.

Rowe, Benedicta J. H. "Henry VI's Claim to France in Picture and Poem." *The Library,* 4th ser., 13 (1932-1933) 77-88.

──────. "Notes on the Clovis Miniature and the Bedford Portrait." *Journal of the British Archaeological Association,* 3rd ser., 25 (1962) 56-65.

Sallier, Claude. "Notice de deux ouvrages manuscrits de Christine de Pisan, dans lesquels il se trouve quelques particularités de l'histoire de Louis d'Orléans," *Mémoires de l'Académie des Inscriptions et Belles-Lettres* 17 (1751) 515-525.

Saxl, Fritz. "Beiträge zu einer Geschichte der Planetendarstellungen im Orient und Okzident." *Der Islam* 3 (1912) 151-177.

──────. "Probleme der Planetenkinderbilder." *Kunstchronik und Kunstmarkt,* n.s., 30, 54 (1918-1919) 1013-1021.

──────. "The Troy Romance in French and Italian Art." In *Lectures.* 2 vols. London: Warburg Institute, 1957.

──────. *Verzeichnis astrologischer und mythologischer illustrierter Handschriften des lateinischen Mittelalters.* Vol. 1, *Handschriften in römischen Bibliotheken* in Sitzungsberichte der Heidelberger Akademie der Wissenschaften, Phil.-hist. Klasse, 6, 7. Heidelberg: Carl Winters Universitätsbuchhandlung, 1915. ─ Vol. 2, *Die Handschriften der Nationalbibliothek in Wien,* Abhandl. 2 (1927). ─ Vol. 3, *Catalogue of Astrological and Mythological Illuminated Manuscripts of the Middle Ages: Manuscripts in English Libraries.* London: The Warburg Institute, 1964.

Schaefer, Lucie. "Die Illustrationen zu den Handschriften der Christine de Pizan." *Marburger Jahrbuch für Kunstwissenschaft* 10 (1937) 119-208.

Scheller, Robert W. "Ensigns of Authority: French Royal Symbolism in the Age of Louis XII." *Simiolus* 13 (1983) 75-141.

―――――. "Imperial Themes in Art and Literature of the Early French Renaissance: the Period of Charles VIII." *Simiolus* 12 (1981-1982) 5-69.

―――――. *A Survey of Medieval Model Books.* Haarlem: Erven F. Bohn, 1963.

Schroeder, Horst. *Der Topos der 'Nine Worthies' in Literatur und bildender Kunst.* Gottingen: Vandenhoeck & Ruprecht, 1971.

Schwarzenberg, Karl. *Adler und Drache. Der Weltherrschaftsgedanke.* Vienna: Verlag Herold, 1958.

Scott, Margaret. *Late Gothic Europe, 1400-1500.* London: Mills and Boon, 1980.

Setton, Kenneth M. *The Papacy and the Levant.* 2 vols. Memoirs of the American Philosophical Society, 114, 127. Philadelphia: American Philosophical Society, 1976, 1978.

Seznec, Jean. *The Survival of the Pagan Gods. The Mythological Tradition and its Place in Renaissance Humanism and Art.* Bollingen Series, 38. Princeton, N.J.: Princeton University Press, 1972.

Sherman, Claire. *The Portraits of Charles V of France (1338-1380).* Monographs on Archaeology and Fine Arts, 20. New York: New York University Press for the College Art Association of America, 1969.

―――――. "The Queen in Charles V's *Coronation Book*: Jeanne de Bourbon and the *Ordo ad Reginam Benedicendam.*" *Viator* 8 (1977) 255-297.

―――――. "A Second Instruction to the Reader from Nicole Oresme, Translator of Aristotle's *Politics* and *Economics.*" *Art Bulletin* 61 (1979) 468-469.

―――――. "Some Visual Definitions in the Illustrations of Aristotle's Nicomachean Ethics and Politics in the French Translations by Nicole Oresme." *Art Bulletin* 59 (1977) 320-330.

Sneyders de Vogel, K. "Une Œuvre inconnue de Christine de Pisan." In *Mélanges de philologie romane et de littérature médiévale offerts à Ernest Hoepffner par ses élèves et ses amis*, pp. 369-370. Paris: Société d'Éditions Les Belles Lettres, 1949.

Solente, Suzanne. "Christine de Pisan." In *Histoire littéraire de France*, 40: 335-415. Paris: Imprimerie nationale, 1969.

Spearing, A. C. *Medieval Dream-Poetry.* Cambridge: Cambridge University Press, 1976.

Spencer, Eleanor. "L'Horloge de Sapience. Brussels, Bibliothèque Royale, Ms. IV.III." *Scriptorium* 17 (1963) 277-299.

Steenackers, François F. *Histoires des ordres de chevalerie et des distinctions honorifiques en France.* Paris: Librairie Internationale, 1867.

Strutt, Joseph. *The Regal and Ecclesiastical Antiquities of England: Containing the Representations of All the English Monarchs.* London: H. C. Bohn, 1842.

Thibault, Marcel. *Isabeau de Bavière, reine de France. La jeunesse, 1370-1405.* Paris: Perrin et Cie, 1903.

Thomassy, Raymond. *Essai sur les écrits politiques de Christine de Pisan, suivi d'une notice littéraire et de pièces inédites.* Paris: Debecourt, 1838.

Thompson, Edward M. "A Contemporary Account of the Fall of Richard II." *Burlington Magazine* 5 (1904) 160-172, 267-270.

Thompson, Henry Yates. *A Descriptive Catalogue of Twenty Illuminated Manuscripts Nos. LXXV to XCIV (Replacing twenty discarded from the original number) in the Collection of Henry Yates Thompson.* Cambridge: University Press, 1907.

———. *Illustrations from the Life of Bertrand Duguesclin by Jean Cuvelier from a Manuscript of about 1400 A.D. in the Library of Henry Yates Thompson. No. C.* London: Chiswick Press, 1909.

Toesca, P. "Le Miniature dell'Elogio funebre di Gian Galeazzo Visconti (Parigi, Bib. Nat., Ms. lat. 5888)." *Rassegna d'Arte* 10 (1910) 156-158.

Tristam, Ernest W. "The Wilton Diptych." *The Month,* n.s., 1 (1949) 379-390; 2 (1949) 18-36.

Tuchman, Barbara. *A Distant Mirror. The Calamitous 14th Century.* New York: A. Knopf, 1978.

Tuve, Rosemond. *Allegorical Imagery. Some Mediaeval Books and their Posterity.* Princeton: Princeton University Press, 1966.

———. "Notes on the Virtues and Vices." JWCI 26 (1963) 264-303; 27 (1964) 42-72.

Vaivre, Jean-Bernard de. "Les Cerfs ailés et la tapisserie de Rouen." *Gazette des Beaux-Arts,* 6ᵉ sér., 100 (1982) 93-108.

———. "Un Document inédit sur le décor héraldique de l'ancien hôtel de Bourbon à Paris." *Archivum Heraldicum* 86 (1972) 2-10.

———. "À Propos des devises de Charles VI." *Bulletin monumental* 141 (1983) 92-95.

Vale, Malcolm G. A. *Charles VII.* Berkeley/Los Angeles: University of California Press, 1974.

Vallet de Viriville, Auguste. "La Bibliothèque d'Isabeau de Bavière." *Bulletin du bibliophile* 36 (1858) 663-687.

Valois, Noël. *La France et le grand schisme d'Occident.* 4 vols. Paris: Alphonse Picard et Fils, 1896-1902.

———. "Un Ouvrage inédit d'Honoré Bonet, prieur de Salon." *Annuaire-Bulletin de la Société de l'Histoire de France* 27 (1890) 193-228.

Vaughan, Richard. *John the Fearless. The Growth of Burgundian Power.* New York: Barnes and Noble, 1966.

Vielliard, Françoise. *Manuscrits français du Moyen Âge.* Biblioteca Bodmeriana Catalogues, 2. Cologny-Geneva: Fondation Martin Bodmer, 1975.

Warburg, Aby. "Italienische Kunst und internationale Astrologie im Palazzo Schifanoja zu Ferrara." In *Gesammelte Schriften,* ed. Gertrude Bing. 2: 459-481. Leipzig: B. G. Teubner, 1932.

Warner, George F. and Gilson, Julius P. *Catalogue of Western Manuscripts in the Old Royal and Kings Collections in the British Museum.* 4 vols. London: The Trustees, 1921.

Wells, William. "A Simile in Christine de Pisan for Christ's Conception." JWCI 2 (1938-1939) 68-69.

Willard, Charity Cannon. "An Autograph Manuscript of Christine de Pizan?" *Studi francesi* 9 (1965) 452-457.

————. *Christine de Pizan. Her Life and Works.* New York: Persea Books, 1984.

————. "Christine de Pisan's 'Clock of Temperance'." *L'Esprit Créateur* 2 (1962) 149-154.

————. "Christine de Pisan's Treatise on the Art of Medieval Warfare." In *Essays in Honor of Louis Francis Solano*, pp. 179-191. University of North Carolina Studies in Romance Languages, 92. Chapel Hill, N.C.: University of North Carolina Press, 1970.

————. "Christine de Pizan: the Astrologer's Daughter." In *Mélanges à la mémoire de Franco Simone. France et Italie dans la culture européenne*, 1: 95-111. Bibliothèque Franco Simone, 4. Geneva: Éditions Slatkine, 1980.

————. "The Manuscripts of Jean Petit's 'Justification.' Some Burgundian Propaganda of the Early Fifteenth Century." *Studi francesi* 13 (1969) 271-281.

————. "A New Look at Christine de Pisan's 'Epistre au Dieu d'Amours'." In *Secondo Miscellanea di studi e richerche sul quattrocento francese*, ed. F. Simone, J. Beck and G. Mombello, pp. 71-92. Chambéry-Torino: Centre d'Études Franco-Italien, 1981.

Winter, Patrick de. "Christine de Pizan, ses enlumineurs et ses rapports avec le milieu bourguignon." In *Actes du 104ᵉ congrès national des sociétés savantes (1979)*, pp. 335-375. Paris, 1982.

Wisman, Josette. "L'Éveil du sentiment national au Moyen Âge: la pensée politique de Christine de Pisan." *Revue historique* 257 (1977) 289-297.

Woledge, Brian. "La Légende de Troie et les débuts de la prose française." In *Mélanges de linguistique et de littérature romanes offerts à Mario Roques.* 4 vols. 2: 313-324. Paris: Librairie Marcel Didier, 1952.

Wright, N. A. R. "The Tree of Battles of Honoré Bouvet and the Laws of War." In *War, Literature, and Politics in the Late Middle Ages*, ed. C. T. Allmand, pp. 12-31. New York: Barnes and Noble, 1976.

Wyss, Robert L. "Die neun Helden. Eine ikonographische Studie." *Zeitschrift für Schweizerische Archäologie und Kunstgeschichte* 17 (1957) 73-106.

Yenal, Edith. *Christine de Pisan. A Bibliography of Writings of Her and About Her.* The Scarecrow Author Bibliographies, 63. Metuchen, N.J., and London: The Scarecrow Press, 1982.

Zeller, Gaston. "Les Rois de France candidats à l'Empire. Essai sur l'idéologie impériale en France." *Revue historique* 173 (1934) 273-311, 497-534.

Index

Plates

1. Christine presenting her book to Louis of Orleans; *L'Epistre Othéa*, Paris, BN MS fr. 848, fol 1r.

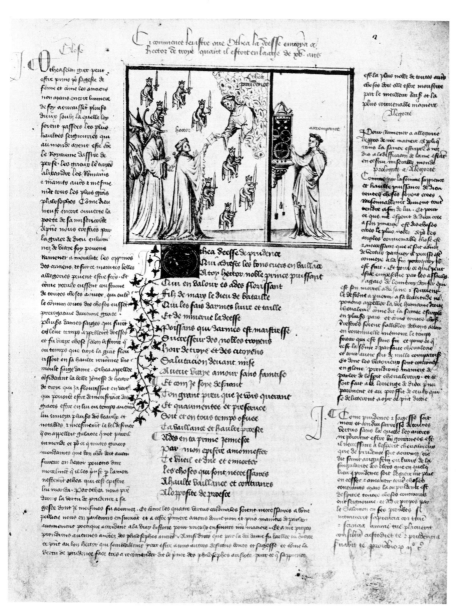

2. Othea giving a letter to Hector; Temperance adjusting a clock;
L'Epistre Othéa, Paris, BN MS fr. 848, fol. 2r.

le roy aynos justice

hercules force

Affin que tout bon cuer sadresce
A acquerir par bonne escolle
Le cheval qui par lair sen volle
Cest pegasus le renomme
Fin de tous vaillans estame
Pour ce que ta condicion
Say par droite inclinacion

3. Minos as judge in hell; Hercules and Cerberus; *L'Epistre Othéa*, Paris, BN MS fr. 848, fol. 2v.

Tres haulte flour par le mode touee
et tous plaisant et de dieu avouee
de lis souef odorant delitable
puissant valeur haute pris surto

5. Christine presenting her book to Louis of Orleans; *L'Epistre
Othéa*, London, BL Harley MS 4431, fol. 95r. See also Plate A.

ou liure parle selon la maniere de parler
des anciens poetes. Et pour ce que deite
est chose espirituelle et esleuee de tres sor
les ymages figurez en nues et ceste pre
miere est la deesse de Sapience.

6. Othea presenting her letter to Hector; *L'Epistre Othéa*,
London, BL Harley MS 4431, fol. 95v. See also Plate B.

tres haulte fleur p̄ le mõde louee
a touz plaisant z de dieu auouee
de lis souef odurãt delictable
puissãt valeur haulte pris sur to⁹
ouenge a dieu auãt œuure soit mise

7. Christine presenting her book to Louis of Orleans;
L'Epistre Othéa, Paris, BN MS fr. 606, fol. 1r. See also Plate C.

8. Othea presenting her letter to Hector;
L'Epistre Othéa, Paris, BN MS fr. 606, fol. 1v. See also Plate D.

9. Minos as judge of hell; *L'Epistre Othéa*, London, BL Harley MS 4431, fol. 98r.

10. Jupiter; *L'Epistre Othéa*, London, BL Harley MS 4431, fol. 99v.

a lathey. V.º capitulo

Venus est planette ou ciel que les payens iadis appellerent deesse damours pour ce que elle donne influence destre amoureux et pour ce sont cy figurez amans qui luy presentent leurs cuers.

texte. Cn.

Venus ne fus tu deesse
Ne te chaille de sa promesse
e poursuiure en est trauailleux

11. Venus; *L'Epistre Othéa*, London, BL Harley MS 4431, fol. 100r.

Se tu en iugement taſſemblee
Saturnus gard que tu reſſembles
A meurs quottivres ta ſentence
Et ne la dōnee en doubtence

12. Saturn; *L'Epistre Othéa*, Paris, BN MS fr. 606, fol. 6v.

13. Apollo and Phoebe; *L'Epistre Othéa*, Paris, BN MS fr. 606, fol. 7r.

14. Mars; *L'Epistre Othéa*, London, BL Harley MS 4431, fol. 101v.

15. Mars; *L'Epistre Othéa*, Paris, BN MS fr. 606, fol. 7v.

Soies aourné de faconde
Et de parole nette e monde:
Ce ta prendra mercurius

16. Mercury; *L'Epistre Othéa*, Paris, BN MS fr. 606, fol. 8r.

17. Minerva; *L'Epistre Othéa*, London, BL Harley MS 4431, fol. 102v.

18. Minerva; *L'Epistre Othéa*, Paris, BN MS fr. 606, fol. 8v.

19. Pallas and Minerva; *L'Epistre Othéa*, London, BL Harley MS 4431, fol. 103r.

20. Penthesilea; *L'Epistre Othéa*, London, BL Harley MS 4431, fol. 103v.

Texte

vec chiere panthassellee
de ta mort sear asoulee
Tel femme doit bien estre amee

21. Penthesilea; *L'Epistre Othéa*, Paris, BN MS fr. 606, fol. 9v.

22. Athamas killing his wife Ino; *L'Epistre Othéa*, London, BL Harley MS 4431, fol. 104r.

23. Diana reading; *L'Epistre Othéa*, Paris, BN MS fr. 606, fol. 13r.

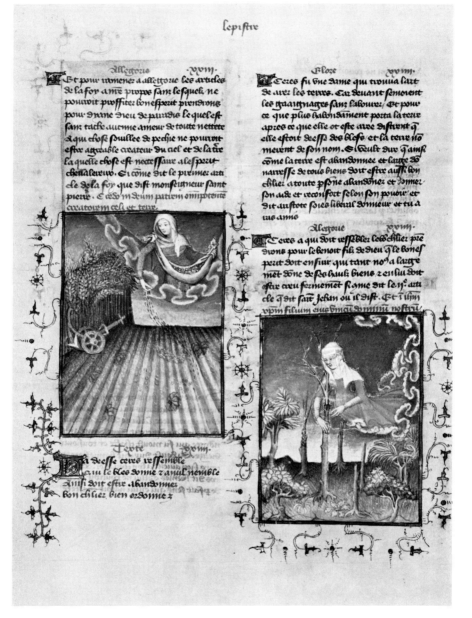

24. Ceres planting seeds; Isis grafting trees; *L'Epistre Othéa*, Paris, BN MS fr. 606, fol. 13v.

25. Cadmus slaying a dragon; Io directing a scriptorium; *L'Epistre Othéa*, Paris, BN MS fr. 606, fol. 15r.

26. Mercury, Argus, and Io; *L'Epistre Othéa*, Paris, BN MS fr. 606, fol. 15v.

27. Pyrrhus avenging Achilles's death; *L'Epistre Othéa*, London, BL Harley MS 4431, fol. 110r.

Lhois que pyrrus ressemblera
son pere. et encor troublera
ses anemis par si cruel les

28. Pyrrhus avenging Achilles's death; *L'Epistre Othéa*, Paris, BN MS fr. 606, fol. 16r.

29. Cassandra praying in a temple; Neptune guiding a ship; *L'Epistre Othéa*,
Paris, BN MS fr. 606, fol. 16v.

30. Atropos-Mors; *L'Epistre Othéa*,
London, BL Harley MS 4431, fol. 111r.

31. Atropos-Mors; *L'Epistre Othéa*,
Paris, BN MS fr. 606, fol. 17r.

32. Memnon assisting Hector; *L'Epistre Othéa*, London, BL Harley MS 4431, fol. 112r.

33. Memnon assisting Hector; *L'Epistre Othéa*, Paris, BN MS fr. 606, fol. 18r.

34. Aesculapius making a diagnosis; Circe spearing frogs; *L'Epistre Othéa*,
Paris, BN MS fr. 606, fol. 19v.

35. Paris slaying Achilles; Busiris's human sacrifices; *L'Epistre Othéa*,
London, BL Harley MS 4431, fol. 114r.

36. Greek messengers before Priam and Helen; *L'Epistre Othéa*,
London, BL Harley MS 4431, fol. 115r.

37. Greek messengers before Priam and Helen; *L'Epistre Othéa*,
Paris, BN MS fr. 606, fol. 21r.

38. Cupid; *L'Epistre Othéa*, Paris, BN MS fr. 606, fol. 23r.

39. Jason fighting the dragon; *L'Epistre Othéa*,
London, BL Harley MS 4431, fol. 120r.

Ne laisses ton sens aborter;
A fol delit ne emporter;
Ta chevance se demande test;
Test; et te mures en medre...

40. Medea handing Jason a coffer; *L'Epistre Othéa*,
Paris, BN MS fr. 606, fol. 28r.

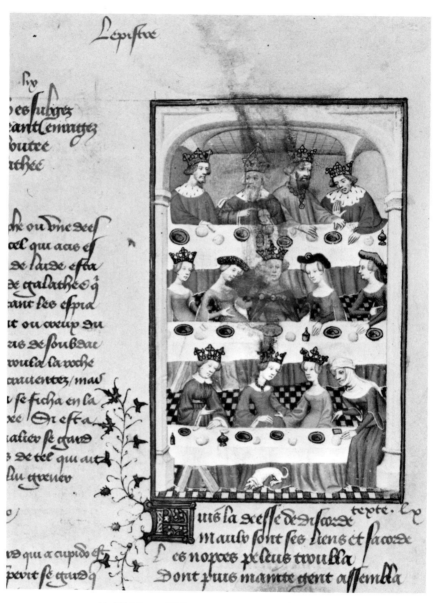

41. Wedding of Peleus and Thetis; *L'Epistre Othéa*,
London, BL Harley MS 4431, fol. 122v.

42. Wedding of Peleus and Thetis; *L'Epistre Othéa*,
Paris, BN MS fr. 606, fol. 28v.

choses faites les quelles condampner est
quaint presomcion On le devons ninterpre
ter en la meilleur partie. Secondement
car nous ne sommes pas certains quels
seront ceulx qui a present sont bons ou
mauuais . a ce propos dist mess en leu
nangile . Nolite iudicare et non
iudicabimini in quo en—iudicio
iudicaueritis iudicabimini mathei vije.

ce que elle promet a maint assez prospe
res et de fait en somme a aucuns z les rent
en petit deue quant il lui plaist Dit au
bon cheualier que il ne se doit fier en ses
promesses ne desconforter en ses aduer
sitez z Dit Socrates les tours de fortu
ne sont comme enigme

allegorie. hophm.

Pour ce que il dit que il ne se doit fier en
fortune poürons entendre que le bon espe
rit doit fuyr et despriser les delices du
monde De ce dit Boece ou tiers liure de
consolacion que la felicite des epicuriens
doit estre appellee infelicite car cest la
vraye plaine et parfaicte felicite qui
peut somme faux souffisant puissa
reuerend sollempnel et ioyeulx Les
quieulx adicions ne pueent point
les choses ou les mondains mettent leur
felicite pour ce dit dieu par le prophete
Populus meus qui te beatum dicunt
ipsi te decipiunt psalre iij. c.

texte. hophm.

En fortune la grant deesse
Ne te fies riens sa promesse
Car en vou deux elle se change
e plus hault souuent mette en fange

glose . hophm.

Fortune selon la maniere de parler des
poetes peut bien estre appellee la grant
deesse Car par elle nous veons le cour
des choses mondaines gouuerner e po

43. Wheel of Fortune; Paris embracing Helen;
L'Epistre Othéa, London, BL Harley MS 4431, fol. 129r.

44. Wheel of Fortune; *L'Epistre Othéa*, Paris, BN MS fr. 606, fol. 35r.

45. Helenus advising Paris; *L'Epistre Othéa*, Paris, BN MS fr. 606, fol. 36r.

personne de leurtlise! Custodi legrem meam
acb confilium creut Brtu anime tue pou
Brozum tezao capitula

Texte   vp
                               nij.

conseil denfant ne tacoudes.

46. Troilus advising Priam; *L'Epistre Othéa*, Paris, BN MS fr. 606, fol. 37v.

47. Andromache warning Hector; *L'Epistre Othéa*, London, BL Harley MS 4431, fol. 135r.

48. Andromache warning Hector; *L'Epistre Othéa*, Paris, BN MS fr. 606, fol. 41r.

49. Queen Ino sowing boiled corn; *L'Epistre Othéa*, Paris, BN MS fr. 606, fol. 45v.

50. Emperor Augustus and the Cumean sibyl; *L'Epistre Othéa*, Paris, BN MS fr. 606, fol. 46r.

Le prologue du songe du viel pelerin adressat au
blanc faucon pelerin couronné au bec et pies dorés

Il est escript en la
sainte euuangile
que Ihuucrist recita
la parabole dun
riche home qui ala en vng grant
pelermage et bailla a ses sergans
ses besans qui en leuuangile sont
appeles talens pour faire marchandie et prester a vsure afin que a
son retour les dis sergans li peu-
sissent ses besans auec toute lusure.
Dont il est assauoir que alun de
ses sergans il bailla v besans a
lautre ij et a lautre vng. Or
auint que au retour du riche home
de son pelermage cellui qui auoit
receu v besans les offri a son
seigneur et autres v de gaigne
et le riche home pour ce quil auoit
bien marchande et saigement preste
a vsure li laissa les x besans et
lordena cheuetaine sur x cites
Et cellui qui auoit receu ij
besans en offri a son seigneur autre
ij de gaigne et le seigneur le loua
grandement et lordena cheuetaine
sur ij cites Mais le tiers sergant
qui ot receu vng besant fu negligent
et doubta son seigneur sans cause
et enfoui son besant en laterre sans
marchander ne prester a vsure
et offri a son seigneur son besant
tout seul dont il fu condampnes
et comanda le seigneur que le besant

li fust ostes et donnes acellui qui
en auoit x. Le tressaint et
gracieux docteur de leglise saint
gregoire en lexposicon de ceste sainte
euuangile dit que le riche home
de la dicte parabole qui ala en pelermage nest autre que Ihuucrist
qui apres son trauaillant pelermage de xxxiij ans ou enuiron
ala ou grant pelermage cest assau-
quant il monta ouciel vestu de
nostre humanite gloriffiee et a ses
sergans cest assauoir a ses creatures
il bailla ses besans pour marchader
et prester a la sainte vsure. Mun
v besans par lesquelz selonc le dit
de saint gregoire sont entendu les
v cens naturelz par lesquelz la
creature humaine doibt saigement
marchander et prester a vsure
adieu principalement a son prouisme
et a soy meismes cest assauoir par
bonnes euuures par bone exemple
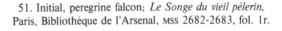
de sainte vie Encores
par les ij besans selonc le dit du
docteur sont entendu en lame raison-
ablement et lentendement et par le besant
seul est entendu lentendement tout
seul. Nul ne se peut doncques
excuser selonc le dit de saint gregoire
qui a le sens entier quil nait
receu le besant de dieu asses suffi-
sant pour faire la marchandie
de lame et prester a vsure mer-
toire car la sainte escripture dit

51. Initial, peregrine falcon; *Le Songe du vieil pèlerin*,
Paris, Bibliothèque de l'Arsenal, MSS 2682-2683, fol. 1r.

52. Flying stag; *Le Songe du vieil pèlerin,*
Paris, Bibliothèque de l'Arsenal, MSS 2682-2683, fol. 34v.

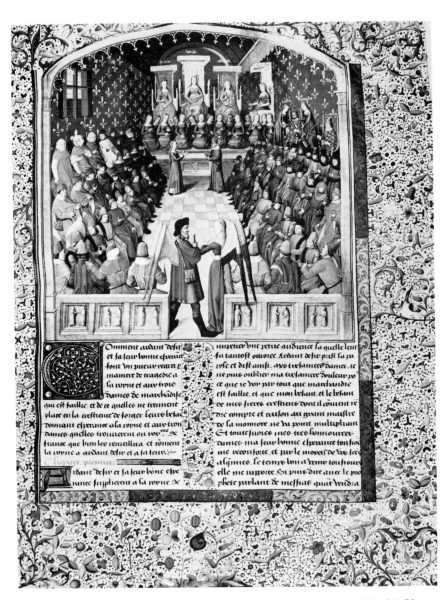

53. Parliament of virtues; *Le Songe du vieil pèlerin*, Vienna, ÖNB Cod. 2551, fol. 73r.

54. Dedication allegory; *Le Songe du vieil pèlerin*, Vienna, ÖNB Cod. 2551, fol. 130r.

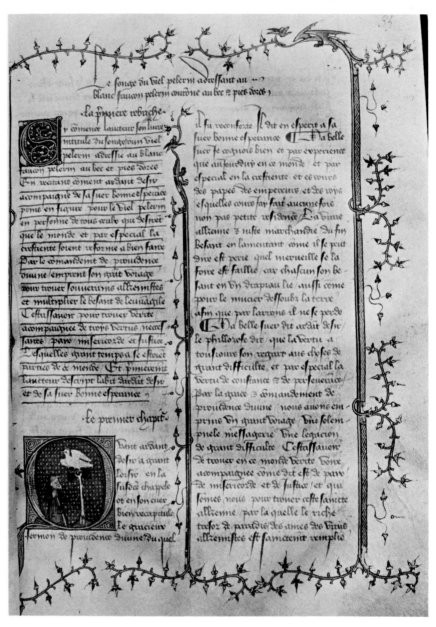

55. Initial, peregrine falcon and old pilgrim; *Le Songe du vieil pèlerin*,
Paris, Bibliothèque de l'Arsenal, MSS 2682-2683, fol. 35r.

56. Frontispiece; *L'Epistre au roi Richart*, London, BL Royal MS 20 B VI, fol. 1v.

The image contains an illuminated manuscript page with medieval French text in Gothic script. The text is largely decorative medieval script within the illumination.

57. Philip presenting his book to King Richard II; *L'Epistre au roi Richart*, London, BL Royal MS 20 B VI, fol. 2r.

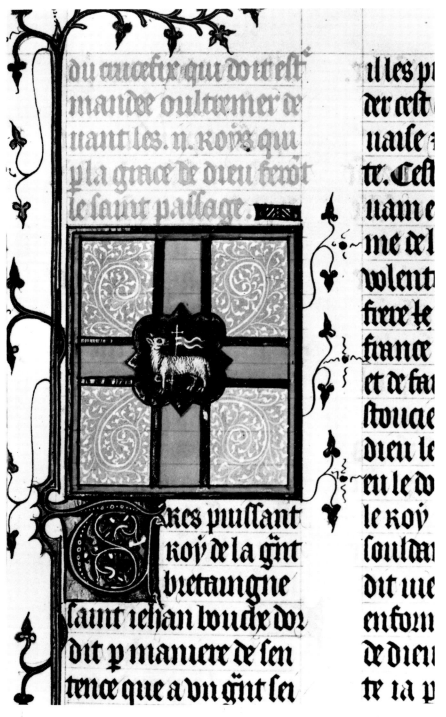

du crucefix qui doit est
mandee oultremer de
nant les. ij. roys qui
p la grace de dieu ferõt
le saint passage.

il les p
der cest
naise
te. Cest
name
me del
volent
fiere le
france
et de fai
stouae
dieu le
eu le do
le roy
souldai
dit me
enfom
de dieu
te la p

kes puissant
roy de la gãt
bretaingne
saint iehan bouche dor
dit p maniere de sen
tence que a vn gãt sei

58. Initial, banner of the Order of the Chivalry of the Passion of Jesus Christ;
L'Epistre au roi Richart, London, BL Royal MS 20 B VI, fol. 35r.

59. Squires carrying banner and shield; *La Chevalerie de la Passion de Jhesu Crist*,
Oxford, Bodleian Library, Ashmole MS 813, p. 2.

60. Prince of the Order; *La Chevalerie de la Passion de Jhesu Crist*,
Oxford, Bodleian Library, Ashmole MS 813, p. 3.

61. Insignia of the Order; *La Chevalerie de la Passion de Jhesu Crist,*
Oxford, Bodleian Library, Ashmole MS 813, p. 7.

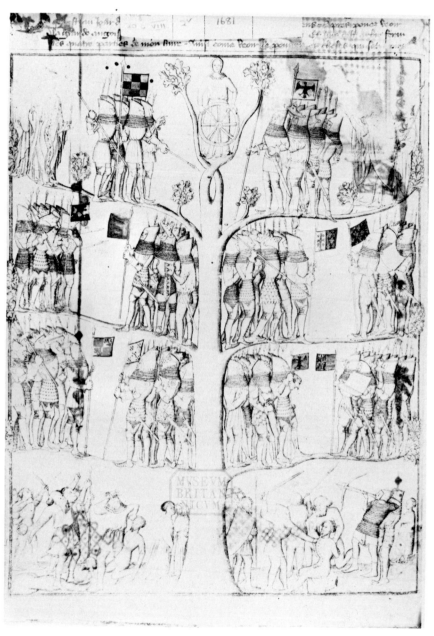

62. Frontispiece; *L'Arbre des batailles*, London, BL Royal MS 20 C VIII, fol. 2v.

63. Frontispiece; *L'Arbre des batailles*,
New York, Pierpont Morgan Library, MS M. 907, fol. 2v.

64. Frontispiece; *L'Arbre des batailles*, Paris, BN MS fr. 1266, fol. 5r.

65. Jehan de Meun speaking to the Jew; *L'Apparition Maistre Jehan de Meun*, Paris, BN MS fr. 810, fol. 9v.

66. Bouvet presenting his book to Valentine of Orleans; *L'Apparition Maistre Jehan de Meun*, Paris, BN MS fr. 811, fol. 1v.

67. Valentine of Orleans and a physician; *L'Apparicion Maistre Jehan de Meun*, Paris, BN MS fr. 811, fol. 8r.

68. Christine presenting her book to Charles VI; *Le Chemin de long estude*,
London, BL Harley MS 4431, fol. 178r.

69. Parliament of queens; *Le Chemin de long estude*,
London, BL Harley MS 4431, fol. 192v.

70. Parliament of queens; *Le Chemin de long estude*,
Paris, BN MS fr. 836, fol. 40v.

71. Equestrian seals of Duke Charles of Orleans (1444) and King Louis XII (1485); Paris, Archives Nationales, Douët-d'Arcq inv. nos. 944, 951.

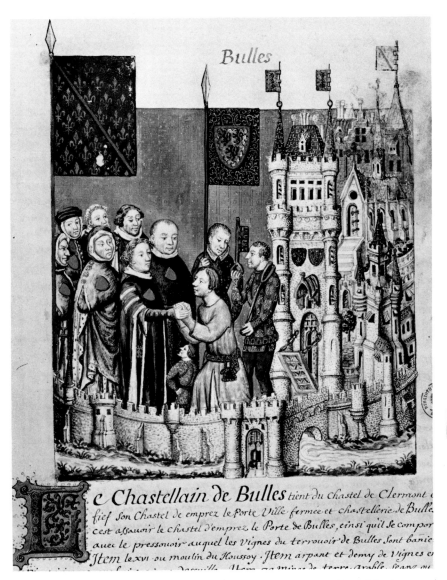

Bulles

e Chastellain de Bulles tient du Chastel de Clermont e
fief son Chastel de emprez le Porte Ville fermée et chastellerie de Bulle
cest assauoir le chastel d'emprez le Porte de Bulles, einsi quil se compor
auec le pressouoir auquel les vignes du terrouoir de Bulles sont banie
Item le xvi ou moulin du Houssoy. Item arpant et demy de vignes e

72. Louis of Bourbon with the knights of the Order of the Gold Shield receiving homage;
Hommages du comté de Clermont, Paris, BN Gaignières MS fr. 20082, fol. 171r.

La sale du soleil estoit
Sur haultes colupnes assise
haultemt? et riche adeuise
Clere com or reflamboiant
Et com propres rungoiät

73. Jupiter; *Ovide moralisé*, Paris, BN MS fr. 373, fol. 24r.

S le fanpture ne me ment
Tout eft voir me enfengnent
Riut quil a ce liures efarpt
Soient bien ou mal fi efarpt

74. Saturn; *Ovide moralisé*, Geneva,
Bibliothèque publique et universitaire, MS fr. 176, fol. 5r.

tympora pulchras vestes et
fixatas z gemmatas habens
rosam in manu. specos z hoñe
stemuens mercurium
Mercurius signatur iuuenis ha
rens iam barbam quia velocius z
plet cursum suum qñ sol z g quare
venus z signat sapientes quasi
sembz simulentur z ptim iullicos
Pingitur autem in figura signante
omnem bonam spem in eo qui na
scitur sub eo. Vnde corona lapidata gemmis signat planitam
clericalem epatum vel abbatiam z Breuitas vo capillorum signat
consuram clericalis Sceptrum signat potestatem z dominium
multorum existentium sub eius regimine virtuoso dignitatis Liber sig
nat sapiam sciat aut homines clericos pauperes abbates hermitas z

Sc signatur mercurius haber faciem medio
crem in omni capillos tuffos z parum erca
os clanideem ad
collum z in ma
nu virgam dupp
licias rami absqz frondibz z libz
clausum in manu honeste inu
ens saturnum in sede colloquy
z ut predicta melius denotent z
Her est forma sui aspectus i
celo ♄
Sol signatur cum quatuor equis
quorum duo sunt masculi z due femine Quorum primus vocatur
rubeus nam qñdo sol oritur primo rubet vel alio nomine dicatur
oriens z est ruteus Secundus dicatur splendens quia post ortum
eius splendet ut' aureus vel circonus vel albens albi coloris

76. Minerva; *Des Cleres femmes*, Paris, BN MS fr. 598, fol. 13r.

Ey fenfuit hÿftoire de Ceres
qui fut lanaenne et trefplan
tireufe delle des bles et roÿne
des ficuliens. La. vij. rubriche.

Eres comme
aucuns dient
et afferment
fut roÿne tres
anaenne des
ficuliens et de

77. Ceres; *Des Cleres femmes*, Paris, BN MS fr. 598, fol. 11r.

78. Isis; *Des Cleres femmes*, Paris, BN MS fr. 598, fol. 16v.

79. Mercury, Argus, and Io; *Ovide moralisé*, Paris, Bibliothèque de l'Arsenal, MS 5069, fol. 7r.

80. Medea directing her brother to kill her children; *Des Cleres femmes*,
Paris, BN MS fr. 598, fol. 27v.

Cy apres senfuit lyftoire
de panthefille royne ama
zones. La .xxxix. rubriche.

Anthefilee vier
ge fut royne
des amazones
et fucceda a o
richie et an
thope roynes

de icellui pays des amazones
Toutevoies ie nay point
leu de queulx parens elle ait es
te engendree et descendue.
Ceste femme comme di
ent les aucuns desirtant la

des et cau
stume de
non des fi
et cheua
merueill
force et d
les aultr
femme n
grant en
quelle te
lusaige i
m congn
comme n
quant el
ce et vertu
elle lame
combien
veu et po
et de rece
uice qui
royalme
titude de l
relles a b
cendy po
grecs aff
opportun
compaig
noble et

81. Penthesilea, *Des Cleres femmes*, Paris, BN MS fr. 12420, fol. 46r.

En dementiers ala tant iaso ql
ala et arriua en lisle ⁊ prist so
escu et sesuure ⁊ se mist lors du bastel ⁊

82. Jason killing the dragon; *Histoire ancienne*, Paris, BN MS fr. 301, fol. 30v.

83. Pope Alexander V; Pierre Salmon's *Demandes et lamentacions,*
Paris, BN MS fr. 23279, fol. 115v.

84. Arms and emblems of Charles VI; Charter of the *Cour amoureuse*,
Vienna, Staatsarchiv, Archives of the Order of the Golden Fleece, MS 51, fol. 2v.

85. Cupid as god of love; *L'Epistre au dieu d'amours*, London, BL Harley MS 4431, fol. 53r.

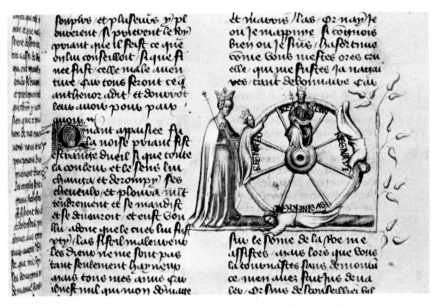

86. Wheel of Fortune; *Histoire ancienne*, London, BL Stowe MS 54, fol. 197r.

87. Andromache warning Hector; *L'Epistre Othéa*,
Waddesdon Manor, Rothschild Collection, MS 8, fol. 48r.

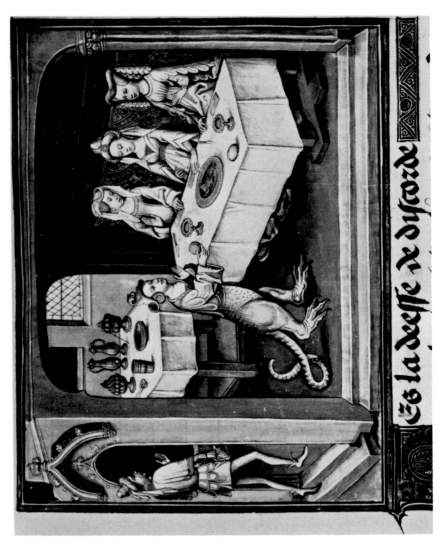

88. Wedding of Peleus and Thetis; *L'Epistre Othéa*, Erlangen, Universitätsbibliothek, MS 2361, fol. 77v.

Vis a toute heure regart
A attropos et a son dart
Qui fiert et nespargne nul ame
Se te fera penser de lame

· Glose ·

Les poetes appellerent la mort attropos pour
ce vuest dire Othea au son cheualier quil doit pen
ser que tousioure ne vinera mie en cestuy monde
mais tantost sen partira Si doit plus vser des
vertus de lame que soy deliter es vicces du corps
Et a ce doit tout vprien penser afm quil ait en
memoire la promission de lame qui dinera sans
fm. Et a ce propoz dist pitagoras que ainsi come
nre comencement vient de dieu comient il que

89. Atropos as a skeleton; *L'Epistre Othéa*, Brussels, BR MS 9392, fol. 37v.

90. Saturn devouring his children; *L'Epistre Othéa*, Brussels, BR MS 9392, fol. 11v.

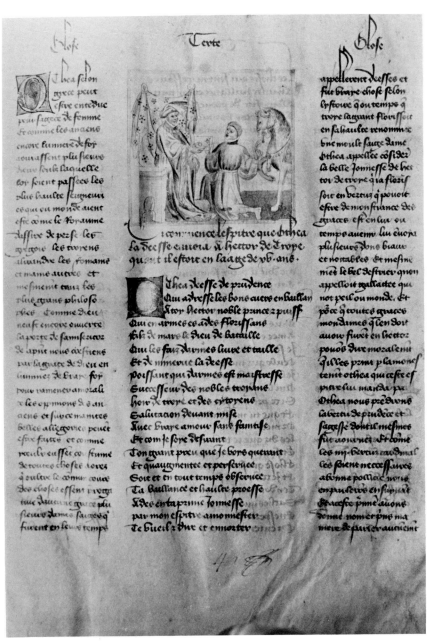

91. Hector receiving his letter; *L'Epistre Othéa*,
Cambridge, Newnham College Library, MS 900 (5), fol. 1r.

Glose

Texte

92. Wheel of Fortune; *L'Epistre Othéa,*
Cambridge, Newnham College Library, MS 900 (5), fol. 38v.

93. Andromáche warning Hector; *L'Epistre Othéa*,
Cambridge, Newnham College Library, MS 900 (5), fol. 45v.

Charles Signeur de Cruſſol, Seneſchal de Poi-
tou.
Tannegui du Chaſtel, Gouuerneur des pays de
Roſſillon, & de Sardaine.

Vltus auos Troiæ.

Louis

94. Porcupine as an emblem of King Louis XII; Claude Paradin, *Les Devises héroïques*
(Antwerp, 1563), Baltimore, The Johns Hopkins University Special Collections, fol. 14r.